WILLIAM STEPHEN GILLY

William Stephen Gilly

An extraordinarily busy life

Hugh Norwood

Edited and completed by **Nicholas Groves**

Lasse Press

First published 2014
by the Lasse Press
2 St Giles Terrace, Norwich NR2 1NS, UK
www.lassepress.com
lassepress@gmail.com

ISBN-13: 978-0-9568758-8-4

Designed and typeset in Adobe Garamond
by Curran Publishing Services Ltd, Norwich, UK

Manufactured in the UK by Imprint Digital, Devon

Contents

Illustrations

Tables

Maps

Figures

Foreword

My father Hugh Norwood died in 2004, ten years before the publication of this book. The book was incredibly important to him, and many times he mentioned that should he not be able to complete it, he would dearly like someone else to finish it, and for the book to be published. As a family we are delighted that it has now reached publication.

Hugh was a constant traveller, and he and his family lived in many countries, including Malawi, Papua New Guinea and New Zealand. Although he greatly enjoyed living abroad, his final years were spent in England, where this book was written. He would sit writing in the top room of his Aylesbury house, overlooking St Mary's Church, and say it was one of the best urban views in England.

Hugh loved Italy and enjoyed his many visits to Torre Pellice, where he met and worked with Gabriella Ballesio, the Waldensian archivist. While in Torre Pellice Hugh and his wife Marilyn stayed at the Foresteria Waldese, and from this base they walked to many of the small Waldensian villages. Hugh died in Italy while on one of his many trips researching this book.

Inevitably family members have been deeply involved with the book's production, Hugh's widow Marilyn typed and retyped, his sister Jenny contacted Dr Nicholas Groves and invited him to complete the book, and negotiated with the publisher, the Lasse Press. Prior to Dr Groves taking on the project we all read early drafts.

Over five years and more, many other people also assisted Hugh with his research and writing. Sadly, the family does not have enough information to thank properly all who helped Hugh. However we would particularly like to acknowledge and thank Viviana Genre for her help and support. We are also deeply grateful to Dr Groves for taking on the task of researching, checking, amending and completing the book. To others whom Hugh would have thanked had he lived, we also give our thanks and our apologies for not naming you.

Charles Norwood
August 2014

Preface

As with so many things in the history of the Church, this book has a complicated origin. It arose out of the curiosity engendered when, while on a walking holiday in the Italian Alps, Hugh Norwood came across the present day Waldensian community, a curiosity that was to occupy much of the last five years of his life. Sadly he died before the final chapter of the book was written. His family decided it should be completed and brought to publication. Early in 2011, I was asked if I would consider taking on the work required. It has proved to be a fascinating task, enabling me to expand my knowledge of the Waldensian Church, but also to engage with the subject of the book, Canon William Stephen Gilly of Durham. He has proved to be an intriguing, if not entirely likeable, character: maybe the one follows from the other!

Gilly, as will emerge, was a very forceful character, and despite a short period apparently becalmed as Rector of a remote Essex parish at the start of his ministry (a parish he seems never to have visited), he quickly rose up the hierarchy of the Church of England to be a Prebendary of Durham. That he did so is testimony to his ability to make use of whatever opportunities for patronage came his way. This was the standard method of promotion at the time, and an ambitious professional had to make his own opportunities if, as in Gilly's case, he did not have any to hand in the form of family connexions. It is still alive and well today, and we call it networking. Gilly was very adept at playing this game: not least the way in which he capitalized on a brief introduction to Shute Barrington, the elderly Bishop of Durham. Having said that, he proved to be an excellent parish priest at his subsequent appointments in Somers Town, Durham and Norham.

Alongside all this, Gilly was riding his 'Waldenisan hobby horse' for all it was worth. So far did he identify with them that anyone else presuming to write about them was quickly put in their place. He managed to visit the valleys six times, a journey taking many weeks each way. He is still rightly venerated there as a great benefactor – and indeed patron. But he had a larger plan in mind: he was convinced that, far from being the Reformed Protestant body they had clearly become in the sixteenth century, the Waldensians were in fact a valid channel of that will-o'-the-wisp of ecclesiastical legitimatists, the Apostolic Succession (something they always have disclaimed to be, and still do). Much of his energy was expended in attempting to make them conform to Anglican practices – including removing three young boys from their valleys and bringing them to be educated in an Anglican ethos at the nascent University of Durham: an experiment, as anyone could have seen, which was doomed to failure.

But there is a side to Gilly which is much less attractive: he was an arrant meddler. This first appears in the 'Irish papers episode', when he broke a confidence and failed to pass on to its intended recipient material which he had been asked to deliver. There was the so-called 'Waldensian crisis', which appears to have been talked up entirely by

Gilly, and which could well have had unfortunate consequences for the very people he was aiming to protect. And finally there was his attempted interference in the foundation of the University of Durham, in which he was kept at arm's length with considerable skill by Archdeacon Thorp.

Hugh wrote of Gilly in Chapter 2, ' … he led an exceptionally busy life during the next forty years'. That assessment seems to be as good a title for the whole book as any.

Hugh had left ten chapters in a draft form, and the original intent was that I should tidy up the main text, and revise the footnotes in their entirety. It became clear at an early stage that there was much more to do than that. Rather as airplanes have made possible in hours journeys that took Gilly weeks, the internet has enabled easy access to all kinds of sources that used to be accessible only by visiting archives and specialist libraries, and thus a certain amount of extra information has come to light. One major revision came to light early on. That is that Gilly's first book, *Academic Errors,* hitherto taken to be autobiographical, turned out not to be so, and thus the relevant section of Chapter 1 has been rewritten to take this into account. I have also subdivided some of the chapters, thus increasing their number to thirteen.

So far as the notes are concerned, the vast majority of those giving references have been recast, and I have seen no need to differentiate here between my work and Hugh's. In this context in particular, I am indebted to a list of material consulted by Dottoressa Viviana Genre (with whom Hugh had been working) in the Archive at Torre Pellice, which has provided explicit references for the material held there. For those notes giving comments and opinions, I have left Hugh's as they were, but mine are initialled, so it is plain whose comments are whose.

Chapter 13 is entirely my own work, although, as noted, it is based on notes supplied by Dottoressa Genre. Tracing Gilly's family after his death was greatly facilitated by the website Ancestry.com, and I am also grateful to Eileen Tristram for assistance with the New Zealand connexions. The Appendices are also mine, and provide explanatory information on a number of points.

A book owes debts to many more people than its author. I am most grateful to the support and interest I have received throughout out the project from Hugh's sisters, Jenny Gladstone and Anna Revill, and his widow, Marilyn Norwood, and I acknowledge the trust they have put in me to finish this work. Marilyn has been most generous in providing material from Hugh's archive. As already noted, much of the information is now available on the internet, but some visits to archives were still needed, among them the Centre for Buckinghamshire Studies, Aylesbury; the Essex Record Office, Chelmsford; the Guildhall Library, London; and the British Library. I am grateful for the assistance of their staffs. Durham Castle has allowed the reproduction of the portrait of Gilly on the cover, which has greatly enhanced the work. Dr Giles Brightwell has been very helpful in providing information about the early history of the University of Durham. Hugh had drawn some of the maps, but others were needed, and I am grateful to Phillip Judge for drawing them and assimilating them so well to Hugh's own style. I am particularly grateful also to Professor William Gibson of Oxford Brookes University for reading a draft of the revised book, and for his comments.

Our thanks are due too to Christ's Hospital Museum for providing a copy of the lithograph reproduced on page 5, to Dr Meg Norman for photographs of Durham and Norham, to the National Portrait Gallery for permission to reproduce the portrait of Thomas James Judkin on page 65, and to all the contributors to Wikimedia Commons whose photographs we have made grateful use of under a Creative Commons licence.

Finally, the thanks of all of us are due to Susan Curran and the Lasse Press for taking on the publication, and, not least, compiling the index.

Nicholas Groves
Norwich, July 2014

Abbreviations used in footnotes, etc.

ASTV: Archivio Storico Tavola Valdese, Torre Pellice.
BL: British Library
CBS: Centre for Buckinghamshire Studies
CCCEd: Clergy of the Church of England Database (online resource)
CUL: Cambridge University Library
DUL: Durham University Library
ERO: Essex Record Office
LPL: Lambeth Palace Library
LVC: London Vaudois Committee
SROB: Suffolk Record Office, Bury St Edmunds branch
SROI: Suffolk Record Office, Ipswich branch.
UCL: University College, London.

Short titles used for Gilly's works:

Narrative = Narrative of an Excursion to the Mountains of Piemont and Researches among the Vaudois, or Waldenses, Protestant inhabitants of the Cottian Alps (1824).
Researches = Waldensian Researches during a second visit to the Vaudois of Piemont (1831).

Portrait of W. S. Gilly, 1834, by Joseph Bouet

Chapter 1

'The place of his birth and the home of his forefathers': childhood and schooldays

William Stephen Gilly was born at Hawkedon Parsonage in Suffolk on 19 January 1789 and was baptised at St Mary's Church in the village on 28 January 1789.[1] His father, also William Gilly, had been born on 17 December 1761 and was Rector of the parish. He had married Anne Oliver from the nearby village of Long Melford on 26 April 1788. His grandfather was William Gilly (1734–1787), Rector of Hawkedon. His great-grandfather, yet another William Gilly (1713–1782), lived at Thurston Hall, and was lord of the manor of Hawkedon and patron of the living. His great-great-grandfather, born on 21 September 1665, was also a William Gilly, who married Elizabeth, daughter and co-heiress of the illustrious Maltyward family (see Table 1.1). All this information is set out in a complex family document discussed in Chapter 2.[2]

'The home of his forefathers': Thurston Hall, Hawkedon. Photo Keith Evans (via Wikimedia Commons).

However, it has been pointed out that nineteenth-century genealogical records do not always tell the entire story, so it is only fair to record that in 1716 a William Gilly was keeping a brew-house in the nearby town of Bury St Edmunds.[3] Whatever their family origins, by the late eighteenth century the Gillys were a clerical and county family with a cousinage throughout the gentry of Suffolk.

Hawkedon is a small village which survived the twentieth century quite well. It lies on the northern side of a gentle valley ten miles south-east of the ancient market town of Bury St Edmunds. The houses are scattered around a large green. In the middle of this green, standing

---

1   SROB, FL579/4/2, Hawkedon Parish Register 1786–1812.
2   *The Pedigree of William Stephen Gilly of Hawkedon in the County of Suffolk, Gentleman. Shewing his Descent from the several heiresses of Everard and Maltyward. Collected from antient Evidences, Monumental inscriptions and Parish Registers with the Blazon of their Respective Arms. Prepared for William Stephen Gilly by George Bitton Jermyne. 19 November 1810.* This complex multi-coloured document, complete with 38 hand-coloured armorial crests, is discussed in Chapter 2. SRO, Bury HA535/4/21.
3   SROB ACC.2220/4, 'Inventory of Goods and Chattels of William Gilly, late of Bury St Edmunds.' 1716.

Table 1.1 Tree to show Gilly's ancestry

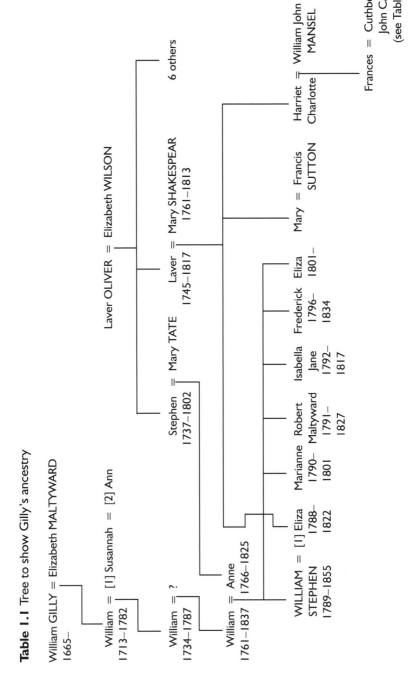

William GILLY = Elizabeth MALTYWARD
1665–

William = [1] Susannah = [2] Ann
1713–1782

Laver OLIVER = Elizabeth WILSON

William = ?
1734–1787

Stephen = Mary TATE
1737–1802

Laver = Mary SHAKESPEAR
1745–1817   1761–1813

6 others

William = Anne
1761–1837 | 1766–1825

WILLIAM = [1] Eliza   Marianne Robert   Isabella Frederick Eliza
STEPHEN   1788–   1790–   Maltyward Jane   1796–   1801–
1789–1855   1822   1801   1791–   1792–   1834
                                  1827   1817

Mary = Francis
       SUTTON

Harriet = William John
Charlotte   MANSEL

Frances = Cuthbert
          John CARR
          (see Table A2.1)

For WSG's second marriage and all descendants, see Table A2.1 in Appendix II.

by itself, is St Mary's Church. In *The Buildings of England: Suffolk*, Sir Nikolaus Pevsner described the church as lacking in noteworthy features.[4] In this instance Pevsner can be ignored, for this fine medieval church has magnificent Jacobean pews, the Gilly memorials and the Gilly vault. When he was in middle age Gilly returned briefly to Hawkedon Church and had a plaque erected:

Church of St Mary, Hawkedon, Suffolk. Photo Susan Curran

As the last memorial of his family in this County and as his farewell testimony of affection for the place of his birth and the home of his forefathers.[5]

Hawkedon parsonage was demolished during the twentieth century, and the site now stands empty. It had a large garden and faced the village green and the church. A drawing of the parsonage has survived.[6] It shows a large house with two gables, entirely fitting for a Suffolk parson and gentleman. It is still remembered by several of the older residents of the village. So William Stephen, who was born nine months after his parents' marriage, spent his childhood in a rectory in a small Suffolk village.

William Gilly senior was educated at Christ's Hospital School in London, and at Gonville and Caius College, Cambridge. In 1788, the year of his marriage, he became vicar of Hawkedon, on the presentation of his grandmother. William junior soon had brothers and sisters: on 16 May 1790 Mary Anna Gilly was born, followed by Robert Maltyward Gilly (29 July 1791), Isabella Jane Gilly (22 September 1792), and Frederick Gilly (1 June 1796).

William's sister Marianne died on 8 April 1801 when she was 10 and he was 12. She was buried at Hawkedon.[7] William may have missed his little sister, because fourteen

4   N. Pevsner, *The Buildings of England: Suffolk.* Penguin Books, 1961, p. 254. [This is not strictly true: Pevsner says the church's 'only noteworthy feature' is its porch, and goes on to note the font, screen, pulpit, stalls, wall-painting, and 'considerable fragments' of medieval glass. NWG]

5   The plaque is in the nave of Hawkedon Church.

6   SROB, HA 535/5/35, Hawkedon Parsonage.

7   Pedigree of William Stephen Gilly. Marianne (also spelled Mary Anne) was probably staying with her maternal grandparents, Stephen and Mary Oliver. However, both Marianne and her maternal grandparents died within eighteen months of each other. Her grandmother died on 26 September 1800 (aged 61), Maianne died on 8 April 1801 (aged 10) and her grandfather died on 19 March 1802 (aged 65). They share a memorial in Hawkedon Church. The memorial records Marianne as aged 11 when she died. However,

years later he named his first daughter after her. However, in November 1801, another sister was born who was baptised Eliza.[8]

The family must have needed money, for on 16 January 1796 William's father sold the advowson of Hawkedon to James Oakes for £800.[9] Thus during the eighteenth century the Gilly family had declined in status from lords of the manor of Hawkedon to normal country clergy, without the right to nominate the next incumbent. William Gilly senior remained as Vicar of Hawkedon, but his son could no longer expect to succeed to the living. Indeed, thirty-seven years later in 1833, the by then elderly gentleman was still Vicar of Hawkedon when the advowson was again sold at the London Auction Mart. On this occasion the prospectus rather unkindly stated that what was being auctioned was 'The next presentation to the Rectory and Parish Church of Hawkedon in the County of Suffolk: subject to the life of the present Incumbent, who is in the 73rd year of his age'.[10]

Christ's Hospital

Gilly was educated, as was his father, at Christ's Hospital, at that time still in the City of London.[11] Christ's Hospital was, and is, one of the best known public schools in England. The school, founded in 1553 during the reign of King Edward VI, contained in 1809 (the year after Gilly left) a thousand boys, most of whom were the sons of City of London freemen or presented by the City of London Companies. One hundred and two of the pupils were the sons of clergymen. John Wilson, in his history of the school, provides the following breakdown for that year:[12]

Source	No.
Presented by companies, parishes, etc	161
Sons of freemen of the City of London	498
Sons of non-freemen	239
Sons of clergymen	102

Later in the century, wealthy parents were to become the rule rather than the exception,

the pedigree records her as born on 16 May 1790, so she would have been five and half weeks short of her eleventh birthday.

8   *Pedigree of William Stephen Gilly.*

9   SROB, HA 535/4/7, 'Indenture of sale of Perpetual Right of Presentation to Hawkedon Rectory', 16 January 1796.

10   SROB, HA 535/4/7 Particulars of sale of 'Next presentation to the valuable Rectory of Hawkedon' at Auction Mart, London. 27 June 1833. While this statement of the sitting incumbent's age might seem callous to us, it was standard practice at the time, if only so that a potential purchaser might have an idea of how long it would be before the living fell vacant.

11   Guildhall Library, MS 12818, vol. 13. Gilly was admitted to the school in April 1797, and 'clothed' in November that year.

12   J. Wilson, *The History of Christ's Hospital*, J. Nichols, London, 1821; p. 69. A problem with this work is that Wilson was unable to consult the Hospital's records: 'I have had the misfortune of undertaking the work at a time when the various duties of the gentlemen connected with the establishment entirely precluded any of them from affording me the least assistance' (p. viii).

but at the time Gilly attended the school, it was still true to its foundation principles of educating children who have no adequate means of financial support. The boys wore a blue uniform which had changed little since the seventeenth century, and indeed is still worn by the pupils today.[13] The school operated a strict entrance policy, and was particularly favoured by the clergy. On the face of it, Christ's Hospital seemed an excellent choice. However, like all English public schools, the educational system concentrated on classical authors, to the virtual exclusion of other branches of learning.[14]

Gilly made the narrator of his first book, *Academic Errors*,[15] attend a thinly disguised Christ's Hospital, and it is safe to assume that the description provides a broadly accurate picture of the school in Gilly's day, although whether he personally experienced everything the narrator of *Academic Errors* did may be questioned. Quite possibly he was conflating episodes from his own experience and those of a number of his fellow pupils.

As an entrance test the narrator was asked to write some Latin poetry, and to his mortification handled the task poorly, as he was no versifier. However the narrator quickly learned to use the same strategy for producing Latin verses as has been used by innumerable other schoolboys in subsequent years:

> I never delivered in a single copy of verses which were my own composition; I obtained them either in return for assistance in other allotments of school business, or by getting old copies which had already been shown up upon the same thesis.[16]

A Grecian (student of the classics) at Christ's Hospital. From Ackermann's *History of Christ's Hospital*, published 1816. Grecians (of whom Gilly must have been one) had longer and better-finished coats than the mathematicians who made up the majority of students. The small cap was worn until about 1860. With grateful thanks to the Christ's Hospital Museum.

---

13 The school was always coeducational. The girls' department, separated in 1902, was reunited with the boys' in 1985. In 1809 there were sixty-five girls.

14 Wilson, *History*, p 88, says that in 1821 the boys were taught 'reading, writing, arithmetic, all classical learning, and Hebrew; part in mathematics and part in drawing'.

15 [W. S. Gilly] *Academic Errors, or Recollections of Youth, by a Member of the University of Cambridge*; London 1817. See Chapter 2 for a discussion of this book.

16 *Academic Errors*, p. 153.

Notwithstanding his knowledge of Latin, the narrator found Christ's Hospital stifling. Latin and Greek texts were studied day after day and week after week:

> While a boy was flogged for his bad metre, or wrong concorde, he was not even questioned as to his proficiency in numbers or knowledge of modern events. ... Nobody was required to know even the name of England's king, or the form of its government. ... Teach a lad first to become a useful and honourable member of society and then inform him how he may be an elegant scholar.[17]

The school appeared to show no interest in cultivating originality. One particularly bright and ingenious youth was subjected to:

> the ridicule of a parcel of blockheads who could not estimate his genius; and with more regret do I relate it, that as often I have witnessed punishments and unjustly inflicted upon him by his preceptors, who from too close an adherence to rule, or from overlooking his peculiar intellectual bias, have inflicted stripes upon him, where applauses were deservedly merited.[18]

A chapter of *Academic Errors* is devoted to the subject of flogging at Christ's Hospital. Gilly abhorred the practice, which he described as 'base, absurd, indecent and degrading', notwithstanding that it prevailed at all public schools.[19]

> The lash is applied so frequently, so indiscriminately, and often so undeservedly, that the mischief it does is infinitely more extensive than the good. ... Upon the first occasion that I beheld a boy hoisted upon the block, I blushed for the master, for the victim, and for myself.[20]

Eighteen-year-old boys were flogged for failing to produce a paper of Greek derivatives; boys knew that they were likely to be flogged when one master had a bout of rheumatism; another would flog boys entirely upon a whim. Gilly, in 1817, wrote, 'Let this abominable instrument be entirely banished from our public seminaries.'[21] On this subject he was 150 years before his time.[22]

17　*Academic Errors*, p. 156.
18　*Academic Errors*, p. 161.
19　*Academic Errors*, p. 162.
20　*Academic Errors*, p. 162.
21　*Academic Errors*, p. 167. There is another detailed account of conditions at Christ's Hospital in Leigh Hunt's autobiography, published posthumously in 1860 (*The Autobiography of Leigh Hunt, With Reminiscences of Friends and Contemporaries*, 3 vols, London 1850, and subsequently revised; ed. R Ingpen, and republished 1903). He entered the school in 1791 six years before Gilly. He too was horrified by the flogging but believed that he acquired quite a good education, albeit largely by his own efforts. Leigh Hunt's account was written when he was an old man, while Gilly wrote when still a very indignant young man. Wilson, *History*, p. 97, writing in 1821, refers to the Monday following Easter Monday as 'Funking Monday', when school resumed after the Easter break. 'The very name of *Funking Monday* cannot fail of recalling to the mind of all Blues (even now the terror of the rod is past) the gloomy aspect of the morning ...'. Did *Academic Errors*, published 1817, have its desired effect?
22　This may be compared with Charles Lamb's essay 'Christ's Hospital five-and-thirty years ago', originally printed in *The London Magazine*, vol. ii, no. xi, p. 483 (1820), and later collected into *The Essays of Elia*.

Gilly was always prudish: many years later he became indignant when the Savoy customs officers laughed at the sight of him travelling through Italy with a young wife while wearing clerical garb. As a schoolboy he deplored the fact that some of his fellow pupils were reading indecent Latin verses. Indeed he became so indignant about this practice of reading about 'Luscious and warm descriptions and voluptuous images' that he wrote, 'I would say, rather commit every vestige of Horace, Juvenal, Anacreon, and the rest of these sensual writers to the flames, than leave it in the power of boys to pore over lines and sentences which cannot fail to contaminate them.'[23] He advocated the setting-up of a government inquiry into the subject.

There is no reason to believe that William Gilly's vivid descriptions of the absurdities and cruelties of the early nineteenth-century English public school system were exaggerations. He was a pupil at Christ's Hospital before the days of Matthew Arnold and the reforming headmasters of the Victorian era:

I may trace many of the sorrows of my life to the errors into which I fell at .... Effrontery, an assumed easiness of manner, and dashing familiarity, characterize the young men who are brought up there, and it would have been very miraculous if I had escaped the general contagion; but had there been a few valuable acquirements to counterbalance these evils, I would then have withheld my censure. I cannot, however, believe that I acquired much improvement from the three years which I passed within its walls; for literary excellence, even allowing that this was attained, can never make amends for the loss of innocence. But it was not my lot to add much to the fund of knowledge which I had previously secured. Latin compositions were not to my taste, and English exercises were so rarely set, that my style was neither amended nor formed by the hints which I had received at ....[24]

He also deplored the fact that modern languages were hardly taught at public schools:

For one of the greatest defects in the education of boys appears to me, to consist in their being brought up in such ignorance of all the modern languages of Europe. There are few girls of sixteen or seventeen, who do not perfectly understand both French and Italian, (among such at least whose minds have been well cultivated), while most boys of the same age have but a smattering of bad French, and know no more of Spanish, Italian or German than they do of the longitude.[25]

Three unhappy years were spent by the narrator of *Academic Errors* at Christ's Hospital. Gilly, of course, spent ten years there, being 'discharged' on 31 October, 1808.[26]

In fact when the term of my scholastic confinement was completed, and I quitted ... to commence a new academic career on the banks of the Cam, I departed from it with this impression, that I had acquired but little where I might have learnt much, and that I have

---

Lamb was a 'Blue' from 1782 to 1789.
23 *Academic Errors*, p. 203.
24 *Academic Errors*, p. 206.
25 *Academic Errors*, p. 210
26 Guildhall Library, MS 12818, vol. 13.

Stained glass from the East Window at Hawkedon Church.
Photo Susan Curran.

been wasting months and years at that kind of institution, which, of all others in the world, possesses the amplest means of diffusing general improvement. With proper regulation and management it might accelerate the progress of the idle, quicken the apprehension of the dull, reform the vicious, and confirm the good.[27]

Gilly's account was not published until 1817, when he was 28. That was nine years after he had left school and five years after he had graduated from Cambridge. The delay in publication may have been because publishers were reluctant to print a work that was so critical of the English public school system. It is doubtful whether the governors of Christ's Hospital[28] ever realized that one of their former pupils was so critical of the education provided by the school, or indeed that *Academic Errors* referred to their school. The school's official record shows Gilly to have been an outstanding scholar, who in 1808 was the only pupil to be awarded an exhibition to the University of Cambridge.[29] Forty-five years later there was an ironic postscript to Gilly's schoolboy years. On 15 June 1853 he was due to preach a sermon before the governors of the school in commemoration of the 300th anniversary of the foundation of Christ's Hospital, but an outbreak of scarlet fever at the school caused this sermon to be cancelled. Perhaps, in the circumstances, it was just as well.

---

27   *Academic Errors*, p. 212.
28   Among whom in 1809 was Shute Barrington, Bishop of Durham (Wilson, *History*, p. 298).
29   Ed. Lockhart, *Christ's Hospital, List of University Exhibitions 1566–1885*, Christ's Hospital, 1885, entries for 1780 (William Gilly, Senior) and 1808 (William Stephen Gilly). There was in fact only one exhibition or scholarship awarded in any year. There were seven at Cambridge, awarded annually, and one at Oxford, awarded every seventh year. The scholarships included the cost of taking the BA and MA degrees. Wilson, *History*, p. 89.

Chapter 2

The young clergyman

Gilly was admitted to Gonville and Caius College, Cambridge, as a pensioner on 19 February 1808, and matriculated there in the Michaelmas Term of that year as a scholar, but soon migrated to St Catherine's College, where he was admitted on 28 December 1808.[1] At this time, St Catherine's was one of the smaller colleges. Here he was under the tutelage of Thomas Turton (1780–1865) who had been elected a fellow of the college in 1806 and a tutor in 1807. He was a notorious pluralist,[2] and later became Regius Professor of Divinity at Cambridge and, in 1845, Bishop of Ely. Turton was a vigorous and controversial writer who defended traditional Anglican values and opposed the abolition of religious tests at the universities. Gilly graduated BA on 18 January 1812 and was ordained deacon, by the Bishop of Bath and Wells, on 16 February 1812. He was priested on 25 September 1814, by the Bishop of London.[3]

While he was at Cambridge Gilly developed an interest in genealogy, and arranged for George Bitton Jermyn to prepare the ornate Gilly family tree which is now in West Suffolk County Record Office. It records:

> The pedigree of William Stephen Gilly of Hawkedon in the County of Suffolk Gentleman shewing his Descent from the several heiresses of Everard and Maltyward. Collected from antient Evidences, Monumental Inscriptions and Parish Registers with the Blazon of their Respective Arms. By George Bitton Jermyn. November 1810.[4]

---

1   Migration between colleges was quite common, and prompted by a number of reasons. Caius is the 'Norfolk' college, and was thus a natural choice for Gilly. What prompted his move to St Catherine's is unknown, but it is worth noting that, between 1713 and 1927, the mastership of the college was annexed to the fourth prebend of Norwich Cathedral: Hawkedon was in Norwich Diocese until 1914. The master (and fourth prebendary) at this time was Joseph Procter (in office 1798–1845).

2   He was Lucasian Professor 1822–26; Regius Professor of Divinity 1827–42; Prebendary of Lincoln 1827–45; Dean of Peterborough 1830–42; Dean of Westminster 1842–45; and Bishop of Ely 1845–64. See further Thompson Cooper, 'Turton, Thomas, 1780–1864', rev. M. C. Curthoys, *Oxford Dictionary of National Biography*, Oxford University Press, 2004; online edn, Jan 2007 (www.oxforddnb.com/view/article/27895, accessed 30 March 2011).

3   Venn, *Alumni Cantabrigiensis, s.v.* Gilly, William Stephen. He proceeded to MA in 1817, and DD (without taking the BD) in 1833.

4   '*The Pedigree of William Stephen Gilly of Hawkedon* ...' (SROB, HA 535/4/21.) George Bitton Jermyn (1789–1857) was a contemporary of Gilly, and his father was an attorney in Halesworth. Jermyn matriculated at Caius in the Michaelmas Term of 1808, although in 1813 he migrated to Trinity Hall, where he graduated LLB in 1814. He was ordained deacon by the Bishop of Norwich in 1813, and priested the following year by the Bishop of Ely. Until 1817 he was curate to Gilly's father at Hawkedon. Genealogical research was his major interest in life. He made voluminous collections for a genealogical history of Suffolk which are preserved in the Bury St Edmunds Museum (see further, Venn, *Alumni Cantabrigiensis*, entry for Jermyn, George Bitton; and Gordon Goodwin, 'Jermyn, George Bitton (1789–1857)', rev. Myfanwy Lloyd, *Oxford Dictionary of National Biography*, Oxford University Press, 2004; online edn, May 2005 (www.oxforddnb.com/view/article/14779, accessed 19 March 2011)).

This family tree contains a coloured coat of arms for each of thirty-eight members of the Gilly family, with descent traced back to the seventeenth century. It is annotated in several places in Gilly's handwriting, and other hands have entered additional information, taking the document forward to the death of Gilly's son, William Octavius Shakespear Gilly, on 10 August 1860. A note by Gilly records that in 1812 he took a journey to Waltham in Essex to search the registers for records of family history but could not find anything, as records previous to 1720 had been destroyed. There is also a pencil note by him that the William Gilly who married Miss Maltyward in 1712 was an officer in the army, quartered in Bury St Edmunds. It is possible that this ornate document may be rather too good to be completely true, as some nineteenth-century genealogists were not above ignoring plebeian ancestors: for example, the William Gilly who kept a brewhouse in Bury St Edmunds in 1716 is nowhere mentioned.[5]

While studying at Cambridge University Gilly suffered from ill health. So,

> For the restoration of my health in the year 1811, I was advised to try the effects of sea air and a change of climate, and was glad to accept the opportunity offered me, by the captain of an 80-gun ship, to take a cruise with him off the southern part of the French coast.[6]

This was no ordinary voyage, for the Napoleonic wars were still in progress:

> On one occasion, in a severe tempest in the Bay of Biscay, a flash of lightening struck the ship and set her on fire. The calmness with which orders were given and obeyed, and the rapidity with which the fire was extinguished, without the least hurry or confusion, made a deep impression on me. This was afterwards increased by the conduct of the crew in the severe gale of wind, when it was necessary to navigate one of the narrow channels, by which the squadron that blockaded Rochelle and Rochfort was frequently endangered. The vessel had to pass between two rocks, so near that a biscuit could have been thrown from the deck on either. An old quarter-master was at the wheel; the captain stood by to con and to direct his steering. At one fearful crisis, every blast threatened to shiver a sail, or to carry away a spar, and a single false movement of the helmsman, or the slightest want of steadiness or of obedience on the part of any man on duty, would have been fatal to the life of everyone on board.[7]

It seems that this exciting sea cruise had its desired effect and brought about an improvement in Gilly's health, for he led an exceptionally busy life during the next forty years.

Gilly's younger brothers embarked on military and naval careers. Robert Maltyward, who had been born in 1791, was gazetted as an ensign of the 67th Regiment in May 1810 and left England to serve in the East Indies in May 1811.[8] Frederick, born on 1 June 1796, entered the navy on his thirteenth birthday and became a midshipman

---

5   SROB ACC.2220/4, 'Inventory of goods and chattels of William Gilly, late of Bury St Edmunds', 1716.

6   W. O. S. Gilly, *Narratives of Shipwrecks of the Royal Navy between 1795 and 1849* (London, 1850), p. ix. (This book, by Gilly's son, has a preface written by Gilly.)

7   *Narratives of Shipwrecks*, p. ix.

8   *The Pedigree of William Stephen Gilly.*

on HMS *Courageous*.[9] In due course he was promoted to lieutenant. Many years later, in 1834, Frederick 'lost his life in a generous attempt to save a vessel from shipwreck on the coast of Sussex'.[10]

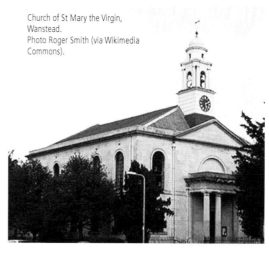

Church of St Mary the Virgin, Wanstead.
Photo Roger Smith (via Wikimedia Commons).

On 19 June 1812 Gilly's father was instituted to the living of Wanstead in Essex.[11] This was on the joint presentation of the Hon. William Pole-Tylney-Long-Wellesley and his wife.[12] William Gilly senior remained, however, as Rector of Hawkedon and thus became a pluralist, something much criticized in the radical press of the period.[13] At Hawkedon he was represented by a licensed curate – from 1813 to 1817, George Bitton Jermyn. After 1812, William occasionally conducted services for his father at both Hawkedon and Wanstead.[14]

---

9   *The Pedigree of William Stephen Gilly.*

10   W. O. S. Gilly, *Narratives of Shipwrecks*, p x. Also ASTV, series V, vol. 35, c. 253: letter from Gilly to Bonjour (Moderator of the Vaudois Church), 9 December 1834.

11   His father (William, 1735–1787, WSG's grandfather) was also Rector of Wanstead from 1759 to 1787, in plurality with Hawkedon (Venn, *Alumni Cantabrigiensis*). Dr Samuel Glasse held the living between the two Gillys.

12   *The Pedigree of William Stephen Gilly*, although the *Clerical Guide* for 1836 lists the husband alone as patron, but they were joint patrons: the faculty of admission of Gilly as rector was 'on the presentation of William Pole-Tylney-Long-Wellesley and his wife, patrons' (ERO, D/DB Q12). William Pole-Wellesley (a nephew of Arthur, Duke of Wellington, 'the Iron Duke') married in 1812 Catherine Tylney-Long, the richest heiress in England: she was heir to Wanstead House and its estate, and thus inherited the patronage of the church with it. Pole-Wellesley then took the name William Pole-Tylney-Long-Wellesley. From 1842 he was known as Viscount Wellesley, until in 1845 he succeeded his father as the fourth Earl of Mornington. The couple were lavish spenders who were bankrupt by 1822. Wanstead House was last rebuilt by Richard Child (created Viscount Castlemaine, and later Earl Tylney), in 1715–22, and was demolished after its contents had been sold to pay their debts. The Earl led such a dissipated life that his obituary in the *Morning Chronicle*, 4 July 1857, claimed that he was 'redeemed by no single virtue, adorned by no single grace'. One wonders how Gilly senior came to his attention. (G. Le G. Norgate, 'Pole, William Wellesley, third earl of Mornington', rev. John K. Severn, *Oxford Dictionary of National Biography*, Oxford University Press, 2004; online edn, Jan 2008.) http://www.oxforddnb.com/view/article/29010, accessed 29 March 2011. The parish church of St Mary was rebuilt in 1789–90 by Thomas Hardwick.

13   Pluralism, the holding of more than one living at the same time, has often been criticized as an evil of the eighteenth and early nineteenth centuries, but was no more widespread then than it had been during the Middle Ages. In both periods, it was in many cases prompted by the need to ensure a decent income, as the stipends of many parishes were poor, and only by holding two or more could a living wage be earned. There were, it is true, 'career' pluralists, who collected rich livings and appointments (such as Thomas Turton: see note 2), and who often paid scant attention to their parishes, but others, as seems to have been the case with the Gillys, ensured that adequate assistant curates were appointed, even if they paid them an absolute minimum. It also rewarded active and conscientious clergy, and helped spread their influence over more parishes.

14   For Wanstead, see ERO 292/1/5 (baptisms 1813–37); 292/1/6 (burials 1813–37); 292/1/7 (marriages

By 1812 William Gilly was 23 years old, held a degree from the University of Cambridge, had almost been shipwrecked, and was an ordained priest of the Established Church. No matter how ancient his ancestors, he would have to make his own way in life because his father had sold the right of the next presentation to Hawkedon when Gilly was aged 7.[15] Wartime agricultural prosperity was ending, and England was entering the post-war years of depression, hunger and repression, which are now remembered for the Corn Laws, enclosures, Peterloo, the Tolpuddle Martyrs, rick-burning and the Luddites. Many parsons were unpopular figures in rural England, as they were closely identified with the gentry by the agricultural labourers, who were lucky if they earned a shilling a day. Another country parson, the Reverend Patrick Brontë, always slept with a loaded pistol by his bed.

In 1813, Gilly became assistant curate to his father at Wanstead while searching for a means to progress in life. Presumably he lived with his parents. Assistant curates[16] were the labourers of the Anglican hierarchy, although incumbents of poorly endowed livings were little better off. Thousands of them were employed by absentee incumbents to do the hard work of conducting baptisms, marriages and funerals; reading the service on Sundays; comforting the sick; and catechizing the children. Frequently they had to find their own accommodation and keep their families on as little as £50 per annum. Many clergymen spent their entire lives as assistant curates. Their widows could expect no pensions, although neither could the widows of beneficed clergy.[17]

Gilly did however have the advantages of an energetic personality, a Cambridge education, a family background rooted in the Suffolk gentry, and an ability to write. On 27 July 1814 he married Eliza Oliver, from Brill in Buckinghamshire, at her parish church.[18] It was a good marriage for Gilly, as the Oliver family were Buckinghamshire gentry, just as the Gilly family were Suffolk gentry.[19] The Olivers lived in Brill House, which was, and still is, the largest house in the village. It was a triple marriage, as Mary Oliver married Francis Sutton,[20] and Harriet Charlotte Oliver married John Mansel,[21] on the same day. Indeed, Gilly was strengthening the ties between the

---

1813–37). For Hawkedon, see SROB, FL579/4/3 (baptisms, 1813–97); FL579/4/7 (burials, 1813–1997); FL579/4/8 (marriages, 1838–1996).

15   SROB, HA 535/4/7, 'Indenture of sale of perpetual right of presentation to Hawkedon Rectory', 16 January 1796, and see Chapter 1.

16   This is the correct term. The curate of a parish is the incumbent – otherwise called rector or vicar – who has the cure of souls. However, in current usage, 'curate' has come to mean the assistant clergy of a parish. A complication arises with perpetual curates, who were effectively incumbents, but with no endowments; they were paid by the diocese, and not from tithes. The exact legal standing of the various parochial clergy is exceedingly complex.

17   See *The State of the Curates of the Church of England: A letter addressed to the Archbishop of Canterbury* by 'A parish priest', published by J. Nisbet, 1828. This passionate plea was in consequence of the publication of Gilly's *Horae Catecheticae* in 1828. Some curates received barely enough money to avoid starvation.

18   CBS, PR 27/1/10, Brill Wedding Register 1813–37 (entry no. 9).

19   There are plaques in both Hawkedon and Brill churches recording eighteenth- and nineteenth-century burials of members of these two county families.

20   CBS, PR 27/1/10, Brill Wedding Register 1813–37 (entry no. 8).

21   CBS, PR 27/1/10, Brill Wedding Register 1813–37 (entry no. 10).

families: reference to Table 1.1 in Chapter 1 reveals that Gilly's wife was the cousin of his mother. The wedding was by licence, with 'consent of the parents', which suggests that Mary Oliver was under age. It is noticeable that, while the others were content with the usual two witnesses, Gilly had six, of whom three were Shakespears: this explains why his eldest son was called William Octavius Shakespear.[22] Gilly took his wife to live with him at Brandean in Hampshire. It was here that their first child was born on 15 March 1816. The baby was named Mary Anna, possibly in memory of Gilly's little sister.[23]

Academic Errors

In 1816 and 1817 Gilly wrote his first book, *Academic Errors*.[24] As outlined in Chapter 1, this radical book was probably based at least partly on his own experiences, and challenged the educational practices of his time. Gilly did not acknowledge having written this book until 1824, when he included it as one of his publications on the title page of his third book, *Narrative of an Excursion to the Mountains of Piemont*.

Hugh Norwood assumed that *Academic Errors*, published anonymously in 1817, was autobiographical, and that Gilly had thus passed through a variety of forms of education, but examination of the Christ's Hospital admission register reveals that Gilly himself was admitted in 1797, at the age of 9,[25] being presented by William Marsh of Knightsbridge, one of the governors.[26] The dates of Gilly's attendance at the school are therefore not conformable with those of the narrator of *Academic Errors* and we should now read the account as literary licence.

The opening 'Advertisement' of *Academic Errors* claims that 'By retracing the courses of study pursued during his early years, and explaining the difference modes of instruction by which knowledge was imparted to himself,' the author would show the weaknesses of various aspects of education of his day. The narrator claims that he was educated at home by his father until the age of 10, when, his parents having to move abroad temporarily, he was enrolled at 'a County Grammar School', run by a Mr P ---. This man and his school have been described as prototypes of Wackford Squeers and his Dotheboys Hall. The narrator was removed from this establishment about a year later by his uncle, who paid a surprise visit, and found him cowed and terrified. This uncle then sent him to board and study with a kindly clergyman, a Mr H---. He stayed there for three years, until Mr H--- was preferred to a better

---

22   The witnesses were William Gilly (WSG's father); Jane Shakespear; Arthur William Shakespear; Mary Anne Shakespear; Richard M[ansel]? – the page is very damaged at this point; and Anna Elizabeth Oliver.
23   *The Pedigree of William Stephen Gilly.*
24   *Academic Errors, or, Recollections of Youth, by a Member of the University of Cambridge*, London, 1817.
25   Guildhall Ms 12818, vol. 13. This is in line with the Regulations 'revised and settled' in 1809, given in J. Wilson, *The History of Christ's Hospital*, London, 1821, pp. 84ff. Regulation no 2 reads: 'No children shall be admitted, but such as shall be between the ages of seven and ten years.'
26   Guildhall Ms 12818, vol. 13. William Marsh (1755–1846) was a prominent banker, who counted Horatio Nelson among his clients. The bank collapsed in 1824 following a fraud perpetrated by one of the junior partners.

living. He was then enrolled at 'a Public School' (at the age of 14): this is a thinly disguised Christ's Hospital.

What we may have in this volume is a text with a purpose similar to that of Swift's *Gulliver's Travels* or Defoe's *Robinson Crusoe*: a means of presenting unpalatable ideas to the reading public, but disguised as autobiography in order to lend it an air of authenticity; there are plenty of other eighteenth-century parallels. Gilly contrasts the extremes of Mr P--- and Mr H---: the one a great 'flogger', who required rote learning of rules and texts without any attempt to explain them or how they could be applied; the other a most pacific man, who instructed by drawing the rule from the example. He also sets the horrors of Mr P---'s County Grammar School and those of the Public School against the much more efficient setting of home education with his father and with Mr H---.

This is not to say that Gilly was inventing what he said. On the contrary, it is entirely likely that schools such as Mr P---'s existed (was it, indeed, modelled on the contemporary Edward VI Grammar School in Bury St Edmunds?), and he may have been drawing on the experiences of boys he knew who had been through one or more of them. The horrors are so uniform and seemingly unending that one cannot help reading them as a conflation, and in some ways an over-drawing. As to Mr H---, that there were plenty of clergy who needed to take in young gentlemen and tutor them in order to eke out their stipends, is well known; that many of them were, like Mr H---, natural and gifted teachers, is equally beyond doubt. So far as its description of life at Christ's Hospital is concerned, it is probably accurate.

Academic Errors thus takes on a much greater significance than previously thought. Far from being mere autobiographical reminiscence, it is a manifesto for the reformation of education at school level. It is all the more intriguing, therefore, that Gilly did not turn his pen to criticize university education, which at the time was equally perfunctory and obsessed with classical authors. *The Gentleman's Magazine* published four paragraphs of the book in April 1818 and described it as 'an entertaining and possibly an useful little volume'.[27] No other review of the book has been traced.

27   *Gentleman's Magazine*, April 1818, vol. 88, p. 343.

'Miserable and isolated': near North Fambridge, Essex. Photo Terry Joyce (via Wikimedia Commons).

Rector of North Fambridge

Once he had been ordained, it is most likely that Gilly intended to progress in the Anglican hierarchy. The key to advancement was patronage. Incumbents were presented to livings by patrons, and as the Gilly family knew full well, the right of patronage was frequently a saleable commodity. Patrons came in many forms, including country squires, Oxford and Cambridge colleges, the sovereign, cathedral chapters, London merchants and dowager ladies. Jane Austen's portraits of Mr Collins and his patron Lady Catherine de Bourgh in *Pride and Prejudice* are not exaggerations. As the advowson of Hawkedon Church had been sold, Gilly would have to look elsewhere. He therefore developed a talent which was to serve him well in later life: the ability to cultivate relations with influential people.

The same influential patron who had presented Gilly senior to his parish in Wanstead now assisted Gilly junior. The Rt Hon. William Pole-Tylney-Long-Wellesley was the son of the Marquis of Wellesley, Member of Parliament for Queen's County in Ireland,[28] nephew of the Duke of Wellington, a former Chief Secretary for Ireland, and Master of the Royal Mint. He had married the richest heiress in England.[29] The Hon. Mr Wellesley was obviously a man of influence. He recommended Gilly to Lord Eldon, the Lord Chancellor of England.[30] The Lord Chancellor is, by right of office, patron of over 800 livings. So, on 17 March 1817, Gilly was presented by the Lord Chancellor to the Rectory of North Fambridge in Essex.[31]

However, North Fambridge was one of the most miserable and isolated parishes in England. It was a tiny village on the Essex marshes with a reputation for being both unhealthy and lawless. It had a small church,[32] a ferry over the River Crouch, an inn, and 148 inhabitants. There was no parsonage. The main occupation was growing oysters on the tidal marshes, and the oyster beds were as carefully tended as any garden.[33] Between the years of 1813 and 1852 there were 150 burials in the parish, of which fifty-four were children aged under 5 years.[34] There were no gentry anywhere near the village.[35] The living was however worth the sum of £283 per annum in 1831.[36] There is no evidence of Gilly ever doing anything for his parishioners. Not one

---

28 Now County Laois.

29 See above, note 12.

30 W. S. Gilly, *The Spirit of the Gospel; Or the four Evangelists Elucidated* (London 1818), p. ii.

31 At this time, unlike today, clergy were instituted privately, often in the bishop's chapel, and not during a public service in their new church.

32 The church, dedicated in honour of the Trinity, is a tiny brick construction of the seventeenth century, consisting of a nave only, although it contains a fourteenth-century font, implying that the current church is a replacement. A west porch was added late in the nineteenth century.

33 E. S. Beach, *Notes on the Parish of North Fambridge,* 1948, typescript, British Library, 1298 m.11 (116). The author was a small girl in the parish in the 1880s.

34 C. Cane, *Brief Notes on North Fambridge,* privately printed, 1909. See also ERO D/P 206/1/7, Burials Register, North Fambridge, 1813–1982.

35 Beach, *Notes on the Parish of North Fambridge.*

36 The *Clerical Guide and Ecclesiastical Directory,* compiled from the 1835 *Report of Commissioners appointed by His Majesty to Inquire into Ecclesiastical Revenues of England and Wales,* London, 1836, p. 77. Hawkedon

of the baptisms, marriages or burials in the parish was carried out by Gilly in person.[37] Indeed, somebody must have complained that North Fambridge was being neglected, for on 1 December 1819 Gilly wrote to William Howley, Bishop of London:

> My Lord
> I will lose no time in endeavouring to comply with Your Lordship's desire, & in engaging a Gentleman to serve my Church at North Fambridge, who shall reside on the same side of the water. – Indeed it was so much my wish to make this arrangement before, that I wrote to Mr Owen, the Curate of Lackingdon to request that he wd undertake the duty, and upon my going to N. Fambridge last month, was very much disappointed in finding that for the present he is prevented by another engagement. Yr Lordship will allow me to add, that I did not offer the nomination to Mr Steel, until I was fearful that further delay should expose me to the penalty, incurred by not having a Licensed Curate.
> Begging your Lordship will accept this Explanation, & the assurance that I will exert myself to procure a proper substitution.
> I remain, My Lord
> Yr Lordship's
> Most Obt humble Servant
> W. S. Gilly
>
> Hawkedon, Nr Bury.
> Dec. 1. 1819 [38]

At no time did Gilly indicate any intention of himself going to live and work in North Fambridge. Financially the living was profitable, as from the annual income he had to pay only expenses of about £50 and a curate's salary of under £100.[39] Gilly's neglect of his small flock of oyster cultivators in the miserable parish of North Fambridge is in sharp contrast with his later life, when the records show him to have been a hardworking and conscientious priest in difficult parishes.

Nonetheless, having obtained a living, no matter how inconsequential, Gilly had taken the first step up the ecclesiastical ladder. The family returned to live in Hawkedon, where he acted as curate to his father, the non-resident Vicar. Here, two

---

was worth £275. This illustrates a contemporary problem: many insignificant livings had high stipends attached, while those of the growing industrial towns were often very poorly endowed.

37   ERO, Parish registers of North Fambridge. Registers of baptisms (D/P 206/1/6, 1813-1981); marriages (D/P 206/1/8, 1813–38, and 206/1/9, 1838–1925; and burials (D/P 206/1/7, 1813–1982). He left so little trace that the village website lists his two curates as rectors, and does not mention him at all.

38   LPL, Fulham Papers, Howley, vol. 17, folio 77, letter from Gilly to William Howley, Bishop of London, 1 December 1819. The registers reveal that C. A. Sage signed as curate from May 1817 to the end of 1818; he was followed by Thomas Steele [sic] throughout 1819; Charles Owen then succeeded as curate until 1832, when Gilly resigned. After that, T. Benson signed as rector. Sage also occurs in the Wanstead registers as 'officiating minister' a few times in 1817 (e.g. ERO, D/P 292, /1/5, 14 September 1817).

39   Report of Ecclesiastical Commissioners, 1835. The Diocese of London had 351 assistant curates, with an average stipend of £100 each: *Clerical Guide* for 1836. This rather pessimistic view of the non-resident clergy should perhaps be balanced by the benefits of non-residence: that it allowed clergy to spread their influence well beyond their benefices, and also of course provided employment for younger curates, enabling them to get a toe on the ladder. [NWG]

more daughters were born: Eliza Henrietta (born 27 August 1818; died 13 October 1818), and Rosalie Emily, born on 18 July 1820.[40] His sister Isabella died at Wanstead on 23 May 1817 at the age of 24. Gilly was to lose his wife, baby daughter, two sisters, and two of his brothers before any of them reached the age of 40.

The Spirit of the Gospel

In 1818 his second book was published. This was entitled *The Spirit of the Gospel; Or, the Four Evangelists Elucidated, by Explanatory Observations*.[41] The book has a dedication to 'The Right Hon. John Lord Eldon, Lord High Chancellor of Great Britain, High Steward of the University of Oxford etc. etc. etc.' It begins as follows:

> I should risk Your Lordship's displeasure, if I were to attempt to express all those feelings of admiration and respect, which have had their share in rendering me desirous of publishing this work under the sanction of Your Name.

This dedication continues for five pages. It appears sycophantic to us, but was the accepted way of expressing indebtedness at the time.

In this book, Gilly set out short texts from the gospels of St Matthew, St Mark, St Luke and St John, and proceeded to explain their purposes. This is a traditional form of Anglican sermons, and the book might well have been a useful volume for parsons searching for edifying words to preach on cold Sunday mornings. Its theme is Christ's love for sinful humanity. It is not an academic tome: the text is succinct, and nowhere does it depart from Anglican orthodoxy. There are no polemics against either nonconformists or Papists. In later life even Gilly's theological adversaries acknowledged that he was a man with a mild disposition who held strong Christian beliefs, had a passion for hard work, and generally got on well with his fellow men.[42]

He did not however, extend his mildness to Islam, and indeed described Muhammed as the 'Impostor of Mecca'.[43] He believed that Christianity would eventually triumph throughout the world, although there would be much travail before this was achieved:

> The service of religion must be an active service: an arduous warfare must be commenced, and all the duties of a resolute man and faithful soldier of the cross performed. We must do violence to ourselves; put a painful constraint upon our inclinations; must resist and

---

40 *The Pedigree of William Stephen Gilly.*
41 W. S. Gilly, *The Spirit of the Gospel; Or the four Evangelists Elucidated*, London, 1818, p. ii.
42 The Reverend James Wheeler (a Roman Catholic priest) complemented Gilly on his 'natural mildness and suavity of disposition' in 1836, when he poked fun at Gilly's 'Waldensian Hobby' in a pamphlet. See J. Wheeler, *A Brief Reply to the Reverend Dr Gilly's Tract*, Durham 1836. In 1875, twenty years after Gilly's death, 'An Old Member of Durham Athenaeum Club' remembered him with this tribute: 'never was there a man more beloved in a parish than was Dr Gilly for visiting the sick, attending to his church duties, and as a plain earnest preacher of the Gospel. He worked harmoniously with Presbyterians and Dissenters. He was no bigot. He would work with anyone and was always anxious to do good.' Letter to *Durham Chronicle*, 24 December 1875.
43 *The Spirit of the Gospel*, p. 30.

strive against our spiritual enemy; press forcibly through the straight and narrow way that leads to heaven, and not expect to arrive there until after a long and violent struggle with opposing forces.[44]

Gilly's writings reflect the social attitudes of his times. He was perturbed that Joseph was only a carpenter, and admired the evangelists for having abstained from recording the business transactions of Christ's youth.[45] He acknowledged that four of the apostles were fishermen:

> But this occupation, so ignoble in our own times, was not considered so in an age and country, where every man followed some employment, and was taught to gain a subsistence by the sweat of his brow, by some handicraft[46]

but they were also quite clearly gentlemen.

Most of the book is easy enough for a lay person to read, but some of the words used are obscure. Only erudite readers would have known that when the disciples were described as subsisting on 'eleemosynary contributions' they did not need to buy food because it was given to them.[47] When discussing Eastern funeral practices, he added:

> The native Irish retain precisely the same form of obsequy: the songs and the chorus are performed alternately by mourners placed at the head and feet of the deceased as described by Homer; and their cry of lamentation, or ullaloo, corresponds with the wulliah woo, spoken of in the 'Narrative of a Residence in Tripoli'. It is from this and other oriental customs, that the aboriginal Irish are supposed to have been derived from some Asiatic tribe.[48]

Gilly knew and loved his Bible, and acknowledged the sinfulness of man. He had read widely, and quoted Josephus, Homer and contemporary theologians with confidence. His belief that people can choose whether to be good or sinful does of course imply that he acknowledged the existence of free will. (This principle is important, for he subsequently spent over thirty years as the champion of the Waldensian Church of Piedmont. The Waldensians had been Calvinists for 260 years, and Calvinists hold the doctrine of predestination. Theologically there was always a considerable gap between Gilly's beliefs and the beliefs of the Waldensian Church.) No review has been discovered of *The Spirit of the Gospel*, and it was never republished.

---

44   *The Spirit of the Gospel*, p. 29.
45   *The Spirit of the Gospel*, p. 245.
46   *The Spirit of the Gospel*, p. 345. Can one detect a foreshadowing of William Morris and the 'Dignity of Labour' here?
47   *The Spirit of the Gospel*, p. 348.
48   *The Spirit of the Gospel*, p. 55.

SPCK and first contact with the Waldensian Church

Gilly's father had for several years been a committee member of the Society for the Promotion of Christian Knowledge (SPCK). On 11 May 1819 father and son attended a meeting of the SPCK in London, where the latter appealed successfully for 'books for the use of the poor of Wickhambrook'. This is a small hamlet five kilometres west of Hawkedon. At the same meeting a very affecting letter was read from Ferdinand Peyrani, minister of Pramol in Piedmont. Pastor Peyrani:

> requested that some aid might be sent in books or money to the ancient Protestant Congregation in the mountains of Piemont, who were struggling hard against poverty and oppression. Of these Vaudois, at that time, I had but imperfect knowledge, but from the moment my mind was thus directed to the subject, it took complete possession of me; and the books to which I now applied for further information, confirmed me in my purpose of visiting this people in their native valleys.[49]

Throughout his life, Gilly was a compulsive writer. Tracing his many publications has proved to be exceedingly difficult, as the habit of publishing anonymously remained with him throughout his life. In July 1821, he possibly contributed an anonymous essay to the *Quarterly Review*. This was about the religious missions of the Reverend Henry Martyn, who died at Tocat in Persia on 16 August 1812 aged 31. Martyn, an exceptionally dedicated missionary, had translated the New Testament into Persian, and left a journal of his life.[50]

---

49 W. S. Gilly, *Narrative of an Excursion to the Mountains of Piemont in the year MDCCCXXIII and Researches among the Vaudois, or Waldenses, Protestant Inhabitants of the Cottian Alps,* 4th edn 1827, p. 4. See also SPCK, *Minutes 1816–22,* July 1821, no. 38, p. 226. Referred to in R. Vigne, 'The sower will again cast his seed. Vaudois and British interaction in the 19th century', in A. deLang (ed.), *Dall'Europa Alle Valli Valdesi,* Turin, 1990.

50 'Memoir of the Rev. Henry Martyn, BD, late Fellow of St John's College, Cambridge, and Chaplain to the Honourable East India Company', *Quarterly Review,* vol. 25, no. 50, pp. 437–53. This essay is identified as being by Rev. W. Gilly (Wanstead) in Hill and Helen Chadwick Shine, *The Quarterly Review under Gifford: Identification of contributors 1809–1824,* University of North Carolina Press, 1949, p. 75. There is a faint possibility that this was written by William Gilly senior, but this is unlikely on stylistic grounds: for instance, Muhammed is referred to as an 'imposter' in both this essay and *The Spirit of the Gospel.* Many years later Gilly wrote a similar, but longer, account of the life of another missionary priest who died young: see Chapter 8. However, the website *Quarterly Review Archive* (www.rc.umd.edu/reference/qr/index.50.html) contains the following information on the article, implying it is by Gilly senior:

> 'The following evidence is published here for the first time. Murray MS., WG to JM, 31 Dec. 1824: 'If you have not Gilly, send to me for it:—Only I must have it again, as it was presented to me by himself.' The authorship of this striking anti-missions article (assuming it is the elder William Gilly) suggests some telling associations. William Stephen Gilly (1789–1855), Gilly's son, had befriended Leigh Hunt at Christ's Hospital; he later visited Lord Bryon at Genoa. These liberal connections seemed to have had little effect on young Gilly for in the same year this article appeared the younger Gilly published his *Narrative of an Excursion to the ... Vaudois.* The Vaudois, an Italian Protestant sect intermittently the focus of Catholic persecution, were perennially the object of English anti-Catholic propaganda (*vide* Milton's 'On the Late Massacre in Piedmont'). On the strength of this book and a flurry of public appearances the younger Gilly became a prominent anti-Catholic crusader. A Church of England clergyman like his father before him, the younger Gilly gained promotion in the church through the sponsorship of Lord Eldon, a

The 'Irish Papers' episode

In January 1824 an intriguing event occurred in Gilly's life, which may help to explain certain other occurrences in later years – notably the Waldensian 'crisis'. Few historians would dispute that the history of England's involvement in Ireland contains many unpleasant episodes. In 1798 an Irish rebellion had been suppressed with brutality. In order to prevent Ireland forming a political alliance with France, in 1800 the British Parliament passed the Union with Ireland Act, and the following year the Act of Union (Ireland), uniting the British and Irish parliaments, was forced through the Irish Parliament by the bribery of Irish politicians.[51] In January 1824, Gilly came into possession (though not ownership) of compromising papers about these episodes. He had been asked to edit them for publication, but instead he tried to sell them to the British Government so that they could be suppressed. Gilly wrote to Robert Peel, the Chief Secretary for Ireland in the British Government:

> My Dear Sir,
> May I beg the favor of your having the goodness to secure for the accompanying letter, addressed to the Earl of Liverpool, a safe passage to his Lordship's hands.
> It relates to some papers that are confided to me for publication. They are the memoirs or reminiscences of a dignitary in the Irish church, a very old man, who is now abroad, but had been much behind the curtain, and knows more of the political intrigues relating to the succession of Bishops, and their Promotion to the Bench, and to the measures which brought about the Irish Union, than ought to be committed to Print.
> But my venerable friend has been persuaded that his anecdotes, which are extremely amusing, will be read with avidity, and his great age renders him less alive to the indiscretion of publishing them, than he would have been in his younger days: there is therefore no doubt that he will persevere in his intentions, and find another person to superintend the press, if I refuse, unless his object can be answered in another way.
> It strikes me that Government might be induced to purchase the manuscript, to add to the collection of State Records, for it really contains valuable materials for future History, however unfit it may be for present publication. If it goes to press now, it will betray secrets that ought not to be revealed, it will place the characters of individuals of high rank and influence in an awkward point of view, & be of great disservice to the Church.
> My letter to Lord Liverpool requests permission to submit these papers to his Lordship's private inspection, and urges what is strictly true, that I have no motive in this proceeding, but zeal for the Establishment of which I am a beneficed member, and a reluctance to see an unnecessary exposure of intrigues either in Church or State.
> Several eminent publishers are mad to get the work into their hands, but I hope to heaven a mode of suppressing it may be devised, which will satisfy my friend that I have consulted his interest, and public expediency at the same time. He has not the remotest idea of the step that I am taking, but I am exceedingly anxious to prevent his committing

leading Ultra-Tory. In the light of his son's evangelical propensities, it is charming to read the elder Gilly's *QR* article as an epistle from of an unzealous Polonius to his son urging him not to join the mission field. J[ohn]M[urray] III's Register: 'Rev. W. Gilly (Wanstead),' but without evidence.

51   The bribery consisted largely of peerages and other honours.

himself, which I am sure he will do, unless something can be put in the scale against the tempting offers which the Booksellers are making for the Copyright.

Pray accept my best apologies for troubling you upon this subject, and believe me, My dear Sir,

Yours most faithfully,

William Stephen Gilly

Wanstead

Janry 26. 1824. [52]

His letter to Lord Liverpool, the Prime Minister, is very similar, though couched in a more formal vein:

The most material part of the memoir relates to the succession of Bishops, and the interest upon which they were promoted to the Bench, and to circumstances connected with the Rebellion of 1798 and to the Irish Union. [53]

Gilly finishes by saying that, although he is 'a perfect stranger to Your Lordship', he begged leave to add that 'I am known to the Earl of St Germains, Lord Maryborough, and the Rt Hon John Villiers', who would vouch that Gilly was not writing on an unimportant matter.

Several different interpretations can be put upon the motives for Gilly's decision. If nothing else, the episode reveals his ability to act duplicitously. Having been entrusted with the papers by their author, and, one assumes, given him his word that he would do as requested, he instead attempted to get them suppressed – acting, as he acknowledged, without the author having 'the remotest idea of the step that I am taking'. But the decision may also be read as Gilly acting in his own interest. By bringing himself to the attention of Peel and Liverpool in this manner (and along the way advertising his noble acquaintance), he was almost certainly hoping for some return for what he perceived as a service to the nation: most likely a 'plum living' in the gift of the Prime Minister. If so, he was disappointed.

The letter to Peel bears a pencil note, probably in the hand of Peel's secretary, which reads 'Dean of Raphoe', prefixed by a sign that is probably to be interpreted as 'Query'. The Dean of Raphoe would fit the picture. This was Richard Allott, who was indeed living abroad at the time. [54] John Smith of Gray's Inn (most likely a pseudonym)

---

52 Manuscript letter, Gilly to Robert Peel, 26 January 1824; British Library, MS Add 40360, Peel Papers, vol. CLXXX, f 220. Gilly's references to the church and Bishops refer of course to the Anglican hierarchy in Ireland, and not to the Roman Catholic clergy who ministered to the majority of Irish people.

53 BL, MS Add 40360, Peel Papers, vol. CLXXX, f 222, letter, Gilly to Lord Liverpool, 26 January 1824. The two letters have hitherto been attributed to Gilly's father (also William Gilly). However the letters are in the handwriting of William Stephen Gilly and signed with his full name. The incorrect attribution was probably caused by similarity in names, identical occupations, and the fact that in January 1824 the young widower and his three children were living with his parents at Wanstead Rectory whilst he wrote his book about the Waldensians and searched for employment.

54 Richard Allott (1745–1832). Admitted to Trinity College, Cambridge, 1762; scholar 1763; BA 1766, MA 1769. He was made deacon in 1767 by the Bishop of Norwich (his priesting is not listed) and appears to

published a book called *A Month in France and Switzerland during the autumn of 1824*, in which he describes the 'English' service at Lausanne, at which 'the Dean of Raphoe (a venerable and gentlemanly old man) read the prayers excellently well'.[55] Allott died at Beaurivage near Lausanne in 1832. He had held the Deanery of Raphoe, and six parishes united to it,[56] since 1795, and was absent with his Bishop's permission 'on account of the embarrassed state of his circumstances, and his advanced period of life'.[57]

How did Gilly encounter the Dean, and why did the Dean entrust the papers to him? It is most probable that they met at Lausanne when Gilly was passing through on his way back from his first visit to the Waldensian valleys (see Chapter 3). Quite how Gilly got his hands on the manuscript must remain open to conjecture, but possibly Allott told him about both it and his plans for publication. Gilly, sensing the possible outcome, may have persuaded the aged Allott that he was the best person to oversee its publication, rather than, as implied in the letters, the Dean asking Gilly to oversee the publication. If this is so, then Gilly sat on the papers for the best part of nine months, between arriving back from the trip in the spring of 1823, and writing to Peel in January 1824.

What became of the papers is unclear. Gilly certainly did not include them with his letters to Peel or Liverpool, and it is not clear what, if any, reaction was provoked from either politician. Further work needs to be done to ascertain their whereabouts, or indeed whether they still exist. According to Venn's entry in *Alumni Cantabrigiensis*, Allott's sole publication was a book of sermons, so it seems that the controversial manuscript was never published.

Family matters

At this time, Eliza Gilly was showing signs of ill health. The nature of her ailment is not known, but it seems to have been a slow wasting disease, probably consumption. Gilly informed the Bishop of London of the situation, and in 1821 he was given a licence of non-residence excusing him from living at North Fambridge because of her ill health.[58] On 24 February 1822 a son, christened William Octavius Shakespear, was born to Eliza Gilly at Wanstead.[59] During the eighteenth and nineteenth centuries, women suffering from consumption continued to give birth, and indeed frequently had the appearance of recovery while they were pregnant; Boswell's wife Margaret is a case in point.

have become Rector of Annaduff, Co, Leitrim, almost immediately, a benefice he held to the end of his life. He took the BD (1776) and DD (1783) at Trinity College, Dublin. He was a Prebendary of Tuam 1771–74, of Armagh 1774–75, Precentor of Armagh 1775–95, and Dean of Raphoe 1795–1832. Venn, *Alumni Cantabrigiensis*.

55   John Smith, *A Month in France and Switzerland during the autumn of 1824*; London, Kingsbury, Parbury, and Allen, 1825; p 159.

56   These parishes formed the income for the deanery, and each was served by a curate.

57   *Papers Relating to the state of the Established Church of Ireland, 1820*, p.100.

58   C. Cane, *Brief Notes on North Fambridge*. Although absentee incumbents were common, they always required a licence to excuse them from living in their parish. The reason Gilly gives is a common one.

59   *Pedigree of William Stephen Gilly.*

However during the spring of 1822 Eliza's health deteriorated further. She was taken to Southend, probably so that she could benefit from sea air.[60] There she died, aged 34. The *Bury and Norwich Post* recorded her death as follows:

On Thursday 6th of June at Southend after a long illness, borne with mildness patience and submis-

Interior of Hawkedon Church, which has memorials to several members of Gilly's family

sion, Eliza, wife of Rev. William Gilly, of Hawkedon and Rector of North Fambridge, Essex.[61]

Eliza Gilly was buried at Wanstead.[62] The widower erected a memorial in the chancel of Hawkedon Church:

IN MEMORY OF
ELIZA
THE BELOVED WIFE OF
THE REVD WILLIAM STEPHEN GILLY M.A.
RECTOR OF NORTH FAMBRIDGE ESSEX
AND ELDEST SON OF THE REVD. WILLIAM GILLY M.A.
RECTOR OF THIS PARISH, AND OF WANSTEAD ESSEX.
SHE WAS THE SECOND DAUGHTER OF

---

60   The same happened to Anne Brontë, who was taken from Haworth to Scarborough on the Yorkshire coast shortly before her death in 1849.

61   *Bury and Norwich Post*, 12 June 1822.

62   ERO, Burial Register, St Mary's Church, Wanstead, 13 June 1822, Entry 262. It seems probable that the Gilly household was infected with tuberculosis. Two other members of the family died in their twenties and thirties and were buried at Wanstead: Gilly's sister Isabella (buried 23 May 1817, aged 24) and his brother Robert Maltyward (buried 4 May 1827, aged 35). It must also be borne in mind that Gilly (and possibly his mother) had been sent abroad to recover their health. Gilly's mother reached the age of 59 before she died on 16 February 1825. Gilly's father, however, managed to live on until the age of 75 before he died on 23 November 1837 (memorial in Hawkedon Church to William Gilly (senior) and his wife). The survival of elderly males and the death of younger family members was a characteristic of tuberculosis in the nineteenth century, the classic example, of course, being the Brontë family of Howarth. Gilly's brother Frederick was drowned at sea in December 1834 at the age of 38 (ASTV, series V, vol. 35, c. 253, letter from Gilly to Bonjour, 9 December 1834).

LAVER OLIVER ESQR OF BRILL HOUSE BUCKS
WAS BORN 12 OCT. 1788 AND DIED 6 JUNE 1822
LEAVING HER HUSBAND AND THREE CHILDREN
MARY ANNA, ROSALIE EMILY AND
WILLIAM OCTAVIUS SHAKESPEARE
SURVIVORS AND DEPLORERS OF HER LOSS.
ON EARTH THOU WERT ALL BUT DIVINE
AS THY SOUL SHALL IMMORTALLY BE
AND OUR SORROW MAY CEASE TO REPINE
WHEN WE KNOW THAT THY GOD IS WITH THEE.

Gilly was now 33 years old. His wife was dead, and he had three small children to look after. His book *The Spirit of the Gospels* had not been noticed by the world. He did not even have a significant parish. The prospects were not bright.

Chapter 3

'The parent church of every Protestant community in Europe': first visit to the Waldensians, 1822–3

The summer and autumn of 1822 must have been miserable months for Gilly, although he had his children to console him, and a home with his parents at Wanstead.[1] He assisted his father in his clerical duties, and possibly paid visits to his own parish of North Fambridge, which was only 40 kilometres away, although he nowhere appears in parish records.

In the autumn of 1822 he was engaged as a travelling tutor (or 'bear-leader', as their charges referred to them) for three youths making the Grand Tour.[2] They were Colville Colverly Jackson,[3] John Savile Hallifax[4] and Robert Dampier Hallifax.[5] Gilly was already aged 33, a parson (at least nominally), an author, a father and a widower. Presumably arrangements were made for Gilly's children to be looked after by their grandparents, the Rector of Wanstead and his wife.

Eighteenth and nineteenth-century travellers were hardy souls, so the party decided to cross France and the Alps during the winter. On 11 December 1822 the group crossed the Channel in a dense fog which continued as their coach trundled towards Paris. They derided 'the imperfect condition of machinery in general' on the road between

---

1   Wanstead Rectory stood in what is now Redbridge Lane West. The site is now occupied by Wanstead High School (W. R. Powell (ed.), *Victoria County History, A History of the County of Essex: Volume 6* (1973), pp. 332–6 (www.british-history.ac.uk/report.aspx?compid=42789 accessed 17 April 2011)).

2   W. S. Gilly, *Narrative of an Excursion to the Mountains of Piemont in the Year MDCCCXXIII and Researches among the Waldensian, or Waldenses, Protestant Inhabitants of the Cottian Alps.* London, 1824; 4th edn 1827. (Henceforth *Narrative*. I (NWG) have used the second edition, available via Google books.) This kind of arrangement was common enough at the time, and for many years afterwards, although the 'responsible adult' was more usually an impoverished schoolmaster or curate. The Grand Tour, as a rite of passage for upper, and increasingly, middle, class youths fell into desuetude after about 1840, with the advent of rail travel. Gilly probably obtained the position in answer to an advertisement. It is not entirely clear whether Gilly had intended to go to the Waldensian valleys, and seized on the Tour as a chance to do so at little or no expense to himself, or whether he first took the position as *cicerone*, and then managed to get the Grand Tour itinerary altered so as to include them.

3   Fourth son of Sir John, fourth baronet, of Arlesey, Beds. Born 1804. At Eton. Matriculated at Trinity College, Cambridge, 1822; left without taking a degree. Entered the East India Company's civil service in Bengal in 1825. Died at Benares, 1858. Venn, *Alumni Cantabrigiensis.*

4   Second son of Thomas, of Finsbury Square. Matriculated at Trinity College, Oxford, 1823; BA 1827, MA 1830. Rector of Groton, Suffolk, 1837 until his death in 1872. Foster, *Alumni Oxoniensis* and Crockford's *Clerical Directory* for 1868. Gilly wrongly spells his middle name as 'Saville'.

5   The son of the Rev. Robert Fitzwilliam Hallifax, of Richard's Castle, Salop, born 1804. He was gazetted an ensign by purchase in the 75th Regiment of Foot in 1823 (*London Gazette,* 30 July 1836), and rose to brigadier-general; died, and is buried, at Karnal, near Delhi. He was a distant relation of John Savile.

Calais and Paris.[6] They deplored 'the hideous-looking crucifixes, erected at intervals along the road side, which seemed more like a mockery, than a record, of the most important event in Christian history'.[7] In Paris they observed 'Processions of priests, and an ostentatious display of popish emblems'.[8] On Sunday 15 December they attended an Anglican service at the British Ambassador's chapel. 'The congregation consisted of about six hundred; and a devout air prevailed among all present.'[9]

On 21 December the party set off south, and travelled through the night to reach the town of Pouilly on Sunday 22 December. Here they were scandalized to observe that 'Strings of carts, herds of swine, and droves of cattle, were passing and repassing as if it were a market day.'[10] Gilly observed none of the solemnities and decorum which accompanied an English Sunday and concluded that 'When we neglect this day as much as our Roman neighbours do, we shall probably become like some of them, degraded in condition, as well as debased in sentiment and principle.'[11]

Yet Gilly's account of France in the December of 1822 is not altogether unsympathetic. He noticed that the French peasants appeared to be more prosperous than the English farm labourers:

> Each cottage had also its scores of poultry before the door, fowls, turkeys, and geese; and adjoining to most of the farm-houses, were large stacks of every kind of corn. This aspect of plenty struck me the more forcibly, from my having observed this same season a very different appearance in England, where few corn-stacks were standing, the pressure of the times having unhappily obliged most of the farmers to thresh out the greater part of their crops, as quickly as they could, to carry the grain to market for an immediate supply of money.[12]

They passed through Palisse, a 'dull country town', on Christmas Day,[13] and reached Lyons on 26 December. Here they stayed for four days. Gilly was impressed with the hospital, and indeed his account is enhanced by a sketch of the design of this institution. It is surely one of the most prosaic plans ever drawn by a traveller (see the figure).

On 29 December, a Sunday, he went to the Protestant service at Lyons and listened to a long sermon which was delivered 'with a propriety of manner and absence from all extravagance'. However, 'Long pauses were made during the sermon, of which the congregation seemed to take advantage, for the purposes of coughing, sneezing etc.;

---

6 *Narrative*, p. 6.
7 *Narrative*, p. 6. While we might well accept that the three boys joined in the derision of the carriages and hunters, it seems likely it was Gilly alone who deplored the religious shortcomings, and was glad to 'turn out of streets where the Sabbath presents no appearance of being a day of rest or holiness' (*Narrative*, p. 7) into the British Ambassador's chapel, where the English Sunday was punctiliously kept.
8 *Narrative*, p. 7.
9 *Narrative*, p. 7.
10 *Narrative*, p. 9.
11 *Narrative*, p. 10.
12 *Narrative*, p. 13.
13 Interestingly, Gilly makes no reference to having either attended a Protestant place of worship (if there were one), or of conducting his own service on this important festival.

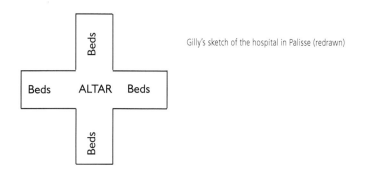

Gilly's sketch of the hospital in Palisse (redrawn)

there was so much of this, that it was pretty clear, colds are almost as general here as in England at the same season.'[14]

On December 30 the party left Lyons and travelled towards the Alps. At the Pont de Beauvoisin they reached the River Guiers, which then formed the frontier between the kingdom of France and the duchy of Savoy. Here they were subject to a strict search by the French customs authorities, who discovered some introductory letters which Gilly was carrying. He was marched off under the escort of a soldier to the post office:

> At the post-office my letters were examined, and myself questioned. The illegality of my being the bearer of a packet of eight or ten letters, some of which were sealed, was strongly urged against me; and a fine of 300 francs for each, and even imprisonment, were thundered in my ears, as the punishment of my transgression. I pleaded the necessity of taking charge of the letters myself, as they were all introductory, and begged they would open those addressed to the British ministers at Florence and Naples, Lord Burghersh, and Mr Hamilton, in proof of my being a true man, and no spy. After some consultation, it was determined that I might go my way in peace; but the letters were demanded, in order that they might be transmitted by the post. This I strenuously resisted; and having succeeded in convincing the gentlemen in office, that letters of introduction could be of little use, unless presented in person, I was permitted to carry away my despatches.[15]

In the 1820s Savoy was an Italian state which then extended to both sides of the Alps, and whose capital was Turin. The kingdom had been restored at the Congress of Vienna in 1814 following the defeat of Napoleon, and the republic of Genoa had then been absorbed into it. West of the Alps the people spoke French, and east of the Alps Piemontese was spoken, which varied from valley to valley.[16] French was widely used throughout Savoy for administrative purposes, and was the language spoken at the court of Carlo Felix, King of Sardinia and Duke of Savoy. Geographically the country included Savoy, Nice, Genoa, Piedmont and the island of Sardinia. When Gilly and

---

14 *Narrative*, p. 25.
15 *Narrative*, p. 31.
16 Gilly gives in an Appendix (no. IX of the 2nd edition), specimens of the Waldensian language compared with French and Italian.

others wrote about 'the Sardinian government', or 'the Savoy government', they were referring to the whole country.

After crossing into Savoy, the party found the countryside attractive and the villages well situated. But this was no rural idyll:

> As the snow lay deep upon the ground, and the wind blew keenly and dismally from the mountains, we could not but pity the condition of a peasantry, whose huts were exposed to all the bitterness of cold, wind, frost, and rain, with unglazed windows, and holes in the walls or roofs, for the exit of the smoke. Their clothing was as bad as their shelter; and their general dirty and squalid appearance, the goitres which disfigured their necks, and the vacant stare of idiotcy [sic], which haunted us in every hamlet, the swarms of beggars, and the eagerness and gratitude with which the poor creatures snatched at the smallest alms, left the most painful impression upon our minds. Sublime as the scenery may be, it is impossible to enjoy it, where the occupiers of the soil are as miserable as they are here; and no person of any feeling can witness their condition, and return home to talk of the happy Savoyard.[17]

On 1 January 1823 they approached the Mont Cenis pass. At Aiguebelle they took refreshments in an inn which contained a party of three French gentlemen and four or five Piedmontese officers. One of the Frenchmen was a merchant of Lyons, an ex-prefect, who questioned Gilly closely and ascertained that he was a clergyman of the Church of England. Gilly was then forced into a theological discussion, conducted in Latin, in which the merchant affected to have the advantage upon every point and kept exultingly appealing to his countrymen and translating the conversation so as to suit his own purpose:

> By way of ending the debate I told them, I hoped there were two ways to heaven, one for the Roman Catholics, and the other for the Protestants. 'Yes, yes' replied the ex-prefect, 'there are two roads, but one goes up and the other goes down; and the latter is the path you take.'[18]

On 2 January they set out from the village of St Michel at 3 am to cross the Mont Cenis pass. They travelled in two light traineaux,[19] one drawn by a horse and the other by a mule. The sun shone on:

> the frozen sides of the cascades, and channels of the torrent, that sparkled under every ray that fell upon them; the pendent icicles of a thousand forms and sizes; the crisp and fringy flakes of snow that hung from the pines .... The road looks as if it were suspended among the clouds.[20]

Although they were travelling in mid-winter, the party had an easy crossing of this famous alpine pass, as they were using the carriage road that Napoleon had hewn

---

17   *Narrative*, p. 32.
18   *Narrative*, p. 37.
19   A species of sleigh.
20   *Narrative*, pp. 39, 41.

out of the rock just twenty years previously. Boswell had crossed the same pass on 6 January 1765, when he had to be carried over by a team of alpine peasants using a specially designed litter.

They arrived in Turin on 3 January. One of Gilly's young friends went into a church and came out amazed at what he had seen: 'he could talk of nothing but the crossings, and bowings, and genuflexions and ringing and tingling, and placing and displacing and replacing the sacred utensils upon the altar, as if the worship of the ministers consisted in a sort of manual exercise, and gymnastic exhibition, and theatrical prostrations, and prescribed and studied obeisances.'[21] Gilly was impressed by this church ceremonial. He wrote that 'The effect of the music, inexpressibly fine in itself ... had an influence beyond the power of language to describe. ... We may go to a Romish cathedral to gratify our taste for music and splendour, but not for sentiments of pure devotion.'[22]

The companions went to the opera, where they gazed upon the royal family of Savoy who moved amongst their subjects 'with very little parade or ostentation'. Gilly contrasted this with an occasion in 1821 when he had attended the London opera:

> when the King of England presented himself before a hearty English audience, who had been waiting with impatient anxiety for his appearance. I thought the magnificent chandelier, suspended over the pit, must have been shaken from its hold, under the acclamations with which the house rang, when George the Fourth entered the royal box.[23]

He was so absorbed by watching the Savoy Royal Family and with his recollections of the British Royal Family that he neglected to describe the performance or indeed give the title of the opera.

On Sunday 5 January 1823, Gilly went to the chapel of the British minister to the Court of Savoy, where he discovered that the Protestant service was not conducted in English or indeed according to the English liturgy, but in French, and after the liturgy of Geneva or Neuchâtel. The minister was 'the learned and excellent M Bert'.[24] M. Bert was a Waldensian from the nearby protestant valleys of Piedmont. Here Gilly also met M. Vertu, a Waldensian merchant.

The Waldensians of Piedmont

The Waldensians, otherwise known as, Waldenses, Valdenses, Valdesi or Vaudois, will feature prominently throughout the rest of this book.[25] They are the most ancient

---

21 *Narrative*, p. 47. He was, says Gilly, 'as much inclined to turn all that he saw into ridicule, as another ... was disposed to set an undue value upon some of the more impressive ceremonials of the Catholic service.' One wonders which was which.

22 *Narrative*, p. 48.

23 *Narrative*, p. 60. Gilly's book is *Dedicated by Express Permission to His Most Gracious Majesty George the Fourth, King of Great Britain and Ireland, etc.etc.etc.* Gilly's first book had also had a fulsome dedication, although not to such an exalted personage.

24 *Narrative*, p. 49.

25 I have chosen to settle on the term 'Waldensian', as it is neither French (Vaudois) nor Italian (Valdesi), and informal research suggests it is more widely understood in English-speaking countries. It is also closer to

surviving Protestant community in the world.[26] They were well-known in eighteenth-century England, and were often cited as Protestant martyrs; very large sums of money were raised for them by church briefs.[27] Gilly had been interested in the Waldensians since he had attended a meeting of the SPCK on 11 May 1819. He had read whatever he could about them, and for four years had been planning to visit their native valleys.

The Waldensians live in three alpine valleys in the Cottian Alps, 50 kilometres south-west of Turin. These are the valleys of Pellice (otherwise known as Luserna), Perosa (or Chisone) and San Martino (or Germanasca), and the total extent of the Waldensian valleys nowhere exceeds 30 kilometres by 30 kilometres. The local language is a variant of Piemontese. In 1823, most of the inhabitants were peasants living in villages and hamlets. The nearest Protestant communities are 190 kilometres to the north in Switzerland. The only town is Torre Pellice, and in 2002 this town still had the appearance of a big village, with population of about 4,000 people. In the nineteenth century, the town was usually called La Tour (French) or La Torre (Italian).

The early history of the Waldensians remains a matter of controversy between theologians and medieval historians, but the following is a brief summary. At the beginning of the thirteenth century Peter Waldo, a rich merchant of Lyons, renounced his possessions and resolved to live a life of primitive Christian simplicity.[28] He attracted adherents throughout Western Europe, particularly in northern Italy. His followers broke away from the Catholic Church and were subject to savage persecution, but some managed to survive as an independent Christian community in the Cottian Alps, taking his name for their own. In the 1530s, the Waldensians held conclaves in the small Angrogna side-valley where they established contacts with the innovators of Wittenberg, Zurich and Geneva,[29] and by the 1560s they were following Calvinist forms of worship. In 1560 and 1561, they survived an attempt at extermination lead by the Conte della Trinità, acting on orders of Duke Emanuel Philibert of Savoy. At this time all their Protestant co-religionists in Calabria were massacred and are now but a memory.

At Easter 1655 the Waldensians faced annihilation by the troops of Duke Charles-

---

the name of their progenitor, Peter Waldo. Gilly tended to use the French 'Vaudois', but it is all too easily confused with the residents of the Swiss Canton of Vaud. NWG

26   We must use the term 'Protestant' with care here, as strictly Protestantism did not come into being until Luther. But insofar as the Waldensians were protesting against the abuses of the Church, then it may stand. A good general history of the Waldensian church and people is P. Prescot Stephens, *The Waldensian Story: A study in faith, intolerance, and survival*, Lewes, 1998. See also Gabriel Audisio, *The Waldensian Dissent, Persecution and Survival c.1170–c.1570*, Cambridge, 1999.

27   See further Tony Claydon, *Europe and the Making of England, 1660–1760*, OUP, 2007, p. 165.

28   This was but one manifestation of a Europe-wide movement at the time, which included the Cathars and the Humiliati; a form which gained official approval is the Franciscan Order.

29   The meeting between the Waldensian leaders and the Swiss reformers Farel and Saunier is traditionally recorded as having taken place at the Synod of Chanforan in the Angrogna Valley beginning on 12 September 1532. Euan Cameron in his book *The Reformation of the Heretics: The Waldenses of the Alps 1480–1580* (Oxford, 1984), challenges the authenticity of the traditional location and date, but does not dispute that in the 1530s meetings were being held between the Swiss Calvinists and the Waldensians in the Angrogna valley.

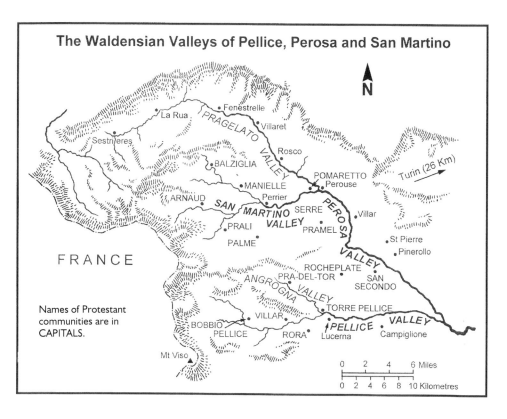

The Waldensian Valleys of Pellice, Perosa and San Martino

Names of Protestant communities are in CAPITALS.

Emanuel II of Savoy. The survivors were saved by the intervention of Oliver Cromwell and the Protestant powers of northern Europe: the Lord Protector threatened to send Admiral Blake to attack the Savoyan port of Nice, and all the continental powers had a healthy respect for the Commonwealth navy. Milton's Sonnet 18, 'On the late massacre in Piedmont', written in response to these events, is one of the bitterest poems in the English language:

> Avenge, O Lord, thy slaughtered saints, whose bones
> Lie scattered on the Alpine mountains cold,
> Ev'n them who kept thy truth so pure of old
> When all our fathers worshiped stocks and stones,
> Forget not; in thy book record their groans
> Who were thy sheep, and in their ancient fold
> Slain by the bloody Piemontese that rolled
> Mother with infant down the rocks. Their moans
> The vales redoubled to the hills, and they
> To heav'n. Their martyred blood and ashes sow
> O'er all th'Italian fields, where still doth sway
> The triple tyrant, that from these may grow
> A hundredfold, who, having learnt thy way,
> Early may fly the Babylonian woe.

Its language has often been likened to the utterances of the Hebrew prophets, combining invective and prayer. 'Stocks and stones' in line 4 relates to the belief, current in Milton's day,[30] that the denomination dated back to Apostolic times, while lines 10–14 refer first to the Parable of the Sower (Mt 13, 3–9), but also to the Classical myth of the warriors who sprang from the dragon's teeth; it has further overtones of Tertullian's statement that 'the blood of the martyrs is the seed of the church'. The 'triple tyrant' of line 12 is the Pope (the reference is to his triple crown or tiara), while in the final line the equation of the papacy with the corrupt Babylon in Revelation (e.g. 14.8) was a standard at this time and for much longer.

In April 1686 the Waldensians were again almost extirpated, and hundreds died in Savoyan prisons. In January 1687 the few thousand survivors were expelled to the Protestant cantons of Switzerland.

But in the very wet summer of 1689 there occurred *La Rentrée Glorieuse*, one of the most extraordinary forced marches in European history (see map opposite). On 16 August 1689, led by their pastor, Henri Arnaud, 900 Waldensian men set out from the northern shore of Lake Geneva to return to their homeland in Savoy. They seized boats and crossed the lake by night, and then marched and fought for ten days through 220 kilometres of alpine passes, torrential rain and hostile Catholic armies, until 700 of them reached their native valleys. There they defended themselves by guerrilla warfare and by a fortified redoubt at Balziglia. In June 1690 the Waldensians were saved by the decision of Duke Victor Amadeus II of Savoy to desert Louis XIV and ally himself with the Protestant William of Orange and the Grand Alliance of European powers, opposed to the French king. Waldensian youths still walk the route of *La Rentrée Glorieuse,* and the starting point is commemorated by a lake-side obelisk near Nyon in the Swiss canton of Vaud.

In the eighteenth century the Waldensians survived by keeping quiet. They were allowed to practise their religion only in their three small valleys. In 1730, a decree was issued that the Protestants of the nearby Pragelato valley must either become Catholics or leave Piedmont. About a thousand of them emigrated to Württemberg, where their descendants still live, while those who remained in the Italian Protestant valleys were subject to penal taxation and forbidden to proselytize. Some of their children were kidnapped by zealous nuns and priests from the convents of the nearby Catholic towns of Luserna and Pinerolo.

A few English travellers reached the Waldensian valleys in the eighteenth century, and some financial assistance was sent for education and welfare by the Protestant cantons of Switzerland, the Dutch Calvinists, the King of Prussia and the Csar of Russia. The British Hanoverian kings sent regular contributions, and indeed there was a Royal Bounty. Unlike the French Huguenots or the English Quakers, the Waldensians had no sympathisers in the local aristocracy and gentry: most were peasants, and remained so until

---

30   And still current among certain Protestant sects, although not among the Waldensians themselves any longer.

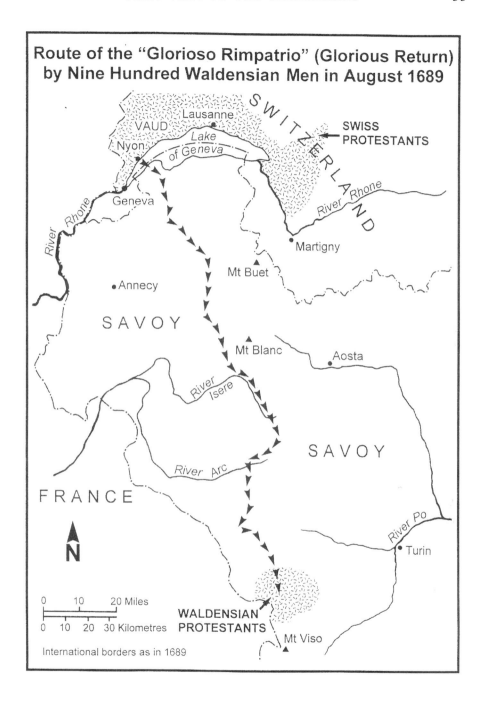

Route of the "Glorioso Rimpatrio" (Glorious Return)
by Nine Hundred Waldensian Men in August 1689

the twentieth century. Their pastors were trained at the Calvinist seminaries in Geneva and Lausanne, as their own training school in the Angrogna valley had been destroyed during the seventeenth-century massacres. In 1630 a plague had killed almost all their pastors, and they had been replaced with French Huguenot ministers. Consequently the language of church services and of the church administration was French, a language which was widely understood in western Piedmont. Napoleon had been intrigued by the Waldensians, and had admired their military prowess and capacity for survival. He had emancipated them and given them a role in the administration of Piedmont, but in 1814 the returning duke of Savoy had reimposed the previous restrictions.

In 1823 most Waldensians were still peasants living in their traditional valleys, where they scraped a living by growing crops, vines and chestnuts, tending their cattle and sheep, and cultivating silkworms. In the upper valleys they lived in hamlets of small stone-built houses, which in winter also accommodated their animals. They also cultivated the fairly fertile flat valley bottoms of the alpine foothills. Some of them had left their traditional valleys, and there was a small Waldensian community in Turin, whose members attended Protestant services at the embassies of northern European powers. A few of these were merchants who had travelled throughout Europe. By 1823, and despite restrictions upon Protestant worship outside the traditional valleys, the Waldensians knew about, and had contacts with, the outside world. Gilly was not venturing into 'unexplored' territory.

Gilly's visit to the Waldensian valleys in January 1823

As noted above, at the British Embassy in Turin Gilly had met Pastor Pierre Bert and Monsieur Virtu, a Waldensian merchant living in Turin. M. Virtu gave Gilly a letter of introduction to his relatives in La Torre (now called Torre Pellice) and to some Waldensian families. He spoke English, as he had lived for a time in Halifax. M. Virtu's son, an intelligent young man of about 20 who also spoke English, then joined Gilly's party for a visit to the Waldensian valleys. The first objective was a visit to Pomaretto, where Pastor Rodolphe Peyrani, the Moderator of the Waldensian Church, lived. On Saturday 11 January 1823, the party crossed the fertile Lombardy plain to Pinerolo and then turned north towards Perosa where they stopped at an inn for a meal. There 'We were shewn into a cold bedroom and had to wait some time before any fire was prepared to warm us.'[31] However they were soon feasting off two ducks, mutton chops, omelette and a dish of small birds followed two or three bottles of rich muscat wine. They were still in Catholic territory.

From Perosa the party had to proceed on foot. They crossed the Perosa River on precarious foot-bridges, and half-an-hour's walk brought them to Pomaretto, the first Protestant village. The scenery had now changed to one of savage disorder:[32]

---

31 *Narrative*, p. 66.

32 The scenery in the twenty-first century is much changed. There is now a road between Perosa and Pomaretto. But fortunately a detailed hand-drawn map has survived in the archives of the Savoy Government which shows the exact route Gilly followed and the rickety bridges the party crossed (Archivio di

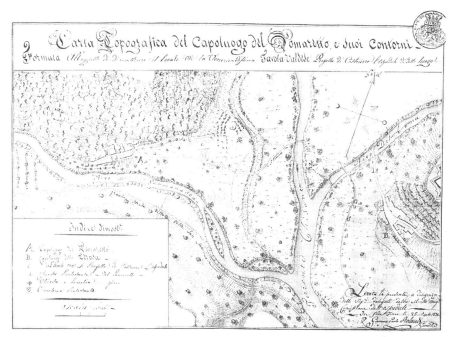

The Pomaretto area: for source see note 32.

huge fragments of rock encumber the ground on all sides, and it seems as if the mountains must have been rent asunder to produce so much nakedness and desolation. The street which we slowly ascended was narrow and dirty, the houses, or rather cabins, small and inconvenient, and poverty, in the strictest sense of the word, stared us in the face at every step we took. In vain did we cast our eyes about, in search of some better-looking corner, in which we might descry an habitation fit for the reception of the supreme capital Pastor of the Churches of the Waldenses. The street was everywhere no better than a confined lane. At length we stood before the *Presbytery* of M Peyrani, for by this name the dwellings of the ministers are known. But in external appearance, how inferior to the most indifferent parsonage in England, or to the humblest manse in Scotland.[33]

Such was Gilly's introduction to the abode of the Moderator of the Waldensian Church, the venerable Rodolphe Peyrani. They found Pastor Peyrani in an untidy bedroom, wearing whiskers and a night cap, and surrounded by packets and books. He was dressed in a shabby black suit and white worsted stockings 'so darned and patched that it is difficult to say, whether any portion of the original hose remained'.[34] Gilly was not discouraged. He later wrote:

The sickly-looking sufferer, in this humble costume, in this garb of indigence, was the

Stato Di Torino, File *Eretico e Protestante, Carta Topografica del Capoluogo del Pomaretto, e suoi Contorni*, 25 Augusto 1834).

33 *Narrative*, p. 67.

34 *Narrative*, p. 69.

moderator of the Waldensian; the successor of a line of prelates, whom tradition would extend to the apostles themselves; the high-priest of a church which is, beyond all shadow of doubt, the parent church of every Protestant community in Europe, and which centuries of persecution have not been able to destroy.[35]

Pastor Peyrani was then 71 years of age, and living on an income of 1000 francs or (in contemporary terms) £40 a year. He was suffering from the effects of a kick from a mule, had a prominent rupture, and was in constant pain. However he spoke good French and could understand, but not speak, English. Gilly and he conversed in Latin. His library was in a muddle and he said he had had to sell many books because of his poverty. Gilly enquired whether there had ever been bishops in the Waldensian Church. Peyrani replied, 'Yes; and I should now be styled bishop, for my office is virtually episcopal; but it would be absurd to retain the empty title, when we are too poor to support the dignity.'[36] The possibility of ancient episcopacy in the Waldensian Church was of great interest to Gilly, and he concluded:

> It was evident that M Peyrani was sincerely attached to the episcopal forms of church government; and I believe he spoke the sentiments of his brethren, as well as his own; but it must be confessed that his predilections lead him to assign more importance to his own office, than his real jurisdiction, and the relaxed discipline of the churches of the valleys, would strictly warrant.[37]

Gilly went on to write:

> I cannot forget, nor must I omit to notice, the evident satisfaction M Peyrani felt in explaining, how closely the doctrines of the Waldensian Church assimilate to those of the Church of England. He pointed to the works of Tillotson, Barrow, and Taylor,[38] which still enriched his book-case, and declared that every time he read them, he was more and more gratified by the light which these English divines had thrown upon truths, for their adherence to which, his poor brethren had been so often obliged to conceal themselves in their mountain fastnesses. 'But remember,' said the old man, with conscious and becoming pride, 'remember that you are indebted to us for your emancipation from papal thraldom. We led the way. We stood in the front rank, and against us the first thunderbolts of Rome were fulminated. The baying of the blood-hounds of the inquisition was heard in our valleys, before you knew its name.'[39]

---

35 *Narrative*, p. 69.

36 *Narrative*, p. 73.

37 *Narrative*, p. 75. This should of course be seen against the lifestyles of the Anglican bishops of the day, notably Shute Barrington.

38 John Tillotson (1630–1694), Archbishop of Canterbury 1691–94. A noted preacher, the general tone of his preaching, being practical rather than theological, and concerned with issues of personal morality instead of theoretical doctrine. Isaac Barrow (1630–1677), first Lucasian Professor at Cambridge, 1663–69, when he resigned it to Isaac Newton, and then devoted himself to divinity. Jeremy Taylor (1613–1667), chaplain-in-ordinary to Charles I. At the Restoration he became Bishop of Down and Connor. All three regarded the Waldensians as Protestant heroes.

39 *Narrative*, p. 78.

Twenty years previously Pastor Peyrani had met Napoleon after the French conquest of Northern Italy. Peyrani recalled the conversation as follows:

N. You are one of the Protestant Clergy?
P. Yes, Sire, and the moderator of the Waldensian Church.
N. You are schismatics from the Roman Church?
P. Not schismatics, I hope, but separatists from scruples of conscience, on grounds that we consider to be Scriptural.
N. You have had some brave men among you. But your mountains are the best ramparts you can have. Caesar found some trouble in passing your defiles with five legions. Is Arnaud's '*La Rentree Glorieuse*' correct?
P. Yes, Sire, believing our people to have been assisted by Providence.
N. How long have you formed an independent Church?
P. Since the time of Claude, Bishop of Turin, about the year 820.[40]
N. What stipends have your Clergy?
P. We cannot be said to have any fixed stipend at present.
N. You used to have a pension from England?
P. Yes, Sire, the Kings of Great Britain were always our benefactors and protectors till lately. The royal pension is now withheld, because we are your Majesty's subjects.
N. Are you organised?
P. No, Sire.
N. Draw out a memorial and send it to Paris. You shall be organised immediately.[41]

Gilly asked Peyrani about details of Waldensian history and the extent of support from the Protestant communities of northern Europe. Peyrani stated that the British Royal Bounty to the Waldensians of 400 francs *per annum* had not been received since 1797, although the Protestant cantons of Switzerland were paying for the education of four students at the seminary in Lausanne, the King of Prussia was giving support for both schools and clergy, the Dutch were sending money for schools, and the Csar of Russia had provided 10,000 francs for the construction of a new hospital at La Torre. Some English assistance had been received for the support of clergy. The Prussian ambassador to the Court of Savoy, Count Waldburg de Truchsess, was very active in his support. The British and Foreign Bible Society and the Baptist Bible Society had sent bibles. It was apparent that, notwithstanding the isolation of the Waldensians and the disruption caused by the Napoleonic wars, the community had not been forgotten by the Protestant nations of northern Europe and the Russians. The assistance reaching the Waldensians was, however, erratic.

Pastor Peyrani had impressed Gilly, despite his poverty and the muddle in his house. When the party left, 'He stood at the threshold, watching our departing steps, and the last sight that I had of his long grey locks, floating in the wind, left an impression that will not soon be removed.'[42] Before leaving, the four Englishmen after some heart-

---

40   For Claude (Claudius), see Chapter 4, note 8.
41   *Narrative*, pp. 81–2.
42   *Narrative*, p. 93.

searching gave Peyrani 'a heart-offering for the purchase of a few of those comforts, which his age and infirmities required'.[43] Gilly proceeded to philosophize that:

> Who knows but, as the flood of time rolls on, some successor of the primate of England may be reduced to the same condition; that the archiepiscopal chair of Canterbury may no longer be filled by a mitred prelate, that the functions and arduous duties may outlive the well appointed dignity of the sacred office, and that some humble pastor, like Rodolphe Peyrani, with the empty title of Bishop, may be obliged to the compassion of strangers for temporary relief.[44]

At the time of Gilly's visit Pastor Peyrani was old and in poor health, and he died eight months after Gilly left.

For the rest of his life Gilly championed the Waldensians. He never revised his belief that the Waldensian Church was the pipeline for true Apostolic Succession[45] without passing through the Roman Catholic Church, and that there were strong historical and theological parallels between the Waldensian and Anglican churches. Later writers have challenged these conclusions as simplistic, and indeed biased, because of Gilly's own position as a High-Church Anglican.[46] In fact the Waldensian Church had followed Calvinist practices since the 1560s. There is no evidence that the church ever had bishops, and even if it had, this would have ceased with adoption of a Calvinistic ecclesiology. It would, therefore, seem that the aged and infirm Pastor Peyrani had set out to please his English visitors. The interview between Peyrani and Gilly is important, but Gilly's conclusions must be treated with reservations.[47]

Following the visit to Pastor Peyrani, Gilly and his companions returned across precarious foot-bridges to the Catholic town of Perosa in a serious and meditative mood. On that Saturday afternoon in mid-January Gilly and his young friends had drunk two or three bottles of wine at lunch, walked a kilometre through difficult terrain from Perosa to Pomaretto, conducted a complex conversation in Latin with an infirm old man and walked back to Pomaretto.[48] They spent the night at an old inn in Pinerolo and had a capital fish supper. However, the four men had to argue with

---

43 *Narrative*, p. 93.

44 *Narrative*, p. 94. Not that Anglican bishops in the 1820s wore mitres – though they were known to carry them.

45 Apostolic Succession: the doctrine that the apostles ordained their successors, and they theirs, and that all bishops, and indeed lower clergy, can thus trace their succession back to at least one of the apostles.

46 See John Pinnington, 'The Waldenses as the Evangelical pipeline', *Australian and New Zealand Theological Review*, vol. 3 (1969), pp. 229–37. (Also published as 'La scoperta dei Valdesi da parte degli Anglicani' in *Bollettino della Societa di Studi Valdesi*, Torre Pellice, December 1969.) This is a well-argued critique of the various nineteenth-century claims for continuous apostolic succession avoiding the Roman Catholic Church. Pinnington's theology and history may be sound, but his geography is shaky, as he locates the Waldensians in 'the French and Swiss Alps'. The Waldensian Church does not claim to be the pipeline for apostolic succession. There is no clear evidence of its existence as an independent church prior to 1200 AD. Many years later a Catholic priest in Durham poked fun at Gilly's 'Waldensian hobby': see Chapter 4.

47 Equally, we have only Gilly's account of it.

48 Again, one is moved to ask what the young men did while Gilly interviewed Peyrani.

the landlord before they could secure separate beds. Gilly's first visit to Waldensian territory had lasted for an afternoon.

Next day, Sunday 12 January, the party headed east on a crisp winter's morning and had an enjoyable drive to the Pellice valley. At San Giovanni they again entered Protestant territory. The peasants, both Catholic and Protestant, were going to church. Gilly claimed to be able to distinguish between the adherents of the two religions: 'it is notorious that the Protestant peasantry may be recognised by the superior cleanliness of their appearance'.[49]

The Waldensian church at San Giovanni was, and still is, an imposing structure. It faces a Catholic church which is situated only 150 metres away across a stream. The two churches have been staring at each other for nearly 200 years. The Protestant church had been built, allegedly at Napoleon's command, in 1806. In 1823 there was a large wooden screen in front of this church which had been constructed on the orders of the Sardinian government in order to prevent Catholics being affronted by the sight of Protestant worshippers.

Gilly and his companions attended service there. The interior of the church was 'perfectly plain'. It had a gallery, and the communion table stood directly in front of the pulpit, which stood 'near the centre of the church'. The congregation was divided by sex, and Gilly notes that they sat 'not in pews, but on benches' – in other words there were not box pews, which were shortly to be swept away from most Anglican and nonconformist churches in England. The interior otherwise was little different from that of most English nonconformist places of worship, as might be expected by the Calvinist influence.

The party proceeded to the lower parts of the Pellice valley, which was 'by far the richest spot which is left in possession of the Protestants'. Here 'Gardens and vineyards, orchards and groves, corn land and pastures, mulberry trees and the stateliest chestnuts, are intermingled in the most picturesque confusion; and the variety of hill and dale, before the acclivities swell into the mountains, complete one of the loveliest landscapes in Piemont.'[50] La Torre was then a village. From a distance it appeared picturesque, but on close examination the party discovered that the streets were narrow and ugly, and the houses poorly constructed and standing close together. The nearest Waldensian church was one kilometre beyond the village at San Marguerita. Gilly was pleased to observe that silence and decency prevailed in the streets, and that the female peasants wore close caps as they did in his native Suffolk.

The party arrived just in time for church. The service was taken by the pastor, Pierre Bert, 'in his gown and band'. It consisted of a gospel reading (Matthew 2 and 3), and an explanation of it; the singing of Psalm 5 (verses 3 and 4);[51] an exhortatory prayer, and extempore intercessions; the Lord's Prayer; a sermon; a long read prayer; the Lord's Prayer again, and the Creed; Psalm 103 (verses 1 and 2); another

---

49   *Narrative*, p. 104.
50   *Narrative*, p. 106.
51   These would appear to be metrical psalms.

A scene in Piedmont with young girls in local costume (source unknown).

exhortation, and a blessing.[52] Anyone attending a Waldensian service today would notice little change. Gilly noted that the congregation of simple people contained no distinctions of birth and rank[53] – and that some of the young women were pretty! Inside the church there was a memorial to Christina Allan from Edinburgh who had died at Turin on 14 May 1817.[54]

The party spent the night of 12 January in a comfortable inn in La Torre. The next day was Monday, and they set out to explore the nearby Angrogna valley. They were accompanied by M. Virtu's brother, who spoke good English as he had spent several years in England. The Angrogna valley is the spiritual and geographical heart of the Waldensian valleys. It is a small valley 10 kilometres long, with steep and well-wooded sides. Clearings in the woods are intensively cultivated, as are small patches of flat ground. It was here that the first contacts between the Waldensians and the Swiss Calvinists had taken place in the 1530s. During the worst persecutions of the seventeenth century, Waldensian peasants had retreated from the main Pellice valley and defended themselves in the defiles of this valley.

The village of Angrogna is situated on a ledge on the eastern side of the valley, and there the party met Pastor Paul Goante. They were also invited to inspect a Waldensian peasant's house. These stone houses have changed little since Gilly's visit. They were grouped in small hamlets and, it being mid-winter, accommodated

---

52 This is very similar to Reformed worship elsewhere, as might be expected with the Genevan influence. See for example N. Yates, *Liturgical Space: Christian worship and church buildings in western Europe, 1500–2000*, Ashgate, 2008, chapter 3, 'The Calvinist and Reformed churches'.

53 In England at least, Anglican and most nonconformist congregations were seated in church according to their secular rank.

54 There are several graves of eighteenth and nineteenth-century English men and women in the Waldensian valleys. Turin was a major city with many foreign merchants and embassies. When Protestants died in Turin, their relatives sometimes arranged for burial in Waldensian cemeteries. Several years later, as a result of reading Gilly's book, Christina Allan's mother sent Gilly a touching letter and a donation to help the Waldensians (*Narrative*, 2nd edn, p. 107, note *d*).

both peasants and animals, separated by a fence. Beds for both animals and people were composed of leaves and straw. In the lower part of the house, a 12-year-old girl was teaching younger children Ostervald's catechism in French,[55] the proceedings watched by a cow, a calf, two goats and four sheep. In the upper part of the house, the children's parents were in a large room with cheese presses, churns, wooden bowls, spinning wheels, a weaving frame, and fourteen large black loaves hanging from the ceiling.

Gilly's picture of the household economy of these alpine peasants is touching. All the adults were literate, and could understand French. He compared their mode of living with the lives of labourers in his native Suffolk, and concluded that 'In their mode of living, or I might almost say, herding together, under a roof, which is barely weather proof, they are far behind our own peasantry, but in mental advancement they are just as far beyond them.'[56] He observed that wheeled transport was rarely used in the Waldensian valleys, and that the peasants owned few carts. In the main Pellice valley ploughing with oxen was possible, but in the steep side valleys, such as the Angrogna valley, most of the cultivation was with spade and hoe.

The Angrogna valley remains largely unchanged since Gilly's time, and Gilly's conclusion still seems apt: 'Peace seems to be amidst these rocks, and health in the air; the ills of society are excluded; but then the barrier which shuts out these evils, is equally effective in shutting out its benefits.'[57]

The party returned for the night to their inn. 'Upon our return to La Torre we took up quarters at our comfortable inn and fed and reposed as well as we could have done in one of the best hotels at Turin.'[58] Gilly would have been much flattered had he known that almost 200 years later the best hotel in La Torre is the *Hotel Gilly*!

During the night of Monday 13 January it snowed, and great flakes continued to float down until 9 am. With the young M. Vertu as their guide, the party set out to walk up the main Pellice valley towards the villages of Villar and Bobbio. They stopped at Pastor Bert's house at the edge of La Torre, and there, to their surprise, met two English boys aged 9 and 12, the sons of a Captain Humphreys of Stockport, who were receiving their education 'under the paternal care of the pastor'.[59] Gilly does

---

55 John Frederick Ostervald (1663–1747), *Catéchisme ou instruction dans la religion chrétienne* (1702); also translated into English and German.

56 *Narrative*, p. 132.

57 *Narrative*, p. 135.

58 *Narrative*, pp. 138–9.

59 This was Salusbury Pryce Humphreys, CB, KCH (1778–1845), Captain RN, who saw action in the French Revolutionary and Napoleonic wars. He married first Jane Elizabeth Tyrel Morin (d. 1808; one son), then in 1810 Maria Brooke Davenport, with whom he had five sons and two daughters. When she succeeded to the Davenport estate at Bramall, Cheshire, in 1838, he adopted the name Davenport. He was eventually promoted to rear-admiral. The sons in question here are the eldest, William Davenport Davenport (1811–1869), who succeeded his father to the Bramall estate, and the second eldest, Trevor Humphreys Davenport (1814–1868), who became a major in the army. It has not proved possible to discover what the connection between the captain and the Waldensians might have been.

not explain how these two young boys came to be so far from their English home.[60] Nor does he inform the reader how he ascertained that 'the virtue of the Waldensian females is beyond all praise'.[61]

When the party approached Villar they passed a small shrine erected in honour of the Virgin Mary. Their guide informed them that 'these idolatrous objects are offensive enough to protestants'.[62] At Villar they found great poverty, with goitres in the necks of many women and children. But the Waldensian church was open, and Pastor Gay was catechizing forty-two boys and twenty-eight girls. The clergy were evidently very poor, and often had to submit to daily labour for their sustenance. Nonetheless, they held church services on Sundays, Mondays, Wednesdays and Thursdays. Throughout the whole of the Waldensian valleys there were only thirteen pastors. The minister at Villar was too busy to spend much time with the visitors, but they noted that he understood English and was teaching it to his children.

The party then arrived at the village of Bobbio, having walked 9 kilometres from La Torre. Here the Waldensian church tower is built upon a rock, and is completely separate from the church and the burial ground. Pastor Muston was busy catechizing fifty-six boys and thirty-two girls. Gilly concluded that the conscientiousness of Waldensian clergy in catechizing children put English parsons to shame.[63] He wrote rather ruefully that 'The Papists are not blind to this truth: they catechise with strict punctuality; and in several cases where I witnessed this service, it was performed with the same patience, good humour and earnestness which we noticed in the Waldensian pastors.'[64]

Pastor Muston invited Gilly and his companions to have a meal with his wife and himself. Gilly described Madame Muston as 'an engaging young woman of about twenty six years of age.'[65] Everything that they ate and drank was a produce of the pastor's smallholding:

> The bread was home baked, the butter and cheese home-made, and the wine home-pressed. The sausages were of pork fatted in his own sty, and the filberts, chestnuts, and white pippins were gathered from his own trees. Nor did he omit to tell us that his wife had prepared the sausages, the apple fritters, and the baked pears.[66]

This excellent cook was descended from the illustrious Jahier family. Her ancestor Bartolomeo Jahier had been a guerrilla leader at the terrible Easter of 1655. Her recipe book, which has survived, gives detailed instructions on how to prepare *Oreille de*

---

60   They had been there 'three or four years'. We can wonder whether this later gave Gilly the idea of educating Waldensian boys in Durham.
61   *Narrative*, p. 144.
62   *Narrative*, p. 150.
63   We can wonder if this may have been one of the factors that prompted him to start a catechism class at St Mary Somers Town (see Chapter 5).
64   *Narrative*, p. 167.
65   *Narrative*, p. 168.
66   *Narrative*, p. 169.

Table 3.1 Population of the Waldensian valleys

Parish	Valley	Protestants	Catholics	Total
San Giovanni	Pellice	1,700	40	1,740
Angrogna	Pellice	2,000	150	2,150
La Torre	Pellice	800	200	2,000
Villar	Pellice	2,000	200	2,200
Bobbio	Pellice	1,700	20	1,720
Rora	Pellice	700	30	730
Pomaretto with Envers Pinache	Perusa	1,100	100	1,200
Prali and Rodoretto	San Martina	1,200	80	1,280
Manglia, Massel, Sabya, and Chabrant	San Martina	1,200	200	1,400
Villa-secca, Richaretto, Faetto, Bovilla, San Martino, Traversa	San Martina	1,200	450	1,650
Paramolo	Perusa	1,200	30	1,230
San Germano	Perusa	1,000	150	1,150
Rocca-piatta, Parostino, Inversa Porta	Perusa	1,800	60	1,860
Totals		**18,600**	**1,710**	**20,310**

cochon, *Omelette au sang de Chevreau*, and *Sauce à la Genevoise pour truite*. Madame Muston was in fact 34, having been born on 1 October 1788.[67]

When the party returned to La Torre, they found an invitation to supper from M. Bert. Gilly's young companions preferred however to go to a dance, so only he dined with the pastor. The young men missed 'a most interesting conversation', lasting 'three or four hours', about church organization and history. Gilly noted the contemporary organization of the Waldensian Church, which was regulated by a synod composed of moderator, thirteen pastors, and one elder from each of the thirteen parishes. He was also given a list of the population of the Waldensian valleys, as shown in Table 3.1.

Later that evening Gilly looked in at the dance, where all the principal families of La Torre were assembled together, young and old. It was a rustic assembly where all was good humour, cheerfulness and frankness. He later wrote that 'austerity forms no part of the religious character of the Waldensians'. He was, as always, susceptible to a pretty girl: 'a female servant of the house had a countenance of rather striking

---

67   The manuscript recipe book of Madame Muston is in the Archivio of the Tavola Valdese, Torre Pellice. Her descent from Jahier is set out in *Bulletin de la Société d'Histoire Waldensiane*, no. 34, April 1915. The legend of her beauty and youthful looks has descended orally, through the generations, to the twenty-first century. (Verbal information from Gabriela Ballesio, Archivista, Tavola Valdese, to HN, June 2001.)

Table 3.2 Summary of Gilly's first visit to the Waldensian valleys

Day	Activity
11 January (Saturday)	Afternoon trip to see Pastor Peyrani in Pomaretto. Return at night to the Catholic town of Pinerolo.
12 January (Sunday)	Visit to San Giovanni, Torre Pellice and San Margarita. Night at La Torre.
13 January (Monday)	Visit to Angrogna valley. Night at Torre Pellice.
14 January (Tuesday)	Visit to Villar and Bobbio. Night at Torre Pellice.
15 January (Wednesday)	Return to Turin.

beauty; the brilliancy of her eyes was Italian, but there was a modesty, and sweetness of expression, peculiar to the Waldensians'.

And so Gilly concluded his first visit to the Waldensian valleys of Piedmont and the party returned to England. The visit had been in mid-winter, which was hardly an ideal time of year for studying an Alpine peasant society. At times the party had been both cold and wet. They visited only the principal villages of Pomaretto, Torre Pellice, Villar and Bobbio, where they were most kindly received by busy pastors. Gilly later wrote vividly about the wisdom of the aged Pastor Peyrani, the catechizing of the children, the industry of the pastors, and the peasants' acceptance of the hard daily grind which formed their lot in life. But he also noted the mean dwellings, the goitres, and the fact that the peasants lived with their cattle to keep warm. He must have been keeping a diary, as he recorded both conversations and menus of meals. He assiduously collected any information which came to hand about Waldensian history, population statistics and church organization. The account is skilfully written, and replete with intriguing details. Nonetheless, examination of his text in conjunction with a calendar for the year 1823 shows that his visit to the Waldensian Valleys comprised the schedule shown in Table 3.2.

That is, he spent a total of three-and-a-half days and three nights in the valleys, which was hardly sufficient to complete a detailed survey of Waldensian society, particularly as it was mid-winter with, at times, falling snow and near-freezing conditions.

Charles Holte Bracebridge, an English country gentleman, visited the Waldensian Valleys in 1825 and later wrote that:

errors have crept into Mr Gilly's book, errors which we cannot be surprised at, from the shortness of his stay in the vallies. I may be allowed to say, that the spirit in which *some* of his remarks and anecdotes are related, is not that of the pastors, and that in deriving his information from an energetic young man living *in* the world, he has given it to the world rather in those terms than after the manner of thinking and speaking universal among the Waldensian clergy; there are consequently some things which have given great pain, though they are fully grateful for the object of the book. ... Four of the best informed of the pastors all agreed in the denial of any episcopal jurisdiction in their church at any time.[68]

Bracebridge's criticisms of aspects of Gilly's account of his visit to the valleys cannot be discounted. Gilly confined his short visit to the easily reached settlements of Pomaretto, San Giovanni, La Torre, Villar and Bobbio, and he made no visit to the San Martino valley. He was always observant, and wrote well when describing people, places, crops, meals and events, but he was not an impartial observer; his own position as a high-church Anglican priest always influenced his writings.

On Tuesday 14 January 1823 the party returned to Turin. Subsequently they made the Grand Tour of Italy and Switzerland, where they 'visited all that was most worth seeing in both these enchanting countries.'[69] Gilly recorded that

in Switzerland and Germany, we observed, very particularly, that mendicity was scarcely seen in any of the Protestant towns and villages, while it prevailed in the Roman Catholic. The truth of this was so glaring, that, in passing from one canton, or state, to another, we used to know that we had arrived in a Roman Catholic community, from the number of beggars, by whom we were infested.[70]

Otherwise nothing is known about the European peregrinations of the four men. They arrived back in England during the late spring of 1823.

We might wonder about the three young men in his charge. According to Gilly,

Often did the companions of my journey thank me for bringing them to these picturesque retreats … and one of them, who never left me, assured me, that no remembrance he could carry home with him, would be more grateful, than that of the days he had spent in the mountains of the Waldensians.[71]

He identifies this one in a footnote as John Savile Hallifax. They must have been

68 C. H. Bracebridge, *Authentic Details of the Valdenses, in Piemont and other Countries*, Hatchard and Son, London, 1827, pp. 45, 47. The book is dedicated to the Bishop of Llandaff. Although it was written by Charles Holte Bracebridge, the author's name is not given on the title pages. Bracebridge was born on 19 March 1799 to Abraham Bracebridge of Atherstone Hall and Mary Elizabeth Holte, and as such was the grandson of Anne Jesson (1733–1799) who had married Sir Charles Holte, 6th Baronet Aston, in 1754. Charles married Selina Mills in 1824, and the pair became internationally known for their extensive travel and love of literature, Charles himself writing several books. They were also very close and influential friends of Florence Nightingale and George Eliot, and very active in local government and campaigns for social justice. (Information from http://myweb.tiscali.co.uk/jessonfamily/biographies.htm, accessed 5 April 2011.) He wrote short pieces about Greek politics, Warwick gaol, Irish poverty, and a denial of the legend that Shakespeare poached deer. After visiting the Waldensians in Piedmont, he travelled to Germany and wrote an account of the Waldensian settlements in Germany. (Information from his publications held by the British Library.) In 1865 he was treasurer of the London Vaudois Committee, and wrote a pamphlet, 'The Waldenses: why they should be supported as the best exponents of anti-popery principles in Italy' (there is a copy in the London Library).

69 *Narrative*, p. 243. This might be how Gilly encountered the Dean of Raphoe – see Chapter 2.

70 *Narrative*, p. 19. This remark should be read alongside the hostile *Literary Gazette* review of *Narrative*.

71 *Narrative*, pp 239–40.

exceptionally serious-minded young men. But, as noted above, once back in La Torre, they were invited to a dance, and the young men decided to go to it early, leaving Gilly to converse with M. Bert, the pastor. 'They lost a most interesting conversation': clearly a serious mind went only so far.

Gilly had found his principal mission in life, and for the next thirty-two years he was the self-appointed international spokesman for the Waldensians of Piedmont.

Chapter 4

The Narrative of an Excursion, *and the foundation of the London Vaudois Committee*

Narrative of an Excursion to the Mountains of Piemont

In May 1823 Gilly returned to Wanstead, where he wrote his third book: *Narrative of an Excursion to the Mountains of Piemont, and Researches among the Vaudois, or Waldenses, Protestant Inhabitants of the Cottian Alps*[1] was published in London in the early summer of 1824 by C. & J. Rivington. The book contains two large folding maps, each mounted on cloth, and nine illustrations, five of which were engraved from sketches made by the Hon. Mrs Fortescue. There are also three facsimile reproductions of ancient Waldensian documents. On the title page of the first edition the author is described as 'The Rev. William Stephen Gilly, MA, Rector of North Fambridge, Essex; Author of *The Spirit of the Gospel, Academic Errors,* &c.'[2] This was Gilly's first acknowledgement of his authorship of *Academic Errors*, the angry attack upon the English public school education system, which he had published anonymously seven years previously.

It is an imposing book, as befits a volume dedicated to the King of England. For the book is 'Dedicated, by express permission, to His Most Gracious Majesty, GEORGE THE FOURTH, King of Great Britain and Ireland etc. etc. etc.' Gilly always had a capacity for cultivating eminent personages.[3] In the three-page dedication he wrote:

> Sensible as I am of the high distinction of being admitted to approach Your August Presence with this volume, I am still more gratefully impressed with the feeling of the prospect it opens to the Vaudois, of obtaining a large share of Your Sympathy.[4]

How Gilly obtained the King's permission for the dedication is not known, but George IV was always susceptible to flattery. Gilly never missed an opportunity to praise his king, even when he was describing his visit to the opera in Turin. Although George IV was not, on the whole, a praiseworthy monarch, this nicely demonstrates Gilly's 'church-and-king' Toryism, which could combine a necessary respect for the office of king with often not approving of its holder.

Gilly wrote vividly when describing the places he had visited, the inns he slept in,

---

1   Henceforth *Narrative*.
2   *Narrative*, title page, first edition only.
3   It is tempting to see Gilly 'going one better': having failed with Peel and the Prime Minister (see p. 21), he went to the King.
4   *Narrative*, p. vi.

NARRATIVE

OF AN EXCURSION TO THE

MOUNTAINS OF PIEMONT,

IN THE YEAR MDCCCXXIII.

AND

RESEARCHES AMONG THE

VAUDOIS, OR WALDENSES,

PROTESTANT INHABITANTS OF THE COTTIAN ALPS;

WITH MAPS,

And an Appendix,

CONTAINING COPIES OF ANCIENT MANUSCRIPTS, AND OTHER INTERESTING
DOCUMENTS, IN ILLUSTRATION OF THE HISTORY AND MANNERS
OF THAT EXTRAORDINARY PEOPLE.

BY

WILLIAM STEPHEN GILLY, M.A.

RECTOR OF NORTH FAMBRIDGE, ESSEX.

" Qui non palazzi, non teatro, o loggia,
Ma 'n lor vece un' abete, un faggio, un pino
Tra l' erba verde e' l bel monte vicino
*   *   *   *   *
Levan di terra al Ciel nostr' intelletto."
Petrarch, Son. 10.

SECOND EDITION,

WITH CONSIDERABLE ADDITIONS AND CORRECTIONS.

LONDON:
PRINTED FOR C. AND J. RIVINGTON,
ST. PAUL'S CHURCH-YARD,
AND WATERLOO-PLACE, PALL-MALL.

MDCCCXXV.

the food he ate, the people he met, the conversations he held and the pretty girls he saw. As already noted, he had spent only three-and-a-half days in the Waldensian valleys, which could hardly provide sufficient material for a quarto book of over 300 pages, plus 210 pages of appendices. So his book contains much additional material about Waldensian history and society interspersed with the narrative. In the course of preparing the book, Gilly consulted every document he could find about the Waldensians, and in particular the manuscripts which had been deposited at Cambridge University Library in the seventeenth century. For instance, in Chapter 8, an account of a meal with Pastor Muston at Bobbio Pellice on 14 January 1823 leads on to a history of the heroic march of Henri Arnaud and his band of Waldensian heroes during *La Rentrée Glorieuse* of 1689. The result could well have been a muddle. But it is not so: the narrative is anchored in the tragedy and glory of Waldensian history. Gilly stressed that the Waldensians were never natural rebels. Historically they had resisted repression, but always wished to be loyal, albeit Protestant, subjects of the Savoy Royal family.[5]

The book is also an appeal for help for the Waldensians. When Gilly met Pastor Ferdinand Peyrani in January 1823, the pastor had drawn attention to the historic

---

5   Again, this quality was likely to appeal to Gilly.

links between the English and the Waldensians, and lamented that the British Royal Bounty had not been paid for several years:

> nothing is so common among the Protestant inhabitants of these valleys as the cry for books. Ask them of what they stand most in need, and the universal reply is, books. One of their ministers, M. Bert, of La Torre, put the following note in my hands. It was a memorandum, that if any were inclined to assist the Waldenses, I might state to such friends their want of books of religious instruction beyond all other necessaries.[6]

Gilly ended his main text with an appeal for British assistance for the Waldensians:

> It cannot then be apprehended that this country will now neglect a community, which has been so supported by us in former years, when the same reasons still exist for holding them in estimation, viz. respect for the cradle of the reformed churches, respect for the descendants of the men, to whom we are indebted for our religious doctrines, and respect for the people themselves, whose faith hath failed not, under persecution, want, or sufferings. There is a sacred debt of justice and gratitude incurred by us, which we cannot be unwilling to redeem; and when it is considered, that there never was a period in English history, when the interests of humanity and true religion were more consulted, than by those who guide the counsels of the nation at this present time, it is not possible to be otherwise than sanguine in expecting, that the claims of the Vaudois, if they are proved to be founded in equity and justice, will be amply recognised.[7]

There are thirteen appendices, amounting to 210 pages. These include a list of Waldensian publications; copies of the manuscripts deposited at the University of Cambridge in the seventeenth century by Sir Samuel Morland (Cromwell's emissary to the Waldensians); an account of Bishop Claudius's writings against the corruptions of Rome in the ninth century;[8] the Duke of Savoy's defence of the repression of 1655; edicts of the Savoy government since 1561; and details of the parochial collection organized by Oliver Cromwell throughout England in 1655 for the relief of the Waldensians. As with the main text, the appendices are both interesting and informative. A reader who starts at the dedication and continues until the end of Appendix XII is both informed and entertained. The book is rounded off with a very good index.

The Times reviewed the *Narrative* on 15 July 1824. It was a shrewd review, the first paragraph of which reads:

> The author of this volume is ambitious of making his appearance in the character of an historian as well as tourist, and under the more attractive form of a traveller's journal, has

---

6   *Narrative*, p. 130.
7   *Narrative*, p. 268.
8   Claudius (*fl* 810–827) was Bishop of Turin 817 until his death, which was probably in 827. His teachings have been held to prefigure the Protestant reformations, probably as he was from a sophisticated urban background, and did not appreciate the provincial modes of worship such as images, pilgrimages and relics. He also held that all bishops are of equal status, and thus the bishop of Rome has no primacy.

A map of tbe Waldensian valleys, 1640

attempted to take his readers by surprise, and to lead them through an elaborate history of the old Waldenses, and their descendants the Vaudois of the Cottian Alps. The subject is new and interesting, and it requires some assiduity to arrange the materials, so as to relate a tale of the present day in the same page that contains allusions to past events, and to digress from incidents that are connected with a personal narrative to details that belong to centuries ago, without breaking the continuity of such narrative. To gratify the taste of those who read for amusement, there are anecdotes in abundance, and frequent descriptions of scenery, manners and customs; and, that nothing may be wanting to make it a book of reference, no pains have been spared in collecting information from ancient manuscripts, official records, and other documents whose authority might be relied on.[9]

The review concluded with an appeal for the restoration of British assistance to the Waldensians.

Not all were so complacent. A further review, published in the *Literary Gazette* in 1824, was far more cutting:[10]

We dislike intolerance from whatever quarter it springs. Till one man, or one sect, can justly claim what will never belong to any man, or to any sect—*perfection*; neither man nor sect are entitled to denounce all others as erroneous, corrupt, or ignorant. What we censure in the fiery Hibernian zeal of a historian (noticed in our Sights of Books, farther on,) we equally condemn in the religious bigotry of the Rector of North Fambridge .... Mr. Gilly, though his volume is dedicated to a King, George IV, whose whole reign has been an example of toleration and liberality, has, we think, gone too great lengths in his hostility to a creed which differs from his own. If the Roman Catholics are bigots, why should a Protestant put himself on the same level? If they foolishly anathematize what they consider to be heresy, why should the more enlightened heretic turn upon them, and fight with the same pointless weapons? There is neither sound sense, nor taste, nor judgment, nor propriety, in such a course.

The reviewer went on to say that:

We have less fault to find with the author's enthusiasm on the peculiar subject of his volume. Among the Vaudois, or Waldenses, the Protestant religion was cradled; and these simple and resolute mountaineers have for many centuries preserved their faith amidst persecutions of the cruellest description. They accordingly offer a noble and inspiring theme for admiration; and we trust Mr. Gilly's efforts on their behalf will be productive of relief and benefit to them. They certainly deserve well of Protestant governments which are able to assist them; and we earnestly recommend the consideration of their wants to the wealthy and powerful, as well as to the legislature of Britain.

After a good deal of theological controversy, the writer concludes by dismissing the style of writing as 'indifferent', and opines that:

---

9   *The Times*, 15 July 1824, p. 2.
10   *The Literary Gazette and Journal of Belles Lettres, Arts, Sciences, etc*; No 400, 18 September 1824, p. 593. (I am grateful to Ms Anne Walker for bringing this to my attention – NWG.)

the author has published a large book where a little one would have been much better. A small octavo volume would have much more effectually pleaded the cause of the suffering Vaudois; instead of provoking irritation where favour should be cultivated, and encumbering the subject with tedious fables as well as partial history.[11]

The most serious criticisms of Gilly's book are that he made factual errors, and that the book has an Anglican bias. These deficiencies are interlinked. Charles Brace-bridge's criticisms of Gilly for factual error were examined in the previous chapter.[12] He demonstrated that there is no empirical evidence to show that the Waldensian Church ever had bishops. Gilly's Apostolic Succession theories cannot be sustained,[13] as there is no proof of the independent existence of the church prior to 1200. In the twenty-first century the Waldensian Church makes no claim of continuous Apostolic Succession, as it has been Calvinist since the 1560s, and the doctrine is thus of no interest to its members.[14]

Nonetheless, Gilly had written a best-selling book. In June 1825 a second edition was published. This was a reduced-size octavo edition, with the illustrations omitted, in order to keep down the cost. A third edition followed in 1826, and a fourth, with the illustrations restored, in January 1827: four editions in three and a half years. Gilly's name was henceforth indissolubly linked with the Waldensians. It was an arrangement of mutual benefit: for the next thirty years Gilly acted as the international spokesman of the Waldensians, while his 'Waldensian hobby' in due course helped his promotion in the Anglican Church.[15]

The London Vaudois Committee

While he was writing his book, Gilly started to campaign on behalf of the Waldensians. This campaign was to last the rest of his life. He drew up and printed statements about their historic links to England, and presented a copy to the Archbishop of Canterbury on 23 February 1824. The next day he sent a copy of the same statement to William Howley, the Bishop of London. He contacted the British Treasury asking that the Prime Minister, Lord Liverpool, should restore the Royal Bounty for the Waldensians of £500 per annum, which had commenced in 1709, but which had not reached Piedmont since 1797 because of the impossibility of sending money to French-occupied territories during the Napoleonic wars.[16]

---

11   *The Literary Gazette and Journal …*, p. 594.
12   See pp. 44–5.
13   This was his 'Waldensian hobby(-horse)': that 'valid' orders, descending directly from the Apostles, came though the Waldensians.
14   Historians increasingly believe that true Waldensianism as such actually ended at the Reformation. See Appendix II, 'Current thinking about the Waldensians'.
15   'As to dismounting you from your Waldensian hobby, believe me, my good Sir, I am not so ill natured as to do any such thing as it is a source to you of much pleasure, besides being a subject of no small amusement to many of your readers.' Extract from a pamphlet addressed to Gilly issued by Father James Wheeler, priest at the Old Elvet Roman Catholic Chapel in Durham, January 1836. (See Chapter 10.)
16   Letter from Gilly to William Howley, Bishop of London, 24 February 1824. LPL, Fulham Papers, Howley,

Gilly was not the only Englishman campaigning for the Waldensians. In 1814 the Reverend Thomas Sims, the domestic chaplain to Her Grace the Dowager Duchess of Beaufort, had visited Ferdinand Peyrani in Pomaretto. Sims had returned to the Piedmontese valleys shortly after Peyrani's death at the age of 71 on 26 April 1823, when Peyrani's sons had given him a series of *Lettres sur les Vaudois*, which Peyrani had written before his death, with the request that they should be published in England. Sims had been lobbying for the restoration of the Royal Pension to the Waldensians since 1814, and had enlisted William Wilberforce, the anti-slavery campaigner, to help him. He had considered setting up an English Committee to help the Waldensians, but Wilberforce had dissuaded him on the grounds that discreet lobbying was more likely to be successful.[17]

On 7 July 1824 Gilly wrote to Bishop Howley expressing his concern that 'The friends, with whom Mr Sims is acting, are likely in their zeal for the Waldensian, to adopt resolutions which may be of disservice to them in the end.'[18] Gilly believed that any move that gave the impression of criticizing the Sardinian government could well have unfortunate consequences for the Waldensians, who had always claimed to be loyal, but Protestant, subjects of the House of Savoy. Gilly was thus, at least outwardly, adopting Wilberforce's advice in advocating discretion and the need for tact, for Sardinian government permission was needed for almost all activities in the Waldensian valleys, including the construction of new buildings and the distribution of literature. But Gilly was probably also worried that Sims might injure his personal interests. He was establishing his credentials as the leading spokesman for the Waldensians in England, and such a position would obviously be an advantage in his own career. Gilly's letter continues:

> the King of Sardinia has permitted his Vaudois subjects to build an Hospital at La Tour, and to apply for public subscriptions to defray the expenses of the same. There are therefore now the best possible grounds on which to form a Committee or Association, for the purpose of raising a Fund. Such a fund would not interfere with the Relief, which it is hoped our Government may extend in the shape of the restored Royal Pension, nor would it be any reason why Government should think it unnecessary to grant that Benefaction; and if any surplus should remain after the Hospital is erected, it might be applied to other wants. A

Vol. 17, folio 79. (Hereafter 'Howley 17'.) Gilly's letter covers all the points made in this paragraph.

17 Sims' account of his efforts to help the Waldensians between 1814 and 1826 is set out in his book *Visits to the Valleys of Piedmont*, London, 1864, pp. 39–45. By 1825 Sims had spent much longer in the Waldensian valleys than had Gilly. He also published, in 1827, *An Apology for the Waldensians, exhibiting an Historical View of the origin, Orthodoxy, Loyalty, and Constancy: to which is added, an Appeal to several European Governments on their Behalf, by the Reverend Thomas Sims, MA, Domestic Chaplain to Her Grace the Duchess of Beaufort*; London, Rivington. Sims was an MA of Queens' College, Cambridge, and Rector of St Swithin, Winchester, 1839–43. In the 1851 Census, he was living with his sister and brother-in-law at 16 Torrington Square, Bloomsbury, where he described himself as 'clergyman of the Church of England not having the cure of souls'. He is missing from the 1861 Census. He published widely, mostly material designed to promote the Protestant cause in Roman Catholic countries, and in 1841 acquired the copyright of G. F. Nott's Italian translation of the Book of Common Prayer.

18 LPL, Howley 17, folio 81.

committee, formed under Your Lordship's sanction, would anticipate and prevent any of the indiscrete measures, which I fear would result from an association composed in the first instance of persons, who set out with imprudent proposals.[19]

In such circumstances the creation of an English Committee to raise funds could hardly be objected to by the Sardinian government, particularly as that committee would be composed of pillars of the English church and state, with the Bishop of London as chairman.

These tactics were successful. In view of William Howley's endorsement of Gilly's arguments, Thomas Sims decided to take no further action on his own schemes to publicize the Waldensian cause in England.[20] In the spring of 1825 the London Vaudois Committee was founded with Howley as chairman and Gilly as joint secretary with the Rev. James Pons.[21] Gilly remained as secretary until he died over thirty years later, and from 1833 onwards he was also the treasurer. The committee still meets regularly, but is now called the English Committee for the Waldensian Church Missions.[22] The minutes of the London Vaudois Committee between 1825 and 1855 are extant,[23] and they show Gilly working tirelessly for the Waldensians, notwithstanding his many other activities. Few committees have been served by such a conscientious secretary for so many years. As noted above, between May 1823 and May 1825, Gilly was living with his parents at Wanstead, which is only 12 kilometres from central London, and thus attendance was easy.

The committee was formed nine months after the publication of Gilly's book, and just prior to the issue of the second edition. The first meeting was at Old Palace Yard, Westminster, on 26 May 1825, with Howley in the chair.[24] The full committee comprised twenty-two eminent people, headed by the Archbishop of Canterbury,[25] and included the Bishop of Winchester,[26] the Bishop of Exeter,[27] the Earl of Clarendon, the Earl of St Germans, and of course Gilly himself as secretary: its composition

---

19 LPL, Howley 17, folio 81.
20 Sims wrote to M. Bert, moderator of the Waldensian Church, in February 1825 saying that he had decided not to publish in England the documents that Ferdinand Peyrani's sons had given him in April 1823. 'Mr Gilly ... earnestly entreats me not to circulate the appeal among the public immediately because he thought it might induce the British Government to refuse to renew the Royal Subsidy, which subsidy the Bishop of London occupied himself in attempting to regain.' Letter, Sims to Bert, ASTV, series V, vol. 33, c. 247.
21 Pons was responsible for the foreign correspondence: *Narrative*, 2nd edn, p, 282. James Samuel Pons was successively chaplain of St Ann Westminster and of the French Chapel in Milk Alley, 1796–1807; curate of St Augustine, Bristol, and the French Protestant Episcopal Chapel in Orchard Street, 1807–10; minister of the French Episcopal Chapel in Crown Street, Soho, 1810–25; and finally preacher at the Dutch Chapel in St James's Palace, 1825–. (Information from CCCEd, Pons, James Samuel, Person ID: *53680*. www.theclergydatabase.org.uk, accessed 7 February 2012.)
22 It publishes *The Waldensian Review* twice a year.
23 Cambridge University Library, ...
24 Minutes of LVC, 26 May 1825. As Bishop of London, Howley was responsible for Anglican churches abroad, especially those in Europe.
25 Charles Manners Sutton.
26 George Pretyman-Tomline.
27 William Carey.

was firmly Anglican. Gilly had succeeded in recruiting some of the most eminent churchmen in England to serve on it, although most of them did not attend meetings: then as now, merely allowing their names to be associated with the cause was sufficient involvement. Bishop Howley, however, was a regular attender. Much of the detailed work was done by a subcommittee which had a quorum of five,[28] and Gilly was also secretary of this subcommittee. The committee and its sub-committee met twelve times between May and December 1825. Initially the treasurer was the Rev. Bewick Bridge;[29] he died in 1833 and Gilly took on the double role. Letters appealing for money were sent to *The Times*, the *Morning Chronicle, John Bull, St James Chronicle* and the *Morning Herald.* One thousand copies of a leaflet appealing for funds were printed and circulated. Pierre Appia, minister of the Waldensian church at Frankfurt, was present at some meetings.[30] By January 1826, £5,000 had been collected. The money raised was vested in public funds with the intention of sending the interest to the Waldensians.[31]

So far as the Royal Bounty was concerned, in September 1823 Lord Teignmouth, president of the British and Foreign Bible Society, had written to William Wilberforce that:

> It is impossible for me to describe the emotions excited by Mr Louther's Letter[32] – pity for the poor, afflicted, pious Waldenses – commiseration, mixed, as it ought not to have been, with indignation, for the bigotted superstitions of their Sovereign and his Papistical subjects ….
>
> It is well for me that Mr Louther has cheered the gloomy prospect of idolatry and superstition, by the account of a truly Christian congregation worshipping God in spirit and in truth. Surely the Lord will not desert his faithful people! … What can we do for them? His Majesty will never refuse the continuance of his stipend; but if he should, I think a hundred persons might be found in this kingdom who would cheerfully contribute their two, or even five pounds each, for the education of the Waldensean [sic] Pastors.
>
> I thought the Bible Society had provided for their wants, in their way: – if not, a moment ought not to be lost in doing it; and, with your permission, I will transmit extracts from Mr Louther's Letter to Mr Owen, to be laid before our Committee at the next Meeting of the 2d of October, omitting his name. – I shall not easily get rid of this heart-rending narrative: indeed, I never wish to forget it. How thankful ought we to be, that we have any liberty and encouragement in this country, once the seat of bigotry and persecution, to worship God in the way He has himself prescribed! [33]

---

28   Besides Gilly, the subcommittee consisted of the Rt Hon. Sir G. H. Ross, MP; Sir Thomas Dyke Acland, Bart, MP for Devon; W. R. Hamilton, esq.; the Rev. Dr Burrow; J. Atkinson, esq.; C. F. Barnwell, esq.; and the Rev. Bewick Bridge.

29   Vicar of Cherry Hinton from 1816 until his death in 1833.

30   Minutes of LVC, May–December 1825.

31   Minutes of LVC, 1825–26.

32   It is not clear who Mr Louther was.

33   *Memoir of the Life and Correspondence of John, Lord Teignmouth*, by Lord Teignmouth, Hatchard, 1843, vol. 2, p. 365. Teignmouth (1751–1834), born John Shore, was the founder and first president of the British and Foreign Bible Society, 1798–1834, and a member of the evangelical 'Clapham Sect'. (See

But there is no further reference to the Waldensians or the Bounty in the correspondence.

On 11 March 1826, Gilly wrote to Lord Liverpool, the Prime Minister:

> Your Lordship is aware that in the spring of last year a Committee was formed in London for the purpose of soliciting and collecting subscriptions for the relief of the inhabitants of the Protestant valleys of Piedmont, commonly called Vaudois or Waldenses.[34]

Gilly's letter asked that the Royal Bounty should be restored. As noted above, this allowance had not reached the Waldensians since 1797. Gilly carried out an investigation of government records, and ascertained that the British Exchequer had continued to disburse the £500 annually between 1797 and 1804. The money had been sent to an agent, a Mr G. W. Dickes, who, it would seem, had pocketed the money between 1797 and 1804. Mr Dickes could not be brought to task for his embezzlement as he had died, insolvent, during the winter of 1808–09.[35]

Gilly also investigated the result of the great parochial collection of 1655, when parishes throughout England had contributed the enormous sum of £38,241 16s 6d. for the relief of those Waldensians who had survived the terrible Easter of 1655.[36] The whole of England had then been outraged by the massacres in Piedmont,[37] and it was then that Milton had written his angry sonnet. Gilly concluded that only £24,908 0s 3d had been sent to the Waldensians before the restoration of Charles II on 29 May 1660. Whether Charles II had spent the balance of £13,343 16s 3d on the Royal Navy or the royal mistresses he was not able to determine.[38]

On Saturday 25 March 1826, Gilly and other members of the subcommittee met Lord Liverpool and the chancellor of the Exchequer, and urged that the Royal Bounty allowance of £500 per annum for the Waldensians should be restored. They were successful. This episode shows Gilly at his best: he had carried out detailed researches into the complex financial history of the English allowances to the Waldensians, sent the Prime Minister a letter clearly setting out the details, and followed up with a delegation to him a fortnight later. Gilly knew

---

further Ainslie T. Embree, 'Shore, John, first Baron Teignmouth (1751–1834)', *Oxford Dictionary of National Biography*, Oxford University Press, 2004; online edn, May 2009 <www.oxforddnb.com/view/article/25452>, accessed 18 April 2011.

34 Letter, Gilly to Lord Liverpool, 11 March 1826, as resolved at the meeting of the London Vaudois Committee on 8 March 1826. Signed by Gilly as secretary.

35 Letter, Gilly to Lord Liverpool, 11 March 1826

36 Letter, Gilly to Lord Liverpool, 11 March 1826. In 2011, this is the equivalent of £2,889,552.30, or in contemporary terms, it would buy 6,000 horses.

37 Local researchers in English towns and villages sometimes discover entries in parish and town accounts for 1655–6 for items such as 'for Savoy' or 'for Piemont'. These are contributions to Cromwell's great collection for the Waldensians.

38 'Very soon after the Restoration these remittances were stopped, but whether the principle sum was paid into the Exchequer or otherwise, or by whom embezzled, is unknown to those who have the honor of addressing your Lordship. Certain it is it never reached the Waldensian.' Letter, Gilly to Lord Liverpool, 11 March 1826.

that any person appealing for money must have the facts of the situation at his fingertips.

The London Vaudois Committee corresponded extensively with the Moderator and Tavola of the Waldensian church, and also established contacts with the Dutch Waldensian Committee. The committee also enquired into the state of the Waldensian settlements in Germany. There is a detailed description of the German Waldensian settlements inserted into the minutes of the London Vaudois Committee for July 1826.[39]

The Committee initially concentrated on raising money for the Waldensian hospital at Torre Pellice and for the relief of the Waldensian clergy. Money was now being received from English local appeals: for example, an appeal at Lichfield raised £390. By the end of 1826 money was being sent to Piedmont for the Waldensian hospital, for the erection of small dispensaries in remote valleys, and for the construction of a girls' school at San Giovanni. The London Committee appreciated the need to coordinate with organizations in other Protestant countries which were also sending help to the Waldensians. The Dutch Waldensian Committee was sending money to assist small schools to stay open during the winter. The Swedes had a Waldensian fund, as did the Prussians, who sent £120 to assist in setting up the hospital in Torre Pellice.[40]

By 1827 the London Vaudois Committee was well established and was beginning to do more than raise money for the hospital, pastors, schools and clinics. In May 1827 M. Bert, the Moderator of the Waldensian Church, wrote to the committee seeking advice on the troublesome case of Pastor de Combe, minister of San Giovanni. Pastor de Combe had been charged by his own vestry with immorality, drunkenness and failure to edify his flock; also, his wife had left him. He refused to resign, and remained in his house. In the end the Sardinian government induced the recalcitrant pastor to leave.[41]

On 19 June 1827 the full committee met in the absence of its secretary. The committee had been in existence for just over two years and had already become the principal exponent of the Waldensian cause outside the valleys of Piedmont. Members unanimously resolved to send their warmest thanks to Gilly for his unrelenting exertions on behalf of the committee. These thanks were well merited.[42]

---

39   This account of the Waldensian settlements in Germany was written by the Rev. Pierre Appia, minister of the French Church at 'Francfurt on Meyne' (*sic*). It is dated 7 November 1826. There are still strong links between the descendants of the Waldensian settlers in Germany and the Protestant valleys of Piedmont. There is a German Waldensian museum at Mühlacker in Baden-Württemburg.
40   Minutes of LVC, 12 March 1827.
41   Letter, Bert to LVC, 26 March 1827. Minutes of LVC, 8 May 1827.
42   Minutes of LVC, 19 June 1827.

Chapter 5

'An active and zealous member of my profession': philanthropic preacher and minister at the new chapel in Somers Town

By 1825 Gilly was well known in England because of his Waldensian works, but he had still made no progress in the Anglican hierarchy. He was Rector of North Fambridge, but the parish records show no sign of him ever doing anything in that parish. But he needed to obtain a more high-profile post: after all, he was approaching 40. Between 1819 and 1823, he had served as assistant curate to his father at Hawkedon and Stradishall. Then, in 1824, he was licensed to the Preachership of the Philanthropic Society, a post he held for two years. The society ran a school, for 'the care of children of convicted parents and the reform of young offenders', which had been founded in 1788 with very distinguished patrons, and incorporated in 1806, in which year a chapel was built.[1]

It is unlikely that Gilly's duties included more than preaching to a fashionable congregation once a fortnight.[2] Once the society was incorporated, the public could be admitted to its services, and collections taken for its support. It was the job of Gilly and his fellow preachers to move the hearts of the congregation to give generously.[3] We might wonder whether this appointment sparked his social concerns, which were to become apparent in his next charge at Somers Town, and later at Durham. It might in some ways seem an odd appointment, but it did at least get him out of the country-side and into the metropolis, and thus into the notice of likely patrons. Indeed, it is possible that he obtained this post by patronage, as the notice of his appointment in the *Christian Remembrancer* states that he was 'Rector of North Fambridge and Chaplain to the Rt Hon. the Earl of Home'.[4] This is the sole mention found so far of his holding the chaplaincy, and no more is known of it at present, but conceivably Earl Home was on the committee of the society and suggested Gilly's name as preacher.[5]

---

1   The school stood in St George's Fields, Southwark; Gladstone Road now occupies its site. In 1849 it removed to Redhill, where it became a reformatory and later an approved school. It closed in 1988. The chapel was taken over by the Church of England in 1850 and became St Jude, Southwark. It was rebuilt in 1899, and closed in 1980. It is currently used by a Pentecostal congregation.

2   He was appointed to the 'alternate morning preachership'. Elected 21 May 1824, licensed 30 June 1824: see Hampshire Record Office, 21M65/A/5, Act Book of Pretyman-Tomline and Sumner, 1824–44.

3   A drawing of a service in the chapel to raise funds in 1809 shows a rectangular building with galleries, box pews and a central pulpit. The two newest 'new boys' stand by the pulpit, presumably to stimulate generosity. (Reproduced in a pamphlet, *The Royal Philanthropic Society's School*, n.d., p. 3.)

4   *The Christian Remembrancer*, vol. 6, 1824, p. 373.

5   Appointment as a domestic chaplain to a nobleman could be, and in many cases was, little more than a

Gilly had also cultivated relations with William Howley, the Bishop of London, who had been chairman of the London Vaudois Committee since the spring of 1825. He had offered Gilly an appointment as a chaplain at Malta, which he had declined.[6] In June 1825 Gilly was still without a lucrative and respectable post in the Anglican church. It was not easy to become the incumbent of an important parish, because livings were freehold, and aged or infirm incumbents could not be removed: they usually retained the living and its income until they died, and employed curates to do the work. There was, however, a growth area in the Church of England at this time. English and Welsh towns were expanding rapidly because of the employment created by the industrial revolution, and 600 new churches were being constructed by the Commission for New Churches to cope with the influx of population. Pevsner sums up the situation:

> There were, it was universally recognised, too few churches, and no churches, so the argument ran, meant no Christianity and hence no law and order. So Parliament voted £1,000,000 in 1818 and another £500,000 in 1824 for the building of churches where they were most urgently needed. These areas of need were of course London and in addition Yorkshire and Lancashire .... Commissioners' churches, as one calls them, are recognisable, if a rough and ready generalisation be permitted, by a minimum Gothic with long, lean windows along the sides, separated by thin buttresses, by no separate chancels or very short chancels, by no towers or thin western towers, and by many clumsy pinnacles.[7]

The Church Building Commissioners decided where new churches were to be built, how much money was to be spent on each church, and the architectural styles to be used.[8] The commission set to work quickly, and by the early 1820s the construction of new churches was well under way. In London the commissioners favoured large churches: several had room for over 1,000 people.[9] Although the commissioners funded the construction of new Anglican churches, there was little or no alteration of the parochial system, and so in legal and administrative terms many of the new churches were but chapels of ease within long-established parishes, even though they were often much bigger than their parish churches.[10]

---

    sinecure. As an earl, Lord Home was entitled to appoint up to five chaplains. See further William Gibson, *A Social History of the Domestic Chaplain 1530–1840*, Leicester University Press, 1997.

6   LPL, Howley 17, folio 79. As noted above, Howley was responsible for European appointments.

7   Nikolaus Pevsner and Edward Hubbard, *The Buildings of England – Cheshire*. Penguin, 1971, p. 30.

8   M. H. Port, *Six Hundred New Churches: A study of the Church Building Commission, 1818–1856 and its church building activities*, rev. edn, Spire Books, 2006. The minutes of the Church Building Commissioners are held by the Church of England Records Centre, South Bermondsey, London, accessible via Lambeth Palace Library.

9   The ideal was for the established church to provide a seat for every parishioner, even though many were members of other denominations.

10 There was also a degree of panic within the established church, as nonconformists were able to erect chapels at will and evangelize the apparently godless masses, while the parochial system and its legal accoutrements, as well as the vested interest of sitting incumbents, made it hard for the Church of England to establish chapels of ease, let alone new parishes.

Gilly had hopes of being appointed priest at the new chapel being constructed in the inner London suburb of Somers Town, near King's Cross, in St Pancras parish. But although this church was finished by the end of 1824, there was a considerable delay in getting it opened.[11] Gilly was impatient. So on 30 June 1825 he wrote to Bishop Howley asking for an appointment to one of the new churches being built in the nearby London suburb of St Marylebone. He enlisted the help of Lord Liverpool, the prime minster, whom he had of course met when he had been the spokesman for the London Vaudois Committee two months previously.[12] Gilly's letter to Howley reads:

2 Tavistock Place, Russell Square,
June 30. 1825

My Lord
    I throw myself upon Your Lordship's indulgence for taking the liberty of informing you, that two applications have lately been made in my favour to the Earl of Liverpool, in reference to the appointments which will take place in St Mary la-bonne Parish, in consequence of the death of Dr Heslop, and the intended erection of another new Church.
    The two friends, who have mentioned my name to Lord Liverpool, have begged that I might be considered in the present or future arrangement, and as the Candidates for Preferment in that Parish are understood to be submitted to Your Lordship's judgement of their qualifications, I earnestly hope for the expression of your favourable opinion, if I should be fortunate enough to obtain Lord Liverpool's notice.
    It has always been my ardent endeavour to acquit myself as an active and zealous member of my profession, and until the present time when I find myself disengaged, in the long and unexpected interval between my nomination to the new Chapel in St Pancras Parish, and the consecration of the Chapel, I have never been without an extensive parochial charge.[13]
I have the honor, to be
My Lord
Your Lordships most obliged
and obedient humble servant
W. S. Gilly
To the Lord Bishop of London.[14]

Gilly's application for the St Marylebone post was unsuccessful. He had to wait for an official position until he was finally appointed minister at the new chapel in Upper Seymour Street, Somers Town, which was dedicated on 11 May 1826.[15] The

---

11   Camden Borough Local Studies and Archives Centre, P/PN1//M/1/ & M/2/, Minutes of St Pancras Select Vestry, 7 December 1825. (Hereafter 'SP Vestry Minutes'.) The ancient parish of St Pancras was eventually, by 1890, split into thirty-three new parishes, many of which have since been reunited.

12   He had also tried to pass the Irish papers on to Liverpool – see page 21.

13   Given that his sole *charge* hitherto was North Fambridge, though he had of course acted as his father's curate, this is a somewhat disingenuous remark.

14   LPL, Howley 17, folio 85.

15   J. A. Baveystock, *The Centenary Book*, London, St Mary's Somers Town, 1926, p. 6. Somers Town Chapel is now called St Mary's Eversholt Street, which has been the name of Upper Seymour Street since about 1912.

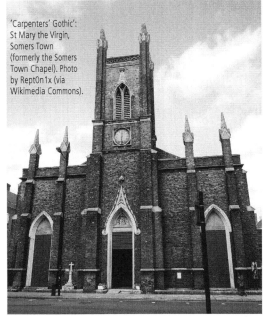

'Carpenters' Gothic': St Mary the Virgin, Somers Town (formerly the Somers Town Chapel). Photo by ReptOn1x (via Wikimedia Commons).

new chapel had been erected quickly. The first stone had been laid on 26 August 1822; the church was finished in December 1824, and cost £13,629 to construct.[16] There was accommodation for 1,030 parishioners in the rented pews, and for 885 people in the free seats.[17] The *Gentleman's Magazine* described the chapel as 'the completest specimen of Carpenters' Gothic ever witnessed. The new church at Mitcham only excepted.'[18] This is of course a highly contemptuous assessment of the building, and the critic went on to say that

upon the first glance at the interior of this edifice, it would appear that the style of the 13th century was aimed at. If this conjecture is correct, the ensuing description must have shewn how totally the imitation has failed.[19]

The architects were William and Henry William Inwood. The building is exactly like many others at the time: internally a large room, to which an external clothing of Gothick was applied – 'external' to the extent that the aisle pillars are made of wood carved and painted to look like stone, and probably have a cast iron core. The side galleries, which made the seating capacity so high, were removed in 1888 by Ewan Christian at the same time as he added the apse, and the west gallery was removed in 1890. Despite its size, the church was but a chapel of ease in the parish of St Pancras, and Gilly was its licensed minister, with a 'district', but not the freehold incumbent with a parish. The small and ancient church of St Pancras still stands, but in 1822 a large new parish church was opened in Upper Woburn Place. Somers Town Chapel was only 500 metres from this church, where Dr James Moore was the vicar, to whom ecclesiastically Dr Gilly was subordinate.[20]

---

16   The site and furnishings were paid for by a local rate, but the building cost was met by a parliamentary grant. 'Somers Town', *Survey of London: volume 24: The parish of St Pancras part 4: King's Cross Neighbourhood* (1952), pp. 118–23. (www.british-history.ac.uk/report.aspx?compid=65570 accessed 13 April 2011).

17   Port, *Six Hundred New Churches*, pp 136–7.

18   *Gentleman's Magazine*, November 1827, p. 393.

19   *Gentleman's Magazine*, November 1827, p. 394.

20   St Mary's became a perpetual curacy (i.e. an independent parish) in 1828. In addition to the Somers Town Chapel and the new church, there were three others built at this time: in Regent Square, Kentish Town and Camden Town, each of which seated over 1,000: *Clerical Guide*, 1836, p. 132. All were by the Inwoods, and all are in classical style. The current St John's, Kentish Town dates from 1845, and is mock-Norman. I [NWG] am grateful to the Rev. Matthew Duckett, formerly assistant priest in the Old St Pancras benefice, with which St Mary has been reunited, for showing me round St Mary's and St Pancras Old Church, and identifying some furniture at St Mary's that survives from Gilly's day.

In 1828, after his move to Durham, Gilly wrote a retrospective account of his work at Somers Town, which he called *Horae Catecheticae, or an exposition of the Duty and Advantages of Public Catechising in Church*.[21] He may have been active in the district before the chapel was officially consecrated on 11 May 1826. The population of St Pancras had increased from 32,000 in 1803 to 50,000 in 1814 and 80,000 in 1826.[22] The parish was entirely outside the boundaries of the ancient City of London,[23] and the only form of local government was St Pancras

Dickensian conditions: 'Over the city by railway' by Gustave Doré, from *London: A Pilgrimage*, 1872. Source: Victorian Web.

Select Vestry, which by the 1820s had become a self-perpetuating oligarchy.[24] Water supply was by parish pumps; the beadles were the only form of police, and they were held to be 'irregular and unsatisfactory' in their conduct.[25] In some streets women 'exposed their persons in a very loose manner'.[26] Exhibitions of wild beasts took place in several parts of the parish, and there were complaints about 'the number of disorderly houses.'[27] Worst of all, and this would have been particularly distressing to Gilly, forty-seven shops opened on Sundays. When the beadles tried to suppress this outrage, William Beeson (grocer) and James Smith (butcher) became abusive.[28]

If these conditions make us think of the word 'Dickensian', it is hardly surprising, as the adolescent Charles Dickens lived at 29 Johnson Street, just around the corner from Gilly's chapel.[29] The refuse tips at Somers Town were notorious, and feature prominently in Dickens' novel *Our Mutual Friend*.[30] Gilly's own description of his

---

21   W. S. Gilly, *Horae Catecheticae, or an Exposition of the Duty and Advantages of Public Catechising in Church — A letter addressed to the Bishop of London*. London, 1828. The book was republished in the USA in 1836 by William Marshall and Co., Philadelphia, with an introduction by George Washington Doane, bishop of New Jersey.

22   SP Vestry minutes, 2 March 1818.

23   It was within the Peculiar of the Dean and Chapter of St Paul's; *Clerical Guide,* 1829, *s.v.* Somers Town.

24   SP Vestry Minutes, 19 March 1819.

25   SP Vestry Minutes, 4 April 1825, 12 November 1828.

26   SP Vestry Minutes, 6 June 1827.

27   SP Vestry Minutes, 5 April 1826, 6 June 1827.

28   SP Vestry Minutes, 12 November 1828.

29   See page 68.

30   HN's notes from the Exhibition at St Mary's Church, Eversholt Street, Somers Town, 21 September 2000. Dickens's house at 29 Johnson Street was demolished during a slum-clearance programme in the 1920s, and Johnson Street has been renamed Cranleigh Street. The topography during the time of Gilly and Dickens can be traced from *Map of the Parish of St Pancras in the County of Middlesex* in *1849*, by E. Daw, London, 1850.

work at Somers Town Chapel gives a sanitized account of the suburb. He acknowledged that, 'for the greater part, the houses were of an inferior description',[31] although he also wrote that there were 'several families of great respectability in the area'.[32]

Somers Town contained dissenters of all sects and many Roman Catholics. Hundreds of French, Spanish, and Italian refugees had come to live in the area.[33] There were also many Irish families. The Catholics were organized with a chapel of long standing 'and well educated priests, who leave no means untried to make proselytes'.[34] When Gilly started preaching at his brand new church he noted:

> A thin congregation, which became much more thin in the afternoon, and free seats not half occupied, constituted no bright prospect. Even those few sheep in the wilderness did not belong to one fold, – the scanty flock was made up of many who came out of curiosity, or from a distance, or with very unsettled notions of unity. It was evidently not entirely composed of persons in regular communion with the Establishment.[35]

He had a zealous assistant minister, the Rev. Thomas James Judkin.[36] The Select Vestry was pleased that the new chapel had been opened at last, but considered that Gilly was being paid too large a stipend.[37]

Gilly and Judkin set about raising the Anglican profile in Somers Town. They had, after all, a large new church to work from and thousands of souls in need of salvation, although only a few of their parishioners were attending Anglican church services. Despite Gilly's anti-Roman stance, he was willing to use their methods against them. He approved thoroughly of the Roman Catholic system of public catechizing both at home and abroad,[38] and gave some examples of how it was handled in the principal London chapels: at the Somers Town Chapel, for example, it was held at 6 pm, and followed by

---

31   *Horae Catecheticae*, p. 89.

32   *Horae Catecheticae*, p. 89.

33   *Horae Catecheticae*, p. 89.

34   *Horae Catecheticae*, p .90; '"and two numerous schools of gratuitous education for the poor", to quote their own report. These form an effective phalanx in the very centre of the position assigned to the district minister': *ibid.*, p. 92. (St Aloysius, Phoenix Road, was founded in 1808, and its school abuts St Mary's.)

35   *Horae Catecheticae*, p. 88.

36   *Horae Catecheticae*, p. 176. Thomas James Judkin (1788–1871) matriculated at Gonville and Caius College 1810 (two years after Gilly); BA 1815, MA 1818; *ad eundem* Oxford 1842. Ordained deacon 1815, priest 1817, both by the Bishop of London. Perpetual curate of St Mary Somers Town 1828–68. Venn, *Alumni Cantabrigiensis*. After Gilly left, the chapel was generally known as 'Mr Judkin's Chapel'.

37   SP Vestry Minutes, 7 December 1825, 25 January 1826.

38   *Horae Catecheticae*, pp. 6, 11. Catechizing, which has its roots in the early church, consists of instructing children (originally, converts) in the essential doctrines of the faith, by means of set questions with fixed answers which have to be learnt by rote: their knowledge is then tested by a public oral examination. It was this examination that people came to see. Gilly used the Church of England Catechism, which is to be found in the Book of Common Prayer. It comprises only a few pages, and is as much concerned with preserving the social order as with instruction in the faith. Howley (and Gilly, following him) rightly recognized that it needed expansion, hence Gilly included teaching on the readings for the day and other matters. (The Catechism of the Roman Catholic Church is a much larger and more wide-ranging document, and was last reissued in 1997.)

Benediction.[39] He noted that the protestant clergy abroad also catechized publicly,[40] but that it had been left off by the Church of England for the previous 150 years.[41] He quoted, with approval, the situation in Barbados where slaves were being given the 'blessing of religion', resulting in 'an increased attendance of the negroes at church, where they behaved with exemplary decorum'.[42] He concluded his book with an appeal:

> The Dissenters boldly measure strength with us; the Roman Catholics openly menace and oppose us – they argue with us, they challenge us to a contest of words, and to a comparison of professional activity. But as long as we are vigilant and true to ourselves we have nothing to fear. Our former triumphs have been achieved by a lively zeal in the diffusion of light and knowledge, by guiding the public mind in the search of truth, and by taking the lead in all pursuits that conduct to it. But having, by the blessing of God obtained our pre-eminence, in part at least, by promoting national education, and religious inquiry, we must now preserve our station by personally superintending their progress, not only in Schools, and among individuals, but in the face of the congregation.[43]

Detail of Thomas James Judkin, by and published by James Scott, printed by Dixon & Ross, after William Fisk. Mezzotint, published 2 June 1834. Reproduced by kind permission of the National Portrait Gallery.

Working with the master of the local Lancasterian school,[44] Gilly set up a system of catechizing children. The schoolmaster marched seventy of his children to the Somers Town Chapel where they were told that:

> their attendance would be required every Sunday morning, at nine o'clock, in the Church, that their first business would be to learn the catechism, and that prayer books would be given, or sold at very reduced prices, to such as should entitle themselves to the privilege by regular application and proficiency.[45]

---

39   *Horae Catecheticae*, p. 21.

40   *Horae Catecheticae*, p. 21. It has been seen that he was impressed with the Waldensian catechizing.

41   *Horae Catecheticae*, p. 28.

42   *Horae Catecheticae*, p. 161.

43   *Horae Catecheticae*, p. 191.

44   Lancasterian schools were run on the monitorial model: senior pupils passed on their knowledge to their juniors. Joseph Lancaster (1778–1838) was a Quaker, and his schools were non-denominational, standing in contrast to the Anglican National Society schools, so it is interesting to find the staunchly Anglican Gilly working with a school of this nature, but the master, a Mr Roberts, was an Anglican and 'sincerely disposed to promote my views' (*Horae Catecheticae*, p. 95). Owing to the possible conflict of interest, Richards resigned as catechist after a few months, but the committee of the school paid 'a young lady' five pounds a year to take on the responsibility (*Horae Catecheticae*, p. 98).

45   *Horae Catecheticae*, p. 97.

Gilly and Judkin rewarded the children who had been successful in learning the catechism:

> partly by tickets of merit, of an assigned pecuniary value, and partly by purchase; and these
> are delivered to them at the end of the service, with a few words of commendation. No less
> than twenty-nine Bibles, five Testaments, and one hundred and twenty Prayer books, have
> been earned by youthful aspirants in this way during the past year, and no doubt they set a
> high value on them after being thus obtained.[46]

The system appears to have been almost identical to the method of catechizing children lampooned by Mark Twain in *The Adventures of Tom Sawyer*.[47] Frederick Miller, a historian of St Pancras, recorded that Gilly and Judkin:

> obtained particular notice and esteem for their zealous and unceasing devotedness in their
> work. At the close of the afternoon service they invariably assembled the children at the
> altar, and catechised them on points of Scripture, particularly in the service of the day, and
> the greater part of the congregation remained. Dr Moore attended on one occasion, and he
> afterwards observed, that, 'the inhabitants of Somers Town had cause to bless God for that
> day which brought these able ministers amongst them.' A meeting was held in the church
> at their instance to consider a plan for relieving the distressed poor in the immediate district
> of Somers Town, Spaniards as well as natives, at their own habitations during the inclement
> season, when about £200 was immediately subscribed.[48]

The children came to church to devote the hours before and after the service to 'religious accomplishments',[49] in other words learning the material for the catechizing itself, which took place immediately after the sermon in the afternoon service. Gilly noted that it had been regularly pursued without any omission, by himself, Judkin or both of them.[50] The Sunday School attendance had, as a consequence, risen from seventy-seven to 280.[51]

Nonetheless, we can see Gilly at work cultivating his connexions in this as in other matters: *Horae Catecheticae* is cast in the form of a letter from Gilly to the Bishop of London,[52] saying how he has taken this activity up expressly as a result of his Lordship's Charge to his clergy: the consecration of St Mary's gave an opportunity 'for making the experiment of public catechizing upon the scale, and with the modifications, which Your Lordship's Charge had recommended'.[53]

---

46 *Horae Catecheticae*, p. 106.
47 'Mark Twain', *The Adventures of Tom Sawyer*, 1876, ch. 4. It is quite possible that Gilly's *Horae Catecheticae*
     was being used as an instruction book for catechizing children in the village of Hannibal, Missouri, where
     the young Samuel Clemens ('Mark Twain') was attending Sunday school in the 1840s. *Horae Catecheticae*
     was republished in the USA in 1836.
48 Frederick Miller, *Saint Pancras Past and Present*, London, 1874, p. 84.
49 *Horae Catecheticae*, p. 159.
50 *Horae Catecheticae*, p. 99.
51 *Horae Catecheticae*, p. 100.
52 William Howley, translated to Canterbury August 1828.
53 *Horae Catecheticae*, p. 85.

Under Gilly's leadership, Somers Town Chapel gained a reputation, and members of fashionable West End society would drive out in their carriages to hear the sermons and watch the proceedings at catechism, which caused a traffic problem outside the church at the beginning of services.[54] But this select company was attracted by rather more than the sermons and the spectacle of children saying their catechism. For the chapel became well known, and indeed to some extent notorious, for the staged public conversions of Roman Catholics that took place within it. Miller records:

> The chapel in Seymour-street, Somers Town, was on Sunday morning crowded to excess, in consequence of its having been announced in several of the public journals, that a Romish priest would then publicly renounce the Roman Catholic religion. The ceremony took place as expected, and was of an interesting character. This proceeding was considered by some inhabitants as in bad taste, being calculated to offend and irritate the many Roman Catholics who had sought refuge in the town.[55]

Using a new Anglican church for such religious conversions could indeed be considered to be in bad taste: the church had, after all, been financed by taxpayers of all denominations. Such events could well fill a church which previously had been almost empty, but they were highly questionable. In November 1826 Father Keane, an Irish priest, renounced his faith and converted to the Church of England at a ceremony in Somers Town Chapel. This certainly attracted a full congregation, but had sad consequences for the former priest, who had no position in the Anglican Church, apart from reading the lessons in Somers Town Chapel.[56] On 3 May 1827, Gilly wrote to Bishop Howley defending his part in the apostasy of Father Keane:

> It was not till after three months' acquaintance with Mr Keane, during which his conduct persuaded me that his mind was fully impressed with the importance of the step, which he was about to take, that I consented to receive his abjuration, and I should not dare to address Your Lordship in his favour now, if I did not think well of him.[57]

Gilly asked Bishop Howley to find some post in the colonies for the unhappy Keane, who had been cast out by his family and friends. What became of him is not known.

Gilly, in his published account of his time at the Somers Town Chapel, did not mention the staged conversions from Catholicism, although these proceedings were later commented upon, with disapproval, by four other writers.[58] He did, however, record that the Catholics were well organized in this teeming parish and that there

---

54   HN's notes from the exhibition at St Mary's Church, Somers Town, 22 September 2000.
55   Miller. *Saint Pancras Past and Present*, p. 85.
56   As a former Roman Catholic priest, his Orders would be considered valid by the Church of England.
57   LPL, Howley 17, folio 89, letter Gilly to Howley, 3 May 1827; written from Durham.
58   See, for example, Miller, *Saint Pancras Past and Present*; St Pancras Borough Council, *Book of Dates, 1827*, 1908, p. 17; Baveystock. *The Centenary Book*, p. 6; *Gentleman's Magazine*, November 1827, p. 395. The conversion of Father Keane took place in November 1826, and not November 1827 as is wrongly recorded in two of the above accounts.

'Master Dickens did not attend in the slightest degree ...' 'He was taken into custody by the police' by Edward G. Dalziel, wood engraving from Dickens's 'Shy Neighbourhoods', ch.10 in *The Uncommercial Traveller*. From Victorian Web, scanned by Philip V. Allingham.

was 'a corps of zealous, able, and well-educated priests, who leave no means unturned to make prose-lytes'.[59] He also accused the 'papists' of circulating ribald anti-Protestant tracts.[60] The Anglicans gave as good as they got in this war of tracts, and the clerk of the Somers Town Chapel was accused of circulating anti-Catholic leaflets.[61] There is no evidence of Gilly himself being involved in this ecclesiastical slanging match, nor were the Catholic priests directly involved. It seems that both sides had followers who were more zealous than their principals.

Unknown to Gilly, there was a very observant child living in a disorganized family just around the corner from Somers Town Chapel. The 12-year-old Charles Dickens had just been released from his degrading employment in a blacking factory, and on 26 December 1824 the Dickens family moved to 29 Johnson Street, 200 metres from Somers Town Chapel, where they stayed until 1828. Somers Town Chapel was thus Dickens' local church, and he attended Gilly's services. Dickens' portraits of the misery and vitality of nineteenth-century English towns are well known, and many of them were based upon the scenes of his childhood and adolescence. Owen Thomas, a friend of Dickens' youth, recorded that in 1826 he met the future novelist one Sunday morning and the two boys attended the morning service at Somers Town Chapel:

> I am sorry to say Master Dickens did not attend in the slightest degree to the service, but incited me to laughter by declaring his dinner was ready, and the potatoes would be spoilt, and, in fact, behaved in such a manner that it was lucky for us we were not ejected from the chapel.[62]

Remarriage, and Bishop Barrington's 'long and curious' will

The years 1825 and 1826 were to be very important in Gilly's life, as they saw him progress in his career. Not only did he gain a new parochial cure, but also a new

---

59   *Horae Catecheticae*, p. 90, note. Gilly's anti-Catholic bias as revealed in the *Narrative* was noted above.
60   *Horae Catecheticae*, p 90.
61   J. Holdstock, *A Reply to a letter addressed to Mr H.H. Breen by Mr Roberts, upon his relapsing into the errors of the Church of Rome*, London, 1828. Holdstock was a Catholic priest and Roberts was clerk of Gilly's chapel. It was alleged that impecunious Catholics in Somers Town were being offered inducements to convert to the Church of England.
62   Baveystock, *The Centenary Book*, p. 11.

wife, and finally, preferment to a stall at Durham. Arguably, none of this would have happened without his coming to know Shute Barrington, the Bishop of Durham.

In County Durham the bishops exercised both ecclesiastical and secular authority, and were known as Prince-Bishops, a legacy from medieval times when Durham Castle had been a fortified bastion against invasion by the old enemy to the north.[63] Shute Barrington, who had been translated to Durham in 1791 at the age of 57, was 90 years old in 1824.[64] He was a redoubtable Protestant, and though willing to grant Roman Catholics 'every degree of toleration short of political power and establishment', he was equally opposed to the more extreme manifestations of evangelicalism. He had outlived two wives, and had no children. By the 1820s he was living in his house at Cavendish Square in London, at his Oxfordshire estate of Mongewell, and at his mansion at Worthing in Sussex,[65] with short residences in Durham.

In 1824, George Townsend[66] became his domestic chaplain. Townsend had written a book, *The Old Testament Arranged in Historical and Chronological Order*,[67] of which the Bishop approved, and Townsend 'accepted the general invitation with which I had been favoured, and repeatedly called in the morning or dined in the evening, as my opportunities permitted … until I had the honour of being appointed chaplain to the bishop in October 1824.[68] The aged bishop's nights were sleepless, and his intellectual, though not his spiritual, powers, were in decay.[69] Townsend respected the bishop for his piety and well-regulated benevolence. He observed, however, that the bishop did not have eminent talents or extensive knowledge.[70]

---

63   Their authority was called 'palatine'. There was a number of other dignitaries with palatine jurisdiction over a county, notably the earls of Chester and the dukes of Lancaster. The Durham palatinate came to an end in 1836. There is a memory of it within the university, which uses a shade of mauve in its academic robes, called 'palatinate purple', and the bishops of Durham still surround their heraldic mitres with a coronet, denoting their former double jurisdiction, temporal and spiritual.

64   Shute Barrington: b. 1734; matriculated at Merton College, Oxford, 1752; graduated BA 1755; elected fellow of Merton 1755, and student of Christ Church 1755; ordained 1756; MA 1757; chaplain-in-ordinary to George III 1760; Prebendary of Hereford 1761–69; Canon of Christ Church, Oxford, 1761-68; DCL 1762; Prebendary of St Paul's 1768–76; Canon of Windsor 1776; Bishop of Llandaff 1769; translated to Salisbury 1782; to Durham 1791; died 1826. He used his patronage at Durham to attract academically distinguished clergy to the diocese, and paid great attention to clerical education. He is credited with being the first bishop to discard the episcopal wig. E. A. Varley, 'Barrington, Shute', *Oxford Dictionary of National Biography*, Oxford University Press, 2004; online edn, Oct 2009 < www.oxforddnb.com/view/article/1534>, accessed 13 April 2011.

65   'Memoir of the Hon. and Right Rev. Shute Barrington', *Imperial Magazine*, June 1826, p. 617.

66   He held the tenth prebend from 1825 to 1857, when he died. He became Perpetual Curate of St Margaret, Durham, in 1839, a living previously held by Gilly until 1831. In 1850 Townsend undertook 'an unusual journey' to Italy with the intention of converting Pope Pius IX to Protestantism. (See further E. I. Carlyle, 'Townsend, George (1788–1857)', rev. Sinéad Agnew, *Oxford Dictionary of National Biography*, Oxford University Press, 2004. www.oxforddnb.com/view/article/27609 accessed 12 April 2011.)

67   London, 1821. A similar work on the New Testament followed in 1825.

68   George Townsend, 'A brief memoir of Shute Barrington, The Late Bishop of Durham', in J. S. Barrington, *The Theological Works of the First Viscount Barrington …*, London, C. and J. Rivington, 3 vols, 1828; vol. 1, p. li. The first Viscount, Shute's father, was a Christian apologist.

69   Townsend, 'A brief memoir' pp. liv, lvii.

70   Townsend, 'A brief memoir', p. xlvi.

No eminent talents or extensive knowledge:
Bishop Shute Barrington, c. 1819, from a portrait by William Owen
in the Balliol College collection.

In 1825 the bishop read Gilly's book on the Waldensians and was impressed by it, particularly by the arguments for continuous Apostolic Succession, and he asked Gilly to call on him. At the beginning of 1825 Gilly was still living at Wanstead Rectory, but during the summer of that year he moved into London, living at 2 Tavistock Place, near Russell Square, about 1,500 metres from Barrington's house in Cavendish Square. Like Townsend, Gilly became a regular visitor to the bishop's house, and the bishop gave money to Gilly for forwarding to the Waldensian Church.[71]

Later in 1825, over five days in December, events moved rapidly in the Barrington household. On Saturday 10 December the Bishop made his will. This 'long and curious' document extended to forty-three sheets.[72] In this will, and a codicil made on the same day, the bishop left £40,000 for the setting-up of the Barrington Society for Promoting Religious and Christian Piety in the Diocese of Durham. He also left legacies to several of his acquaintances and servants, which included the following:

> Mansion at Warwick House, Worthing (including stables, coach house, furnishings): life interest to Anne Colberg.
> Bishop's portrait and china: to Anne Colberg.
> £100 to Gilly and to Townsend respectively.
> Plate, silver, etc: to Anne Colberg.
> £500 to Anne Colberg.
> £500 to the Waldensian Church.
> £500 to Roland Colberg (at twenty-one), Anne Colberg's nephew.
> £500 to Frederick Colberg (at twenty-one), Anne Colberg's nephew.
> £1,000 per annum to Anne Colberg.
> £100 each to Ann Kennicott and Ann Franklin. When they died, their annuities were to be paid to Anne Colberg.

71   *Imperial Magazine*, June 1826, p. 617.
72   J. Nichols, *Illustrations of the Literary History of the Eighteenth Century*, 6 vols, London, 1817–31; vol. V, p. 621, where the will is described as 'long and curious'. The *Gentleman's Magazine*, January–June 1826, p. 518 also gave an account of the will, as did the *Durham Advertiser*. The full text of the will is on microfilm at the Family Records Centre, London, Prob. 11.1711, Quire 203. It was proved in the Prerogative Court of Canterbury on 12 April 1826 by the late bishop's great-nephews. We might ask why the bishop waited until he was 91 before making his will.

Anne Elizabeth Colberg, who was 50 years old at this time, had lived for many years in the household of Bishop Barrington. Although she and her relatives were not the principal beneficiaries, nonetheless they did very well out of the bishop's will. In the will, Barrington acknowledged 'the unceasing attention and unvarying kindness of the said Anne Elizabeth Colberg to my late dear wife and myself during a period of twenty-five years'.[73] Thus Anne Colberg, the Bishop's former companion, became a very wealthy woman.

Two days after the will was signed, on Monday 12 December 1825, Gilly married Anne Colberg's niece Jane.[74] Her brother, Roland Colberg, was a trustee of the marriage settlement.[75] Two days after that, on Wednesday 14 December 1825, George Townsend resigned his chaplaincy to Gilly.[76] Townsend had become a prebendary of Durham in August 1825,[77] and he officiated at Gilly's marriage to Jane Colberg.[78]

When the marriage took place, Gilly's third book was, unlike its predecessors, being widely read by the British public, so Jane Colberg was marrying a clergyman of repute. Gilly's second wife was just 21 years old when she married, while he was a 35-year-old widower with three children, the oldest of whom, Mary Anna, was aged 9. The wedding took place at the new church of All Souls in Langham Place, London, which had been completed in 1824. This fine church was designed by John Nash to close the vista at the north end of Regent Street. It was one of the Commissioners' Churches, that is, a church constructed with money provided by Parliament for the building of new churches in crowded areas.[79]

Eight weeks later, about 12 February 1826, Barrington suffered a stroke. Townsend, who had been in Brighton, hastened back to London, but he was refused admittance to the sick chamber, as the bishop was increasingly ill, so that it was felt 'advisable that he should see no-one but his physician, and the members of his family'.[80] By the time Townsend was allowed in, Barrington failed to recognize him. The bishop died at his

---

73 It would be interesting to know exactly what her position was in the household, but she was probably a 'companion'.

74 Jane Charlotte Mary Colberg, was born at St Helier, Jersey, on 3 November 1804. She was the only daughter of Colonel Samuel Thomas Colberg of the 90th and 58th Regiments, and her grandfather was Captain Samuel Colberg, barrack-master at Liverpool. (Inscription on Jane Gilly's gravestone at Norham Churchyard, Northumberland. See also White and Armytage, *The Baptismal, Marriage and Burial Registers of the Cathedral Church of Christ and Blessed Mary at Durham*, pp. 29, 136.) Gilly's remarriage is recorded in *The Gentleman' Magazine,* July–December 1825, p. 640, and see also E. A. White and G. J. Armytage (eds), *The Baptismal, Marriage and Burial Registers of the Cathedral Church of Christ and Blessed Mary at Durham 1609–1896,* Harleian Society. vol. RS 23, 1897, p. 29.

75 DUL Archives and Special Collections; Probate Records, Will of William Stephen Gilly, 5 November 1852.

76 Townsend, 'Brief memoir', p. lviii: 'I resigned my chaplaincy to my friend Mr Gilly'.

77 www.british-history.ac.uk/report.aspx?compid=35866 accessed 21 December 2011. And see App. I.

78 *Quarterly Theological Review and Ecclesiastical Record*, vol. 3, 1826, p 256. Townsend is described as Prebendary of Durham, and Gilly as Rector of North Fambridge. All Souls had had its own rector since earlier in 1825, Dr George Chandler (later Dean of Chichester).

79 See p. 60 for an account of Commissioners' Churches.

80 Townsend, 'Brief memoir', p. lviii.

house at Cavendish Square on 26 March 1826. He lies, with his second wife, in a tomb in the roofless nave of Mongewell Church beside the River Thames.[81]

On 25 February, Barrington had added a codicil to his will to ensure that his mansion at Worthing passed to Anne Colberg without any financial encumbrances, and which required the executors to pay all outstanding charges on this house from the estate.[82] Anne Colberg did not, however, go to live at Warwick House in Worthing. She made a financially beneficial arrangement with the trustees for the sale of the mansion, and went to live with Gilly and his new wife.[83] She was still living with the family[84] when she died at the age of 57 on 31 October 1832.[85]

Bishop Barrington had no close relatives. The executors were his great-nephews, the Hon. William Keppel Barrington and the Hon. Augustus Barrington. His will was proved in the Prerogative Court of Canterbury on 12 April 1826, less than three weeks after his death. There is no reason to believe that the executors were unhappy about the legacies to Anne Colberg and her relatives. Indeed, they co-operated with her in reaching a settlement about the mansion at Worthing in which she had been given a life interest. The rapid sequence of the making of the Bishop's will, Gilly's marriage to Miss Colberg's niece (and possibly the resignation of the chaplaincy by Townsend to Gilly) is remarkable. It would be charitable to believe that the Bishop, despite his extreme age, was still in control of events, but it is also pertinent to ask why Anne Colberg's nephews received bequests. Overall it is difficult to avoid the conclusion that the aged Bishop's will-making was at least influenced, and possibly manipulated. If so, it seems probable that both Anne Colberg and Gilly himself were in agreement about the eventual use of the Bishop's money to be left to Anne, and that Gilly's marriage to Anne's niece Jane helped to cement the understanding. There is no proof that either Gilly or Anne Colberg were involved in manipulating Barrington's will-making, and Gilly is remembered for the excellent ways he used the substantial amounts of money to which he obtained access in the late 1820s.

---

81   A visit to the Bishop's modest grave in this ruined and deserted church in a copse of trees beside the Thames is a moving experience. There is a sharp contrast with the splendid statue of the Bishop in Durham Cathedral, and the imposing portraits in the Bishop's Palace at Bishop Auckland and Balliol College, Oxford.

82   Nichols, *Illustrations of Literary History*, vol. V, p. 629.

83   Nichols, *Illustrations of Literary History*, vol V, p. 623.

84   Details of Gilly's remarriage and of Anne Colberg's residence and death at Gilly's house on 31 October 1832 are in White and Armytage, *The Baptismal, Marriage and Burial Registers...* pp. 29, 137.

85   When Anne Colberg made her own will on 12 January 1828 she appointed Gilly as a trustee. Her will was witnessed by George Townsend and by James White, butler to Gilly. Family Records Centre, London, Prob. 11.1808, Quire 745. See also White and Armytage, *The Baptismal, Marriage and Burial Registers ...* p. 136. On 12 February 1833 Gilly paid £5 17s 8d. to William Jobling, mason, for constructing a vault for the late Miss Colberg. DUL Archives and Special Collections, S.R.A./9/4, Account book of ninth stall, 1833.

The rising star

By late 1826 Gilly had become a prominent London clergyman. His book about the Waldensians was selling well; he had founded the London Vaudois Committee; his church was well known. He had at last attracted attention. On 9 April 1827 he preached the sermon at the fifth-third anniversary of the Royal Humane Society in the church of St Martin-in-the-Fields; the previous year's sermon had been preached by no less a person than Bishop Howley. Gilly had come a long way in the six years since the bishop had reprimanded him for neglecting his parish at North Fambridge.

Gilly took as his text verses 19 and 20 of the fiftieth chapter of Genesis, which records the deliverance of the biblical patriarchal families. He praised the activities of the Royal Humane Society in saving lives, and exhorted his audience to give generously to the society. Three days later the Committee of the Society unanimously resolved that 'the most sincere Thanks of this Committee be given to the Reverend William Stephen Gilly, MA, for his excellent sermon'. It was also resolved that the sermon should be printed.[86] Gilly continued as the minister at Somers Town Chapel for several months, probably until the spring of 1827.[87] From May 1826 he must have been very busy, as not only had he been appointed to Somers Town Chapel on 11 May, but on 13 May he became a Prebendary of Durham.

---

86   W. S. Gilly, *Sermon Preached before the Royal Humane Society in the Church of St Martin-in-the-Fields*, Sunday 18 March 1827. Printed for the Society.

87   LPL, Howley 17, folio 89, letter Gilly to Howley, 3 May 1827; written from Durham. Judkin was installed as Perpetual Curate in 1828.

Chapter 6

Durham: the early years

Canon Gilly of Durham

Barrington had nominated Gilly to a Prebend at Durham Cathedral, but he died before Gilly could be formally admitted (collated).[1] His successor, the new (and last) Prince-Bishop, William van Mildert, was under no legal obligation to honour Barrington's nomination of Gilly, and this could have been a major setback for the rising clergyman. Van Mildert did honour the nomination, however, and Gilly was collated to the Prebend on 13 May 1826, and formally installed on 19 May. As a Prebendary of the Cathedral, Gilly was entitled to a house on Durham College Green[2] – a secluded close to the south of the Cathedral – a substantial income and free coal. On 27 May 1826 the *Durham Advertiser* recorded that:

> The Reverend Stephen Gilly was installed Prebendary of Durham Cathedral on Friday last on which occasion the bells of that church rang a merry peal; and on Sunday the Reverend Gentleman read the morning and evening service, with the customary declarations of conformity to the forms and ceremonies of the church as by law established.[3]

Gilly's new place of employment, Durham Cathedral, is one of the finest buildings in England. The great Norman cathedral was substantially complete by 1140. Together with Durham Castle, also Norman and also magnificent, it forms the heart of a defensive site which for hundreds of years stood as a bastion against invasion by the Scots (see the map opposite). In the twenty-first century Durham is one of the few English medieval hill towns. It has never been a centre for heavy industry, and the visitor can still stand beside the Cathedral and look over the chimney-pots of the small city to the fields beyond.

As already noted, for centuries County Durham had been governed by 'Prince-Bishops'[4] who, under the King, held both ecclesiastical and lay authority, and in medieval times the Bishop had his own parliament and issued his own coinage. A small standing army was maintained until the end, and Barrington, somewhat

---

1   It was probably a promise of the next vacant prebend, rather than to any specific one: there was at this time rarely more than a day or two between a prebend becoming vacant and its being filled. Gilly's predecessor in the ninth stall, J. B. Sumner, moved to the fifth stall on 11 May 1826: as noted, Gilly was collated to the ninth two days later.

2   The house attached to the ninth stall was rebuilt by William Sancroft during his tenure (1662–74); he was later Archbishop of Canterbury. The house was taken down after Gilly's death, as the stall was suspended. See Appendix V, p. 236.

3   *Durham Advertiser*, 27 May 1826.

4   Despite this common usage, the bishops were not princes, but earls.

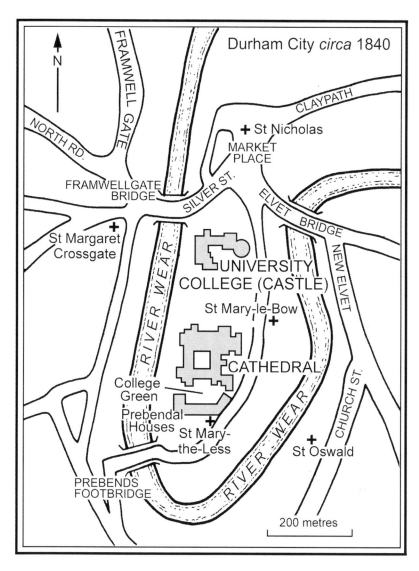

Durham City *circa* 1840

uncharacteristically, dispatched it in 1812 to put down a miners' strike at a colliery in Chester-le-Street which belonged to the Dean and Chapter. Barrington was Bishop of Durham and Earl Palatine for thirty-five years until his death on 25 March 1826. When in Durham, the bishops lived in state at the castle. They also had a castle at Bishop Auckland, 15 kilometres to the south-west. Barrington was a traditionalist, distrusting radicals and distrusting change. He believed that the French Revolution had been brought about by the corruption of the Roman Catholic Church.[5]

---

5   S. Barrington: *Vigilance: A Counterblast to Past Concessions and a Preventive of Future Prodigality. Recommended in two charges and a letter to the clergy of the diocese of Durham.* London, 1806, p. 1.

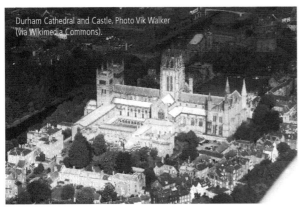

Durham Cathedral and Castle. Photo Vik Walker (via Wikimedia Commons).

The Durham Chapter consisted of a Dean and twelve canons or prebendaries, each of whom received income from assets specific to his stall (his prebend). Gilly's stall, the ninth, was the poorest, with an annual income of only £396 per annum. But he also received as his dividend of the Chapter's profits £1,491 per annum, as well as the free house on College Green and free coal. Gilly's front parlour looked out on Durham Cathedral in all its splendour. As a cathedral canon, he had tenure for life, which meant that he was free to speak his mind at meetings of the Chapter. In the 1830s he not infrequently did so, and there were quite heated disagreements between members of Durham Cathedral Chapter. He remained Minister of the Somers Town Chapel until 1828, and was also still receiving £333 per annum as non-resident Rector of North Fambridge, from which sum he had to pay the wages of a curate.[6] Most of the twelve canons of Durham also held other appointments: see Appendix V, Tables A5.1 and A5.2.

The Dean and Chapter of Durham owned much land in County Durham, beneath which are a large coalfield and also lead mines. The colliery owners leased land from the Dean and Chapter and sank mines. The pitmen hewed the coal which was transported by road and on horse-drawn tramways to the ports on the Rivers Tyne, Wear and Tees, whence it was exported all over Europe, as the industrial revolution had stimulated the demand for coal throughout the continent. The Chapter charged the colliery owners substantial rents for the right to extract the coal on their land, and these rents were regularly reviewed. The pitmen had a sturdy independence of spirit, and worked long hours in conditions of great danger: colliery explosions and accidents were frequent in County Durham, as they were in all coal mines. In the south of the county, Quaker merchants were financing the construction of a revolutionary new form of transport between the collieries near Darlington and the port of Stockton: the railway.[7] Both the Bishop and the Dean and Chapter benefited from all this activity, as the railway ran over their land. The rents they collected made Durham the wealthiest diocese in England.

---

6   *Report of the Commissioners appointed by His Majesty to Inquire into Ecclesiastical Revenues of England and Wales*, 1835: Durham, Table 3. The house had been built in 1694, and was demolished soon after Gilly left it, but the roof line can still be seen on the wall of the adjacent house. See J. T. Fowler, *Rites of Durham*, Surtees Society vol. 107, Durham, 1903; *Notes on Prebendal Houses*. Details of North Fambridge are contained in the Commissioners' report on the Diocese of London, 1835.

7   The Stockton & Darlington Railway (S&DR). Initially built to carry coal to Stockton, it opened as the first public passenger railway in 1825. Durham was reached in 1839 (the current station dates from 1857).

Van Mildert, elected Bishop in 1826,[8] was like his predecessor a believer in traditional values. But he was also sensitive to criticisms, and prepared to accept such changes as would not undermine the position of the church. Criticisms of the established church were widespread. There was much poverty, and indeed at times hunger, in County Durham, and much of the housing in the city was squalid. Yet the prebendaries of the cathedral drew large incomes, and most of them were pluralists, holding other senior positions in the church.[9] It would, however, be both simplistic and unfair to equate nepotism and pluralism with indolence and corruption in the Church of England. Many of the eminent clergy worked very hard and were passionately

William van Mildert, after Thomas Lawrence, from the Durham University collection

devoted to the liturgy and traditions of the church. They could also, on occasions, be innovative: in the 1830s the Chapter created the new University of Durham from within its revenues.[10] The alternative would have meant following the model of the Roman Catholic Church, whose clergy at that time were poverty-stricken and ill-educated, and drawn from the lowest classes of society.

Prebendary of the ninth stall

The minutes of the Cathedral Chapter show Gilly to have been regular in his attendance at meetings, and he took his full share in the administrative duties. On 28 September 1827 he was elected as Receiver of the Cathedral, and he frequently took services.

Initially, Gilly divided his time between Somers Town and Durham. The coach journey between London and Durham took at least two days. He had to be in Durham when he was the canon-in-residence, which did not happen until May 1827.[11] The

---

8 Although 'elected' is the term used, bishops are appointed by the Prime Minister acting for the Crown, so van Mildert was in fact appointed by Lord Liverpool.

9 E. A. Varley, *The Last of the Prince Bishops,* Cambridge, 1992. This is a detailed biography of van Mildert. John Banks Jenkinson, the Dean of Durham, was also Bishop of St David's and a cousin of the Prime Minister (Lord Liverpool), while Henry Phillpotts, a Prebendary, was also Bishop of Exeter. See Appendix I on the composition of the Chapter and their pluralities at various times.

10 To be accurate, the Chapter was effectively forced to do so, or to have a large portion of its ever-increasing revenues confiscated by Parliament. See Chapter 8.

11 The prebendaries or canons residentiary of the various cathedrals take it in turn to be canon-in-residence, and are responsible for the services during the period of their 'residence', a technical term referring to this duty. Nowadays all the canons may well be living in their prebendal houses, but the 'residence' still rotates

date of the Gilly family's removal to Durham was probably late 1826 or early 1827, but certainly by 3 May 1827 he was dating his letters from Durham, and by the spring of 1827 Gilly and his household (which now included Anne Colberg) had settled into Durham. He resigned as Minister of Somers Town Chapel in 1828, and his erstwhile deputy, Thomas Judkin, became its first Perpetual Curate, and continued the policy of confrontations with the local Catholics.[12]

At Wanstead, Gilly's brother Robert died at his father's rectory and was buried on 4 May 1827.[13] He was 36 and had gone to the East Indies as an ensign in 1810, from where he had probably been invalided home. Gilly's first wife, his mother, his sister and his brother were all now interred in Wanstead churchyard. Gilly's father continued as Rector of Wanstead and non-resident Rector of Hawkedon for another ten years, until his death in 1837.

The opening of St Cuthbert's tomb

Gilly was present at the opening of the tomb of St Cuthbert, which is on the eastern side of the high altar screen in the cathedral, on the site of his shrine. St Cuthbert, the best-loved saint in the north of England, had died on the holy island of Lindisfarne on 20 March 687, and for the next 300 years devoted monks had protected the saint's uncorrupted body from Danish marauders, and at various times had carried the coffin to Norham, to Chester-le-Street, to Ripon and finally to Durham, where it had been interred in the cathedral's predecessor, 'the White Church', on 4 September 999. Between 1093 and about 1130, the great Norman cathedral was built around the saint's shrine.

At the Reformation the shrine was demolished, but the saint's body was reinterred beneath the shrine site.[14] In 1827 the tomb was opened for the first time since 1540. On 17 May Gilly, in the company of the sub-dean (Nicholas Darnell), the verger, three officers of the cathedral, four masons, two carpenters and four labourers, gathered to open the tomb.[15] Inside they found a stone grave, three separate coffins

---

among them. In Gilly's day, as most had other livings, they often lived in their prebendal house only during their term of residence, a period which was fixed by the Chapter, and depended on the number of its members. In the 1820s, the period of residence at Durham appears to have been one month. In 1841, the Ecclesiastical Commissioners Act fixed residence terms at eight months for deans, and three for residentiary canons, at all cathedrals. This same Act reduced the number of prebendaries – in Durham's case, from twelve to six. See Table A1.4.

12   *Horae Catecheticae*, p. 176. Judkin remained as perpetual curate until 1868; he died in 1871.

13   ERO, D/P 292/1/6, Parish of Wanstead, Burial Register 1813–37.

14   There is the predictable 'conspiracy theory' story that the monks buried a substitute in the grave, and the real body elsewhere, whose whereabouts is known only to a select few. It seems that the opening was promoted by a desire to lay the rumour to rest (C. J. Stranks, *This Sumptuous Church: The story of Durham Cathedral*, London 1973, p. 83), but it still has its adherents.

15   J. Raine, *Saint Cuthbert: With an account of the state in which his remains were found upon the opening of his tomb in Durham Cathedral, in the year MDCCCXXVII*, Durham, 1828, pp 181–6. However, an account by 'FCH' in *Notes and Queries*, 3rd series, IV, 18 July 1865, p. 44, based on what Gilly had told him, corrects this by saying that the tomb was in fact opened privately by Raine and Darnell, and that Gilly, far from being there, was 'engaged in the service of the quire', as he was prebendary in residence, and on

within each other, human bones, a seventh-century cross of gold, an ivory comb, and the saint's complete skeleton wrapped in a shroud of silk. The remnants of the earliest coffin were removed before the body was reinterred. This coffin and the various other artefacts are now displayed in the Cathedral Treasury. However, the already fragmentary remains of St Cuthbert's coffin are not quite intact: for, sad to say, Canon William Gilly purloined a small piece of it.[16]

On 7 February 1829 Gilly and the Sub-Dean reported to the Chapter that 'In our inspection of the Treasury Offices, we had reason to see that the papers in some of the cupboards were in a great state of intermixture and confusion.'[17] Gilly was then authorized to tidy up this muddle, and on 4 April 1829 he reported: 'A great number of Rolls, Charters and other documents which were lying in confusion and in a decaying state about the floors of the Treasury have been brought into the Chapter Room, many of these have been dried and cleaned and preserved from further mischief, but some are irreparably damaged.' By 10 October 1829 he was able to report that these ancient documents had, so far as possible, been sorted out.

St Margaret's Church, Crossgate

On 28 September 1827 the Dean and Chapter nominated Gilly as Perpetual Curate of St Margaret Crossgate, a Durham city church sited at the bottom of Crossgate, a steep hill leading into the city by Framwellgate Bridge over the River Wear (see the map on page 75).[18] The church is a fine Norman building with later medieval additions, and a spectacular view of Durham Cathedral and Castle. Gilly described his new parish:

> The population of the Parish amounts to more than 3000; and is of a very indigent and fluctuating character. Being a detached suburb of a considerable town, and abounding in mean houses, which are, moreover, in a multitude of instances, divided into tenements occupied by distinct families; – it naturally becomes, for these reasons, the abode of the poorest orders; and, on some other accounts, also attracts very many of the vagrants, and loose and suspicious characters, who pass along the great North-road.[19]

---

hearing the noise, 'ran thither in his surplice as soon as the service was over, to see what was going on'. Gilly (unsurprisingly) took charge of the situation, demanding witnesses be brought in from the town and from Ushaw College (the Roman Catholic seminary nearby). He descended into the grave and brought out the vestments, plate, etc.

16 Letter from Gilly to the Hon. George Liddell, 25 September 1841, in which he enclosed a piece of the coffin. Gilly incorrectly dated the opening of the coffin as 27 May 1827. Manuscript letter in Durham Cathedral Chapter Library.

17 Durham Cathedral Chapter Minutes, 7 February 1829.

18 It started life as a chapel of ease to St Oswald, becoming independent in 1431 – an interesting, if much earlier, parallel to St Mary, Somers Town. Crossgate was one of the main pilgrimage routes to Cuthbert's shrine. The church was refurnished in 1865 and 1877. Gilly's predecessor was William Nicholas Darnell, Prebendary of the sixth stall, who was also present at the opening of the tomb, and who had been John Keble's tutor at Oxford (Stranks, *Sumptuous Church*, p. 83.) The parish was extremely large, extending well out onto the moors around Durham (www.stjam.f9.co.uk/St%20Margaret's%20Church.htm).

19 *Horae Catecheticae*, p. 182.

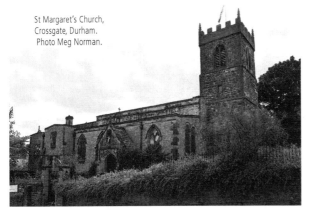

St Margaret's Church,
Crossgate, Durham.
Photo Meg Norman.

He made full use of the experience he had gained at Somers Town. Fortunately, his curate at St Margaret's, the Rev. Patrick George,[20] had been working at the church for sixteen years and was respected by the congregation, although the afternoon service[21] was indifferently attended, and there were only sixty children in the Sunday school. Gilly and George set about catechizing the children on the plan he had adopted at Somers Town, and within ten weeks had increased the number of children in the Sunday school to 160. By 1828 Gilly felt so satisfied with his success in catechizing children, at both Somers Town and in Durham, that he published his fourth book: *Horae Catecheticae – or An Exposition of the Duty and Advantages of Public Catechising in Church.*[22]

This latest book attracted criticism. For an anonymous parish priest published *The State of the Curates of the Church of England – a letter addressed to his Grace Archbishop of Canterbury in consequence of the publication of the Reverend WS Gilly's Horae Cathecheticae.*[23] In this pamphlet the author pointed out that:

> A great number of parishes in the country are under the spiritual care of curates appointed by Pluralist Incumbents, who allow them for their services a sum that is often barely sufficient to keep them from starvation; in many cases, where they have large families, it will not do it ...

The pamphlet is well written and indignant. It was directed principally against the nepotism and pluralism which was endemic in the Church of England during the 1820s. The author quoted one case where the living of a parish produced £1,200 for the nominal vicar who held two other parishes, and who did nothing whatsoever except draw his stipends and employ a curate to whom he paid £105 per annum, from

---

20 George was also Vicar of Great Aycliffe from 1821 to 1831, when he succeeded Gilly at St Margaret (*Clerical Guide*, 1829, 1836), although the Great Aycliffe website omits him from its list of incumbents (www.aycliffehistory.org.uk/html/incumbents.htm). The Aycliffe baptismal register (available online at www.aycliffehistory.org.uk/html/Baptisms1800s.htm) shows that all were performed by James Humphrey Brown, 'curate', as do the marriage and burial registers, and George's name does not appear. This implies that he was an absentee incumbent, something he had in common with Gilly at North Fambridge.

21 Until quite late in the nineteenth century, Evening Prayer (evensong) was normally read in the afternoon, and evening services were uncommon.

22 *Horae Catecheticae – or An Exposition of the Duty and Advantages of Public Catechising in Church. In a Letter to the Bishop of London*, London, C. and J. Rivington, 1828. For a discussion of this, see Chapter 5.

23 Published August 1828 by James Nisbet, London; p. 10. The BL catalogue says Gilly was the author, but this seems very unlikely.

which the curate had to pay £40 per annum for lodging for his wife and himself. The Church of England could not expect to command the respect of the population while it contained such abuses. This criticism must surely have struck a sensitive note with the now affluent Canon Gilly, for he was himself a pluralist, currently with three posts.[24]

The Society for the Suppression of Mendicity

Soon after Gilly arrived in Durham he became involved in the affairs of the small cathedral city, and he was to be a well-known figure in Durham for the rest of his life. There was much poverty and squalor in the narrow streets. Conditions were particularly grim in the twenty-eight common lodging-houses. Durham was on the Great North Road which links London with Scotland, and every year thousands of Scotsmen journeyed south to seek their fortunes. By the time they reached Durham many of them were indigent. In the 1820s the problems of vagrancy had been growing worse throughout the British Isles, and Durham was no exception.

On 28 December 1827 Gilly convened a public meeting to consider the problem of beggars in Durham, at which it was resolved to set up a 'Society for the Suppression of Mendicity', with an annual subscription of five shillings, and a committee composed of two representatives from each vestry in the city.[25] Gilly, perhaps unsurprisingly, was elected president. The society was founded 'for the purpose of removing vagrants and impostors from the City and securing relief only to those who are really distressed'.[26] Any person importuned for alms was requested to refrain from giving the beggar money, but to give them a ticket issued by the society instead. The mendicant would then take the ticket to the office of the society where the deserving poor would be given assistance, while the undeserving poor would be sent on their way out of Durham. A Vagrant Office was opened in Claypath, with Mr William Emmerson as the Superintendent.

The *Durham Advertiser*, the conservative local newspaper, welcomed the establishment of the Mendicity Society:

> It may be safely promised that the streets of this town will shortly be cleansed of the nuisance of common beggars, if the charitably disposed will abstain from giving alms to unknown applicants, and will take the trouble to refer them to the superintendent, whose duty it will be to let no real distress go unrelieved, and to compel vagrants to quit the place without delay. Members of the committee will take an early opportunity of collecting from house to house, to solicit contributions of the inhabitants.[27]

Gilly was, as ever, a good organizer. By February 1828 there were over 150 Durham

---

24 His chaplaincy to Lord Home qualified him to hold another two benefices in addition. See W Gibson, *A Social History of the Domestic Chaplain, 1530–1840*, p 4.

25 The vestry was the governing body of a parish (so called because it met – technically at least – in the vestry of its parish church), and still had at this time a good deal of secular power, notably in dealing with paupers and beggars. Much of these powers were to be gradually taken away during the nineteenth century by new state-run bodies such as the Poor-Law Unions.

26 *Durham Advertiser,* 19 January 1828.

27 *Durham Advertiser,* 19 January 1828.

residents subscribing to the society, and the Dean and Chapter had made a donation of ten guineas. The society was not sympathetic to poverty: the fourth annual report in 1832 concluded that 'vagrancy is too often a matter of choice rather than necessity'.[28] Gilly remained chair of this society for seven years, and he worked very hard to get it organized and operating efficiently. He had, with his usual drive, taken decisive action upon an acute social problem in Durham. The references in the Durham press of the time were to the need to clear beggars off the streets, and we might wonder, even allowing for the differing standards of the time, how much this was a cosmetic exercise under a thin veil of philanthropy. To modern eyes the stated aims of the Society may appear to lack sympathy for the plight of the poor, but they must be seen within the context of the times. The ancient system of relying upon parishes to relieve the poor was not working, as many parishes would refuse to help vagrants who originated from outside their boundaries. Five years later, in 1834, Parliament took the matter in hand and passed the notorious Poor Law, which in due course led to the grim workhouses castigated by, among many others, Charles Dickens in *Oliver Twist*.

Gilly's name comes up whenever researchers study social conditions in Durham between 1827 and his death in 1855. He was one of a group of prominent people involved in the day-to-day affairs of the ancient city. He was a member of the Athenaeum Club, and in 1875, twenty years after Gilly's death, an old member of the club wrote to the *Durham Chronicle* giving a sympathetic, but not uncritical, account of his energy and character:

> Dr Gilly was another true friend of the Athenaeum. I remember his first appearance in our city. He was a curate in London. I had it from a friend of my own in London, that never was there a man more beloved in a parish than was Dr Gilly for visiting the sick, attending to his church duties, and as a plain, earnest preacher of the Gospel. No man better deserved promotion than Dr Gilly. In Durham he was useful, as rector of Norham he was greatly beloved, and he worked harmoniously with Presbyterians and Dissenters. He was no bigot. He would work with any one, and was always anxious to do good. I watched him for years very closely, and was often brought in close contact with him, and only differed with him once, which was during the discussion on negro emancipation. He proposed to recompense the slave-owner for giving the liberty to the slave which he had no right to take from him, while the slave himself never received a farthing for his wrong; again, what I considered an inconsistency was his voting Tory in Durham and Liberal in Northumberland.[29] Dr Gilly was not an angel, but he was a good, Christian clergyman, and conscientiously, I believe, did his duty. In him the Athenaeum lost a true friend. I remember a lecture by Dr Gilly on the 'Troubadours' he quoted from the song 'Tom Bowline',[30] and I would apply the quotation to himself:
>
> > Faithful below he did his duty,
> > and now he's gone aloft.[31]

---

28   *Durham Advertiser*, 10 February 1832.
29   Under the rules then in force, Gilly had two votes: one as Prebendary of Durham, and one as Vicar of Norham.
30   More usually 'Tom Bowling'.
31   *Durham Chronicle*, 24 December 1875.

Confirmation of this assessment of Gilly's character is demonstrated by his part in the following two meetings. On 24 October 1828, Gilly was in the chair at a crowded meeting of the Durham Auxiliary Bible Society and Association.[32] Catholic emancipation was then a subject of considerable political debate, and it was a very sensitive subject in Durham, as Ushaw College had been opened for the training of Catholic priests in 1804,[33] and Old Elvet, an inner-Durham suburb, had retained a Catholic presence throughout the penal years.[34] Gilly made a highly emotional speech appealing to his audience to 'abstain from any language on the present occasion which might savour of bitterness against those who differed from them'. Nonetheless, the sentiments expressed by other speakers were strongly anti-Catholic.[35] Two years later, on 28 October 1830, Gilly addressed a meeting of Durham citizens in the Town Hall, at which it was agreed that a petition should be presented to the House of Commons, urging that:

> No further delay should be interposed to the total and final abolition of slavery than is necessary to complete the proper arrangements for this purpose, and that in the meantime, such measures may be taken for the mitigation of the sufferings of the slaves, and for their moral and religious instruction as may prepare them for the enjoyment of liberty.[36]

The new Canon had, within a few years of arriving in Durham, made a decided mark on the city's life. In his ministry at Somers Town and at St Margaret Crossgate he had established a thriving catechism; and at Durham he had moved into the sphere of public service. Comparing this with his neglect of North Fambridge, we might be tempted to the conclusion that his guiding text was that of Matthew 5:16, one of the offertory sentences in the Prayer Book Communion service: 'Let your light so shine before men, that they may see your good works, and glorify your Father which is in heaven.' Fambridge, possibly, did not provide enough 'men' before whom his light could shine. We must assume Gilly was aware of the final clause of the verse.

---

32 This was to support the work of the British and Foreign Bible Society (BFBS), which was ecumenical and non-sectarian, and thus included nonconformists as well as Anglicans (although, through their own choice, not Roman Catholics). It was set up to provide affordable copies of the Bible for all, and also spearheaded a translation programme. In the United Kingdom supporters soon organized themselves into local 'Auxiliary Bible Societies', which provided a large part of the Society's income, and were also a channel for home distribution. The Durham Auxiliary was formed in 1821.

33 In full, St Cuthbert's College, Ushaw. It started life in 1568 as the English College at Douai, but was forced to leave France in 1795, and was established at Ushaw in 1804. It was the Roman Catholic seminary for northern England, and was affiliated with Durham University from 1968. It closed in 2011, owing to a lack of vocations.

34 J. M. Tweedy, *Popish Elvet*, Durham, 1981.

35 *Durham Advertiser*, 25 October 1828.

36 *Durham Advertiser*, 29 October 1830.

Chapter 7

'Going to renew old acquaintanceship': the second visit to Piedmont, 1827–31

By 1826 the London Vaudois Committee was well established as the English link with the Protestants of Piedmont. Gilly remained as secretary, despite the fact that he was now living in Durham, some 400 kilometres from London. The Committee was supporting a hospital at La Torre and subsidizing schools in the Protestant valleys.

The minutes of the London Vaudois Committee for 1 January 1827 contain a detailed factual account of the Waldensian settlements in Germany. These had been established in the eighteenth century, when refugees from Piedmont had been given sanctuary in Würtemberg and other Protestant states. By 1826 all these communities had been absorbed into the German Protestant churches, and with one exception, the village of Dornholzthausen, were using German in their services. The London Vaudois Committee was now meeting less frequently, probably because it had become an established institution, with its secretary living in Durham. It met seven times in 1827, thrice in 1828, twice in 1829 and 1830, and once only in both 1831 and 1832. Gilly was present at five of the meetings in 1827, and all the other gatherings except in 1831. One of the meetings which Gilly did not attend was on 19 June 1827, at which the other members then resolved to send their warmest thanks to him for his untiring exertions on behalf of the committee.

By May 1828 the committee had received donations of £6,500 to help the Waldensians. Distributions were made with caution: indeed, the committee distributed only the interest upon the donations received, which amounted to £214 in 1828.[1] Surgical instruments were sent to assist the hospital at La Torre, and small amounts of money were sent to assist with ministers' salaries and to help in improving the education system.

General John Charles Beckwith

In the summer of 1827 Colonel (as he then was) John Charles Beckwith became interested in Waldensian affairs, and his name is still revered in the Waldensian valleys.[2] Beckwith, one of the great British eccentrics of the nineteenth century, had been born in 1789 as one of fourteen children of a United Empire Loyalist family

---

1   LVC Minutes, 6 May 1828.
2   The Waldensian radio station is called *Radio Beckwith Evangelica*. In 2000 it gave timely warnings of the floods which caused great damage in Piedmont. For more on Beckwith, see H. M. Stephens, *Beckwith, John Charles* (1789–1862) rev. James Lunt, *Oxford Dictionary of National Biography*, Oxford University Press, 2004; online edn, May 2008 (www.oxforddnb.com/view/article/1912, accessed 26 April 2011).

in Halifax, Nova Scotia. His mother, when a girl, had fled from New York with her family at the time of the American Revolution of 1776. At the age of 14 he entered the British army, and served with distinction under the duke of Wellington during the Napoleonic wars. In 1815 his left leg was shattered at the Battle of Waterloo, and three months later it was amputated without anaesthetic.

The survival of this traumatic experience led Beckwith to believe that God had preserved him for a purpose in life. He remained as a half-pay officer, but the lack of a leg was obviously a disadvantage in a military career. In the summer of 1827 he read Gilly's *Narrative*,

General Beckwith (source unknown).

probably while sitting in Apsley House library waiting to see the Duke of Wellington, and his purpose was revealed to him: for the next thirty-five years Beckwith devoted his life to helping the Waldensians. During most years he spent several months in the Protestant valleys. His first visit to Piedmont was in the autumn of 1827; he returned for seven months between October 1828 and April 1829, and eventually took a house, La Torre in Rémont, where he lived until his death. He was a practical man, concerned to improve the lot of the peasants. He learned to speak the local language, and could talk to the farmers about turnips and to young girls about knitting. He was always proud of his military rank in the British army, and was promoted to the rank of general while he was on half-pay. In 1857 Beckwith resigned his pension, and received a letter of one sentence from the British War Office, which must surely be one of the most laconic which has ever been sent by that august institution. Hitherto unpublished, it reads in full:[3]

The War Office, London.
28 December 1857

I am directed by Lord Palmerston to acknowledge the receipt of your letter of the 21st instant in which you resign the pension of £300 per annum which was granted to you in

---

3   We await the publication of a critical biography of this hard-working, efficient, dedicated, dogmatic and eccentric man. When he was in his late 60s he asked the Tavola to find a Waldensian wife for him. His only daughter, Charlotte, was born posthumously: he never knew that his wife was pregnant. There is one sympathetic account of his life: J. P. Meille, *General Beckwith: His Life and Labours among the Waldenses of Piedmont*, published by T. Nelson, London, 1873 (original in French, trans. W. Arnot).

consideration of the loss of a leg at Waterloo, and to acquaint you that in compliance with your request your name has been removed from the list of officers who are in receipt of military pensions.

I have the honour to be
Sir
Your most Obedient Servant

B Harvey
Under Secretary of State for War,
War Office, Pall Mall, London, S.W.[4]

Beckwith was a High Church Anglican by both birth and the inner conviction of his heart,[5] but his correspondence shows that he considered the Pope to be the Antichrist: in a letter to the secretary of British and Foreign Bible Society, he wrote, 'There cannot be much difficulty to find where Anti Christ has his seat.' The recipient has endorsed this letter 'Must be used with caution'.[6] He was convinced that the Waldensian Church would, in due course, be the catalyst for the conversion of Italy to a form of Protestantism. He studied the Revelation of St John the Divine (the final book in the New Testament) and believed that 'The study of prophecy is a legitimate exercise for the Christian mind, and is not only a right but a duty.'[7] He liked his own way, and usually got it. He once wrote, 'I do not pretend to teach ladies and gentlemen – I take in hand only the lower orders.'[8] By 1829 he had started the construction of small primary schools, many of which are still standing, although they are no longer used as schools. His methods would have pleased Samuel Smiles.[9] Each community was told, 'You, my friends, will provide the site and the labour, and I will provide the money for materials.'

Gilly, who led a busy life in England, and Beckwith, who increasingly lived in the Waldensian valleys, formed an efficient partnership. Both were High Church Anglicans, whereas the Waldensians had been Calvinist for nearly 300 years, and in later years there were to be tensions as the two Englishmen tried to persuade the Waldensians of the virtues of Anglican practices. On one occasion an exasperated Beckwith wrote to a correspondent in Scotland:

> I must tell you however that this Presbyterian form has not much meaning in it, for in a close despotism civil and religious men are under the operation of a regular system of espionage, which poisons and subverts the whole frame of society.[10]

4   ACCV, Beckwith Papers.
5   See Appendix IV as to the meaning of 'High Church' at this time.
6   CUL, Archives, British and Foreign Bible Society; letter, Beckwith to BFBS, 30 September 1844.
7   ACCV, Beckwith papers.
8   Letter, Beckwith to Muston, 25 March 1834. Quoted in Meille, *General Beckwith*, p. 233.
9   Samuel Smiles (1812–1904) was the author of a runaway best-seller *Self-help, With Illustrations of Character and Conduct* (1859), followed by others called *Character* (1871) *Thrift* (1875), *Duty* (1880) and *Life and Labour* (1887). [NWG]
10   Letter, Beckwith to the Rev. William Robertson, Stirling, 'North Britain' [*vidz*, Scotland], 22 January

The second visit to Piedmont, May to August 1829

On 16 May, 1829, Gilly went to London for the Meeting of the London Vaudois Committee, held at 2 Argyle Place, Bloomsbury, and informed the Committee that he proposed to visit Piedmont during the summer. He was requested to make particular inquiries about the state of the four girls' schools supported by the committee, and was authorized to spend up to £100 in improving church buildings.[11]

Gilly's second visit to the valleys was far more comprehensive than his initial short visit in January 1823, when he had stayed there for only three-and-a-half days. In the summer of 1829 he travelled with his wife, and was later joined by his brother Frederick. William and Jane Gilly arrived on 22 June 1829 and left on 20 August 1829. During these two months they made arduous journeys through the valleys of Piedmont, and also in neighbouring parts of France. This visit was made with a clear purpose. Anne Colberg, who was now living in Gilly's household, and who had inherited a great deal of money from Shute Barrington, was prepared to donate several thousand pounds of her inheritance for the establishment of a theological college in the Waldensian valleys. Gilly never revealed the source of this financial benevolence to anybody, not even to the London Vaudois Committee.[12] He had a carefully formulated plan. He intended to liaise with leaders of the Waldensian community about the construction of a college in the valleys, but also for the reform of their liturgy. The story of the financing and construction of the college during 1829 and the 1830s shows Gilly at his best, for he was a hard-working administrator with a talent for persuading many diverse individuals of the merit of his proposals.

William and Jane Gilly set off for Piedmont at the end of May 1829:

We arrived at Paris on Monday night, June 1st, and there I had the good fortune to meet Colonel Beckwith, whose long residence in the Valleys during the last autumn and winter, enabled him to form a most accurate estimate of the present condition and wants of the Vaudois. He was so good as to let me transcribe his notes upon the state of public instruction, the hospital, the resources, of the pastors, and other matters connected with the object of my journey; and I should be doing injustice to this judicious and zealous friend of the cause, were I not to state, how much I am indebted to him for the information and suggestions with which he favoured me. Unlike some of my countrymen who have visited the Valleys, he did not come away disappointed and dissatisfied, at not finding the Vaudois far above all human beings, in the scale of virtue and religion; but he judged of them fairly, according to their advantages and disadvantages, their lights, their means, and opportunities, and their local statistic position in society.[13]

1843. ACCV, Beckwith papers.

11 LVC Minutes.

12 On 20 March 1830 Gilly reported to the Vaudois Committee that he was not at liberty to divulge the names of the benevolent individuals who were financing the proposed Waldensian Training College (LVC Minutes).

13 W. S. Gilly, *Waldensian Researches During a Second Visit to the Vaudois of Piemont*, 1831, p, 168 (subsequently *Researches*).

This was the beginning of a partnership between these two High-Church Anglicans which was to last until Gilly's death twenty-six years later. As noted in this account, Beckwith, in his methodical way, had already compiled notes upon the state of affairs in the Waldensian valleys, and these detailed notes, written in Beckwith's clear hand-writing, are still preserved in the archives of the Waldensian Church.[14] They record the number of schools in the valleys (one grammar school, fifteen great schools, 126 small schools, four girls' schools, and one private school); the income of the ministers; the success of the hospital established at La Torre in 1824; and details of the finances of the Waldensian Church. The notes show that the Waldensians, although poor, were already a well-organized community before they began to benefit from the activities of Gilly and Beckwith. Some Waldensians had become successful merchants and lived, admittedly on sufferance only, in Turin.[15] Thanks therefore to Beckwith's notes, Gilly was well informed about the state of affairs in the Waldensian valleys.

On Friday 12 June, Gilly and his wife arrived in Geneva, where they had hoped to meet three Waldensian students studying at the Calvinist seminary, but the students had already left for the vacation. Following the destruction of the school for *Barbes*[16] in the Angrogna Valley during the massacres of the seventeenth century, pastors had received their training in seminaries at Geneva and Lausanne in the French-speaking Protestant cantons of Switzerland, where they were supported by scholarships funded from Holland. Gilly disapproved of this practice, and indeed referred to 'the evils of the present system'.[17] He wanted the pastors to be trained again in their own valleys:

> I can make no hesitation in expressing my opinion, that new habits, new wants, and wishes, and new opinions, injurious to native simplicity, cannot but be acquired by lads who leave their rustic and secluded habitations on the mountains, and pass the greater part of seven or eight years, from fifteen and sixteen years of age, in a foreign town. Formerly the Vaudois pastors were educated at home, but when the college, or establishment for education at Angrogna, of whatever kind it may have been, was destroyed, the candidates for ordination had no other resource than to betake themselves to Switzerland.[18]

On Monday 15 June the party sailed to Lausanne by steamer, and met M. Monastier, who was a professor at the theological college there, and a Waldensian by birth. M. Monastier agreed with Gilly's plan, and indeed:

> further stated, that he did not know of any better plan for ameliorating the general condition of the Vaudois, than this, that the friends and protectors of the Waldensian Church should combine their efforts, and establish an institution, where efficient instruction may be given,

---

14 ACCV, Beckwith Papers.
15 *Researches*, p. 547, footnote.
16 *Barbes* is the name given by the Waldensians to their ministers. The word *barba* in Piedmontese means 'uncle', but is also used as a term of respect. It seems to have taken on a specifically religious term among the Waldensians in the fifteenth century. See further Audisio, *The Waldensian Dissent*, pp. 125 ff.
17 *Researches*, p. 171.
18 *Researches*, p. 170.

not only to the young people who are intended for the ministry, but to those also who are destined to be the regents or masters of the village schools. By this means general improvement will be secured, and they who are to preside over education will be well grounded in those branches of knowledge, which are most essential for a population like that of the valleys.[19]

On Wednesday 17 June William and Jane Gilly left the Protestant canton of Geneva and entered the Catholic Kingdom of Sardinia:

As soon as we crossed the barrier, and had passed out of the Swiss into the Sardinian states, pauperism and mendicity, dirt and discomfort, scanty productions, and inferior cultivation, proclaimed the change of masters more than that of soil.[20]

At the frontier town of Chambéry their passports were examined. The Sardinian customs officers were in a jovial mood because a *fête* was in progress. They reacted predictably when they encountered William and Jane Gilly (aged 40 and 24 respectively). Gilly indignantly recorded:

The transport or hilarity of the occasion had so intoxicated the man of office, whose inspection and permission were necessary to the continuance of our route, that when he saw my party described in the passport as an ecclesiastic travelling with his wife, he excited a loud laugh among his colleagues at the idea of a married clergyman, and humorously or insolently contrived to word the *billet* which he gave me in exchange for my passport, so as to make it contain an affronting *équivoque*.[21]

On Saturday 20 June they arrived in Turin, and booked into an hotel overlooking the main piazza. Gilly does not record going to church on 21 June,[22] but he has left a precise description of all that was going on in the grand piazza of Turin on that Sunday morning:

In one part, soldiers were paraded and marched off to their posts. In another, a religious procession extended its lines from one side of the square to the other. Here a fellow who presided over a blacking stall was holding forth upon the excellency of his commodity, with all the earnestness and fluency of a senator. There a quack-doctor had collected a crowd by the sound of his trumpet, and was dispensing his advice and his medicine out of a four-wheeled open carriage drawn by one horse. At one moment he was haranguing in stentorian tones, which could be heard distinctly in our room: at another, blowing a blast with his trumpet scarcely more loud. We saw him draw the tooth of one patient, and dress

---

19   *Researches*, p. 174.
20   *Researches*, p. 176. This seems to have been something of a King Charles's head with Gilly. We might wonder quite how he reconciled it with the 'pauperism, mendicity, dirt and discomfort' etc. in Protestant Durham which his Mendicity Society was combating [NWG].
21   *Researches*, p. 177. The '*billet*' seems not to have survived.
22   There were places for Protestant worship in Turin, over which a Waldensian pastor (M. Bonjour) presided (see below) but Gilly probably read the Book of Common Prayer Morning Service with Jane in his room [NWG].

the wounds of another, as much to the amusement as to the edification of the bystanders.
Not far from him a conjuror was exercising his lungs and his ingenuity, and tempting idlers
away from the parade, the procession, and the empiric. The clamours of these rivals for
public applause, the buzz of voices, the rattling of arms, and the sound of military music,
mingled strangely with the bells calling to Church, and with the chanting of the priests in
procession. Nowhere is religion more ostentatious, or even more obtrusive than at Turin,
and yet the whole of the Lord's day presents the spectacle of a fair, rather than that of a
holy convocation, and glad were we to think, that one day more, and the short distance of
less than thirty miles, would bring us to the valleys, and restore us to a state of things more
resembling those to which we are accustomed at home.[23]

The next day, Monday 22 June, at 7 pm they reached La Torre. Gilly's second visit to
the Waldensian valleys had begun:

> I cannot adequately describe my feelings, as I approached the well-remembered spots, which
> are almost as dear to me as my native soil. As the mountains neared upon us, after travelling
> the long plain, and straight line of road which extends from Turin to Pinerolo, it was more
> like the sensation of returning home than of going to renew old acquaintanceship.[24]

They stayed with Pastor Bert in the hamlet of San Margarita on the outskirts of La
Torre, and used his house as their base for the next two months whilst they visited
each of the fifteen Waldensian communes, as well as the adjoining Protestant valleys
of France. Bert took great trouble to look after his guests:

> Our dinners consisted generally of *potage*, a small piece of beef or veal, not remarkable for
> fatness of flavour, poultry, trout caught in the Pellice, and some preparations of eggs, rice,
> vegetables, or pastry. The substantial dish as supper was a flowing bowl of milk rich as
> cream, or of custard pudding with some preserved fruit.[25]

They also had fruit in abundance, baked cakes, curds, and sausages.
   Within three days of Gilly's arrival he was visited by pastors from Bobi, Villar,
San Giovanni, Rora and Angrogna, and the master of the Latin school also called.
Thanks to Beckwith's detailed work, Gilly now had particulars of the organization
of the church, schools, health facilities and society throughout the valleys. He also
knew precisely what assistance was reaching the valleys from the Protestant countries
of Northern Europe and from Russia. Language was a problem, and Gilly stated the
matter succinctly:

> The vernacular tongue of the Vaudois is a barbarous dialect between Latin, French, and
> Italian, more like the Spanish perhaps. The language of the state is Italian, and that, in
> which they receive instruction is French, without the means at present of acquiring it gram-
> matically. It is astonishing therefore that a population should be grounded and rooted in a

---

23   *Researches*, p. 179.
24   *Researches*, p. 180. And this after a previous visit of just three-and-a-half days [NWG].
25   *Researches*, p. 182.

The bridge at San Margarita: one of Jane Gilly's illustrations published in WSG's *Researches* (via Google Books)

faith, the knowledge of which is communicated to them under every possible impediment; and it is hard to determine how the difficulties of having to learn the principles of religion in a language, not the spoken language of the province, are to be met.[26]

On Sunday 28 June, the church service was conducted by M. Bert according to the

---

26   *Researches*, p. 200. Piemontese is a distinct language of the north Italian group, and not merely a dialect of Italian.

liturgy of Geneva: the service lasted one and a half hours. Psalms were sung 'with more earnestness perhaps than harmony'.[27] Gilly was pleased to learn that 'One of the younger pastors has undertaken to open his church for a third Sunday service, at which he reads the prayers and Scripture himself, and gives a familiar explanation of some scriptural passage.'[28] He commended the ministers and the people for their example and wrote:

> I am persuaded that nobody, who has been in the valleys, can accuse our Protestant brethren there of profaning Sunday, as it is profaned among ourselves, by entertainments, which employ our servants from morning till night, and by those licentious scenes which disgrace the streets of almost every populous town in England.[29]

On 29 June Gilly's brother Frederick arrived, on leave from his post as an officer in the Royal Navy, and the party was further increased by the arrival of M. and Mme Bonjour. M. Bonjour, a Waldensian, lived in Turin, where he was Protestant chaplain to the British, Dutch and Prussian ambassadors to the kingdom of Sardinia. Protestant services could only be held in this Catholic city at foreign embassies.[30] Pastor Bonjour was Pastor Bert's son-in-law, and they were both important personalities in the Waldensian Church.

On Wednesday 1 July the annual fair was held at La Torre. Gilly was apprehensive 'lest anything disgraceful should occur upon an occasion so trying to morals .... I could not forget our English fairs or their demoralising effects.'[31] But the great fair was a happy occasion: 'the road filled with moving objects, with buyers and sellers in their various costumes, and arrayed in their best apparel'.[32] He noted, with pride, that the cottons of Manchester and the hardware of Birmingham were being sold in the booths.

On Monday 6 July, with Gilly and his brother on foot and his wife on a pony, the party set off to explore the mountains to the north of La Torre. They spent an energetic day searching for the Castelluzza cavern where, according to legend, the Waldensians had taken shelter in times of persecution, but they were unsuccessful. The next day they visited the Waldensian hospital which, with assistance from Protestants in northern Europe and the London Vaudois Committee, had been established in the hamlet of Copia in 1824. The hospital had accommodation for fourteen patients, and was run on economical lines. 'The average expenditure, independently of the salaries, is at the rate of one franc or ten-pence a day for each patient, including

---

27 *Researches*, p. 220.
28 *Researches*, p 242.
29 *Researches*, p. 243.
30 Precisely the same arrangements as had existed, *mutatis mutandis*, for Roman Catholics in Britain for many years [NWG].
31 *Researches*, p. 260.
32 *Researches*, p. 260.

charges for food, medicine, fuel and wine.'[33] Gilly was fascinated by the accounting system used at the hospital, which he considered to be 'one of the most perfect models of accuracy and perspicuity which I have ever examined'.[34] He also visited the nearby Waldensian grammar school, and was most agreeably surprised to find the master 'well-informed, zealous, active and successful in his labours, far beyond any thing which I was prepared to expect'.[35]

The week of 7 to 11 July was spent visiting the various communes in the Pellice valley. At the hamlet of Puys a new school had been established by Beckwith. At Bobi Gilly met Pastor Muston, the Moderator of the Waldensian Church. He noted that Waldensian society was egalitarian: there were no seigniorial rights, and while the peasants deferred to their clergy and to the elders of their church, there was no distinction of family or class. There were no chateaux or big houses, and nobody in the valleys had any claim to noble birth. Given their origin in the twelfth century as 'the Poor of Lyons', this shows remarkable tenacity to their founding ideals.

On Friday 10 July Gilly walked to Rora, an isolated Waldensian mountain village with a population of 800. It was here that, in the seventeenth century, the worst massacres had occurred.[36] The pastor, M. Monastier, conducted three services each Sunday. As Gilly walked back to La Torre in the evening, he was fascinated by the fireflies:

> The brilliant lights which they emit, their rapid flitting motion through the air, and the cheerfulness which they impart to the spirits, by engaging us to watch for their playful illumination, are quite indescribable. There is no difficulty in catching them; and I had the satisfaction of carrying one home with me, and gazing at its mysterious lamp without doing it injury.[37]

Gilly had now spent three weeks in the Waldensian valleys. Thanks to Barrington's will and his wife's aunt, Anne Colberg, he had access to a substantial amount of cash:

> These were not any part of a public subscription, but private funds, over which I had the sole control,[38] and which I might appropriate in such manner, as should appear to me to be most beneficial to the Protestant cause in the valleys of Piemont. After much reflection and long deliberations with persons competent to give an opinion, I was encouraged to hope that a scheme which combined the endowment of a college, with the restoration of

---

33 *Researches*, p. 310.
34 *Researches*, p. 311.
35 *Researches*, p. 320.
36 Samuel Morland, *History of the Evangelical Churches of the Valleys of Piemont* ..., London, 1658. (Republished 1982).
37 *Researches*, p. 361. The fireflies of the Pellice valley still fascinate visitors in the twenty-first century.
38 This is an extraordinary remark. Until the passing of the Married Women's Property Act in 1882, a married woman had no control over her property, as she surrendered her legal identity to her husband: thus Gilly had control over Jane's money. Unmarried women and widows, on the other hand, did have control. As Anne Colberg was unmarried, this implies that she had given some of her money to Gilly, and this appears to be borne out by a later letter – see note 59 [NWG].

an uniform church service and discipline, upon old Waldensian principles, would be sanctioned and promoted, not only by the Vaudois pastors individually, but also by the officers of the Table, in their official capacity, as the constituted authorities of the community, and by the people at large. In this there was nothing new or offensive to common prejudices, it was simply a recurrence to the ancient order of things.[39]

There was a hidden agenda to Gilly's scheme for a college. As already noted, before the massacres of the seventeenth century, the Waldensians had had a college of their own in the Angrogna valley which they remembered with fondness, although a not a vestige of it remained. Gilly envisaged that eventually the new institution would take its place, and supplant the then-current practice of training pastors in Geneva and Lausanne, whence the students returned to their native valleys with their Calvinism reinforced. Gilly wrote, 'The present ecclesiastical government of the Vaudois, is, in some degree, like that of the Presbyterian Church, but more relaxed and indulgent. Anciently it was episcopal.' Gilly's unequivocal assertion about the episcopalian origins of the Waldensian Church is mere wishful thinking: a similar claim in Gilly's first book about the Waldensians had been challenged by Bracebridge and by the Waldensian pastors, while sixteen years later Ebenezer Henderson, another English visitor to the valleys, wrote: 'No trace of an episcopal hierarchy is to be found in any of their ancient documents.'[40]

Gilly set out clearly his aspirations for the establishment of a new training college:

> It was naturally a great object with me, not only to obtain the general consent of the Vaudois for the introduction of a uniform liturgy, but that this liturgy should be formed, in part at least, after the model of that of the Church of England.[41]

Between Monday 13 and Thursday 16 July, Gilly, his brother, M. Bonjour and a guide named Melo walked over the Alpe de Julien to the San Martino valley, and thence to Roderetto and Baliglia, where in 1690 the Waldensians had constructed a fortified redoubt. (Jane Gilly remained at Pastor Bert's house in San Margarita.) This expedition involved crossing four alpine passes and much energetic walking. Each night the party stayed with pastors in isolated Waldensian villages and hamlets. Gilly recorded vividly the mountain scenery, the lives of the peasants, the church structure and the village schools. At Perrero, a predominantly Catholic village:

> We were hailed in by a Roman Catholic surgeon, who invited some of his neighbours to

---

39   *Researches*, p. 379.
40   *Researches*, p. 383. See also C. H. Bracebridge, *Authentic Details of the Valdenses ...*, London, 1827; E. Henderson, *The Vaudois; comprising observations made during a tour to the Valleys of Piedmont, in the summer of 1814: together with remarks, introductory and interspersed, respecting the origin, history and present condition of that people*, London, 1845, p 208. See also Chapter 3 of this book. Episcopacy was a major tenet of Gilly's High Churchmanship.
41   *Researches*, p. 385.

join us, and placed a repast before us, on the strength of which we might have proceeded till night. The kindness and genuine frankness with which the three Vaudois clergymen, and the English strangers, (whose Protestantism was known to have brought them here,) were received by these members of the other community, added one more to the many convictions on my mind, that there is no reason why Protestants and Roman Catholics should not dwell together amicably, wherever pains, and penalties, and disabilities for religion sake are removed.[42]

As the party descended to the village of Pramolo, Gilly fell and dislocated his finger. There they stayed with Pastor Vinçon, whose Swiss wife had once lived in England, and in Ireland as a governess in the family of an Anglican archbishop. She had cheerfully adjusted to life in the Waldensian valleys, although she had retained 'many of those English habits which give a charm to domestic life'.[43] Thanks to the kindness of a Miss Burroughs, an English lady, Madame Vinçon had a well-stocked medicine chest from which she dispensed medicine and good cheer to the local sick.

From Pramolo Gilly crossed into the Angrogna valley, and from thence back to Pastor Bert's house at San Margarita. He recorded with pride:

> I had traversed on foot the whole length of the valleys, and in such a direction as to give me a good idea of the localities of all the parishes and hamlets. I had become acquainted with notables of the community, and had learnt their sentiments upon many important topics. I had seen the manners of the pastors, and principal inhabitants, and of the poorest peasants, under different circumstances. My favourable opinions are all strengthened. If there were some few things which vexed me, there were many which gave me pleasure.[44]

Gilly had now visited most of the parishes in the Waldensian valleys, and had discussed his proposals for a college with the pastors of each of these communities. Upon his return to Torre Pellice, he drew up a set of papers for consideration by the pastors of the Waldensian Church:

> I propose, (upon certain conditions, and under certain regulations,) to apply funds at my disposal to the endowment of a school, or college, which shall serve for the instruction of young persons intended for the ministry, for regents, schoolmasters, &c., &c., and which shall, as far as it is possible, be equally beneficial to the three valleys. In the promotion of this object, I engage to furnish five thousand francs towards building a house for the proposed establishment, provided that the Vaudois will themselves give the site, within the commune of La Torre.
>
> To give a stipend of 1500 francs a-year to the head-master.
>
> To give ten exhibitions of 100 francs each to students of the ten communes, situated at the greatest distance from La Torre.
>
> To make these permanent endowments, if the college goes on satisfactorily.
>
> To make a communication of these intentions to the London Vaudois Committee, and

---

42 *Researches*, p. 416. Is Gilly overstating the religious divide here? [NWG]
43 *Researches*, p. 421.
44 *Researches*, p. 423.

The view from Pastor Bert's house in San Margarita, Pellice valley: a drawing by Jane Gilly from *Waldensian Researches* (via Google Books)

to the Dutch Committee, under the hope that the former may supply the means of raising a salary for a second master, and that the latter may consent to transfer the stipend and services of the master of the grammar-school of La Torre, to the proposed college, by which a third mastership may be established.

To assign 2000 francs for the purchase of books, of my own choice, for the use of the students of the proposed establishment; under the expectation that the pastors will contribute from their own stock of books towards the foundation of a library.

I engage also, to assign 500 francs annually to the Officers of the Table, to enable them to meet the expenses of annual visitation, -

To the Moderator	200
To the Moderator adjoint	150
To the Secretary of the Table	150

upon condition that they visit the college twice a year, and they also visit the parishes as heretofore.

To assign also 1300 francs annually, in equal allotments, to the pastors, to enable them to meet the casual wants of the poor, or of the schools of their several parishes, upon condition that they deliver a report in writing to the Moderator, every year, in answer to the queries proposed at his visitation.[45]

Gilly obtained the signatures of fourteen pastors to his proposals.

This exercise again shows Gilly' s organizing genius. The Waldensian pastors knew that Gilly had access to a considerable amount of money, and were naturally pleased that it would be used to revive their ancient church. Gilly, for his part, made it quite

---

45   *Researches*, p. 427.

clear that he wished to work with the local community. But it is also evident that Gilly hoped to wean the Waldensians from their traditional Calvinist practices and induce them to move to a liturgy (and presumably theology) similar to that used in the Church of England. He had in mind the practices in the Swiss canton of Neuchâtel, where he believed that Anglican practices had, in part, replaced Calvinist procedures.

Between 17 and 22 July Gilly stayed with Pastor Bert at San Margarita, while his dislocated finger healed. On Wednesday 22 July he walked to Pra del Tor, hoping to find some vestiges of the ancient college of the *Barbes*, but could find nothing. Nor could he find the caves which had, according to tradition, been used as lecture rooms for this college in the fourteenth and fifteenth centuries.

Visit to the French Protestant valleys, 25 July to 4 August 1829

In late July and early August Gilly and his wife made an expedition to the remote valleys in the Dauphine on the western side of the Alps – Val de Queiras and Val de Frassinière. Gilly wanted to establish contacts with these French Protestant communities which, because of their isolation in remote valleys, had survived Francis I's attempt to exterminate the Huguenot church in the sixteenth century, and also the revocation of the Edict of Nantes by Louis XIV in 1685. Gilly had been briefed about the Protestants of the Dauphine by Francis Cunningham, Rector of Pakefield in Suffolk,[46] who had spent several months in 1826 visiting their villages and hamlets.[47]

Felix Neff: a portrait from the cover of a later biography

These communities were even more isolated than the Waldensian communities of Piedmont. Felix Neff, a young clergyman from Geneva, had devoted his short life to helping these remote villagers prior to his early death from cancer in 1826: he acted as pastor, schoolmaster, engineer and agriculturalist, and was so successful that he changed the character of the district and its inhabitants. Gilly was later to write a 'Memorial' of him.

46   Cunningham was Rector of Pakefield from 1814–56. His wife Richenda was a sister of Elizabeth Fry (www. pakefieldchurch.com/history2nd.htm).

47   F. Cunningham, *A letter to the Right Hon. Lord Bexley containing a statement made to the committee of the British and Foreign Bible Society as to the relations of that institution with France, the Valleys of Piedmont, Switzerland, and Germany*. London, 1827.

William and Jane Gilly were accompanied by a guide. A pony carried Mrs Gilly, and an ass had been hired to carry the luggage. In places they knew they would find only sour wine to drink and rye bread to eat, so they loaded the ass with:

> three large cloaks, one of which was water-proof; a water-proof bag, (these articles we found to answer the purpose most faithfully, and against some pitiless storms they stood proof); an inflated air bag, to serve as a seat or pillow; some tea, sugar, chocolate, biscuits, and brandy. We added the equally necessary changes of linen and clothes, and a basket containing books and drawing materials and three staves shod with iron.[48]

William and Jane Gilly were embarking upon an arduous expedition into mountainous regions without roads. Jane Gilly, who was no mean draughtswoman, was carrying her sketch book.

The party set out from Bobi before 7 am on Saturday 25 July. They journeyed uphill towards the French frontier, which was marked by the dismantled Fort Miraboca. By midday they reached Bergerie du Pra, where there was a small inn. The route they were following was the one that, according to tradition, had been followed by Hannibal when he crossed the Alps in 218 BC. The inn was crowded, as word had got around that a Protestant service was to be held the next day, but they managed to find accommodation. On the morning of Sunday 26 July:

> at nine o'clock, a man ascended the roof of the auberge, and blew a loud and long blast with a conch-shell, – this he repeated at half-past nine, and at ten. The summons, I was told, might be heard at a great distance. After the first blast, we saw people approaching from different quarters, and this picturesque gathering continued for more than an hour. The service then commenced, and never did I behold a more attentive congregation. M. Bonjour's text was from Isaiah lii.7.[49]

After this moving service, the party continued through torrential rain, and spent the night at Abries. They had now entered France and were in the Val de Queiras, a remote and largely Huguenot valley. Here they were heartened to note that two new Protestant churches had recently been constructed:

> we went into most of the villages and hamlets where Neff had laboured, and never shall I forget the proofs which we witnessed of the strong devotional feeling, and pure Christian spirit implanted among the Protestant families, in Val Queiras and Val de Frassiniere. Neff's name is so reverenced, that it cannot be pronounced without producing a sigh or a tear, and a blessing upon his memory.[50]

On Wednesday 29 July they crossed the River Durance and ascended the Val de Frassinière, one of the most remote valleys in France. Here most of the popula-

---

48   *Researches*, p. 453.
49   *Researches*, p. 464. (The text reads: 'How beautiful upon the mountains are the feet of him that bringeth good tidings …'.)
50   *Researches*, p. 467.

tion was Protestant. After passing through the villages of Violin and Mensals, they reached the remote hamlet of Dormilleuse. Gilly recorded that 'No Dormilleusian ever bowed his knee before an image of the Roman church'.[51] At four of the villages, when their guide made it known that Gilly was a Protestant clergyman, 'the inhabitants left their houses, and their work in the fields, and flocked round me to entreat me to preach to them'. However, 'I pleaded my imperfect knowledge of French, and they reluctantly gave up the point.'[52] This visit to the remote Queiras and Frassinière valleys confirmed Gilly in his belief that 'when the primitive Churches were supplanted by the Roman church in the plains, there were branches of the old stock which still flourished in the remote mountain hamlets. Some few of these have survived.'[53]

William and Jane Gilly were now seasoned travellers. They decided to return to the Waldensian valleys by turning north and following the road constructed by Napoleon from Briançon to the Val di Pragela. This is a valley of bitter memories for the Waldensians of Piedmont, for it had once contained thriving Protestant communities, but all the Waldensians had been expelled during the eighteenth century. They migrated to Germany, where their descendants still live. Gilly later wrote:

> The Waldenses of the valley of Pragela have been exterminated, in conformity with a secret compact made between Louis XIV and Victor Amadée, but in violation of the most binding treaties between the Bourbons and the Waldenses. And where are the Bourbons now? Righteous art thou, O Lord![54]

He mournfully recorded that 'every vestige of the Waldensian church is effaced in the Valley of Pragela'.[55]

On Saturday 1 August the Gillys reached Fenestrelle, where they were hospitably received by M. Coucourde, a Waldensian resident of that town. From there the party returned to La Torre, after again visiting the San Martino valley. At Pomarretto Gilly visited Pastor (Rodolphe) Peyrani's grave. He recorded the inscription: *J. R. L. S. Peyran, Pasteur et Moderateur né le 11 Dec. 1752, Mort le 26 Avril, 1823*. This visit was important for Gilly, because his meeting with Pastor Peyrani on 11 January 1823 had been the turning point of his life. Here they also examined the large Waldensian church erected with the help of the Csar of Russia, and inspected the dispensary which

---

51   *Researches*, p. 468.
52   *Researches*, p. 468. His written French was highly competent. I suspect he did not wish to preach extempore, something he would regard as a mark of extreme evangelicalism. [NWG]
53   *Researches*, p. 469. As with his theory of Waldensian episcopacy, he was seeing what he wanted to see. [NWG]
54   *Researches*, p. 480. Gilly was travelling before the French Revolution of 1830 which overthrew Charles X, the last of the direct line of the Bourbon monarchy. Gilly published his account of the expedition in 1831, when Louis Philippe, 'the Citizen King', ruled France. Louis Philippe was a Bourbon, although not in the direct line of descent. Victor Amadeus was a descendant of the Stuart dynasty and a distant claimant to the British throne, and thus a hate-figure among Protestants.
55   *Researches*, p. 482.

was being assisted by the London Vaudois Committee. From thence they travelled up
the San Martino valley to Prali.

By now they were very tired indeed: 'we were both so ill, and suffering so severely
from the effects of our rough journey into Dauphine, as to be apprehensive of the
consequences of being laid up in this remote village'.[56] Their journey was still not
completed, for they diverted to San Germano where, in the Protestant cemetery,
Gilly discovered the grave of the father-in-law of one of his school friends with an
inscription as follows:

> Beneath this stone are deposited the remains of Capel Loft, who was lord of the manors of
> Troston and Stanton, in the county of Suffolk, England, born in London, 25th November,
> 1752, died at Moncalière, 26th May, 1824.[57]

English gravestones were not rarities, for when Protestant tourists, traders or diplomats
died in north-east Italy, their bodies were often buried in the Protestant cemeteries of
the Waldensian valleys.

The party arrived back at La Torre on Tuesday 4 August, justly proud of having
successfully carried out an exceptionally arduous expedition. Gilly recorded:

> I have now planted my foot in every village, which is most sacred in Waldensian history;
> and have surveyed most of those spots, which in their seclusion or natural strength, have
> been the asylums of the persecuted.[58]

The next week they remained based at San Margarita, but made excursions to nearby
villages. On 14 August Gilly, his brother and two Waldensian men again tried to find
the cavern of Castelluzzo. They did find a large cave in the traditional location, but Gilly
was not able to satisfy himself that it contained sufficient space for 400 people to seek
refuge during the days of persecution. The party carved their initials on a wall of the cave.

Between 16 and 20 August Gilly met several Waldensian pastors at La Torre, when
they considered sending a petition to the King of Sardinia for the amelioration of the
restrictions on the community. On 20 August William and Jane Gilly said goodbye
to their hosts and set out for home. It had been an arduous journey, but Gilly had
succeeded in persuading the leaders of the Waldensian community of the soundness
of his proposal for a college in the valleys. He recorded:

> when I was entrusted with the disposal of a private fund for their benefit,[59] I thought
> it right to apply it in such a manner, as should strengthen the weak hands – and be of

56   *Researches*, p. 495.
57   *Researches*, p. 501.
58   *Researches*, p. 504.
59   This is an interesting sentence. The money we know to have been Anne Colberg's, and it suggests that
     either she was equally as keen as Gilly to convert the Waldensians to a more Anglican viewpoint, or that
     Gilly had persuaded her that she was. It would be very enlightening all round to know more about her
     views. [NWG]

service in a religious point of view. A college, or superior school, where young men intended for holy orders may be grounded in the true principles of the Waldensian Church, and where all, who are likely to fill influential stations in the valleys, may receive the love of the truth – a revived system of ecclesiastical discipline, consistent with ancient practice, – and an uniform liturgy, may, with the blessing of God, have the effect of providing a remedy against errors, which might otherwise creep in. I am happy in being able to report, that the proposals which I made to the Pastors, and Notables, and to the Table, and which were accepted, before I took my departure from the valleys, are likely to be carried into effect, so as to meet my views in every respect. Had it been otherwise, I should have been under the necessity of withdrawing the offers which were made.[60]

England again – Waldensian affairs

In the autumn of 1829 Gilly returned to his house on College Green in Durham. In March 1830 he went to London for the meetings of the Vaudois Committee which were held on 20 and 22 March. The minutes of those meetings record that:

> Mr Gilly reported to the Committee that measures were being taken on the part of certain benevolent individuals, whose names the Secretary was not at liberty to divulge, with the knowledge of the Vaudois Table for the erection and endowing of a college at St Jean.[61]

From September 1829 Gilly was corresponding regularly with Pastor Rostaing, who had become Moderator of the Waldensian Church in 1828, about his schemes for a college and the revision of the liturgy. His letters, which are in good French, were written from his house in Durham.[62] Although Gilly had talked to many people during his summer visit, there were still formidable problems to be overcome, including the selection of a site for the college, the drawing-up of regulations for its conduct, financial matters, and the need to obtain permission from the Sardinian government.

Gilly was also pressing for reforms to the Waldensian liturgy. This was a sensitive subject, in view of the considerable theological differences between the Anglican and Waldensian churches. He was also concerned that the Calvinist outlook of the Waldensian Church was at times intolerant. On 1 March 1830 he wrote to the Moderator as follows:

> Risquerai-je respectueusement d'attirer l'attention de La Table à certains évènements tristes dans la Commune de St Jean qui portent l'esprit d'intolérance? Tels mouvements choquent tout le monde Protestant, et aliennent les affections et l'intérêt des Vaudois! Les Vaudois, deviennent-ils Persecuteurs?[63]

---

60   *Researches*, p. 526.
61   LVC Minutes.
62   ASTV, series V: Letters from Gilly to the Tavola: 23 September 1829 (vol. 34, c. 298); 28 November 1829 (vol. 34, c. 290); 14 December 1829 (vol. 34, c. 282); 1 March 1830 (vol. 34, c. 382); 30 June 1830 (vol. 34, c. 361); 6 September 1830 (vol. 34, c. 348); 15 November 1830 (vol. 34, c. 341); 12 January 1831 (vol. 35, c. 2); and 30 January 1831 (vol. 35, c. 7). His facility with written French makes all the odder that he refused to preach in the language.
63   ASTV, series V, vol. 34, c. 382. (trans. NG). Both Gilly and Beckwith complained that the Calvinist

[Dare I risk respectfully drawing the attention of the Tavola to certain sad events in the community of St-Jean which carry the spirit of intolerance? Such developments shock the whole Protestant world, and alienate the goodwill and interest of the Waldensians! The Waldensians: are they to become the Persecutors?]

There had indeed been sad events in the parish of St Jean (San Giovanni). For there had been divisions in that village between those who advocated an evangelizing form of Protestantism, and those who believed that evangelism would only cause problems for the Waldensians. These tensions had resulted in the pastor calling in the Sardinian police. A scuffle had ensued, and a man had been killed by the police. These events had been reported throughout Europe.

The second Waldensian book, *Researches*

During 1830 and January 1831, Gilly was occupied in writing his fifth book, on which much of the previous section relies. *Waldensian Researches During a Second Visit to the Vaudois of Piemont* was published by C. & F. Rivington in 1831. This time he had a good deal of material, for, as has been seen, he had spent two months in the Protestant valleys compared with the three and a half days of January 1823, carried out arduous expeditions to remote areas, and had discussed Waldensian affairs with many people. The book contains many intriguing details about the people he met, the church services in remote areas, the weather, the state of the mountain tracks, and the wretchedness of some of the inns where he and Jane spent their nights. Gastronomically Gilly's two books about his travels are only surpassed by Boswell and Hašek.[64] There is a good map of the Waldensian valleys and the adjacent parts of France, but the book has no index and no appendices. There are twelve competent, but quite heavily drawn, illustrations by Jane Gilly.

The first four chapters of the text consist of an inquiry into the antiquity and purity of the Waldensian Church, an account of the traditions of the church, and a testament of the history of the church gathered from adversaries of the church and various early writers. This is hard going for any reader who is not interested in theological and historical arguments. Gilly's personal narrative does not start until page 157, and the text becomes much more readable, and indeed in places quite witty, though Gilly's penchant for detail can be fascinating on one page and tedious on the next. As an example of the latter, precise particulars of the forms used for the monthly account keeping at the Waldensian hospital are inserted into the text in full.[65]

It would have been a much more accessible book had Gilly arranged it differ-

---

outlook of the Waldensian Church could be intolerant at times. See above and note 10 of this chapter for Beckwith's exasperated comments.

64   Boswell's works are well known. Malone tried to persuade Boswell to excise the gastronomic details, but fortunately for posterity they survived in the text. The present author (HN) has successfully recreated and eaten some of them. Hašek's *The Good Soldier Schweik* is, in places, a cookery book of the last days of the Austrian Empire.

65   *Researches*, pp. 311–13.

ently, using the opening chapters to describe his travels, together with particulars of the food he ate, the people he met, the wretched inns he stayed at, and the weather. Descriptions of historical documents, particulars of accounting systems, and details of his proposals for administering the college could then have been left to a set of appendices, to be read only by those interested in such matters. The book's failure to be republished is probably owing to its awkward structure, for, unlike Gilly's previous book about the Waldensians, it is not easily readable. This was recognized in a long and perceptive review in *The British Critic, Theological Review, and Ecclesiastical Record* of 1833, which found the format confusing and opined that 'we so very much prefer Mr. Gilly's narrative to his ratiocination'. The reviewer poked fun at Gilly's Apostolic Succession beliefs, and concluded that Gilly at times interpreted his evidence to justify his conclusions.[66] This criticism is just – and of course the same criticisms had been made of Gilly's first book about the Waldensians.[67]

66 *The British Critic, Quarterly Theological Review, and Ecclesiastical Records*, Vol. XIII, 1833, pp 183-200.
67 See Chapter 3.

Another of Jane Gilly's illustrations for *Researches* (via Google Books)

Chapter 8

'A university to be attached to our college': the foundation of the University of Durham, 1829–36

Durham has a long history of links with higher education, and with Oxford in particular. Of especial relevance is Durham Hall, later College, Oxford (in full, 'The College of the Holy Trinity, the Blessed Virgin Mary, and St Cuthbert'), which was founded in 1291 by Durham Priory for some of its monks to study theology at the university.[1] Closed in 1544, its site is now occupied by Trinity College, founded in 1555, although some of its buildings survive there as Durham Quad.[2] Less directly, two other Oxford colleges have Durham links: Balliol College was founded in 1263 by John Balliol under the guidance of the bishop of Durham, while University College is now generally accepted to have been founded by William of Durham in 1249.[3]

Henry VIII considered founding a university in Durham, and Oliver Cromwell actually did found a college there in 1650. This institution, called New College, was effectively operational from 1656 to 1659, and was the outcome of long-standing agitation for a northern university. A number of other towns had been proposed as its seat, but as the Chapter of Durham had been dissolved in 1649, New College was to occupy its premises in the Close. Cromwell signed letters patent giving it formal existence in 1657,[4] and Parliament granted it the right to award degrees in 1659.[5] It was dissolved in 1660, it would appear on grounds of pure anti-Cromwellian prejudice, and probably also under pressure from Oxford and Cambridge, which did not wish their monopoly to be broken.[6] The idea that a northern university would actually be beneficial was not, it seems, ever considered.[7]

---

1   Founded as Durham Hall for monks alone in 1291, it became a college in 1380, when it was formally endowed by Thomas Hatfield, Bishop of Durham 1345–81, and included secular students as well as monks. Hatfield is commemorated in the name of the second-oldest of the Durham colleges, and his arms form part of the university's arms.

2   The funds of Durham College reverted to the newly established Dean and Chapter; see below.

3   Claims that it was founded by King Alfred are not usually entertained seriously these days.

4   Richard Brickstock, *Durham Castle: fortress, palace, college*. University College Durham Trust, 2007, p. 55.

5   J. S .Brubacher and W. Rudy, *Higher Education in Transition: A history of American colleges and universities*, New Brunswick and London, 4th edn, 1997, p. 21.

6   They had already seen off several other competitors throughout the Middle Ages, notably Stamford and Northampton.

7   Contrast this with the situation in Scotland, where St Andrews (1411) and Glasgow (1450) were joined by King's College, Aberdeen, in 1495 – founded precisely for the convenience of students in northern Scotland. Wales, on the other hand, despite continuous lobbying, had no places of higher education at all until St David's College, Lampeter, was founded in 1822.

In 1833 Durham became a university city again, and it has since developed into one of the foremost centres of learning in England. Durham Castle, formerly the palace of the prince-bishops of Durham, is now part of the university, as are other historic buildings around Palace Green, exactly as Cromwell and his advisors had envisaged. The university is integrated into the small city.

Until Durham was founded, there were only two universities in England, Oxford and Cambridge. Oxford refused to teach both nonconformists and Roman Catholics, although it was generally agreed that the dissenters and papists missed little by this exclusion. Cambridge allowed nonconformists to attend lectures, but they could not matriculate, and thus could not proceed to degrees. This was because both universities were Anglican institutions, and membership of the university required membership of the Church of England.[8] The 'godless institution in Gower Street'[9] known as London University (later renamed University College London) opened in 1828, and admitted anyone to its classes and lectures, regardless of creed – or lack of one. However, it could not award degrees,[10] and its 'aggressively secular' stance led to the founding of the equally 'aggressively Anglican' King's College London in 1829. These two became the first colleges of the federal University of London in 1836, which has continued the tradition of imposing no religious tests on its students or graduates to this day.[11]

In Wales, Thomas Burgess founded St David's College at Lampeter in 1822.[12] It forms an instructive parallel to Durham, its near contemporary, in that both were Anglican foundations, but whereas Durham was well-funded from the start, being based on the excess wealth of the Chapter, Lampeter was not, being founded on subscriptions and donations. The object of Lampeter was to provide a university-level education principally for those intending to become clergy in the diocese of St David's, who could not afford to go to Oxford or Cambridge, although it always had a few students who did not plan to be ordained. Alongside the usual classics, mathematics and theology, it taught scientific subjects, English and Welsh. Its exact status – was it a university or not? – remained unclear really until it became part of the federal University of Wales in 1971. It gained only limited degree-awarding powers in its own right, and those comparatively late (BD in 1852; BA in 1865).

Burgess himself had strong Durham links,[13] and his successor as bishop from 1825

---

8   The difference between the two was that Oxford required the relevant oaths to be taken on matriculation, whereas Cambridge did not require them until graduation.

9   So called by Thomas Arnold.

10   Again, owing to pressure from Oxford and Cambridge to prevent its doing so.

11   For a good general history of the University of London and its genesis, see Negley Harte, *The University of London, 1836–1986: An illustrated history*, London, 1986.

12   On the history of St David's College, see D. T. W. Price, *A History of St David's University College, Lampeter*, vol. 1, to 1898, Cardiff, 1977; vol. 2, 1898–1971, Cardiff, 1990.

13   Thomas Burgess (1756–1837), chaplain to Shute Barrington at Salisbury 1785, then at Durham, 1791; Prebendary of the ninth stall of Durham (later to be Gilly's stall) 1791–92; of the sixth stall 1792–1820; of the second stall 1820–25; Bishop of St David's 1803–25; Bishop of Salisbury 1825–37. See further D. T. W. Price, 'Burgess, Thomas (1756–1837)', *Oxford Dictionary of National Biography*, Oxford University Press, 2004; online edn Oct. 2009 (www.oxforddnb.com/view/article/3985, accessed 10 May 2011).

to 1840, and thus as visitor of the college, was John Banks Jenkinson, also Dean of Durham from 1827 to 1840. Jenkinson played a major part in getting St David's College off the ground;[14] he corresponded with other bishops and academics about the statutes, and consulted with van Mildert about the length of the course (van Mildert thought four years, Jenkinson five). Certainly his experience with the nascent college at Lampeter was put to good use when the university was founded at Durham. Indeed, his affections seem to have been transferred there once he was made dean in 1827, the year Lampeter opened. But while Lampeter certainly kept an eye on progress at Durham, the favour was not necessarily returned.

Mention might be made also of a third institution, St Bees College in Cumberland.[15] This was founded in 1816 by George Henry Law, the bishop of Chester. Never endowed – the principals were also the proprietors, as well as rectors of the parish – and without proper buildings or degree-awarding powers, nonetheless it lasted until 1895, and educated many hundreds of clergy. (It provided a general 'arts' education as well as specific theological and pastoral training, and in 1850 it had more students than either Durham or Lampeter.) It was mentioned in national legislation in 1840, along with Oxford, Cambridge, Lampeter and Durham. The Durham founders must therefore have been aware of its existence, a mere 140 kilometres away.

Between 1760 and 1830 the industrial revolution had transformed northern England. Cotton and woollen mills were built in Yorkshire, Lancashire and Derbyshire, where the new industrial towns expanded rapidly. The Durham coalfield was developed, and the seaports at the mouths of the rivers Tyne, Wear and Tees expanded. The world's first steam railway was built in 1825 between Stockton and Darlington in the south of County Durham. Parliament had become concerned that the rapidly expanding urban areas lacked religion, and, as explained in Chapter 5, the large new Commissioners' churches had been built as a result. Yet there was still no university in the north of England. Schemes for establishing universities at Liverpool, York, and Newcastle had been considered at various times, but many northern industrialists were sceptical of such proposals, as the graduates of the two ancient English universities appeared to have little practical knowledge: the curriculum consisted almost entirely of the classics, with a greater (Cambridge) or lesser (Oxford) amount of mathematics, and some divinity. Again, UCL broke this mould, as it had chairs in chemical engineering, chemistry, psychology, electrical engineering and zoology, as well as in Egyptology, English, French, geography, German, Italian and phonetics – all subjects regarded as 'not proper subjects' by Oxford and Cambridge.[16] It also boasted the first real chemistry department in England.

---

14   See Price, *History of St David's University College*, vol, 1, pp. 29 ff. Although Burgess laid the foundation stone in 1822, the college did not open until 1827, after his translation to Salisbury: unlike Durham it did not have ready-made buildings to move into, but was built from scratch.

15   On the history of St Bees, see T. Park, *St Bees College: Pioneering higher education in 19th century Cumbria*, St Bees, rev. edn 2008. See also www.stbees.org.uk/publications/college/index.htm

16   Cambridge was one of the last English universities to make provision for teaching English as an academic subject, for example: the Tripos was not established until 1917, and even then it was founded in a study of the classics. See R. Williams, 'Cambridge English and beyond', *London Review of Books*, vol. 5, no.

In the late 1820s and early 1830s there was a mood of radicalism throughout the country. The House of Commons still did not represent the country as a whole. Many MPs had been elected by so-called 'rotten boroughs', which contained a handful of electors who could be bribed, while the rapidly expanding northern cities were hardly represented in Parliament. In the 1831 election, of 406 members, 152 were chosen by fewer than 100 voters. The county of Yorkshire, with a population of over 1 million, returned two members, as did the rotten borough of Old Sarum, with a population of three, while Manchester (population 60,000) had no representation at all. Two Bills for the reform of the House of Commons were debated in 1831. Most of the bishops, all of whom sat in the House of Lords, opposed this reform. William van Mildert, Prince-Bishop of Durham, voted against the reform, and his effigy was burned within sight of his palace gates. He fared better than his episcopal brother of Bristol, where a mob burnt down his palace.

The miners, whose hard and dangerous work produced the wealth of Durham, were discontented. In the early 1830s there were strikes and sporadic violence in towns and country areas throughout England.[17] In June 1832 the Reform Act finally passed through Parliament, and the cautious reform of the composition of the House of Commons commenced.

Alongside parliamentary reform there was a call for reform of the established church. In 1821 the *Durham Chronicle* published an editorial alleging that the established church 'stinks in the nostrils'. Shute Barrington successfully sued for libel on the clergy.[18] The editor of the *Durham Chronicle* was ably defended by Henry Brougham, who became Lord Chancellor in the reforming Whig government which came to power in November 1830.[19] As such, he had considerable powers of church patronage.[20] Until 1828, the member of Parliament for County Durham was 'Radical Jack' Lambton, who believed that reform of both Parliament and the established church was long overdue.[21] He became Lord Privy Seal in the 1830 Whig government, in which his father-in-law, Earl Grey, whose country seat was at Howick in Northumberland, was Prime Minister. The extremely rich diocese of Durham was under pressure from powerful politicians who had strong local connections.

Earl Grey believed that a northern university should be created, while Brougham had been closely involved in the creation of London University in 1828, and had been

---

12, 7 July 1983, p. 3. With regard to the introduction of new subjects at Cambridge, Williams says 'A conventional majority could usually be mobilised for the status quo, by one after another established and prejudiced authority.'

17 In Northern England the disturbances were largely confined to towns. In total nine men or boys were hanged, about 400 were imprisoned and about 450 were sentenced to transportation, many for life.

18 J. A. Williams, *Trial of John Ambrose Williams for a Libel on the Clergy,* Durham, 1822, p. 6.

19 A government of which it was said that none of the senior members were serious or orthodox Anglicans.

20 Including, among others, the living of North Fambridge.

21 John George Lambton (1792–1840). MP for County Durham 1812–28; Baron Durham 1828; privy councillor and Lord Privy Seal, 1830; resigned 1833, and became Viscount Lambton and Earl of Durham. Married twice, the second time in 1816 to Earl Grey's daughter, Lady Louisa Grey.

active in the movement for popular education in the 1820s. The wealthy clergy of Durham Cathedral realized that, if they did not use their wealth for better purposes, then it was likely that Parliament would intervene and bring about radical reforms, which would include confiscating the better part of their revenues. There was even talk of disestablishing the church. Bishop van Mildert was by nature a defender of 'the church by law established', but he perceived the need for change.

The small city of Durham did not appear to be particularly well suited for the creation of a university.[22] It had, of course, the magnificent cathedral and castle, but the streets of the city were narrow and steep, and many houses were crowded close together. The city was considered to be unhealthy, and contained much poverty. On the other hand, the Bishop and the Chapter had large incomes, and they owned imposing buildings around Palace Green and College Green. Furthermore, the church did not really need so many buildings in Durham city, for the Bishop had a second palace at Bishop Auckland, 13 kilometres away, and each Canon had a fine prebendal house on College Green.

By 1829, Canon Gilly's household at 9 College Green included the wealthy Anne Colberg, a butler and several other servants. Gilly had come up in the world, and there was a lady in his household with a good deal of cash to spare. He was looking for useful ways to spend that money, and what better project could there be than the funding of a college?[23] Gilly may have discussed the concept in general terms with other members of the Durham clergy. He may well also have been in touch with Robert Southey, the poet laureate, who in April 1829 published the following ambiguous sentence in the middle of a long review article about Surtees' *History of Durham*:

> The time, it may be hoped, is not far distant, when a northern university will be founded; and in lasting honour will the memory of that excellent lady be held, who has made known her intention of contributing to it with a munificence unequalled in later times, and unsurpassed in former ones.[24]

Southey certainly knew of Gilly. As young men they had both published attacks upon the practice of flogging in public schools,[25] and in January 1826 Southey had published

---

22   Lampeter and St Bees were both smaller, as well as far more remote, towns, although the railways did alleviate this later in the century. (NWG)

23   He was already exploring the possibility of establishing a theological college for the Waldensians with this money – see *Researches*, pp. 379 and 526, and this book, pp. 93–6.

24   *Quarterly Review*, vol. 39, 1829, p. 389. The sentence is all the odder as it is inserted into a paragraph about Cromwell's college. Although this essay was published anonymously, it was written by Southey. He acknowledged authorship in a letter dated 9 May 1829 to Caroline Bowles. See E. Bowden (ed.), *The Correspondence of Robert Southey with Caroline Bowles*, Dublin, 1881. Southey had already written an essay in the January edition of the *Review*, in which he stated that 'a munificent lady in Yorkshire has recently offered to subscribe 50,000£ towards the endowment of an university *in that county*, and a Noble Earl has professed his willingness to give a similar benefaction'. Southey went on to express 'some doubts' as to whether 'the site of the new university for the north would be best selected in Yorkshire': *Quarterly Review*, vol. 39, 1829, p. 127. Possibly the 'excellent lady' was not Anne Colberg. [NG]

25   *Academic Errors, or, Recollections of Youth* by 'A member of the University of Cambridge'. (i.e. W. S. Gilly).

a long and eulogistic review of Gilly's *Narrative of an Excursion to the Mountains of Piemont* in the *Quarterly Review*.

But Anne Colberg's money was not to be used to fund Durham University, and Gilly's role in the foundation of the University of Durham was, in the end, marginal. The moving spirits in the foundation of the university were Bishop van Mildert and Charles Thorp, Prebendary of the second stall and Archdeacon of Durham, and they worked closely together on this grand project. That neither of them trusted Gilly is clear from their correspondence.[26] They correctly believed that if Gilly had his way, a theological college would be created in Durham, rather than a true university. Gilly might well have access to the money to fund such a college, and indeed he eventually did so, but it was not in Durham, or indeed in England. Gilly's desire to found such a college may well have had its roots in the fact that at Ushaw, just four miles up the road, a Roman Catholic seminary had opened in 1808.[27]

Charles Thorp was, like Gilly, an energetic Anglican clergyman. He had been born in 1783 and had succeeded his father as Rector of Ryton, a large village 15 miles north-west of Durham, where he had helped to establish the first English savings bank. Van Mildert had made him a Canon of Durham Cathedral in 1829, and Archdeacon of Durham in 1831; he was also chaplain to Earl Grey.[28] Much of Thorp's correspondence survives.[29] He realized that, with careful planning, it would be possible to fund a university from within the considerable resources of the Bishop and of the Chapter. He pointed out that, when the Chapter had been created at the Reformation in the sixteenth century, one of its objectives had been education. Thorp's concept was brilliant. Cash would be provided by using the incomes from three or four of the rich cathedral stalls. The buildings already existed: the Bishop and the Chapter would vacate Durham Castle and some other buildings around Palace Green. Thorp had in mind the situation at Oxford, where the Cathedral is the chapel of Christ Church, the Dean of Oxford is the head of house, and the stalls were attached to chairs in the university.

Some members of Chapter expressed doubts: specifically, they felt that the surplus funds should go to augment poor livings. Thorp pointed out that part of that surplus was in fact the funds which had, until the Dissolution, belonged to Durham College, Oxford, and which had always been intended to be used for higher education in Durham.[30]

Published by A. and J. Valpy in 1817 (see Chapter 1). R Southey, *The Flagellant*, privately printed, London, 1792.

26   Balliol College, Oxford, Jenkyns Papers. DUL, Thorp correspondence.

27   There were no Anglican seminaries (theological colleges) as such until several years later: the first of them, Chichester, opened in 1849. Lampeter and St Bees were concerned with providing a general education, but we can wonder whether Gilly took inspiration from them.

28   See C. D. Watkinson, 'Thorp, Charles', *Oxford Dictionary of National Biography* Oxford University Press, 2004; online edn, Oct 2009 (www.oxforddnb.com/view/article/27373, accessed 10 May 2011).

29   Balliol College, Oxford, Jenkyns Papers. DUL, Thorp correspondence.

30   C. J. Stranks, *This Sumptuous Church: The story of Durham Cathedral*, London, SPCK, 1973, p. 87.

On 11 July 1831 Thorp wrote to the Bishop as follows:

> I would fain bring before you the project of a university to be attached to our College.[31] A slight extension of the establishments & a few Professorships founded by the body in the Cathedral would effect the object. It would gain to the Dean & Chapter strength & character and usefulness, – preserve the revenues to the Church and to the north, – & prevent the establishment of a very doubtful academic institution which is now taking root in N'castle.[32] I trust you will not think me a projector beyond what the times require.[33]

The Bishop was enthusiastic. The proposal was submitted to the Chapter on 28 September 1831. Gilly was Sub-Dean that year; the Dean, John Banks Jenkinson, was 300 miles away in West Wales, where he was carrying out his duties as Bishop of St David's. The Chapter minute reads:

> Present in chapter, the Sub-dean (Mr. Gilly), Mr Durell, the Bishop of Chester, Mr. Ogle, Mr. Gisborne, Mr. Townsend, and Mr Thorp.
>
> Resolved unanimously, A plan of an academic institution, to be called Durham College, in connexion with the dean and chapter, and to be provided for by their funds, proposing an annual charge upon future incumbencies of one fifth of the value of the deanery and stalls, and a present annual vote of supply not exceeding 2,000£, (made up of an additional 1,700£, and of 300£, already voted for the purposes of education,) until the funds destined for its support become available; and proposing also, on the part of the Bishop of Durham, a limitation of some of his patronage to the purposes of the institution, having been received from the dean;
>
> That the sub-dean be desired to state to the dean the readiness of the chapter to accept the plan with these changes, viz., for 'dean and a master or principal,' reading 'a master or principal,' and for 'dean with the approbation of chapter,' reading 'dean and chapter,' and for 'dean and master (principal),' reading 'dean and chapter and master, (principal),' and to take it into their earliest and most favourable consideration, and to take measures which may be necessary, in the first instance, with a view to the early accomplishment of the object; and that the sub-dean be desired to express to the Bishop of Durham the thanks of the chapter for communication of his liberal intentions through the dean.[34]

The minute declares the intention of establishing an academic institution or 'college': there is no mention of a university, nor indeed of the aims of the new institution. It

---

31 That is, the Chapter. In this sense, 'college' means a body of people living some kind of communal life, and forming a corporation: thus we can speak of the 'college of canons of Durham'. Long before the 1820s any communality of life in cathedral chapters had dwindled to merely worshipping together.

32 This institution was adumbrated in two papers read in April and June 1831 by the eminent surgeon T. M. Greenhow to the Literary and Philosophical Society of Newcastle upon Tyne, on 'The expediency of establishing in Newcastle an academical institution of the nature of a college or university for the promotion of literature and science'. See further W. H. G. Armytage, *Civic Universities: Some aspects of a British tradition*, London, 1955; repr. 1977, p. 170.

33 Jenkyns Papers, Balliol College, Oxford, Box IVA, Envelope 6, Letter, Thorp to van Mildert, 11 June 1831. Thorp's handwriting is very difficult to read.

34 Durham, Dean and Chapter Minutes, 28 September 1831. The Chapter were footing the bill for the new institution, and they were clearly determined to have their say in its governance.

had not yet been determined whether it was to be a university or an Anglican theological college. Therein lay the seeds of much dissension in the Chapter during the ensuing months and years.

The same day Gilly wrote a letter to Lord Brougham, the Lord Chancellor:

Confidential
College – Durham
Sep. 28th 1831
My dear Lord,

I have the greatest satisfaction possible in communicating a piece of intelligence to your Lordship, which will be after your own Heart. The Chapter of Durham have this day minuted a Resolution, which will lead to the Establishment of a Northern College or University out of their own Resources. It will be upon a scale worthy of our Reputation as an endowed Body but it is not sufficiently developed at present to permit me to say more.

   Your Lordship will oblige me by receiving this as a Confidential Communication at present. Perhaps I ought not to have divulged it yet – but with all my own enthusiasm in behalf of Education Institutions, I could not keep it from such a Friend to the Principle as yourself. I shall be grateful for any suggestions which your Experience in such matters may enable you to offer.

I have the honor to be, My Lord
Your Lordships most grateful Servt.
W. S. Gilly
   [To:] The Lord High Chancellor[35]

In January 1832 Gilly submitted a scheme to the Bishop and the Chapter whereby the new institution would be oriented to promote the cause of Protestantism by a professorship which he offered to fund. He assured the Chapter that he had the financial backing of 'wealthy persons'. Gilly left the sex of his financial backers indeterminate, but almost certainly he proposed to use Anne Colberg's money. Some members of the Chapter were enthusiastic for Gilly's scheme: they did not want to turn down hard cash. But van Mildert and Thorp were implacably opposed to his proposals. They wanted the new university to be a centre of learning, not a sectarian college. From January 1832 there were tensions in the Chapter. On 24 January 1832 the Bishop wrote to Thorp:

I know not *what sort of friends* Mr Gilly has, who are disposed to be such magnificent benefactors. *Sed timeo Danaos*. The party he is connected with, (including other members of the Chapter with himself) would, I doubt not, be very ready to contribute largely, for the sake of that *influence* among us, which may subserve their purposes. In the project, as stated to me, I instantly saw the danger of our being, in the outset, entangled with a party whose zeal perpetually outruns their discretion, and a probability of turning our Institution

---

35   UCL, Brougham Papers, letter, 28 September 1831, Gilly to Brougham. Note that Gilly introduced the term 'university'. As with the Irish Papers, can we again see Gilly currying favour behind people's backs?

(which aught to be most strongly characterised by sobriety and wisdom) into an arena for those unseemly displays of energy which are daily breaking forth in disputatious meetings, and answering as I conceive, no good practical purpose.[36] As to the Institution of an office like the C[hris]tian Advocate at Cambridge,[37] I should augur little or no good from it. Nor can I as yet conjecture any other scheme for the public benefit, which may not better be attained by our own present plan. I will not, however, *prejudge* the matter – still less am I inclined to give offence. But again I say, *Beware.* … Pray *burn* this letter. Yours affectionately, W. Dunelm [38]

So Gilly's scheme for the new college to be a purely theological institution was rejected. Gilly was, however, a forceful member of the Chapter. Notwithstanding the tensions with the Bishop and Thorp, he backed the proposals for a university at Durham, and accepted the concept of funding from within the considerable resources of the Bishop and Chapter. On 22 July 1833 he again wrote to Lord Brougham:

Durham, July 22 1833

My Lord Chancellor,
    Your Lordship will be happy to learn that the good ship, The Durham University, was launched on Saturday last.
    The Ships Company will consist of
        Warden
        Divinity
        Greek   } Professors
        & Mathematical
Lecturers in: Medicine
                 Law
                 Hebrew & Oriental Languages & Literature
                 History
                 Moral Philosophy
                 Natural Philosophy
                 Chemistry
                 Modern Languages & Literature
Two Tutors
Twenty Foundation Students
Bursar

Almost all the appointments are filled up, and we open in October next.
    The Lecturer in Chemistry, a man of 100 Testimonials, is a Presbyterian; pretty well this for Electors, who according to the Times Newspaper are 'Brutes & Bigots'.

---

36   Here van Mildert is referring to the Evangelicals, who were given to emotive displays of religious feeling.
37   This was a term used for the Hulsean Lecturer or Preacher at Cambridge, who is charged with the annual task of delivering an address to answer objections against Christianity. The post was inaugurated in 1803. A Durham version of this is clearly the 'professor' that Gilly had in mind.
38   DUL, Thorp correspondence. The Latin quotation in the second sentence is from Virgil: *Timeo Danaos et dona ferentes*, 'I fear the Greeks, even when they offer presents', in other words that a foe is most dangerous when he feigns friendship.

I trust your Lordship will have no difficulty in the way of your noble proposal to endow the University with the Chancellor's Livings in these parts.

I have the honor to be

My Lord

Yr Lordships most faithful Sevt.

W. S. Gilly

[To:] The Lord Chancellor[39]

Gilly's letters to Lord Brougham give the impression that he had a major part in organizing the new institution. But of course this was not the case: Thorp remained the leading spirit, ably backed by van Mildert. The reference to the Presbyterian lecturer in chemistry is to the chemist and educationalist James Finlay Weir Johnston. In this appointment the Chapter, reluctantly it seems, agreed that knowledge of chemistry was more important than theological soundness.[40]

The early years of Durham University were very difficult. Canon Thorp was appointed warden of the university and did his best to develop the new institution. The Bishop vacated Durham Castle so the new university had, like the two ancient universities, large, ancient and draughty buildings, with a magnificent medieval hall. The bishop, however, reserved for himself a suite of rooms in the castle which included a bedroom, sitting room, servant's room, water closet and still room. Other buildings around Palace Green were also handed over to the new university. There exists a fine coloured plan showing how the property division was made.[41] Put briefly, the Archdeacon's Inn on Palace Green housed the undergraduates, and the song school, writing school and almshouses were turned into lecture rooms.[42] The castle was turned over to the university in 1837 to become University College; Thorp was appointed master.[43]

But the new institution did not attract as many students as had been hoped, and some of the staff were unhappy at being subject to control by the Bishop and Chapter of Durham. In particular Hugh James Rose,[44] the Professor of Divinity and a

---

39   UCL, Brougham Papers, letter, Gilly to Brougham.

40   Born in Paisley, 1796; after graduating at Glasgow he opened a school in Durham, so was well known locally. He was one of the founders of the British Association for the Advancement of Science, and was elected FRS in 1837. He died in 1855 at Durham. See further David Knight, 'Johnston, James Finlay Weir (1796–1855)', *Oxford Dictionary of National Biography*, Oxford University Press, 2004. (www.oxforddnb. com/view/article/14942, accessed 9 May 2011).

41   Ecclesiastical Commissioners for England, papers relating to the University of Durham. 1839, no. 23A. (Henceforth 'ECE Durham'.)

42   The almsfolk were rehoused, it is a relief to note!

43   Stranks, *This Sumptuous Church*, p. 88.

44   One of a group of pre-Tractarian High Churchmen, Hugh James Rose (1795–1838) was professor of divinity at Durham for a year only, resigning on health grounds. He was Christian Advocate (Hulsean Lecturer) at Cambridge 1829–33, and his influence in that university has been held to be almost as great as that of Newman at Oxford. In 1836 he was appointed principal of the Anglican King's College, London. See further Peter B. Nockles, 'Rose, Hugh James, (1795–1838)', *Oxford Dictionary of National Biography*, Oxford University Press, 2004; online edn, May 2006 (www.oxforddnb.com/view/article/24094, accessed 13 May 2011).

distinguished theologian, was restless, and in June 1834 he wrote to Henry Jenkyns, the Professor of Greek:

I say nothing of the C[hapter] of D[urham] in particular – for I believe many of the[m] to be most honourable men. But I am equally sure that *one* who leads them says one thing today & another tomorrow. And when I remember the way in w[hi]ch he spoke of Peile's sacrifices of income at Liverpool & his *good* fortune in getting what he

The Great Hall, University of Durham. By A. D. White Architectural Photographs, Cornell University Library (via Wikimedia Commons).

has at Durham, I will never put myself into his power without having bread to eat totally independent of *him*.[45]

The reference to 'one who leads them' is almost certainly a reference to Gilly. Rose was concerned that in June 1834, nearly a year after the university had opened, the scheme for financing university professorships by the allocation of three cathedral stalls to specific professorships had not been approved by Parliament. So, as Professor of Divinity, he was dependent on the goodwill of the Bishop and the Chapter for his salary. He was apprehensive that the Bishop, who was 68 years old and in poor health, might die, and he distrusted Gilly's influence over the Chapter. In October 1834 Rose resigned and went back to London.

In February 1835 the university finances were in a parlous state and dependent upon a private contribution of £2,000 per annum by the Bishop. At this stage the Archbishop of Canterbury arranged for the Ecclesiastical Commission to inquire into the University of Durham.

By April 1836 the university had been operating for two-and-a-half years. But only ninety-six students had enrolled, and it had received no contributions from industrialists, who continued to believe that universities taught academic subjects of no serious relevance to the practicalities of life in the north of England. The evidence to the

---

45   Balliol College, Oxford, Jenkyns Papers, Box IVB, bundle [c], letter, Rose to Jenkyns, franked 2 June 1834. Thomas Williamson Peile (1806–1882) was senior tutor at the university from 1834 until 1841, when he became headmaster of Repton School. He had previously been headmaster of the Liverpool Collegiate School, chaplain to Lord Westmorland, and Perpetual Curate of St Catherine's, Liverpool. Even though the Dean and Chapter appointed him Perpetual Curate of Croxdale in plurality, he probably had a sharp drop in income. See further the *ODNB*.

Ecclesiastical Commissioners revealed the tensions which existed in the Chapter.[46]

On 14 February 1836 van Mildert died. He had been unwell for some time, and had become despondent at the wrangling in the Chapter about the university, yet without his consistent support, Durham University would not have been launched.[47] On 15 March 1836, Thorp submitted a memorial to the Commissioners, with the official seal of the Chapter affixed, pointing out that the university was under-funded and that Parliament had still not authorized the transfer of the incomes of three prebendal stalls from the Chapter to the university.[48] Henry Phillpotts, who was also Bishop of Exeter, submitted evidence on 22 April 1836 that Thorp's memorial was improperly submitted, as it had not been approved by a quorum of the Chapter.[49] Gilly supported Phillpotts.[50] On 30 May 1836 Thorp wrote to Jenkinson, expressing his 'astonishment and disgust' at Phillpotts' evidence to the Commissioners.[51] Gilly described the action of affixing the seal as 'an unfortunate piece of irregularity'.[52]

Gilly and Thorp also clashed in evidence to the Commissioners as to precisely what had happened in the deliberations of the Chapter in the early 1830s. Gilly gave evidence on 22 April 1836, stating that he thought it would have been best if the funds available had been applied to a theological institution instead of a university. He also commended the location of the university in Durham Castle:

> Very conveniently and beautifully situated; nothing can be so good for the purpose; it stands so well; it is so commanding and so convenient; it contains a noble range of apartments, and such a hall as there is not in either University of Oxford or Cambridge.[53]

Thorp passionately defended the university before the Ecclesiastical Commissioners. He contradicted both Phillpotts' and Gilly's evidence, and accused Phillpotts of being 'at variance … with the documents upon the most important points'.[54] Concerning Gilly's evidence to the Commissioners, Thorp stated:

> I am unwilling to trouble your Grace and the Commissioners unnecessarily, and shall only observe, as to some points of Dr Gilly's evidence, that they are by no means sustained by the books of the Chapter.[55]

Thorp then produced the various minutes of the Chapter to the Commissioners to

46   ECE Durham, 1839.
47   He is commemorated by Van Mildert College, founded in 1965.
48   ECE Durham, no. 1.
49   ECE Durham, no. 13. Phillpotts was notoriously litigious.
50   ECE Durham, no. 14.
51   DUL, Thorp Correspondence.
52   ECE Durham, no. 14.
53   ECE Durham, no. 14. 'Appearance is all at Vanity Fair', clearly.
54   ECE Durham, no. 18.
55   ECE Durham, no. 18.

prove his point. He was passionately opposed to turning the new university into a theological school. He cited the support of the late bishop for a full university and concluded:

> As to the proposal of a theological school, I trust your Grace and the Church Commissioners will reject it. … it contradicts the terms of the engagement upon the faith of which the University of Durham was established; and it proceeds upon the vicious principle, than which none is more noxious to the church and to society, that the clergy in their early habits, studies and pursuits, are to be separated from the mass of the community with whom they are to live …. And now, my Lord, the fate and fortunes of the University of Durham seem to rest with you and with the Board of Church Commissioners. It is probably in your power to establish it on that scale of befitting efficiency and splendour which the late Bishop of Durham, with the concurrence of his dean and chapter, intended it to have, or to reduce it to an inferior establishment for clerical purposes.[56]

Thorp's emotional appeal for a full university status was successful. The university was not reduced to the status of a theological college, and the transfer of funds from cathedral stalls to the university received the consent of Parliament. In the late 1830s student numbers improved when James Johnston, the lecturer in chemistry, developed pioneering scientific courses, notably in engineering.[57]

Gilly was actively involved in the discussions and arguments which accompanied the setting-up of the university, but in the end his role was a minor one. Van Mildert distrusted his motives, as did Hugh Rose. Thorp pointed out that Gilly's support, at meetings of the Chapter, for the concept of a university was contradicted by his subsequent statements to the Ecclesiastical Commissioners that he would have preferred the creation of a theological college as an initial step. There is no evidence that any of Gilly's fellow canons knew anything of his two letters to Lord Brougham. It is difficult to reconcile the enthusiastic tone of these letters with his later evidence to the Ecclesiastical Commissioners, beyond the fact that Gilly had been adroitly sidelined by Thorp, and he did not care to be anywhere other than centre-stage. There is no question but that Thorp was the dominant figure in the university's early years. Hence, maybe, Gilly evolved his own scheme which, if accepted, would have put him back in the centre of things.

Durham Castle
Photo Meg
Norman

---

56   ECE Durham, no 18. Many of these arguments were to be used again later in the century against the new theological colleges, many of which were founded in small cathedral cities such as Wells and Chichester, indeed 'separated from the mass of the community with whom they are to live', ostensibly so that their ordinands would remain 'unspotted by the world'.

57   They were ultimately unsuccessful, as industrialists 'refused to recognize paper qualifications from a university'. *ODNB*, s.v. Johnston.

Chapter 9

Vicar of Norham, Canon of Durham, and 'philoprogenitive theory-monger': Norham and Durham, 1831–40

Notwithstanding his other activities, Gilly remained active in the affairs of both Durham Cathedral and city. On 20 November 1830, he was elected Sub-Dean for 1831.[1] On 6 February 1831 Jane Gilly gave birth to her first child, a boy, who was named Frederick Dawson Gilly.[2] The baby already had two half-sisters and one half-brother – Mary Anna (aged 14), Rosalie Emily (9) and William Octavius Shakespear (8). So 9 College Green, now contained Canon and Mrs Gilly, Anne Colberg, one teenager, two children, a new baby, a butler, a lady's maid for Miss Colberg, a cook and other maids. Anne Colberg had been suffering from a 'severe and long illness' since 1829.[3] Gilly's next move, to the countryside, may have been prompted by a desire to escape overcrowding, and to avoid disturbing the invalid.

On 20 July 1831 the Dean and Chapter passed two resolutions:

1. That the Reverend W. S. Gilly be presented to the vicarage of Norham, vacant by the cession of the Rev. W. N. Darnell, and his presentation was sealed accordingly.
2. That in future no one be presented to a Living in the gift of the Dean and Chapter but on the understanding of Residence, and that any person holding a Chapter Living presented to another in the gift of the Chapter do resign the first Living forthwith.[4]

The wording of the second resolution is worth noting: it had the effect of making Gilly resign as Perpetual Curate of St Margaret Crossgate, and of making him go to live at Norham. He also resigned, at long last, as Rector of North Fambridge.[5] The parishioners of St Margaret's Church were sorry to see him leave, and 117 of them

---

1   The Sub-dean, Treasurer, and Receiver were elected annually.

2   E. A. White and G. J. Armytage (eds), *The Baptismal, Marriage and Burial Registers of the Cathedral Church of Christ and Blessed Mary at Durham 1609–1896,* Harleian Society, vol. RS 23, 1897, p. 29.

3   Will and codicil of Anne Colberg, 12 January 1829 and 3 November 1829. Family Records Centre, London, Prob. 11. 1808, Quire 745. This will was witnessed by James White, butler to Gilly. The second codicil of 3 November 1829 states that she was suffering from a 'severe and long' illness.

4   Durham, Dean and Chapter Minutes: 20 July 1831.

5   He was succeeded at St Margaret by Patrick George, who then resigned Great Aycliffe (*Clerical Guide,* 1839). His successor at Fambridge, Thomas Benson, seems to have been resident, as he signed the various registers from 1832 (ERO, PR 206/1/6, Baptisms 1813–1981.)

subscribed to a silver presentation plate and signed their names to a finely decorated certificate which reads:

> To the Revd. William Stephen Gilly, M.A.
> Revd. Sir,
> We whose names are here subscribed, most respectfully request your acceptance of the piece of Plate presented with these lines, as a small token of gratitude and respect for the zeal and unwearied attention which you have on all occasions displayed for our temporal, and more especially for our spiritual welfare, as is particularly evinced by your establishing a gratuitous Evening Lecture during your incumbency.
> St Margaret's Vestry, Durham, Sept. XXVII, MDCCCXXXI.[6]

The *Durham Advertiser* carried a full account of the various addresses at the leave-taking ceremonies.[7] He had been a successful minister in a difficult parish. He remained as Canon Gilly, Prebendary of the ninth stall of Durham Cathedral, and was the English friend of the Waldensians of Piedmont. He was about to start new activities on the Scots border. In Durham he was heading for controversy.

Norham

St Cuthbert's Church, Norham,[8] is 1,400 kilometres from the Waldensian valleys, 130 kilometres from Durham City, and 200 metres from the Kingdom of Scotland. Gilly had exchanged the busy city parish of St Margaret's, Durham, for one of the most remote parishes in England. He was Vicar of Norham for the remaining twenty-four years of his life. He is still remembered as an outstanding vicar who took an active, and at times controversial, interest in current social issues, and in the lives and problems of his parishioners.[9] This is in sharp contrast to the total lack of interest he displayed in the equally remote parish of North Fambridge, of which he remained nominally the Rector until he moved to Norham in 1831.

As a Prebendary of Durham, Gilly could have hoped for better things than such a parish, although its income was generous, at £597 a year. Four of the twelve canons (Jenkinson, Grey, Sumner and Phillpotts) were diocesan bishops, and several of the other canons held senior church benefices (see Appendix 1, Table A2). Possibly he moved because there were tensions within the Chapter, although in September 1831

---

6   The original is held by Mr Roland Bell, Gilly's descendant, who has kindly allowed the author (HN) to copy it.

7   *Durham Advertiser*, 25 November 1831.

8   Pronounced 'norrum', not 'nore-um', it is of enormous historical significance. It was where Aidan crossed the Tweed on his way from Iona to Lindisfarne. When the monks left Lindisfarne, Norham was the first place where they stopped with the body of St Cuthbert, but a church already stood there, which had been built to house the remains of King Ceolwulf. They stayed there for forty years, before Viking raids propelled them on their way, eventually ending at Durham. The castle, now ruined, is of the same age as the church, and was the chief border stronghold of the 'Prince-Bishops' of Durham; they were built by Ranulph Flambard, Bishop 1099–1128.

9   In Berwick-upon-Tweed Museum there is a life-size effigy of him preaching an indignant sermon, complete with a 'voice-over' in a strong local accent – which is odd for a man brought up in the Suffolk countryside.

A life-size effigy of Dr Gilly preaching (from Berwick-upon-Tweed Museum – see note 9)

these were not yet serious. It was unlikely that Bishop van Mildert would recommend Gilly for promotion to a bishopric: the bishop's correspondence makes it clear that he was no friend of Gilly's.[10] A charitable interpretations might be that 9 College Green was too crowded, and Gilly wanted to escape from the watchful eye of the invalid Anne Colberg, who was still living in his household, or maybe he wished to emulate the poet Southey, who had retreated to Crosthwaite near Keswick in order to write in peace. At Norham Gilly did not lead a tranquil life, but write he certainly did.

Henceforth Gilly had two establishments to maintain: 9 College Green in Durham, and Norham Vicarage. Norham was a day's journey by coach from Durham.[11] But as noted above, the second resolution had the effect of getting Gilly out of Durham, except for his periods as Canon in Residence, and this might have been the underlying cause.[12] It affected none of the other prebendaries unless they held a Chapter living, and not even then if they were already in post. It may have been also a case of Chapter seeing which way the wind was blowing, as in 1838 the Pluralities Act was passed, which abridged the holding of benefices in plurality, and it was enacted that no person should hold under any circumstances more than two benefices. This privilege was

---

10   DUL, Thorp Correspondence; Balliol College, Oxford, Jenkyns Papers. Both are manuscripts. Extracts from the former were published in 1998 by Durham University, edited by Fowler. It is advisable always to consult the originals of this correspondence, as Thorp's handwriting was dreadful and is susceptible of different readings, although the Bishop's writing is generally decipherable. The two collections form an entity which is frustrating for any researcher who finds it difficult to be simultaneously in Durham and Oxford.

11   Although Gilly occupied the poorest stall in the Cathedral, the ninth, which in 1841 was worth £312 p.a., Norham was worth £529, so possibly the motive was financial.

12   Although we do have to ask, given the date and the new insistence upon residence, if it was not to get him out of Durham while the university was being founded.

Church of St Cuthbert, Norham. Photo by Meg Norman

made subject to the restriction that the benefices were within 10 statute miles of each other, and required residency on the benefice. (In 1850 the restriction was further narrowed, so that no spiritual person could hold two benefices except the churches of such benefices were within three miles of each other by the nearest road, and the annual value of one of such benefices did not exceed £100.)

Norham is a border village. It lies on a bend of the River Tweed facing the Kingdom of Scotland. North of the Tweed, the established Church of Scotland is Calvinist, which is of course the same version of Christianity as that in the Waldensian valleys, although the Waldensian version of Calvinism is more cheerful than the Scottish variety. Norham, however, is an English village with an English church, an English vicar and a village green. Norham Castle is one of the great border castles which historically had been maintained by the Bishop of Durham to protect England from invasion by the old enemy to the north. The village is the main settlement in the rural district of Norhamshire which, together with the coastal district of Islandshire, formed North Durham, an outlier of County Durham north of Northumberland[13] (see map overleaf) The small fortified coastal town of Berwick-upon-Tweed is 13 kilometres east of Norham. Berwick was a county in its own right (but not to be confused with Berwickshire), being in neither England nor Scotland.[14]

---

13   James Raine, *The History and Antiquities of North Durham as sub-divided into the Shires of Norham, Island and Bedlington*. London, JB Nichols, 1852.

14   Berwick-upon-Tweed has a highly involved history, having been annexed alternately by the English and by the Scots. Since 1482 it had been administered by England, although not officially merged with it, and in 1551 was made a County Corporate, which status it retained until 1885, when it was merged with

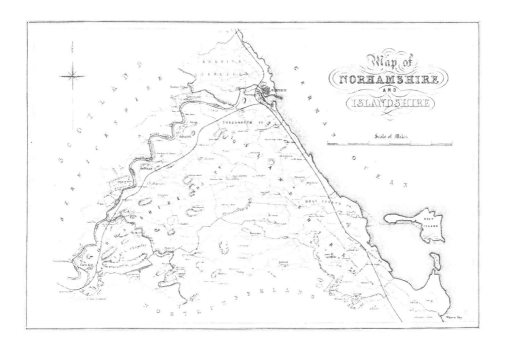

Norhamshire and Islandshire: above, from Raine, *History of North Durham* (opposite p. 2). Below, drawn by Phillip Judge.

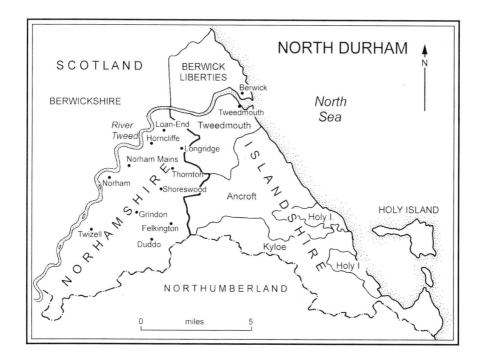

Norham Castle. Photo Meg Norman

North Durham was within both the ecclesiastical and the secular jurisdictions of the Prince-Bishops of Durham. Obviously the situation was anomalous, but far from unique, as several counties had detached portions within other counties. Gilly, of course, tried to tidy things up. Archdeacon Charles Thorp, who had no love for Gilly owing to their policy disagreements over the University of Durham, attended a meeting of the North Durham magistrates in April 1834. On 8 April Thorp wrote to Bishop van Mildert:

The North Durham magistrates go home in very good humour, particularly with your Lordship, but not well pleased with *Dr Gilly* who, they say, first proposed the scheme of annexation. He flew at me with much heart and good-will but made little of it, and probably discovered that he does not stand so strong with the Bench as he expected.[15]

Gilly's 'scheme of annexation' was that Norhamshire and Islandshire, together with Berwick-upon-Tweed, should be amalgamated to form a new English county,[16] and he promoted this scheme at local meetings throughout the 1830s. But this was one argument which he did not win. On 6 August 1844, Norhamshire and Islandshire were incorporated into the county of Northumberland, and North Durham disappeared after an existence of over 800 years. The *Berwick-upon-Tweed*

Northumberland. The declaration of the Crimean War in 1853 was made by England, Scotland 'and the town of Berwick-upon-Tweed'. We still hear stories that Berwick is still at war with Germany 'as it was omitted from the declaration of peace' in 1945 – it was, of course, not in the declaration of war either!

15   DUL, Thorp correspondence.

16   We could almost expect that it might have been called Gillyshire.

Advertiser reported that Gilly was the last man in the district to surrender on the issue.[17]

Gilly was familiar with a rural environment, as he had spent his childhood in Hawkedon, but there is a great difference between rural Suffolk and the Scots Borders. North Durham was a land of large estates and few settlements. The pattern of agriculture centred on villages, each with its own church and parish, which existed in most of central and southern England, was rare on the Borders. Some of the estates were broken up into large farms operated by tenant farmers. These farmers employed many labourers – the hinds of the Borders. The hinds were landless labourers. They, and many of their families, were employed on short-term contracts, and every few months they moved to new employment and new houses. Consequently there was no incentive for improvement of the hinds' dwellings, as they knew that they were likely to be 'flitting' in a few months' time. The hinds were not servile: most were literate, and every household had its Bible; many families had fine pottery and household possessions such as long-case clocks.

Gilly's large new parish had a population of about 3,000, living in Norham village and in scattered farms and hamlets such as Duddo, which is 7 kilometres from Norham (see the map).[18] Most of his parishioners worked on the land or served the rural community in occupations such as blacksmith, miller, cobbler, butcher, brewer or baker. From the 1831 census, we learn that in the township of Norham itself there were 819 people and 174 inhabited houses. Classification of the occupations of males over the age of 20 showed four described as 'Capitalists, Bankers, Professional, and other Educated men'; eighty employed in retail and various skilled trades; ten employed in 'making things'; and eighty-nine employed as farmers, farm workers, or fishermen.[19]

In Norham the public houses included the Black Bull, the Masons' Arms, the Wagon and Horses, the Swan and the Salmon. Apart from agriculture, there was a small colliery at Duddo, another at Ladykirk across the border, and there was also seasonal employment in the salmon fisheries of the River Tweed, which is still a famous salmon river. Norham is not on a main road, and every Saturday the delightfully, but we must hope not aptly, named John Snail, the carter, made a return journey to Berwick-upon-Tweed. St Cuthbert's was the only Anglican church in this geographically large parish, although there was also a Presbyterian church serving the many Scotsmen who had migrated across the border. Gilly's vicarage was a large late Georgian house 100 metres from the church.[20]

In addition to his income as a Prebendary of Durham, Gilly now had also a stipend as

---

17   *Berwick-upon-Tweed Advertiser*, 15 September 1855.
18   The parish of Norham had, besides the township of Norham itself, eleven other townships: Duddo, Felkington, Grievestead, Grindon, Horncliffe, Loan-End, Longridge, Norham Mains, Shoreswood, Thorton and Twizell. Many of these now consist of a single farm building (pers. comm., Dr Paul Coxon).
19   See http://freepages.genealogy.rootsweb.ancestry.com/~agene/norhamvi.htm (accessed 9 January 2012).
20   *Parson and White's Directory, Norhamshire*, 1828; *Whellan's Directory, Norhamshsire*, 1855.

Vicar of Norham.[21] He employed two curates, and maintained a large household. There was a governess, Mary Shields, for the children of his first family.[22] He was a substantial man in the community, and as a Canon of Durham he was the social equal of the local gentry. He became a magistrate. Frederick Dawson Gilly, his first child with Jane, was baptised in Durham Cathedral on 23 June 1831. William and Jane appear to have decided that a teenager, a baby and two other children were sufficient for the time being, as there was a thirteen-year gap before their next child was born.[23]

In 1833 Gilly proceeded Doctor of Divinity at the University of Cambridge.[24] He did no academic work for this distinction; at that time the degree was effectively given on application to senior clergymen who had distinguished themselves in some way. Gilly was a Prebendary of Durham Cathedral and had written three successful books, and thus was eminently suitable to apply for the degree.[25]

Good incumbents become involved in local matters. Even if Gilly had never taken an interest in Waldensian affairs, and had never been a Prebendary of Durham, he would still be remembered for his efforts to improve his parish and ease the hard lives of his parishioners.[26] On 31 December 1837, Dr Walter Ainslie, a popular local surgeon, was drowned while trying to ford the River Tweed at Norham.[27] Gilly started a campaign to construct a bridge over the river, which was eventually built in 1839. He agitated for improved schooling in the parish, and contributed £350 to help establish

---

21 Report of the Ecclesiastical Commissioners for England and Wales, 1835.

22 The 1841 Census shows that Gilly was resident at Norham Vicarage, with his wife Jane, their children Mary Anna (wrongly given as aged 20), Rosalie Emily, William Octavius Shakespeare and Frederick Dawson, together with three male and four female servants. There was a 'schoolmistress', Martha Hall, and Mary Shields, described as 'Ind[ependent means]'. In 1851 he was there with Jane, and their children Alice Ann and Charles Pudsey. Mary Shields was a 'governess', and there were a housekeeper, a cook, a nursery-maid, a house-maid, a kitchen-maid, a footman and a groom. Also listed was Bolton Simpson, described as 'Minor canon without cure of souls'. Simpson, a BA of Queen's College, Oxford, was vicar of Bossall and Buttercrambe, Yorks, from 1854 to 1875 (Forster, *Alumni Oxoniensis*). Did he act as Gilly's curate? The copy of Gilly's *The Crown or the Tiara* (1842) at Cambridge University Library bears Shields' signature, as do six of Gilly's sermons bound together in that library. (CUL 2100.d.1868). In 1830 Gilly had three children aged between 8 and 14. A governess would have been needed at Norham until his death in September 1855. Gilly's youngest child, Charles Pudsey, was born in November 1845, when his half-sister Mary Anna was 29, and his other half-sister Rosalie Emily was 25, and married with a year-old baby.

23 Naturally, there is no information about any still-births or miscarriages Jane Gilly may have suffered during this period.

24 Joseph Romilly, *Graduati Cantabrigienses*, Cambridge, Deighton, Bell & Co, 1856, p. 152. Also Venn, *Alumni Cantabrigiensis*, which reveals he did not take the BD first.

25 The degree, both at Cambridge and other universities, is still awarded on the basis of published scholarly works. He was also awarded a Durham DD, but seems never to have used it. See *Durham University Calendar, passim*.

26 A contemporary example for comparison is the Rev. Francis Witts, Rector of Upper Slaughter. *The Complete Diary of a Cotswold Parson: The diaries of the Revd. Francis Edward Witts 1783–1854*, 10 vols, ed. Alan Sutton; Chalford, Amberley Publishing, c. 2008. I am grateful to Prof. William Gibson for bringing this to my attention. [NWG]

27 Dr Ainslie's friends erected a plaque in Norham Church to commemorate him. He was 36 when he drowned.

a school at Shoreham Wood. He started a girls' school at Norham.[28]

Gilly was concerned about the dilapidated state of Norham Church, but also worried that the more remote parts of his parish, such as the hamlet of Duddo, were far from their parish church. So he enlisted the help of Ignatius Bonomi, who had been architect to Durham Cathedral since 1827. Bonomi has been described as 'the most important architect to practise in nineteenth century Durham'.[29] He had been born into an Italian Catholic family in 1787, and he formed a lasting friendship with Gilly. Whenever Gilly needed buildings designed or repaired, he turned to Bonomi, and he was probably influential in persuading Bonomi to become an Anglican in middle age. In later years Bonomi designed churches for the Waldensians in the Piedmont; his wife Charlotte wrote a bad novel whose hero spent much of his time in the Waldensian valleys.[30]

St James's Chapel, Duddo (now redundant).
Photo by Northumberland County Council.

The hamlet of Duddo is 7 kilometres from Norham. It had neither church nor chapel. Nearby there was a small colliery. In 1832, only a few months after Gilly had arrived in the parish, a new chapel-of-ease was constructed 'by the exertions of the present vicar';[31] it was designed by Bonomi. Gilly drew upon his experience of church financing methods at Somers Town, where the large chapel of St Mary had been funded by taxpayers under the Church Buildings Act of 1819: he used the same source to finance the construction of the chapel of St James the Great at Duddo. Gilly laid the foundation stone on 6 April 1832,[32] and the opening ceremony took place on 28 August 1832. The chapel could seat 250 people, all seats were

Ignatius Bonomi (source unknown).

---

28 *Berwick-upon-Tweed Advertiser*, 15 September 1855.
29 June Crosby, *Ignatius Bonomi of Durham*, City of Durham Trust, 1987, Preface.
30 Charlotte Bonomi, *Edith Grey; or, Ten Years Ago*, London, Vertue & Hall, 1859.
31 James Raine, *The History and Antiquities of North Durham ...* Duddo.
32 June Crosby, *Ignatius Bonomi of Durham*, p. 84.

free, and the congregation had to sit on open benches, not in square ('box') pews. A curate employed by Gilly conducted the services.[33] The neo-Norman chapel bears the arms of the Bishop of Durham.[34] Gilly had built his first church for a total cost of £250.3s.10d.

Norham parish church, St Cuthbert's, was a fine Norman church, but it had fallen into decay: in 1320, it had been occupied and fortified by Robert Bruce while besieging the castle, and in 1619 it was re-roofed after being roofless for over a hundred years, but it had fallen into disrepair again. Gilly set out to remedy the situation with the help of Bonomi. The restoration was somewhat heavy-handed, as alas were so many nine-teenth-century church 'restorations': but Simon Jenkins says that 'Norham's saviour, if restoration is salvation, was the Victorian vicar, William Gilly'.[35] Work started in the mid-1830s and continued intermittently until the 1850s.[36] This included rebuilding the tower in 1837, and taking down the aisle walls and rebuilding them farther out to create wider aisles. He also rescued some of the fine seventeenth-century furnishings from Durham Cathedral, installed by Bishop Cosin, which were then being thrown out: their date made them unfashionable and 'incorrect'. They include the pulpit, the lectern and a stall.

Gilly always had antiquarian interests; he examined Norham churchyard, which is large and lies in a prominent position between the village and the River Tweed, and, with his usual self-confidence, started excavating. He later wrote:

> In the winter of 1832, and again in December 1833, workmen were employed to remove the earth on this spot, and at irregular depths of from three to four feet below the sods, tracings were found of an ancient building, the original destination of which antiquaries have not been able to determine. Most probably this was the site of the Saxon church of Egfrid, and previously of a Roman Temple. ... One of the carved stones is the fragment of a Saxon tombstone, and still retains the letters 'P. Anima Aelf;' another contains the figure of a monk giving the benediction.[37]

These stones he later set into a 'pillar' in the north aisle of the church, to prevent them being taken away or otherwise misused. The churchyard includes fragments of standing crosses as well as grave markers.

He took a lot of trouble to improve this fine churchyard, believing that it 'should be a place to which a villager would willingly resort for a contemplative stroll'.[38] It remains unaltered today. Both William and Jane Gilly are buried there.

---

33   Probably Bolton Simpson – see note 22.
34   N. Pevsner, *The Buildings of England – Northumberland,* Penguin, 1957, p. 139.
35   S. Jenkins, *England's Thousand Best Churches,* Penguin, 2000, p. 512.
36   June Crosby, *Ignatius Bonomi of Durham,* p. 87.
37   W. S. Gilly, 'Our churches and churchyards: Norham', in *Proceedings of Berwickshire Naturalists' Club,* Vol. 2, 1846, p. 177. The inscription can be interpreted as '[Orate] p[ro] anima Aelf...': Pray for the soul of Ælf...' – a number of Anglo-Saxon names share that first syllable, so the name cannot be completed.
38   Walter White, *Northumberland and Border,* London, 1859, p. 294.

Family affairs

In December 1834 Gilly lost his second brother in a storm off the south coast of England. Frederick Gilly (born 1796) had served as a naval officer all his adult life. In 1829, while on leave from the Navy, Frederick had accompanied his brother on journeys through the Waldensian valleys (see Chapter 7). When the news of Frederick's drowning reached Gilly, he was lying in bed at Durham with a broken leg. On 9 December 1834 he wrote a poignant letter to M. Bonjour, the Moderator of the Waldensian Church:

> Vous vous rappellez de mon Frère, le compagnon de notre voyage, et de notre séjour à La Tour – Dieu s'est plû à nous éprouver en nous otant ce Frère chéri, et d'une manière très pénible. Dans l'attente trop hasardeuse de sauver un vaisseau naufragé sa petite barque ne pouvant résister à la violence de la mer, fut renversée – et en un instant, fut enseveli dans les ondes, il périt, avec tout l'équipage de son bateau – Les nouvelles inattendues de ce triste Evênement me trouvèrent dans un état déjà souffrant. Car, m'étant cassé la jambe me voilà, depuis six semains étendu sur mon lit, incapable de faire le moindre mouvement. Mais je rend grâces à Dieu qu'il m'a supporté par les consolations de son St Esprit et par les précieuses promesses de sa Parole, et qu'il m'a permit de reconnaitre sa main paternelle dans ces pénibles châtiments et de crier 'Tu es juste, O Seigneur, et droit dans tes jugements'.[39]

> [You will recall my brother, the companion of our journey, and of our stay at La Tour – God has been pleased to test us by removing from us this beloved brother, and in a very distressing manner. During the extremely hazardous attempt of saving a shipwrecked vessel, his small ship could not withstand the violence of the sea, was overturned, and in an instant was buried in the waves, he perished, with all the crew of his boat – The news of this unhappy event found me already in a state of suffering. For, having broken my leg, I had been for six weeks been laid on my bed, incapable of the least movement. But I give thanks to God that he has supported me with the consolations of his Holy Spirit and by the precious promises of his Word, and that he has allowed me to recognize his fatherly hand in these distressing chastisements, and to cry 'Thou art just, O Lord, and righteous in all thy judgments'.]

Gilly's eldest son, William Octavius Shakespear Gilly, was now 13,[40] and Gilly sent him to Harrow School in September 1835, where, from April 1836 until 1844 the headmaster was Christopher Wordsworth, a nephew of the poet William Wordsworth. Wordsworth reformed Harrow: he tightened up the discipline, which had become lax, and took a personal interest in raising the academic standards of the boys' work on an individual basis, but his reform of the school led to the governors requesting his resignation in 1844. He moved to a canonry of Westminster, and in 1868 to the See of Lincoln.[41] In November 1836 the 14-year-old W. O. S. Gilly was described

---

39   ASTV, series V, vol. 35, c. 253, letter Gilly to Bonjour. Trans NWG. The quotation is an altered form of Ps 119, v. 137.
40   He was born on 24 February 1822, just two-and-a-half months before the death of his mother.
41   Margaret Pawley, 'Wordsworth, Christopher', *Oxford Dictionary of National Biography*, Oxford University

as 'headless', 'volatile' and 'backward', and was a cause of much worry to his father. So Gilly wrote to Wordsworth pleading that his son 'should not lose caste by being denied remove to a higher form'.[42] It is only fair to record that in later years William Gilly junior made good and became an official of the Admiralty, where he wrote a book about shipwrecks of the Royal Navy.[43] He took over as secretary of the London Vaudois Committee after his father's death in 1855.

In December 1837 Gilly's father died at Wanstead. He was 75 and had outlived his wife and four of his six children, and was still both rector of Wansted and non-resident rector of Hawkedon. With his death the Gilly family's links with the village of Hawkedon were severed after 300 years; the parish church contains the family vault, with the remains of Gilly's infant daughter, and memorials to his ancestors and to his first wife. Gilly arranged for a memorial to be erected to his parents at Hawkedon church. This includes the words

> THIS TABLET IS ERECTED BY THEIR SON
> WILLIAM STEPHEN GILLY D.D.
> PREBENDARY OF DURHAM AND VICAR OF NORHAM
> AS THE LAST MEMORIAL OF HIS FAMILY IN THIS
> COUNTY AND AS HIS FAREWELL TESTIMONY
> OF AFFECTION FOR THE PLACE OF HIS
> BIRTH AND THE HOME OF HIS
> FOREFATHERS.

At the end of December 1838 Norham vicarage caught fire, and Gilly lost many of his records. The building was saved from complete destruction by the stalwart efforts of his parishioners, who probably formed a bucket chain from the River Tweed to the vicarage. Gilly wrote to M. Bonjour on 27 December 1838:

> Nous venons de subir un grand malheur. Notre maison à Norham a manqué d'être brûlée toute entière, mais Grâces à Dieu, et aux efforts bien zélés et bien dirigés de mes paroissiens, le feu fût éteint après avoir détruit la chambre de Madame Gilly, et tout ce qu'elle contenait. Ce que je regrette le plus c'est le mal fait à mes livres, papiers, manuscrits etc. en les emportant hors de la maison pour les conserver.[44]

> [We have just suffered a great misfortune. Our house at Norham just escaped being entirely burnt, but thanks be to God, and to the very zealous and well-directed efforts of my parishioners, the fire was extinguished, having destroyed Mrs Gilly's room and all its contents. What I most regret is the harm done to my books, papers, manuscripts, *etc*, in carrying them out of the house in order to save them.]

Press, 2004; online edn, Sept 2010 (www.oxforddnb.com/view/article/29971, accessed 5 January 2012).

42 R. G. Welch (ed.), *The Harrow School Register, 1801–1835*, 1834, p. 109. LPL, Wordsworth papers, MS2141, No. 173, letter from Gilly to Christopher Wordsworth, 30 Nov. 1836.

43 W. O. S. Gilly, *Shipwrecks of the Royal Navy between 1793 and 1849*, London, J. Parker, 1850. His father wrote a preface which provides valuable information about his early life.

44 ASTV, series V, vol. 37, c. 164, letter, Gilly to Bonjour (trans. NWG).

His eldest daughter, Mary Anna, was 21 on 15 March 1837, and still living at home. She suffered from ill-health, but married the Rev. Lewis Morgan in 1847.[45] Rosalie Emily was four years younger, and lived at home until her marriage in 1841. William left Harrow School probably in 1840 and started work in the Navy Office in London, so by the late 1830s all Gilly's first family were leaving home. Mary Shields, the governess, stayed to look after the young Frederick Dawson Gilly, born in June 1831.

Throughout the 1830s Gilly lived the life of a busy Anglican incumbent, concerned for the welfare of his parishioners in a large, poor, rural parish. By the end of the decade he was well established locally. Politically he was a Conservative, and paid an annual subscription of a guinea a year to the Durham Conservative Association.[46] But he realized the need for change, and was becoming increasingly concerned about the wretched conditions in which many of the hinds were living. So at the beginning of the 1840s he started to agitate on behalf of the peasantry of the border.

Durham

The main event in the City of Durham during the 1830s was the founding of the university. As outlined in Chapter 8, Gilly would have liked to have had a major role in founding a college in the city, but was prevented from doing so, as his views on the type of institution were too narrow. Neither Bishop van Mildert nor Archdeacon Thorp, the effective founders of the university, had confidence in him. There were tensions in the Chapter concerning the university until the late 1830s, and Gilly must have known that he was not a favourite of the Bishop. As he had no aristocratic connections, and was not a leading theologian, he had little prospect of advancing further in the church: it was highly unlikely that he would be made a bishop, although a deanery or archdeaconry might have come his way. Canon Gilly of Durham he was to remain: but as such he had tenure for life, and was quite free to write and campaign on those matters that concerned him.

Anne Colberg continued to live at 9 The College, where she had been suffering from a 'severe and long' illness since 1829,[47] and she died at there in October 1832, aged 57.[48] There is no record that she ever went to live in Norham. Indeed, the removal of the large Gilly family and their servants may have provided peace and quiet for the last few months of her life. Gilly arranged for her body to be buried in the nave of

---

45   Morgan was born in Dublin in 1819, and attended Trinity College there (BA 1841, MA 1846). Ordained by the bishop of Durham (deacon 1846, priest 1847), he was chaplain to the University of Durham (BA *ad eundem*, 1845, MA *ad eundem* and LTh, 1846). In 1860, he became Vicar of West Bradenham, Norfolk; in 1876 Vicar of St Mary, Summerstown, Tooting (not to be confused with Gilly's earlier cure of St Mary, Somers Town, King's Cross); in 1887 Vicar of Ainstable, Cumberland (*Crockford's Clerical Directory, passim*). Mary Anna probably died at Summerstown in 1888.

46   DUL, Archives and Special Collections, SRA/9/4-6, Accounts of the Ninth Stall, 1826–55.

47   Second codicil to the will of Anne Colberg, 3 November 1829, Family Records Centre, London. Ref. Prob. H. 1808, Quire 745. This refers to 'my severe and long illness'.

48   G. Armytage (ed.), *The Baptismal, Marriage and Burial Registers of the Cathedral Church of Christ and Blessed Mary the Virgin at Durham 1609–1896*. Harleian Society, Register Section, 23 (1897), 136.

Durham Cathedral, and paid William Jobling £5 17s 8d. for the construction of the vault.[49] She died in obscurity. The Waldensians never knew that it was her money Gilly had used to finance the construction of a college at Torre Pellice. She willed her personal effects to her niece, Jane Gilly, and the residue to be divided between her two nephews and Jane Gilly. Gilly was appointed a joint executor of the will, which had been witnessed by James White, his butler. She left nothing to her father, because she had already given him £500.[50]

Most of Gilly's personal papers disappeared after his death, so it is impossible to unravel his finances completely. The account books for the ninth prebendal stall show he received dividends of £1,296 11s 11¾d. in 1826, which rose to £1,960 11s 7¾d. in 1837. He also received £597 as vicar of Norham.[51] From these sums he had considerable expenses to pay, including the wages of curates at Norham. Between 1831 and 1840 he sent an average of £380 each year to Messrs Glyn & Company in Lombard Street in London, for forwarding to the Waldensians. The account books of the ninth stall also show that he paid £105 on 21 January 1832 towards the cost of the construction of a memorial for Shute Barrington; seven shillings for a dog on 2 November 1833; and an annual subscription of one guinea to the Durham Conservative Association; as well as numerous donations to charities such as the Durham Infirmary, the Antiquarian Society of Newcastle, the restoration fund for St Oswald's Church, the Asylum for the Blind and Deaf, and the Society for Propagating Christianity amongst the Jews. He also paid a wine bill of £41 3s 8d. on 4 April 1832, and made half yearly payments of £6 11s 9d. for window tax. These account books are of course not a full record of his finances: they show only items Gilly decided to pay through the stall accounts, and include no information about the finances of Jane Gilly or Anne Colberg.

The City of Durham Society for the Suppression of Mendicity must have taken up much of Gilly's time: he had been president since its foundation. The sixth annual

---

49 DUL, Archives and Special Collections, Accounts of the Ninth Stall, SRA/9/4, 12 February 1833. See also Armytage, *The Baptismal, Marriage and Burial Registers of the Cathedral Church of Christ and Blessed Mary the Virgin at Durham 1609–1896*, p 136. There is a mystery about Anne Colberg's tomb. C. M. Carlton, *Monumental Inscriptions of the Cathedral, Parish Churches, and Cemeteries of the City of Durham*, vol. 1, Durham, 1880, p. 15, records an inscription on a plain slab in the centre of the nave 'Here rests of the body of Anne Elizabeth Colberg who died October 26th 1832 aged thirty-seven years'. Carlton got her age wrong, for she was 57 when she died, though in some styles of lettering used on monuments, '3' and '5' are easily confused. However when the Friends of Durham Cathedral checked on site in 2002 they discovered that the inscribed slab had been removed and replaced by a blank stone (pers. comm. to HN, Miss Lilian Groves). The enigma remains: who removed the slab containing the inscription? And why was it done? (It might have been a casualty of the re-orderings under Salvin in 1840, or Scott in 1870.)

50 Second codicil to the will of Anne Colberg, 3 November 1829. See p. 72, note 85.

51 *The Report of the Ecclesiastical Commissioners for England and Wales,* 1835 shows Gilly receiving £1,491 as his share of Dean and Chapter income, plus £312 as income specific to the ninth stall after deductions. His income as Vicar of Norham was £597 gross, from which there were deductions of £68. His income as a Canon of Durham rose during the 1830s, as the Chapter received increased payments from the coal mines on Chapter land in County Durham. (In contrast with his relatively poor ninth stall, the 'Golden Stall' was the eleventh, which yielded £1,587 in 1835.) Gilly also had his prebendal house and Norham vicarage – both rent free, and there were also free coals at Durham.

meeting of the society was held in Durham Town Hall on 21 January 1834.[52] It was reported at the meeting that in 1833 12,402 'Strangers, chiefly Trampers', who did not apply to the society for relief, were received at the four Durham lodging houses,[53] whereas 2,744 applied to the society for relief, of whom 2,416 were relieved.[54]

There was much poverty and indeed distress in the city during the 1830s, exacerbated by the many Scotsmen and Irishmen who passed through Durham as they migrated south.[55] The *Durham Advertiser* of 5 February 1836 carried a report of the eighth annual meeting of the society. The number of common lodging houses had been reduced from twenty-five in 1828 (the year of the Society's foundation) to eight, while the number of vagrants in the same

City of Durham.

AT THE SIXTH

ANNUAL MEETING

OF THE SOCIETY FOR THE

SUPPRESSION OF

MENDICITY

Held in the TOWNHALL, January 21, 1834.

THE REVEREND
W. S. Gilly, D. D. Prebend of Durham,
PRESIDENT.

It was Reported — That the Number of Strangers, chiefly Trampers, but not applying at the Office of this Society for Relief, received into the Lodging Houses between January 1st and December 31st, 1833, were as under:

Framwellgate	2358
Gilesgate	4886
Elvet	1109
Claypath	4049
Total	12,402

Being an Increase on the preceding Year of 532.

It was Reported—That the Number of Applicants at the Office amounted to 2744.

Women	446		2416 were relieved and lodged.
Children	564		175 relieved but not lodged.
Labourers	597		36 lodged without other relief.
Seamen	162	of	117 dismissed without any relief, not being objects who were thought
Soldiers	1	these	to require the Society's assistance.
Mechanics	974		
	2744		2744

It was Reported—That the Number of Irish and Scotch were,
Irish........ 3341 the Increase upon the last Year being 647.
Scotch ...... 1622 the Increase upon the last Year being 170.

period had shrunk from 15,018 to 9,890 in 1835, of whom only 1,995 applied for relief, forty-six of them being turned away. The comparatively low numbers applying for relief may reveal a desire not to accept charity, or it may reveal the rigour with which the applicants were known to be assessed. The society congratulated itself in 1836 that the annual expenditure for the previous year was 'only' £103, which included the superintendent's salary of £42. That gives an average expenditure of 8½d per successful applicant.

During the 1830s, the population of the city was increasing at a rate of 2 per cent a year.[56] Durham was an insanitary town with a feckless town council, composed of

---

52 The report of the society was widely distributed as a handbill in Durham. There is a copy in DUL
53 Claypath, Framwellgate, Elvet and Gilesgate.
54 Of the 2,744, 597 were labourers, and there were 446 women, 564 children, 162 seamen, 974 mechanics, and one solider. 117 were 'dismissed without relief, not being objects who were thought to require the Society's assistance'. Some were lodged, some 'relieved' (i.e. given money), some lodged and relieved.
55 In 1833, 3,341 Irish and 1,622 Scots were received into the Durham lodging houses – in each case an increase on the previous year's tally.
56 G. T. Clark, *Report to the General Board of Health on a Preliminary Inquiry into the Sewerage, Drainage and*

twenty-four councillors and aldermen, which could trace its origin back to 1179.[57] In 1835 Parliament passed a Municipal Corporations Act, but this resulted in no serious improvement in the administration of Durham City. The civil economy of the city was supposed to be administered by about 120 commissioners, but they were self-elected, irresponsible and incompetent.[58] Parts of the city were undrained and in a very filthy condition. Gilly's society, usually called the Mendicity Society, was at least trying to do something about the acute misery and sanitary problems in the city. Gilly and his friend the architect Ignatius Bonomi were major players in attempts to improve social and health conditions in Durham between 1827 and 1855. Their names come up whenever researchers study conditions in the city during these years.[59]

On 21 February 1836 Bishop van Mildert died at the age of 70. He had been in ill health for several years. His body was interred with much pomp in Durham Cathedral. The procession included officers of both the See and of the Palatinate; the Mayor and Corporation; the local nobility and gentry; members of the university; about sixty clergy from the diocese, and the end was brought up by 'gentlemen, tradesmen, etc'. Gilly was one of the four pallbearers, with Townsend, Wellesley and Ogle, and thus walked beside the coffin fully robed.[60]

The procedures for appointing bishops in the Church of England have hardly been altered since the Reformation. The idea that the cathedral chapter elects the bishop had become a mere notion long before that date, and although a *congé d'élire* was, and still is, issued to the relevant chapter, they merely 'rubber-stamp' the choice of candidate presented to them. (This stage of the process was mocked by Ralph Waldo Emerson: 'The King sends the Dean and Canons a *congé d'élire*, or leave to elect, but also sends them the name of the person whom they are to elect. They go into the Cathedral, chant and pray; and after these invocations invariably find that the dictates of the Holy Ghost agree with the recommendation of the King.'[61]) After the Reformation, the Crown arrogated to itself, as Supreme Governor of the Church of England, the right to nominate bishops. During the eighteenth century, the appointment had come to be exercised by the Prime Minister acting on behalf of the Crown. Thus, the

---

Supply of Water, and the Sanitary Conditions of the Inhabitants of Durham, London, Stationery Office, 1849. This report was reprinted as D. J. Butler (ed. and intro.), *Public Health Act, Report to the General Board of Health on Durham*, Durham County Local History Society, 1997.

57   Clark, *Report to the General Board of Health*.

58   'Report on the sanitary condition of the labouring population of Great Britain. A supplementary report on the results of a special inquiry into the practice of interment in towns'. Made at the request of Her Majesty's Principal Secretary of State for the Home Department, by E. Chadwick. House of Lords Sessional Papers, Session 1843, vol. 32, p. 20. This famous report was particularly critical of sanitary conditions in Durham, and of the failure of the local authorities to take any remedial action. Clark, *Report to the General Board of Health*, para. 21.

59   It may be telling that the University of Durham introduced a Licence in Sanitary Science (LSSc) in 1887, and also degrees in Hygiene (BHy, DHy) – what would now be called Public Health.

60   *Durham Advertiser*, 26 February 1836.

61   R. W. Emerson, *English Traits*, XIII, London, 1856.

Dean and Chapter of Durham needed to go through the formality of electing a new bishop, who had already been chosen. The Chapter minute of 19 March 1836 reads:

> Dr Gilly requested that the following protest should be entered 'Considering that the act of electing a Bishop, as the law now stands, is not a free act on the part of the Chapter, but one of compulsion, I protest against the use of any expression in the forms adopted upon this occasion, by which the Holy Name of God is invoked or which implies freedom of election. I make this protest without any feeling of disrespect towards the distinguished Prelate nominated by the King and in reference solely to the deed of nomination, which under any circumstances would be imperative on us, in the present state of the Law, and according to the exigent of the law.'

Gilly's protest was a courageous act, and one which was hardly likely to endear him to the new Bishop, Edward Maltby. Van Mildert had been the last of the Prince-Bishops of Durham, for on 21 June 1836 the Palatine jurisdiction of Durham was separated from the Episcopal and vested in the Crown, and henceforth the Bishops of Durham no longer had secular authority in County Durham, but they remained powerful ecclesiastical figures and still sat in the House of Lords.[62]

In the late 1830s Gilly continued to attend the Chapter meetings regularly. He was sub-dean again in 1839.[63] He kept up his interest in antiquarian curiosities. In 1835 he was studying medieval manuscripts with a view to their publication by the Surtees Society.[64] In 1839 he made a study of the bells and of the medieval chantry priests of the Cathedral.[65]

Writings, 1830–40

Gilly was a compulsive author. When he wrote about the interesting things he had done, his travels, people he had met, and the poverty of his parishioners, he wrote well, but he could not resist the temptation to insert extraneous material into his publications. He was not an academic theologian, and did not entertain doubt. He had firm beliefs about the nature of God, the superiority of the Anglican Church, and apostolic succession through the Waldensian Church. In his beliefs about Apostolic Succession, Gilly was largely on his own: no leading theologian supported him. Two contemporary writers who had visited the Waldensian valleys challenged Gilly's assertions that the Waldensians had once had bishops.[66]

---

62 The Bishops of Durham, along with those of London and Winchester, as well as the two Archbishops, sit by right in the House of Lords, while the other bishops gain their seats dependent on their seniority as bishops. With the Bishop of Bath and Wells, Durham is one of the two 'supporters' of the new monarch during the coronation ceremony.

63 Dean and Chapter Minute Book, 26 February 1836.

64 Dean and Chapter Minute Book, 28 February 1835.

65 Dean and Chapter Minute Book, 16 March 1839.

66 Charles Holte Bracebridge, *Authentic Details of the Valdenses, in Piemont and other countries; with abridged translations of 'L'Histoire des Vaudois' par Bresse, and La Rentrée glorieuse, d'Henri Arnaud, etc.,* London, 1827. (See Chapter 3 of this book.) Ebenezer Henderson, *The Vaudois; comprising observations made during*

In November 1831 he published, anonymously, an essay on education amongst the Waldenses in the *Quarterly Journal of Education*, published by the Society for the Diffusion of Useful Knowledge. This is an account of the traditional village schools in the Waldensian valleys and the establishment, with funding from Gilly, of the Ecole Superieure. The school had been opened in Torre Pellice on 1 March 1831 in temporary quarters, and closed by the Piedmontese authorities almost immediately as unauthorized, although it had been allowed to reopen on a restricted basis on 27 May 1831. The article made no mention of the work of Colonel Beckwith in extending and upgrading the village schools.[67]

In 1832 he published another best-selling book. *A Memoir of Felix Neff* is the account of the short life of Neff, a Swiss pastor, who was born in Geneva in 1798, spent most of his life working in remote French Huguenot villages of the Dauphiné, and died of cancer in 1829.[68] Pastor Neff devoted his life to helping some of the poorest rural communities in France. He was remembered with love by his parishioners. Gilly never met him, but in the summer of 1829, only a few weeks after Neff's death, William and Jane Gilly had made an arduous journey to the remote French Huguenot villages in the Val Queiras and the Val Fressinière where Neff had laboured. Everywhere he was remembered with affection. After Neff's death, his journals had come into the possession of Miss Mary Elliott of West Field Lodge. She had given Gilly access to them, which enabled him to write his book. Gilly acknowledged Miss Elliott's help in the first edition of this book. This mention evidently upset Miss Elliott, for the second edition states:

> I could not have done justice to my subject, had I not been indebted to the great kindness of a lady, whose name I am not permitted to mention here, for the journals of Neff himself.[69]

The book contains a good fold-out map, but once again there is no index.

Neff was a remarkable man, whose name is still remembered and honoured in the history of the French Huguenot church. Gilly's is not the only account of his life. There is, as usual, much extraneous matter in the first edition, but this was pruned for the smaller second edition, published in 1834 – possibly as a result of the review quoted below. The book sold steadily and went to five editions. Southey published a long and laudatory review of the book in the April 1833 edition of the *Quarterly Review*. A more perceptive and critical review was published in the Anglican *British*

---

a tour to the Valleys of Piedmont, in the summer of 1814: together with remarks, introductory and interspersed, respecting the origin, history and present condition of that people, London, 1845. (See Chapter 7 of this book.) Both of these visitors discussed Waldensian history with local pastors, and both concluded that the Waldensian Church had never had bishops.

67   The article is authenticated as being by Gilly in a letter written by him to the secretary of the Society for the Diffusion of Useful Knowledge 18 October 1831. UCL, SDUK archives.

68   W. S. Gilly, *A Memoir of Felix Neff, Pastor of the High Alps, and of his labours among the French Protestants of Dauphiné, a remnant of the primitive Christians of Gaul*, London, 1832. See also p. 96.

69   Gilly, *A Memoir of Felix Neff*, 2nd edn, 1833, p. 13.

Critic in the same year. It reads, in part:

We cannot but think that his Biographer would have done him greater justice if he had allowed him more fully to tell his own tale, and had avoided the huge admixture of extraneous matter which now assists to swell this volume. ... When once a favorite notion obtains despotic mastery over the fancy, we believe that the orgasm which impels to its propagation is almost irresistible; and that the philoprogenitive theory-monger, like a frog during the first warm days of Spring, unconsciously drops his sporn of hypothesis upon every spot to which it is at all likely to adhere. Mr Gilly has adopted a belief that primitive Christianity, like primitive rocks, may be found in almost all the mountainous regions of Europe; and so incontinent is he of this fancy, that there is scarcely a page before us which is not in some degree impregnated with it. ... We earnestly *hope* that Mr Gilly has yet before him many years of life; we *think* that his intervals of authorship (slightly to vary a favourite quotation) will be neither few nor far between; and we are *quite certain* that he will never put pen to paper without some notice of those many Churches which he supposes have preserved their original purity even from Apostolic times. ... The style of this volume is perplexed and cumbrous.[70]

A

MEMOIR

OF

FELIX NEFF,

PASTOR OF THE HIGH ALPS;

AND OF

HIS LABOURS AMONG THE FRENCH PROTESTANTS

OF DAUPHINE,

A REMNANT OF THE PRIMITIVE CHRISTIANS OF GAUL.

BY

WILLIAM STEPHEN GILLY, M.A.

PREBENDARY OF DURHAM, AND VICAR OF NORHAM.

" There are very few habitations in Dormilleuse which are not liable to be swept away, for there is not a spot, in this narrow corner of the Valley of Fressinière, which can be considered absolutely safe. But terrible as the situation of the natives is, they owe to it their religion, and perhaps their physical existence. If their country had been more secure, and more accessible, they would have been exterminated, like the inhabitants of Val Louise. — NEFF'S JOURNAL.

LONDON:

PRINTED FOR J. G. & F. RIVINGTON,

ST. PAUL'S CHURCH YARD,

AND WATERLOO PLACE, PALL MALL.

1832.

There was an imposing sequel to this best-selling book. Frederick, the fifth Lord Monson, was so impressed that he visited the French Protestant valleys and published *Views in the Department of Isère and the High Alps, chiefly designed to illustrate the Memoirs of Felix Neff by Dr Gilly* in 1840.[71] This book contains a set of lithographs

---

70   *The British Critic, Quarterly Theological Review, and Ecclesiastical Record*, Vol. 13, 1833, pp. 357 and 360.

71   *Views in the Department of the Isere and the High Alps, chiefly designed to illustrate the Memoir of Felix Neff by*

drawn by Louis Haghe. Haghe was born in Belgium in 1806, but lived in England. The lithographs are very impressive, but they are very large and can only be properly examined if the book is opened on a large flat table. Lord Monson's was not the first collection of imposing lithographs to be published about the Protestant valleys, for in 1838 William Beattie had published *The Waldenses* which included fine lithographs: this book is discussed in the next chapter.

Gilly's book on Neff was not free from controversy, for in 1833 T. S. Ellerby wrote another biography of Neff.[72] Ellerby, a Congregationalist minister in Canada, was scathing of Gilly's work. He had published a short memoir of Neff in the *Congregational Magazine* in April 1832, which 'excited interest' and he had started to collect information for a fuller biography. He commented:

> Before Mr Gilly's work on the same subject appeared, he [i.e. Ellerby] had actually announced his intention, and made a rough sketch of the greater part of the following pages. The publication of that volume, however, rather added decision to his design than otherwise, inasmuch as it appeared to him extremely defective, not merely with regard to some of the important occurrences in the life of Neff, but more especially as to those views of theology, to the influence of which, there can be no doubt, we owe much of that ardent zeal, and those various and incessant labours, by which the pastor of the Higher Alps was so eminently distinguished.[73]

Ellerby went on to say:

> the very extensive revival, of which [Neff] was the highly honoured instrument, [Ellerby] found, was spoken of as a mere improvement; whilst the numerous meetings for prayer and mutual exhortation established by him, and of whose importance he was, to the last hour of his existence, a most decided advocate, were condemned, or, at most, spoken of in the language of doubt and suspicion.[74]

The prayer meeting, a gathering, usually in a private house, at which extempore prayer is offered, was and is an important part of nonconformist religious culture.[75] To Gilly, an orthodox High Church Anglican for whom all worship had to take place within the confines of a liturgy such as the set forms of the Book of Common Prayer, led by an ordained clergyman or other authorized person, such gatherings were anathema. As Ellerby noted, the difference in theological views between Gilly and Neff made it almost impossible that one should be an impartial biographer of the other. Ellerby then proceeds to justify the prayer meeting from Scriptural sources, and enquires how Gilly can object to something which St Paul had approved. Again,

---

    Dr. Gilley [sic], *lithographed by L. Haghe from sketches by ... Lord Monson*. London, 1840. The copy in the British Library is bound in leather and bears the Royal Coat of Arms.

72   T. S. Ellerby, *Memorials of Felix Neff, the Alpine Pastor*, London, Manchester and Liverpool, 1833.

73   Ellerby, *Memorials*, p. vii.

74   Ellerby, *Memorials*, p. viii.

75   Such meetings were to be found among the Evangelical part of the Church of England, as well.

Gilly appeared to be seeing what he wished to see, in this case Neff as an Anglican *manqué.*

Gilly published two sermons at this time. In 1833 *The Enduring Obligation of the Sabbath* stressed the need for strict observance of the Lord's Day:

> There is but one way of securing the Sabbath to the working classes; that is, by consecrating it according to God's appointment by making it 'holy unto the Lord'. Once break down the religious barriers of the Sabbath, and business, pleasure, avarice and unfeeling tyranny would soon complete the work.[76]

This was followed in 1834 by *The Power of Prayer.* There was a cholera scare in Britain during that year. Gilly wrote:

> The pestilence has been abroad, threatening first one, then another. … Is it not time, then, to humble ourselves before the most High, and to have recourse to the power of prayer?[77]

In 1835 he published a pamphlet (priced 'fourpence, or three shillings the dozen'), *Our Protestant Forefathers*, in which he justified his Apostolic Succession beliefs and his conviction that there had been a continuous succession from Christ's apostles to the nineteenth century without having passed through the Roman Catholic church: Gilly maintained that the true Apostolic Succession had been through the Waldensian church.[78] It sold well, and was later reprinted several times by the Society for Promoting Christian Knowledge. The publication of the pamphlet led to a local controversy, which must have enlivened life for Durham citizens. Early in 1836, the Reverend James Wheeler, priest at the Roman Catholic chapel in Old Elvet, published a twopenny pamphlet entitled *A Brief Reply to the Reverend Dr Gilly's Tract.* This witty pamphlet complimented Gilly on his well known 'mildness and suavity of disposition', but poked fun at Gilly's determination 'to have none but Protestant forefathers'. Wheeler went on to write:

> As to dismounting you from your Waldensian (Vaudois) hobby, believe me, my good Sir, I am not so ill-natured as to do any such thing, as it is a source to you of much pleasure besides being a subject of no small amusement to many of your readers'.[79]

Wheeler also pointed out that Gilly, in castigating the medieval church for its wealth, was on dangerous ground, as everybody knew that the canons of Durham had large incomes and enjoyed very comfortable lifestyles. Apostolic succession was an argument that Gilly lost. His theories about there being continuous Apostolic

---

76   Published in *Family Sermons.*
77   Published in *Sermons Contributed by Clergymen of the Church of England in Aid of the fund for the relief of clergy of the Church of Ireland.*
78   W. S. Gilly, *Our Protestant Forefathers*, London, 1835 (2 editions). The third edition was published by the Society for Promoting Christian Knowledge, Religious Tracts, etc., vol. 4, 1836, no. 51.
79   Wheeler, *A Brief Reply*, p. 17.

Succession through the Waldensian Church were accepted by few of his contemporaries in the Anglican Church, and by almost nobody in the twentieth century. The Waldensian Church (now La Chiesa Valdesi) has never accepted the theory: as noted above, that Pastor Peyrani agreed with Gilly was possibly due to an aged sick man's not wishing to disagree with his guest, or possibly to Gilly hearing what he wished to hear.[80]

In 1836 Gilly published *God Is With Us*, a sermon preached before the Society of the Sons of the Clergy of Northumberland North of the Coquet at Alnwick on 31 August 1836. He defended the Reformation in England as 'a cleansing of the temple, and not a demolition of it'. He added that 'there is an over-ruling Providence which upholds the national Church and which evermore cleanses and defends it'.[81] The pamphlet then proceeds to make a passionate appeal for assistance for widows and orphans of Anglican clergy, many of whom were living 'in a wretched state of penury and humiliation'.[82] At the back of this pamphlet is a list of Gilly's publications, which includes *Academic Errors,* the angry denunciation of brutalities of English public schools which Gilly had published anonymously in 1817.[83]

On 7 November 1837 *The Globe*, a London evening daily newspaper, published an open letter from Gilly to the Bishop of London pointing out that the Anglican service for 5 November had 'an improper exciting tendency' and suggesting that more temperate language should be substituted. He signed his letter *Sanctae Theologiae Professor*.[84] The service referred to was one of the four State Services, 'annexed to' the Book of Common Prayer. A proclamation at the beginning of each reign authorized a form to commemorate the accession of the sovereign, and the other three were included by Acts of Parliament, and commemorated the beheading of Charles I in 1649 (30 January); the restoration of the Royal family in 1660 (29 May); and the Gunpowder Treason of 1605 (5 November), which is the one Gilly was anxious about: or to quote its full title, *A Form of Prayer with Thanksgiving to be used yearly upon the Fifth day of November, For the happy Deliverance of King JAMES I and the three estates of ENGLAND, from the most traiterous and bloody-intended Massacre by Gunpowder*. All of these made even more obvious the bond between Church and State – specifically, the Stuart State, although the service for 5 November also includes a later addition to give thanks for 'the happy Arrival of his Majesty King William on this Day, for the Deliverance of our Church and Nation'. All of them, save the accession service, were abolished in 1859.

Gilly was particularly exercised by those parts of the Gunpowder service which could upset Roman Catholics, such as the reference to the royal family being 'by Popish treachery appointed as sheep to the slaughter, in a most barbarous and savage

---

80   See page 36.

81   W. S. Gilly, *God is With Us*, published at Warder Office, Berwick-upon-Tweed, 1836.

82   Gilly, *God is With Us*, p. 35.

83   See pages 55–8.

84   The letter can be identified as by Gilly because he published two further letters in *The Globe* using the same pseudonym on 25 November 1837 and 11 December 1837. *Sanctae Theologiae Professor* is a Latin version of Doctor of Divinity.

manner', or (with reference to the arrival of William of Orange) to 'the deliverance of our Church and Nation from Popish tyranny and arbitrary power'. The day itself is marked in the calendar at the front of the book as 'Papists' Conspiracy' – and as a 'Red Letter Day': in other words it is of equal standing with Easter, Christmas and feasts of the Apostles. In contrast a single-sheet pamphlet entitled *Tender Mercies of the Papists*, a reprint of two more open letters by Gilly to *The Globe,* published on 25 November and 11 December 1837 (addressed to Lord Durham), contains extensive references to the persecutions of the Waldensians by the Roman Catholic church.[85]

In 1837 he published *The Church of England in her Strong and Weak Points.* This is the text of a sermon he preached in Berwick-upon-Tweed on 21 September 1837, on the occasion of the visitation of Edward Maltby, the new Bishop of Durham. It is a passionate sermon preached by a man who now had extensive parish experience of the slums of Somers Town, the squalid alleys of Durham, and rural poverty in the Borders. Gilly took the opportunity to attack the Anglican Church for its failure to maintain day-to-day links with the ordinary people, and particularly with the millions who had come to live in the rapidly expanding towns:

> We have not sufficient provision to meet the religious wants of a rapidly increasing population … I might tell you of thickly populated districts in the Metropolis, containing parishes of above 20,000 each, but having church room for only one twentieth of the whole population …

In this statement, however, he was being disingenuous. 'Church room' refers specifically to Anglican churches, and does not take cognizance of the fact that many of the people chose to go to the churches of other denominations – or indeed religions. The concept of the Church of England as a national church was to fade during the course of the nineteenth century.[86]

Gilly, rather unusually for a clergyman of the Church of England, denounced pews:

> Nothing can be more unseemly in the temple of God, than pews with locks upon them … The introduction of pews into our churches cannot be too highly reprobated, whether we consider the selfishness of the practice, or its encroachment upon architectural beauty…. I trust the hour will come when there will not be a pew in any church in England.[87]

By 'pews' Gilly meant the old square 'box pews', which were either rented by, or were

---

85   Gilly is assumed to be the author, as he used the pseudonym *Sanctæ Theologiæ Professor* to sign both, and by the subject matter. The copy in CUL (Syn 6.84.52) is bound with eight other pieces of his work, and was in the possession of Mary Shields, the governess.

86   This was highlighted by the Religious Census of 1851, which showed that, although the Church of England was the largest single denomination, taken together the nonconformist denominations had greater numbers – and that there were as many as the two put together, if not more, who attended no place of worship.

87   W. S. Gilly, *The Church of England in Her Strong and Weak Points.* Pub. at Warder Office, Berwick-upon-Tweed, 1837.

the outright property of, the richer members of the congregation. Pew rents formed a significant part of an incumbent's income. Within fifty years of this sermon, most churches did away with them, replacing them with the now-familiar open benches (often miscalled 'pews'.)

In 1838 Gilly was involved in an obscure but polemical local dispute. So far it has not been possible to untangle the details, because the participants wrote anonymously and the record is incomplete. The argument began with the publication of a pamphlet in Newcastle-on-Tyne by 'Layman'.[88] It was entitled *An Epistle to the Priesthood of the Apostolical Succession.*[89] It was probably an attack on Gilly's Apostolic Succession beliefs. A reply was published entitled *Who is the Arian?* This was published in Berwick-upon-Tweed and is signed 'Presbyter'.[90] This pamphlet defended the Anglican doctrine of the Trinity. It is well written and avoids polemics, and stylistically it could well have been written by Gilly.

The publication of *Who is the Arian?* raised the temperature. In November 1838 'Layman' published *A Second Epistle to the Priesthood with a Postscript to the Presbyter of Berwick-upon-Tweed and a word to the Wise man of Newcastle.*[91] This polemical pamphlet is in part an attack by name on Gilly, who was described as 'A rich Prebendary of Durham, and a pluralist besides'.[92] Gilly was also accused of repudiating *Who is the Arian?* although 'Layman' believed that he had in fact written the tract.[93] Gilly probably wrote a riposte entitled *Sabbath or No Sabbath*.

So far it has not been possible to untangle this obscure dispute. However it was in part a personal attack on Gilly, particularly in the addenda to the postscript of

---

88 'Layman' was the pseudonym of Richard Burdon Sanderson. Born in Newcastle 1791, the son of Sir Thomas Burdon, he graduated BA at Oriel College, Oxford in 1812. The following year he was elected Fellow of Oriel, and also appointed Secretary of Presentations by his uncle Lord Eldon, the Lord Chancellor. In 1815 he married Elizabeth Skinner Sanderson, and changed his name to Burdon Sanderson. He resigned his post as Secretary of Presentations, disgusted by the graft and corruption of the patronage system in the Established Church, in 1816. From 1833 he was active as a nonconformist lecturer, pamphleteer and religious teacher. In 1837 he was (re-)baptised by the Rev. J. A. Methuen at Otterburn Dene: Methuen was a member of the Plymouth Brethren. He lived at Otterburn Dene and Jesmond, and bought a chapel at the latter place where he conducted services. He died in 1865 at Hampstead. Information from www.stanford.edu/group/auden/cgi-bin/auden/individual.php?pid=I1598&ged=auden-bicknell.ged, accessed 21 June 2011, and also Lady (Ghetal) Sanderson, *Sir John Burdon Sanderson, a memoir*, Oxford, 1911, p. 14. The British Library lists seventeen publications by him, mostly of a polemical nature: examples are *The Church of England identified, on the authority of her own historians chiefly, with the Second Beast, as described in the Book of Revelation, chapter XIII. verses 11-18*(1836); and *Babylon; or the Conservative system: with the comparative anatomy of each as developed in the world at large and in the Word of God, etc*; (1837).

89 'Layman' (Richard Burdon Sanderson), *An Epistle to the Priesthood of the Apostolical Succession, on certain points of doctrine hitherto but imperfectly developed. Under cover of a letter to the Lord Bishop of Durham, by a Layman of his Diocese*, Newcastle and London, 1838. The DUL copy (XL 080 YOR/7) is inscribed 'From the Author a weak man called Burdon the son of Sir Thos Burdon of Newc.'

90 'Presbyter' (prob. W. S. Gilly), *Who is the Arian?*, Berwick-upon-Tweed, 1838.

91 'Layman', *A second Epistle to the Priesthood [contending that the Law of the Sabbath is not a commandment of Christ], with a postscript [subscribed, 'The Layman'] to the Presbyter of Berwick upon Tweed [W. S. Gilly], and a word to the wise man of Newcastle, etc*, Newcastle, 1838.

92 'Layman', *A second Epistle*, p. 30

93 'Layman', *A second Epistle*, pp 46–8.

'Layman's' pamphlet. But the episode does not cast discredit on Gilly, for it is no disgrace to anyone to be the subject of a personal attack (assuming Gilly did in fact write *Who is the Arian?*) *Who is the Arian?* is a quite well written but a very obscure pamphlet. The same cannot be said for 'Layman's' attack, which is largely invective. But the episode does show that in the late 1830s Gilly was a controversial and public figure in north-east England.

On 20 January 1839 Gilly preached a sermon at his former church of St Margaret Crossgate, based on Acts 16:9, called *The Cause of Missions, the Cause of God*, which was published in New York in March 1839. It is largely a plea for help for the Society for the Propagation of the Gospel. It was published in New York because an American, identified solely by his initials CF, heard the sermon, and was so impressed by it that he decided to publish it on his return home. The publisher's introduction states that 'In England the name of Dr Gilly is well known.'[94]

On 19 January 1839 Gilly was 50. The young priest keen to make a name for himself in the Anglican Church had matured into an experienced clergyman, fully aware of the miserable lives led by so many of his countrymen, and concerned to do his best to try and improve the living conditions of the common people. He was a forceful man, who was not liked by everybody, and as he aged he became more passionate, more topical and more controversial. Nationally, he was known for his work for the Waldensian Church. Politically he was a Conservative, and a stalwart defender of the national church, yet he was increasingly concerned about the conditions in which many of his fellow men and women lived, be they hinds of the Border, the beggars of Durham, the widows of the clergy or the peasants of the Waldensian valleys – and even in some circumstances Roman Catholics. He was never reluctant to speak his mind, and held views which were at times controversial. Several of his publica-

Durham Cathedral. Photo Meg Norman

tions had sold well and been reprinted, although his writings had attracted criticism because he appeared to have reached conclusions which were hardly justified by the facts: this was especially so for his beliefs about the Apostolic Succession.

---

94   W. S. Gilly, *The Cause of Missions, the Cause of God*, New York, Swords, Stanford & Co, 1839.

Chapter 10

Trinity College, Torre Pellice: Waldensian affairs, 1830–39

Throughout the 1830s Gilly remained very active in Waldensian affairs, and much was achieved in difficult circumstances. During the decade he persuaded the Waldensian Church to introduce a new liturgy; he inspired, and largely financed, the construction of the Waldensian College in Torre Pellice; and he assisted in raising educational and social standards throughout the valleys. Yet his only visit to Piedmont between the summer of 1829 and the spring of 1851 was in June 1837. The London Vaudois Committee met in most years, and he kept the Committee informed of developments. But the Committee was no longer the driving force, for thanks to Bishop Barrington's legacy to Anne Colberg, Gilly had an appreciable amount of money at his disposal. The achievements of these years were due to three factors.

First, the Waldensians realized the need for progress. A spirit of liberalism was gathering throughout Western Europe, to become in the 1840s a wind of change. In

France the revolution of 1830 overthrew the reactionary Charles X, and Louis Philippe, the 'Citizen King', sat on the throne. In Italy the kingdom of Sardinia, which then comprised Savoy, Genoa, Piedmont and the island of Sardinia, was the most respected of the Italian states, with an ancient, but quite progressive, monarchy. However, the Catholic Church remained very influential at the Sardinian court in Turin, and was considered to be reactionary by many liberals, of whom there were many in Italy at this time.

Second, Gilly had money to distribute, and he had firm links with the Waldensian moderator and the Tavola. During his visit to the valleys in 1829, he had spent much time talking to the pastors and had visited most of the villages. He did not try to interfere in local matters, such as choosing the

The Waldensian church in Torre Pellice

best location for the proposed new college. His objectives were to get a Waldensian college built, and a new liturgy introduced, which he wanted to be compatible with the Anglican liturgy. He tried to discourage links with the Calvinist training colleges in the republican cantons of Switzerland.

Third, and probably most important, there was Colonel Beckwith. Gilly might have become remote from the Waldensians were it not for Beckwith's presence in the valleys. They both believed that they had a mission to revive the Waldensian Church, and that this revived (and Anglicized) church would, in God's good time, be the catalyst for 'the pure Church of Christ to resume her seat in those Italian states, from which Pontifical intrigues have dislodged her'.[1] Little direct correspondence between the two men has survived. It is, however, evident that Gilly in England, and Beckwith in Piedmont, coordinated their activities closely throughout the 1830s, and this must have been mainly by letter. Each year Beckwith visited England for several months, when he stayed in London and sometimes travelled north to stay with Gilly at Norham.

Beckwith had considerable financial resources at his disposal, independent of Gilly. He was spending money in the valleys to build schools from the 1830s until his death in 1862. In later years he spent considerable amounts on churches and other projects, such as houses for the professors at the college. Beckwith's finances have not yet been unravelled: it has been suggested that the British Freemasons or even the British Secret Service may have had a hand in all his endeavours to build up Protestant institutions in Piedmont.[2] Certainly the State Archives in Turin show that the Sardinian government was keeping his activities under surveillance.[3] Beckwith always took care to avoid offending the Sardinian authorities, while the Waldensians themselves claimed to be loyal, but Protestant, subjects of the Sardinian Royal Family. Both Gilly and Beckwith were strong royalists: Gilly's adulation of George IV, surely one of the least praiseworthy of all British monarchs, has been commented on in earlier chapters.[4]

Although during the 1830s Beckwith and Gilly worked together, there were tensions between Beckwith and the Waldensian Tavola at the end of the decade. Both Gilly and Beckwith held that before the Reformation there had been Waldensian bishops who had maintained the precious remnant of the pure Church of Christ from biblical times. The Waldensians realized that their church needed reviving and they

1   W. S. Gilly, *Waldensian Researches during a second visit to the valleys of Piemont*, London, Rivington, 1831, p. 158.

2   Clare Pakenham, *General John Charles Beckwith: The Man behind the Myth*: Lecture to Waldensian 'Away Day', May 1998. Photocopy courtesy of the author.

3   Archivio di Stato di Torino, manuscript file *Eretico e Protestante*. This bulky file contains reports on the activities of Englishmen in the Protestant valleys. It also contains comments upon Gilly's *Narrative of an Excursion to the Mountains of Piedmont in the year 1823...*, notably that the book is factually incorrect in places – as Bracebridge pointed out in 1827. (See Chapter 3.)

4   See in particular Chapter 3. 'Never in modern times has a sovereign died so unlamented, nor the person of the monarch retained so little respect after death, as George IV': Steven Parissien, 'George IV and posterity', *History Today*, March 2001, pp. 9–16.

wanted help, but they had been Calvinists for over 250 years, and there was a long tradition of their ministers being trained at Geneva and Lausanne, which cities were in Calvinist and republican cantons of Switzerland.

At the end of the decade, Beckwith tried very hard to persuade the Waldensians to appoint their Moderator for life. They could see no great difference between a 'moderator for life' and a bishop, and so refused to make the change.[5] Beckwith, in a mood of frustration, went to live in England between the autumn of 1839 and October 1841.

Gilly was more diplomatic. He tried very hard to wean the Waldensian Church from its Calvinist traditions and to induce it to adopt some episcopalian practices. This theme can be observed in matters discussed in this chapter, including the naming of the new college, the reform of the liturgy, the attempts to stop students for the ministry being trained in Switzerland, and the saga of the three Waldensian students sent to the strongly Anglican University of Durham.

It is pertinent to consider what would have happened if the Scots rather than the English had been the first to establish close contacts with the Waldensians in the 1820s, for they too were Calvinists. But the Scottish Church had its own internal problems, which culminated in the Disruption of 1843, resulting in the formation of the Free Church of Scotland, an independent Scots Calvinist church which had great missionary zeal and soon did establish contact with the Waldensians. But if the Scots had preceded the English in establishing contacts with the Waldensians in the 1820s, they too would have found much in need of reform. For the Waldensians had a relaxed view of the Lord's Day, and indeed played games on their Sunday rest-day. Unlike the Scots, they did not regard the Sabbath as a day of abstention from 'worldly' pleasures, turning it, in some eyes at least, into a 'day of gloom'.[6] This laxity also offended Gilly, of course, though his idea of Sabbath observance was possibly not quite so strict as the Scottish one.[7]

---

5   This hinges largely on the difference between the Anglican concept of three degrees of *ordained* ministry – bishop, priest and deacon – inherited from the pre-Reformation church, while the Reformed churches recognized only one, variously called minister, pastor, etc., though they have other forms of ministry – elders, deacons, etc.

6   See Chapter 12 for Gilly's concern about Scots contacts with the Waldensians from the early 1840s. In 1842 the Rev. Robert Stewart, a minister of the Free Church of Scotland, was horrified when he discovered that on Sundays 'After the services of the morning, the Sabbath is converted into a day of amusement … they may be seen congregating in groups, singing, dancing and pursuing their other favourite pastimes, as though the day were their own.' R.W. Stewart, 'On the present condition and future prospects of the Waldensian Church', in *Lectures on Foreign Churches delivered in May 1845 in connection with the objects of the Committee of the Free Church of Scotland on the state of Christian Churches on the Continent and in the East.* Edinburgh, 1845, pp 205–68.

7   See e.g. Gilly, *Narrative* (1824), p. 11. Again, a theological difference is at work here. The Waldensians were interpreting Exodus 20: 8–11 literally (and probably as intended): 'you shall not do any work'. The Scots (and indeed most Anglicans at this time) took the end of verse 11 ('therefore the Lord blessed the sabbath day and consecrated it') and interpreted 'consecrated' to mean that only religious activities were permissible. (Quotations from the *New Revised Standard Version*.) This also overlooks Jesus's own statement, 'the Sabbath was made for man, not man for the Sabbath'.

William Beattie's visit

The Waldensian valleys are picturesque, although the scenery does not have the grandeur of the high Alps. The few large villages, such as Bobbio Pellice, lie in the bottom of these valleys, while many of the small hamlets, where peasants and cattle lived in close proximity, were on steep hillsides. Most peasants still wore their traditional costumes, and thus to British visitors they conformed to the romantic image of the time. The Waldensians lived only 80 kilometres from Turin, so British travellers visited the valleys not infrequently. Most of these visitors would have read at least one of Gilly's books, and some carried sketchbooks – and some published their experiences.

One of these was William Beattie, MD. He visited the valleys, and also the nearby Protestant valleys of France, in 1836. When he returned to England, he published a large book about his travels entitled *The Waldenses or Protestant Valleys of Piedmont and Dauphiny, and the Ban de la Roche*.[8] The text is uninspiring, and much of it appears to be based on Gilly's books. But there are also seventy-three engravings in the book, which were drawn by William Henry Bartlett and William Brockedon from Beattie's sketches. They are very well drawn, and show the villages, the hamlets, the churches, and peasants engaged in everyday activities such as haymaking, tending their goats and going to church. This fine book is still keenly sought by collectors of engravings.

---

8   London, 1838. Beattie was a highly successful and well-connected physician, who was also a prolific author. See further P. B. Austin, 'Beattie, William (1793–1875)', rev. Patrick Wallis, *Oxford Dictionary of National Biography*, Oxford University Press, 2004 (www.oxforddnb.com/view/article/1833, accessed 27 June 2011).

One of the engravings from Beattie's book on the valleys

Launching a Protestant College in Piedmont: the Maison Brezzi

Gilly's second involvement in founding a college was, in the end, successful. In Durham he was frozen out of the process by the distrust of both Bishop van Mildert and Archdeacon Thorp. But in Piedmont, after many difficulties, he succeeded. The foundation of a Protestant college in an overwhelmingly Catholic state was no mean achievement, and Gilly is commemorated at the college in Torre Pellice as *Fondateur du Collège, Historien, Bienfaiteur et Ami des Vaudois.*[9]

The Waldensians knew nothing of Gilly's attempt to become involved in the foundation of Durham University, and there is no reason to believe that the rest of the Durham Chapter knew that he was founding a college in Piedmont. The two projects were however contemporaneous. It is very difficult to found a college at the best of times, as is evident from the early problems at the University of Durham. Where will it be built? How will the site be acquired? What will be taught? Who will provide the cash for both construction and maintenance? How will the students be selected? Where will the students live? How will existing institutions be affected? Who will draw up the plans? What permissions are needed? How will the college be governed? Where will the lecturers live? Which language(s) will be used? Who will pay the lecturers' salaries? How will the students be funded? What support facilities are needed? How is a library to be formed? And specific to Gilly's foundation, will Protestant books be allowed into an overwhelmingly Catholic country? Furthermore, the founder and sponsor was an Englishman, living 1,400 kilometres away in north-east England; the local language was a dialect of Piemontese; the Waldensian Church conducted its business in French; and the Sardinian state used choice Italian to conduct its affairs.

There was already a Latin school in the Luserna Valley which had been subsidised for many years by the Calvinist Dutch Waldensian Committee, which was suspicious of Gilly's intentions and refused to cooperate, stating that they preferred the existing system, whereby talented pupils from the Latin school went on to study at Geneva or Lausanne. Gilly accepted that he would have to proceed without their help.[10]

Gilly had £5,000 (125,000 Sardinian francs) available to fund the new institution. To the Waldensians this was a great deal of money, but Gilly's funds were limited. He wisely stayed out of the arguments about where the new college should be located; that decision he left to the Tavola. Delicate negotiations took place between protagonists for the San Martino valley, for San Giovanni and for Torre Pellice. Each community wanted the new institution to be located in its valley. On 1 March 1830, Gilly wrote to Pastor Rostaing, the moderator:

> ... Il faut accepter le local qui pourrait être de plus grand convenance pour toute la population Vaudois. ... Mais je laisse cela a vôtre choix. ...[11]

---

9   Plaque, first floor of college building at Torre Pellice.
10   ASTV, series V, vol. 34, c. 282, letter, Gilly to Rostaing, 14 December, 1829.
11   ASTV, series V, vol. 34, c. 382, letter, Gilly to Rostaing, 1March 1830 (trans. NWG).

[It is necessary to accept the locality which can be of the greatest convenience to the whole Vaudois population .... But I leave that to your choice.]

By mid-1830 he was becoming impatient at the failure of the Tavola to decide a location. On 30 June 1830 he wrote to Pastor Rostaing:

Si les Vaudois ne peuvent pas l'accepter par le rivalité, qui regne parmi leurs communs il faut le donner une nouvelle destination et les consigner à la cause Protestante ailleurs.[12]

[If the Waldensians cannot accept it [i.e. the money], on account of the rivalry which exists between their communities, it will be necessary to give it a new destination and consign it to the Protestant cause elsewhere.]

This was no empty threat, for Southey had already published his essay referring to 'an excellent lady' willing to contribute to the funding of a new college in northern England.[13]

1830 was a difficult year for the Waldensians. The troubles in San Giovanni had been publicized throughout Europe,[14] and now the different parishes were quarrelling about where the new college should be located. However, in September 1830, a suitable building for a temporary college was found in Torre Pellice: the Maison Brezzi, which still stands in the centre of the town. Gilly accepted the choice 'si l'édifice est solide et stable'. He sent 5,000 francs so that the building could be repaired and fitted up for teaching.[15]

On 15 November 1830 Gilly sent Pastor Rostaing 'une liste des réglements que je crois d'être indispensibles au bien être du college'. Regulation No. 9 read:

L'Instruction Religieuse sera parfaitement conformée a l'ancien Catechisme, au formulaire de la doctrine Vaudois datté de l'an 1100, et à la confession de foi, et la Manifeste publiée de l'an 1655, et ces formulaires seront les fondement d'un Cours Annuel de la Theòlogie par le principal Professeur de l'Establissement.[16]

[Religious instruction shall conform completely to the ancient Catechism, to the Waldensian doctrinal formulary dating from the year 1100, and to the confession of faith, and to the manifesto, published in 1655, and these formularies shall be the foundation of an Annual Course of Theology by the principal teacher of the Establishment.]

So Gilly had a major part in drafting the regulations for the new institution. But these regulations would be based on *his* interpretation of ancient Waldensian practices, rather than on the Calvinist forms which had been used since the middle of the

---

12   ASTV, series V, vol. 34, c. 361, letter, Gilly to Rostaing, 30 June 1830.
13   *Quarterly Review*, April 1829. See page 108.
14   See Chapter 7.
15   ASTV, series V, vol. 34, c. 348, letter, Gilly to Rostaing, 6 September 1830.
16   ASTV, series V, vol. 34, c. 341, letter, Gilly to Rostaing, 15 November 1830.

seventeenth century. This of course left open the question exactly what the ancient forms had been.

From 1830 onwards Gilly did his best to weaken links between the Waldensians and the Calvinist colleges in Geneva and Lausanne. But he was not opposed to links with the Swiss canton of Neuchatel, for although Calvinist, it was a monarchy under the king of Prussia until 1848 and included prayers for the king in the liturgy.[17] In the early 1840s he was very upset when he discovered that the Waldensians were in touch with the strongly Calvinist Free Church of Scotland.[18] Again we see the two persistent patterns in all the works of both Gilly and Beckwith for the Waldensians: first, to discourage Calvinism, and second, to encourage episcopalianism on the Anglican model.

On 1 March 1831 the new College opened at the Maison Brezzi in Torre Pellice under the name of *L'Ecole Supérieure*.[19] In order to forestall objections by the Sardinian government, Catholics were not permitted to enrol. However, when the news reached the Sardinian Minister of the Interior in Turin, he promptly sent the Intendant of the province to shut the college down,[20] upon which the Waldensians cited their ancient privileges regarding freedom of religion within their ancient limits.[21] A compromise was reached on 27 May 1831, probably after the intervention of the Prussian ambassador in Turin.[22] So the new institution was allowed to open, still at the Maison Brezzi, subject to the number of students in the first class being no more than fifteen, and the right of the Intendant to examine all the text books and to veto any staff appointments considered unsuitable. The Intendant of the province was also appointed as a Visitor, to ensure that nothing was taught which could be seen as subversive to the Catholic religion or the Sardinian state.[23] So by mid-1831 Gilly had succeeded in establishing a small Protestant teaching institution, albeit in temporary accommodation, at Torre Pellice.

House of Commons debate, 1832

Since its inception in 1825, the London Vaudois Committee had consisted of bishops, peers, gentlemen and politicians, all of whom were Anglican. Amongst the latter was Sir Robert Inglis, a country gentleman and barrister, who sat in the House of

---

17 'Nous te prions aussi pour les puissances superieures, & en particulier pour le Roi notre souverain Seigneur …' [We pray also for the superior powers, and in particular for our sovereign Lord the King …] La Liturgie ou la manière de célébrer le Service Divin, qui est établié dans les Eglises de la Principauté de Neuchâtel et Valangin, Neuchâtel 1789; and still in use in 1830. The Swiss canton of Neuchâtel did not free itself from the Prussian king until the local revolution of 1848.

18 See Chapter 12.

19 W. S. Gilly, 'Education among the Waldenses', *Quarterly Journal of Education,* vol. II, July–Oct 1831, pp. 201–15; p. 212.

20 Gilly, 'Education among the Waldenses', p. 214.

21 Gilly, 'Education among the Waldenses', p. 215.

22 Gilly, 'Education among the Waldenses', p. 215.

23 Gilly, 'Education among the Waldenses', p. 215.

Commons as MP for Oxford University. He was a much respected and very able Tory politician, well known for his distrust of Roman Catholicism. On 24 January 1832 Sir Robert initiated a short debate on the Waldensians in the House of Commons. He gave a detailed account of Waldensian history, praised Gilly's work in the valleys, lamented the restrictions imposed on the Waldensians, and asked for British government help to ameliorate their grievances. Sir Robert's motion was seconded by David O'Connell, the leader of the Irish Nationalists and a Roman Catholic. Viscount Palmerston, the Foreign Secretary, assured Sir Robert that the British government would 'exert every interference that it could legitimately employ, for the protection of the Waldensians from ill usage or persecution'.[24] (Palmerston's use of the word 'interference' seems odd in the context of this debate, as he went on to say that he knew of no evidence of 'any injury being suffered by these people at present', but the word is a standard nineteenth-century diplomatic usage, especially in relation to affairs in other countries.)

Reforming the liturgy

The Waldensian liturgical reforms of the early 1830s were largely inspired by Gilly, but not organized by him, and culminated in the new Waldensian liturgy of 1837. The Tavola knew that a reformed liturgy was needed, as different liturgies were used in the various parishes. In the 1820s six parishes used the Neuchâtel liturgy, seven parishes used the Geneva liturgy, and two parishes used the Lausanne liturgy.[25] Since the seventeenth century, French had been the language of church services and administration. The local dialects differed between the San Martino and Luserna valleys, and there was still no standardized Italian language or unified Italian state. So it seemed sensible to retain French, which was understood by most local people, for church services. The Waldensian synod set up a commission for the reform of the liturgy. On 28 November 1829 Gilly wrote to the moderator: 'Je suis charmé d'entendre que cette affair ne peut souffrir aucun difficulté.'[26]

Gilly did not attempt to supervise the preparation of this new liturgy. The format that resulted from the lengthy deliberations of the commission remained basically Calvinist, but there are Anglican influences in the wording.[27] There is the following prayer for the Sardinian king and the royal family:

Souverain Maître du mond, Toi qui fais la destinée des nations, nous te prions pour tous les Rois, les Princes, et les Seigneurs à qui tu as confié le gouvernement des peuples et l'administration de la justice. Nous t'adressons particulièrement nos vœux pour le Roi *N.*, nôtre

---

24   The debate is to be found at Hansard, HC Deb 24 January 1832, vol 9 cc799–808. (Available online at http://hansard.millbanksystems.com/commons/1832/jan/24/the-vaudois. Accessed 28 May 2013.)

25   Gilly, *Researches*, p 229.

26   ASTV, series V, vol. 34, c. 290, letter, Gilly to Rostaing, 28 Nov 1829 ('I am delighted to hear that this affair can suffer no difficulty' – trans. NWG).

27   *La Liturgie Vaudoise, ou la manière de célébrer Le Service Divin, comme elle est établie dans les Eglises Evangéliques des Vallées du Piemont.* Edinburgh, 1837.

auguste Souverain, et pour toute la famille royale; répands sur eux tes bénédictions; dirige leurs vues et leurs enterprises, et fais que sous le regne de S[a] M[ajesté] nous puissions te servir librement, dans la paix et la prosperité.[28]

[Sovereign Master of the world, who settest the destinies of the nations, we pray to thee for all kings, princes, and lords to whom thou hast committed the government of the peoples and the administration of justice. We address our prayers to thee especially for King *N* our noble sovereign, and for all the royal family; pour out thy blessing upon them; direct their thoughts and their enterprises, and grant that under the reign of his Majesty we may serve thee freely, in peace and in prosperity.]

This may be compared with the second Collect for the Sovereign at Holy Communion in the 1662 Book of Common Prayer:

Almighty and everlasting God, we are taught by thy holy word that the hearts of kings are in thy rule and governance, and that thou dost dispose and turn them as it seemeth best to thy godly wisdom: we humbly beseech thee so to dispose and govern the heart of *N* thy servant, our King and Governor, that in all his thoughts, words, and works, he may ever seek thy honour and glory, and study to preserve thy people committed to his charge, in wealth, peace, and godliness: grant this, O merciful Father, for thy dear Son's sake …[29]

Gilly tried to steer the commission away from the liturgies used in the republican Swiss cantons of Geneva and Vaud towards the liturgy used in the Calvinist Swiss canton of Neuchâtel, which he believed to be in many ways akin to the Anglican liturgy. Certainly *La Liturgie de la Sépulture des Morts* is a very close parallel to the BCP *The Burial of the Dead* (see Table 10.1). The Lord's Supper, on the other hand, not surprisingly bears no relation to the Anglican liturgy at all.

Gilly arranged for the new liturgy to be printed in Edinburgh in 1837, and met most of the printing costs himself. The work was done by Andrew Shortrede, a well-established printing firm of that city. (The fact that it was printed in Edinburgh has no theological significance: the Scottish capital had a long-established tradition of printing, and it is the nearest large town to Norham.) The result was an imposing volume suitable for use in church, bound in sheepskin, gilt, and with the façade of a church embossed on the front cover. The 1837 *Liturgie* was designed for church use. A smaller version, for family use, was printed in Lausanne in 1842.[30]

Building the college

On 27 May 1834 the Tavola decided to proceed with the construction of a new college at Torre Pellice.[31] The foundation stone was laid on 12 August 1835 by M.

---

28   *La Liturgie Vaudoise*, p. 3 (trans. NWG. I have attempted to be as close as possible to the original, while at the same time using or echoing parallel phrases from the BCP).
29   Other parallels are to be found in the various prayers for the sovereign in the Accession Service.
30   *La Liturgie Vaudois … etc;* Par ordre du Synode, Lausanne, 1842.
31   J. P. Meille, *General Beckwith: His Life and Labours among the Waldenses of Piedmont*, T. Nelson, 1873, p. 82.

Table 10.1 Relationship between the Book of Common Prayer, 1662 and La Liturgie Vaudoise, 1842

Book of Common Prayer,	La Liturgie Vaudoise
Sentences:	
I am the Resurrection…	Je suis la résurrection …
I know that my Redeemer …	Je sais que mon rédempteur …
We brought nothing into this world …	Nous n'avons rien apporté …
Psalms 39, 90.	*Psalms* 39, 90, 6, 23, 38, 51, 102, 130, 143
Reading: I Corinthians 15, 20-end	*Reading*: I Corinthians 15, 20–end
Antiphon: Man that is born of a woman	
Prayer: Forasmuch as it hath pleased Almighty God …	
Antiphon: I heard voice from heaven saying …	
Lord have mercy …	
Our Father …	
Prayer: Almighty God, with whom do live the spirits of them that depart hence …	
Collect: O Merciful God, father of our Lord Jesus Christ, who is the resurrection and the life …	*Prayer*: O Dieu, très-miséricordieux, père de nôtre Seigneur Jésus-Christ, qui est la résurrection et la vie …
Our Father …	
Grace	*Grace*

Bonjour, the Moderator.[32] The site chosen was an open one at the western end of the small town. The building, a solid one which still stands, was designed by M. Roland, a surveyor, and the building work was entrusted to M. E. Gastaldi.

On 23 February 1835 Gilly wrote to the moderator:

> Permittez moi de vous suggester, que le nom le plus convenable a la nouvelle Institution serait 'Le Collège de la Sainte Trinité'. Le Titre marquera la caractère de l'etablissement – le rendra plus respectable aux yeux de vos voisins de la église Romaine, et de Christiens Etrangers, et il servera d'attester l'adhérence des Eglises Vaudois aujourd'hui à la Foi de leurs Ancêtres.[33]

> [Allow me to suggest to you, that the most suitable name for the new Institution would be 'The College of the Holy Trinity'. That title will indicate the character of the establishment – and will render it most respectable in the eyes of your neighbours of the Roman

---

32   Meille, *General Beckwith*, p. 82. There is a carved Latin inscription in the basement of the building recording the event.

33   ASTV, series V, vol. 35, c. 280, letter, Gilly to Bonjour, 23 February 1835 (trans. NWG. 'Christiens' is more usually 'Chrétiens').

Church, and of foreign Christians, and it will serve to attest the adherence of the Waldensian Churches [*sic*] today to the Faith of their ancestors.]

The name of the college was important: the Kingdom of the Two Sicilies and the Roman Catholic Church would think twice before objecting to an institution called the College of the Holy Trinity. It was hardly a Calvinist name,[34] but, of course, the majority of the costs were not being borne by Calvinist sources, most of the money needed for the new building being provided by Gilly. He sent 100,000 francs (£4,000), plus some additional money for maintenance; an additional 25,000 francs was raised by contributions from the different Waldensian parishes and from collections; and Colonel Beckwith made a contribution, as did the Waldensians living in Turin.[35] Gilly had made a substantial contribution, but the college was not a gift from him: the Waldensians themselves raised substantial sums.

Colonel Beckwith was closely involved in the design and construction of the college. In July 1835 he was in England, when he discussed progress with Gilly. He returned to Torre Pellice in the autumn of that year, and henceforth he appears to have taken control of the construction of the college, paying particular attention to the building of the library.[36] Gilly arranged for suitable books to be sent from England. He took care that none should be sent which could offend the censors when they passed through the Sardinian customs upon arrival at the port of Genoa.[37]

Initially the college was a modest institution, and indeed, despite being housed in an imposing building, it taught little more than had been taught at the Maison Brezzi. There were only two lecturers, and the college failed to attract the number of students that had been hoped for. On 10 December 1835, Gilly wrote to the moderator, 'La diminution du nombre des étudiants me fait la peine.'[38] In the summer of 1836 he sent 130 books for the college library, including *Sermons of English Divines*,[39] nine copies of the bishop of Chester's *Works*,[40] and a technical book on silk manufacturing. On 9 December 1836 he wrote to M. Bonjour, the Moderator, stating that he proposed to visit the valleys in 1837.[41]

---

34 Equally it was not a 'Romish' one either, which have might been the objection if a saint were named. Many new Anglican churches founded at this time were called 'Trinity' or 'Christ Church'. Both Oxford and Cambridge have a Trinity College, and Dublin's only college is Trinity. Durham, interestingly, does not have one.

35 Meille, *General Beckwith*, p. 38.

36 Meille, *General Beckwith*, p. 88.

37 CUL, Manuscript file Add. 2612, *Correspondence relating to the Library at La Tour*, 1838–1855. This is an important record, for it contains informal letters from Gilly to his friend the Rev. R. Potts of Trinity College, Cambridge. The file also contains reference to the Waldensian boys sent to Durham in the late 1830s and the 'Waldensian crisis' of the early 1840s (see pp. 186 ff).

38 ASTV, series V, vol. 35, c. 399, letter, Gilly to Bonjour, 10 December 1835 ('The reduction in the number of students pains me').

39 Possibly J. Brown (ed.), *The Evangelical Preacher; or, a Select collection of doctrinal and practical sermons, chiefly by English divines of the eighteenth century, etc*; 3 vols, Edinburgh, 1802–06.

40 It is unclear which Bishop of Chester this is: possibly G. H. Law (Bishop 1812–24); C. J. Blomfield (1824–28); or J. B. Sumner (1828–48). Sumner was also a member of the Durham Chapter.

41 ASTV, series V, vol. 36, c. 116, letter, Gilly to Bonjour, 9 December 1836.

William Palmer's visit to the valleys

Gilly's visit was preceded by that of a rather odd Englishman, William Palmer. Palmer was a very advanced high church Anglican, only 25 years old at the time of his visit. He was a fellow of Magdalen College, Oxford,[42] and had been the first classical tutor at the University of Durham between 1833 and 1836, where he knew Gilly. He was widely recognized in his

The Waldensian Centre in Torre Pellice. Photo by Jan Szturc (via Wikimedia Commons)

own time as a learned, if controversial, Anglo-Catholic theologian, who published extensively about Russia and the Levant, and during the early 1840s had attempted (but failed) to establish better formal relations between Anglicans and the Russian Orthodox Church. After considering conversion to both Russian and then Greek Orthodoxy, in 1855 he was received into the Roman Church, and went to live Rome, where he died in 1879.

Palmer kept a detailed diary, in French, of his visit and the many conversations he had with Waldensian pastors, Catholic priests and friars, and the Bishop of Pinerolo. Palmer was in Torre Pellice while the Waldensian College was being constructed, and his diary provides an intriguing picture of the personalities of the time. On 10 June 1836 Gilly wrote to Pastor Bonjour, the Moderator, anticipating Palmer's visit, and describing him as 'C'est un jeune homme très instruit – tant soit peu opiniâtré mais la conversation malgré cela vous fera plaisir.'[43]

Palmer was, like Gilly, fascinated by the Waldensians, and admired their fortitude and steadfastness. However three years later, on 15 November 1839, he wrote to Gilly about the Waldensians:

> Now they are, I suppose, either the descendants of heretics or of persons first instructed by heretics …. I think the first step for the Vaudois to take towards legitimately gaining or recovering a place in the visible Catholic Church is, clearly, to seek the communion of the bishops in whose sees they are.[44]

So Palmer clearly did not accept Gilly's hypothesis of the Waldensians as the non-Roman conduit of Apostolic Succession: the word 'heretic' here implies

---

42 He is usually known as 'William Palmer of Magdalen', to distinguish him from his Oxonian contemporary, 'William Palmer of Worcester [College].' See further Leon Litvack, 'Palmer, William', *Oxford Dictionary of National Biography*, Oxford University Press, 2004 (www.oxforddnb.com/view/article/21224, accessed 28 June 2011).

43 ASTV, series V, vol. 36, c. 51, letter, Gilly to Bonjour, 10 June 1836. ('He is an educated young man, albeit rather obstinate, but despite that his conversation will appeal to you.')

44 *Journal of William Palmer.* LPL, Palmer Papers, No. 2816.

Protestant or Reformed doctrines, and he advocated that the Waldensians should put themselves under the spiritual authority of the Bishop of Pinerolo. Anyone who knew anything about Waldensian history would have known that this was impossible, but Palmer was concerned with restoring the outward and visible unity of all the branches of the church, and for him this meant the various Protestant and Reformed denominations reuniting with Rome – or possibly with the Orthodox, but his experiences with them a few years later were to leave him less sanguine about that.

Gilly's visit to the Waldensian valleys, June 1837

This was Gilly's only visit to the Waldensian valleys between 1829 and 1851. Although he was well known in England for his work for the Waldensians, and he had had considerable influence in the valleys for over thirty years, between 1823 and 1851 he made only three visits there, so to many Waldensians he must have seemed a remote, if benevolent, figure.

On 1 May 1837 Gilly wrote to Pastor Bonjour setting out his plans for the visit. He was to travel with his family: there were seven in the party, including Mary Shields, the family governess. The party would leave England on 1 June 1837 and sail to Rotterdam, and then proceed to Wiesbaden, so that Gilly's 21-year-old daughter Mary Anna, who was in delicate health, could drink the waters. They would then travel to Torre Pellice, where they would stay at the Coron d'or, as Gilly felt it would be very difficult for any of the pastors to accommodate such a large party.[45]

He also arranged for London agents to send over 200 books for the library at the new College, including twenty-five copies of the new Waldensian liturgy which had just been published in Edinburgh. Also included were *Sermons* by John Henry Newman,[46] and twenty-eight volumes of *Tracts for the Times*.[47] The choice of these books for the library seems odd at first sight, but the earlier tracts protested against the claims of Rome to be the sole repository of truth, and also tried to show that the Church of England was a branch of the true Catholic Church; several were reprints of earlier works by Anglican divines of the seventeenth and eighteenth centuries. This teaching would be acceptable to Gilly, although he, along with many other 'orthodox high churchmen', was later to express his disapproval of the 'Romanizing' tendency of the Tractarians and their successors. It was the later tracts, notably numbers 80 and 87 ('On reserve in communicating religious knowledge') and 90 ('Remarks on certain passages in the Thirty-nine Articles'), that caused outrage, and brought the series to an abrupt end.

There is no detailed record of this, Gilly's third visit to the valleys. There were discussions about the liturgy, the future of the college, and Gilly's hopes that the

---

45 ASTV, series V, vol. 36, c. 175, letter, Gilly to Bonjour, 1 May 1837.

46 *Parochial and Plain Sermons*, vol. 1, published 1834; all others were published too late. (There were eight volumes altogether.) Newman was not received into the Roman Church until 1845.

47 There were to be ninety tracts in all by 1837, of which seventy-seven had been published by the end of 1836. As some were mere pamphlets of four pages, it may be that the twenty-eight 'volumes' included all seventy-seven bound up as one volume.

Waldensians would become less Calvinist and more akin to the Anglican Church. He almost certainly held discussions with Colonel Beckwith. He submitted a one-page report on his visit to the meeting of the London Vaudois Committee held, twenty months later, on 8 March 1839, when he reported upon the completion of the College of the Holy Trinity, the introduction of the new liturgy, and the educational work being carried out in the valleys by Colonel Beckwith.

The party returned to England via Switzerland and France. They spent three days in Geneva, and one in Lausanne, where Gilly held discussions with the professors of the Calvinist College about the Waldensian students studying there. He was of course hoping that the links between the Waldensians and the Calvinists in republican Swiss cantons would be weakened, and if possible severed, for he had other plans in mind for the overseas training of the Waldensian students. From Lausanne the party travelled to Paris, and returned to Durham after a stay with Gilly's aged father at Wanstead.[48] This was the last Gilly saw of his father, who died on 23 November 1837, aged 75. He is buried at Wanstead Church and commemorated by memorials in both Wanstead and Hawkedon churches.

Controversies: 1838

In October 1837 the *Dublin Review*, a Roman Catholic magazine, published a thirty-five-page attack on the Waldensians in general and Gilly in particular. This article was mainly based on a book published in Paris in 1836, entitled *Récherches Historiques sur la Véritable Origine des Vaudois et sur le Caractère de Leurs Doctrines Primitives*. Although it was anonymous, it is known that André Charvaz, the Bishop of Pinerolo, wrote it. The *Dublin Review* article was polemical, and accused the Waldensians of causing 'confusion and havoc' and fomenting 'constant rebellions'.[49] Gilly's habit of publishing historical defences of the Waldensians was the subject of a sarcastic paragraph:

> Enter the library of the British Museum – you will see them there each with his quire of foolscap spread before him, and at his elbow a host of works penned and published on his side of the question years ago, but now dead and forgotten; biographical dictionaries and encyclopaediae complete his munition. From these he is culling, with all the spirit of penmanship, whole passages of a length so formidable, that in a few days he has obtained almost sufficient matter for his single duodecimo volume, hot-pressed, and quite enough to authorize his publisher to announce the approaching appearance of a new work on the Vaudois, or on the Albigenses, or on the Culdees, or whatever else the subject may chance to be. That any such will take the trouble to peruse our pages, – or, perusing them, will have the candour to abate their foregone conclusions, – at least, until they have made the experience of a more

---

48   ASTV, series V, vol. 36, c. 200, letter, Gilly to Bonjour, 7 July 1837.
49   *Dublin Review*, vol. III, October 1837, pp. 357, 358. It forms part of a review (Article III, pp 325–59) of four books on the Waldensians. The *Review* (not to be confused with the current literary magazine the *Dublin Review*) was a Roman Catholic periodical; it was founded by Michael Quin, Nicholas, Cardinal Wiseman and Daniel O'Connell. Published in London (the title 'Dublin' was chosen as the city was regarded as a centre of Roman Catholic culture), it ceased in 1969.

careful search into authorities, – we cannot hope. Our purpose is not with them, but with their readers. If we shall have been the means of putting them in possession of a more honest and unglossed account of the state of the Vaudois question, than they are likely to derive from the shallow pages of English polemics, or of pointing to those sources of information whence a purer truth may be imbibed, than their Gillys will supply them with.

This public and personal attack on Gilly succeeded in shaking him out of his normal equanimity. It was a far cry from the witty criticisms of Gilly's 'Waldensian hobby' which Father James Wheeler had made in 1835. Gilly reacted. He wrote two long open letters to Lord Durham which were published in the *Globe* daily evening newspaper on 25 November and 11 December 1837. These letters were reprinted in a large single-page pamphlet entitled *Tender Mercies of the Papists*. Gilly signed them with the pseudonym '*Sanctae Theologiae Professor*'. Lord Durham, who between 1813 and 1828 had been MP for County Durham, had recently made a speech in Durham City in which he had advocated full civil rights for English Catholics. Gilly quoted extracts from *The Dublin Review* article. He continued:

> Such, my Lord, are the sentiments and language of a publication, which is considered to be the mouth-piece of the Roman Catholics of Great Britain and Ireland. ... a new Sardinian code comes into force in January next, which will absolutely expose the Vaudois to the severalties exercised against them in the persecuting times, unless certain unrescinded edicts of the ancient Dukes of Savoy shall be formally repealed. ... I have laid before you the unworthy invectives which they have employed to bring a defenceless and unoffending community of Protestants into contempt and hatred, at a time when it greatly stands in need of sympathy and kindness.

Gilly's two letters published in the *Globe* were not as polemical as the attack that had been made against him, but they do show that he was very upset. He also started work on a new book about the Waldensians. There is no evidence that this book was ever published, but nonetheless 103 pages of proofs were printed and the only copy that is known to have survived is corrected in Gilly's hand.[50] In this book he set out his purpose in writing as follows:

> I depart from the rule I had laid down for myself, and I appear as a polemic when it was my wish to reserve myself for the calmer duties of the Historian. But time and investigation –will continue to enlarge my qualifications for the task – and I do not regret the present interruption.[51]

---

50   There is no title page: HN quotes it as *Present State of the Waldenses*, deduced from the heading of Chapter 1. The author's name is not stated, nor a date. The only known copy of this untitled publication is the book of various Waldensian-related items bound together, in Cambridge University Library, CUL Syn.6.84.52. It contains nine items: 'The Waldenses or Vaudois, Protestants of Piedmont', statement by the London Committee (1826); Catalogues of ancient Waldensian MSS (18–); Bible extracts in French and Vaudois; two articles on the poems of the Poor of Lyons by A Herbert (1841); *The Crown or the Tiara?* (1842); Statement of the grievances of the Waldensians (1843); an edition of *La Noble Leyçon*, possibly by WSG (18–); *Tender Mercies of the Papists* (183–).

51   *Present State of the Waldenses*, p. 3.

The book is a defence of both the Waldensians and their king:

> Charles Albert, himself, the reigning master of the Vaudois, has testified his opinion of their good conduct, by numberless acts of equity and benevolence. His heart yearns towards them with paternal affection, and his hand is open upon all occasions when appeals are made to his private generosity.[52]

To Gilly the villains were clearly in the Catholic hierarchy in Piedmont, and the king was absolved from all blame. He followed his praise for the Sardinian King:

> If the Temporal Head of the Government had been less favourable to them, the Spiritual Authorities of Piedmont would at least have concealed their increasing envy; but now such a tempest is impending over the Church of the Waldenses, as has not darkened upon it for a century and a half.[53]

He accused the Bishop of Pinerolo of having 'raked up every calumny ... to injure these Mountaineers'.[54] In the greater part of this work, Gilly reverted to his role as an historian, but, as in previous publications, he was never an impartial one: for example, the Roman Catholics are described as 'the adherents of the Roman Apostasy'.[55] Gilly's belief in the continuous existence of a Protestant Church in Piedmont prior to 1200 AD is reiterated: 'We deny that the Protestants of Piedmont derive their origin from the Citizen of Lyons.'[56]

It is probably significant that the two letters to the *Globe* were published anonymously and that the longer work appears never to have been published. Both were written for British readers, and there is no evidence that the Waldensians themselves were concerned about a new wave of persecution in the years 1837 and 1838. Indeed, it must be remembered that a few years previously, the Sardinian government had permitted the erection of a Protestant college at Torre Pellice only 80 kilometres from the royal capital of Turin. The controversy of these years appears to have been largely between Anglicans and Roman Catholics in the British Isles: the matter was to flare up again in the 1840s.

Colonel Beckwith

Following the introduction of the new liturgy in 1837, Colonel Beckwith had been urging the Waldensians to appoint a Moderator for life, with no parish duties. Traditionally, the Moderator had been appointed by the synod for five years and selected alternately from the Luserna and San Martino valleys. Beckwith wanted the Waldensian Church to become 'An Episcopal Church with a Presbyterian constitution',[57]

---

52 *Present State of the Waldenses*, p. 6.
53 *Present State of the Waldenses*, p. 7.
54 *Present State of the Waldenses*, p. 7
55 *Present State of the Waldenses*, p. 19.
56 *Present State of the Waldenses*, p. 39: Gilly is maintaining that there was a Protestant church in Piedmont prior to 1200 AD, when Waldo ('the Citizen of Lyons') was active.
57 Meille, *General Beckwith*, p. 173, note. It is far from clear quite what Beckwith intended by this phrase:

but the Waldensians stuck to their Calvinist traditions. At the Synod of April 1839 nobody supported the proposal for a Moderator for life. Beckwith, obviously in a bad temper, wrote, 'All who remain to you are Dr Gilly and myself. Think what a burden we have to bear! … You are, in our eyes, anarchists and children of rebellion and schism.'[58]

But, although Gilly was being cited as Beckwith's supporter during this unfortunate argument, he seems to have taken no part in this dispute. His letters during the late 1830s are about the college, Waldensian students training overseas, sending funds, and his concerns about restrictions on the Waldensian community by the Sardinian government. It is quite possible that when Beckwith went to live in England between 1839 and 1841, Gilly had a calming effect on the (at that time) Colonel.[59] Beckwith was much loved by the Waldensians. His achievements were considerable, but he did on occasions hector their leaders. Gilly believed that more could be achieved by a quieter approach, but he too was quite prepared to lecture the Waldensians on occasions. However, on a fine day in October 1841, Beckwith's well-known post-chaise returned to Torre Pellice after an absence of two years. He was welcomed back by his many friends in the valleys.[60]

The Synod of 1839 and increasing problems

1839 and 1840 were difficult years. The new college in Torre Pellice suffered the same problems as had the University of Durham in its early years: it failed to attract sufficient students. Gilly was kept informed of developments through his correspondence with the moderator and by Colonel Beckwith. The Synod of the Waldensian Church, held between 23 and 25 April 1839, declared the unity of the church and the approval of the 1837 liturgy. The Synod resolved that all pastors must receive ordination in the valleys. On 10 June 1839, Gilly wrote from Norham to his friend Dr Robert Potts at Trinity College, Cambridge:

> Last week I had letters from the valleys, which reported the proceedings of the Synod, held in April. The Acts of Synod related principally to a new code of ecclesiastical discipline, which will place the Waldensian Church on a more respectable footing than she has held for 150 years. The pastors declared the unity of their church and the adoption of the new liturgy – the necessity of subscribing to the Confession of Faith of 1655, and of admitting none to officiate in their parishes but those who received orders at home. They would have advanced a step or two nearer to the Anglican Church but for the interference of the Popish Bishop of Pignerol [Pinerolo] who knows that every approach towards episcopal discipline will strengthen their cause – His intrigues therefore prevented their taking other measures which were in contemplation. You are to understand that the Vaudois cannot hold a Synod without the presence of the King's Commissioner who keeps them in check.

Presbyterianism and Episcopalianism are mutually contradictory church orders.
58   Meille, *General Beckwith*, pp. 169 and 171.
59   He was promoted to Colonel 1837, Major-General 1846.
60   Meille, *General Beckwith*, p. 172.

With an orthodox liturgy – and an orthodox confession of faith, the Waldensian Church is at the present crisis the most orthodox of all Presbyterian churches, and if we will go on discreetly, without noising abroad, the advantages we are gaining, we may yet see the little flock of the mountain side restored to episcopal government. With such feeble instruments it is wonderful to think what a strong and moral and religious affect has been produced within a few years.[61]

Gilly was sending money regularly for the upkeep of the college in Torre Pellice, but there were still only a few students: in the late summer of 1839 there were fewer than eight.[62] In December 1839 Gilly was alarmed to receive a letter from the Moderator telling him that a regulation had been introduced at the college stating that its aim was to educate young men to the stage where they could be admitted to study philosophy in other academies – which could only be abroad. He wrote indignantly to the Moderator:

Je désire de répéter encore ce que j'ai déjà dit bien fais. Le but du College n'est pas seulement de conduire les jeunes gens jusqu'à un certain point, et de s'arrêter là, mais le dernier et le plus important *but* de l'Institution est de fournir de tels moyens d'instruction dans les vallées qu'il ne soit plus absolument nécessaire pour les jeunes Vaudois d'aller aux Académies Etrangères pour finir leur Education … Si les Vaudois continuent d'envoyer leurs fils dans la Suisse, et de refuser de leur fournier la moitea des moyens de la seminarization, et de recevoir leur Education dans leur pays, le College deviendra pour la plupart inutile et les espérances du fondateur seront frustrées.[63]

[I desire to repeat again what I have already said better. The aim of the college is not solely to get the young people to a certain point, and to stop there, but the last and most important *goal* of the institution is to furnish such a means of instruction in the valleys that it should not be absolutely necessary any more for the young Vaudois to go to foreign academies to finish their education …. If the Waldensians continue to send their sons to Switzerland, and to refuse to furnish them with the means of training, and of receiving their education in their own country, the college will become for the most part useless and the hopes of the founder frustrated.]

The modest Waldensian revival of the 1830s and the building of the new college between 1835 and 1837 produced a Catholic response. Gilly believed that Carlo Alberto, the King of Sardinia, was an enlightened monarch, but that there were reactionary forces in his court at Turin. In January 1838 the Sardinian government introduced a new code of laws which, Gilly believed, 'would be fatal to the religious and civil liberties of the Waldenses'.[64] So he wrote to Lord Palmerston, the Foreign

61   CUL, MS Add 2612, letter, Gilly to Potts, 10 June 1839. Robert Potts (1802x4–1885) was a private tutor in the university. LL.D College of William & Mary ?1846. See further ODNB.

62   ASTV, series V, vol. 37, c. 309, letter, Gilly to Vinçon, 12 September 1839.

63   ASTV, series V, vol. 37, c. 395, letter, Gilly to Vinçon, 23 December 1839. ['Moitea' is questioned by HN; I have left it, but suspect it may be 'moitié' – NWG.]

64   Printed report of the London Vaudois Committee meeting held 8 March 1839.

Secretary, asking that the British government should intervene to protect Waldensian liberties. Lord Palmerston replied that the government would keep a careful watch on the situation.[65]

Gilly was becoming more concerned about what he considered to be threats to Waldensian liberties. On 2 August 1839 he wrote from Chester to Potts in Cambridge:

> I am now on a journey of business and I catch at a small interval of rest to confer with you on the subject of common interest. ... The priests and the Government are more zealous than ever of the Vaudois – and watch most carefully anything from England. – Books more than all things else excite their suspicion. – It is feared that a heavy blow impends – and that we shall ere long be alarmed for their very existence. Under these circumstances we must not send them a volume which will not be useful and unsuspected at this present moment.[66]

The scheme for sending Waldensian students to Durham

Gilly had persistently opposed the traditional practice of sending Waldensian youths for training at Calvinist seminaries in Geneva and Lausanne. On 14 July 1835 he told the London Vaudois Committee that this practice existed 'at the hazard of their religious principles'.[67] What Gilly really objected to was Swiss republican Calvinism. If the Waldensians could be persuaded to stop sending their sons for training in Calvinist and republican cantons of Switzerland, he and Beckwith reasoned, Calvinism would wither in the Waldensian valleys of Piedmont. However, Lausanne and Geneva were only 180 kilometres from the Waldensian valleys, the language of instruction at the colleges was French, and the climate on the Swiss Riviera was generally benign.

The College of the Holy Trinity at Torre Pellice was not yet able to provide theological instruction, and in any case the Sardinian government, which was watching the new institution closely, would be unlikely to give approval for a full-scale Protestant theological college only 80 kilometres from Turin. So Gilly devised an alternative training scheme: to send young men to the new Durham University, which was of course a firmly Anglican institution under the control of the Dean and Chapter of Durham. He discussed this proposal with the Tavola when he visited the Waldensian valleys in June 1837. The Tavola agreed to the scheme, particularly as Gilly and other Englishmen would be bearing all the costs. Three Waldensian boys were chosen, each of them the son of a Waldensian pastor: Henri Muston, Joseph Monastier and Charles Vinçon. They were aged 15, 13 and 12: presumably the theory was that adolescent boys would be less set in their ways than older students. Little thought seems to have been given to the 1,100 kilometres distance from the Waldensian valleys; the fact that Durham is cold, wet and dark for much of the year; and the language problems. Also, at that time, Durham was still an insanitary and overcrowded medieval city. The boys were too young to enter Durham University, so they were enrolled at Durham

---

65   Printed report of the London Vaudois Committee meeting held 8 March 1839.
66   CUL, MS Add 2612, letter, Gilly to Potts, 2 August 1839.
67   Printed report of London Vaudois Committee, 14 July 1835.

Grammar School with the intention that they should progress in due course to the university. On 19 June 1838 Gilly wrote to Potts:

> Your observation that the cause of the Waldensian Church has excited considerable interest at Cambridge encourages me to inform you that we are now proposing to educate a few Vaudois boys in England, under the belief that English instruction and example may be of service in preparing them for the Ministry. I have now three of the ages 15, 13 and 12 whom I am about to place in the Grammar School at Durham, and shall afterwards enter at Durham University, if they promise well and if the funds for their maintenance enable me to do so. I reckon that the expense of each will be about £60 a year – and I have suggested that five or six friends might undertake the cost of one. For example if six persons engaged to provide £10 each and to make up to £60 they can lighten the responsibility by taxing their acquaintances in small sums of £1 or £2. The promises which I have already received will not allow me to doubt that I shall be successful.[68]

It was arranged for Colonel Beckwith to accompany the boys to England. On 20 May 1838 he wrote a letter to the Tavola seeking formal authorization to deliver the boys to Dr Gilly in Durham.[69] Taking a 12-year-old child from his parents and sending him to a strange, cold, wet and dark city seems heartless when viewed from twenty-first-century perspectives, but Beckwith had left his parents to enter the army at the same age, and Gilly's brother had become a midshipman in the navy at the age of 13, while Gilly himself had been separated from his parents and put in the care of sadistic schoolmasters at the age of 10.

The party arrived safely in Durham, and Gilly arranged lodgings for the boys in Durham City at the house of Mrs Shields, the mother of the Gilly family governess. On 13 July 1838 Gilly wrote from Norham to the Moderator stating that the boys seemed happy, although Charles was a little homesick.[70]

Throughout 1839 Gilly wrote regularly to the Moderator reporting that the boys were doing quite well in their studies. Presumably they soon learned to speak both English and Geordie.[71] Although they did not live in his prebendal house during term times, they stayed with Gilly at Norham vicarage during much of their vacations. Gilly must have financed the three boys largely from his own funds, for one of the principal English benefactors withdrew in the spring of 1839.[72]

The London Vaudois Committee

Throughout the decade Gilly remained as secretary of the London Vaudois Committee which he had set up in 1825. The first treasurer was the Rev. Bewick Bridge; on his

---

68   Letter, Gilly to Potts, 19 June 1838. CUL MS Add. 2612.
69   ASSV, carte Beckwith, fasciolo 1, letter, Beckwith to Tavola, 20 May 1838.
70   ASTV, series V, vol. 37, c. 75, letter, Gilly to Bonjour, 13 June 1838.
71   Strictly not Geordie, as this applies only to the dialect used in Newcastle, Gateshead, and North and South Tyneside. The Durham dialect is properly called Pitmatic or Yakka. The confusion exists solely from a southern perspective. Pers. comm., Dr Paul Coxon, of Newcastle – NWG.
72   CUL MS Add 2612, letter, Gilly to Potts 10 June 1839 (dated from Norham).

death in 1833 Gilly took over as treasurer, and henceforth, until his own death in 1855, Gilly was both secretary and treasurer of the committee. In addition to his other duties, the treasurer collected the annual Royal Bounty of £277.1s.6d. from the Treasury, and forwarded it to the Waldensians in half-yearly sums of £138.10s.9d. each January and July. The role of the committee declined during the 1830s, but its reports and minutes provide a valuable record of Gilly's activities in helping the Waldensians during the decade.

William Howley, who as Bishop of London had played an important part in the early days of the committee, became Archbishop of Canterbury in 1828, and ceased to attend meetings, but remained interested in Waldensian affairs. The Bishop of Winchester, Charles Richard Sumner, took over as chairman.[73] The committee remained firmly Anglican. It included Henry Phillpotts, a Prebendary of Durham and Bishop of Exeter from 1831 to 1869.[74] He was notorious for having published a pamphlet in 1819 supporting government action after the Peterloo massacre.

Between 1830 and 1840 the committee met only eleven times.[75] Partly this was because the committee had served its purpose of drawing the attention of the British public to the Waldensians, but a more important factor was that Gilly no longer needed the committee. For, thanks to Bishop Barrington's will and Anne Colberg, he had money available, with complete discretion over how to use these funds. The accounts of the committee show that the amounts it remitted to Piedmont during the 1820s were modest. Subscriptions received were invested in government stock, and only the interest was sent to the Waldensians. At the meetings on 20 and 22 March 1830, Gilly reported that during the year £214 had been sent for ministers' stipends and £40 sent to the girls' school. Gilly reported to the same meeting that 'certain beneficial individuals whose names the secretary was not at liberty to divulge, were prepared to erect and endow a College at St Jean'.[76] The London Vaudois Committee was being bypassed.

The meeting of the committee on 19 July 1833 resolved to stop supporting

---

73   Bishop of Winchester 1827 to 1869.

74   Phillpotts had been a Prebendary of Durham from 1809 to 1820; he then held another prebend from 1831 in plurality with the See of Exeter in order to supplement the episcopal income, holding both until his death. He was a noted High Church controversialist, and is best known for a dispute with G. C. Goreham over baptismal regeneration. See further Arthur Burns, 'Phillpotts, Henry', *ODNB*, Oxford University Press, 2004; online edn, May 2006 (www.oxforddnb.com/view/article/22180, accessed 3 July 2011).

75   There were meetings of the London Vaudois Committee on 20 March 1830 (sub-committee), 22 March 1830, 3 June 1831, 19 May 1832, 13 June 1833 (sub-committee), 19 July 1833, 14 July 1835, 9 May 1836, 15 July 1837, 8 March 1839 and 16 May 1840. Attendance dwindled during the decade: only three members attended the meeting on 8 March 1839. Gilly was present at all the meetings except 1831. Beckwith was present in 1832 and 1835. The manuscript minutes of each meeting are extant. Printed reports are extant for the meetings on 19 July 1833, 14 July 1835, 9 May 1836, 8 March 1839 and 16 May 1840. Reports of the other meetings might have been printed, but if so, they have not yet been located. Prior to 1833 the only printed document of the committee as yet located is the letter to Lord Liverpool (the Prime Minister) of 11 March 1826, signed by Gilly as secretary of the committee, and as resolved by the committee on 8 March 1826.

76   LVC Minutes, 22 March 1857.

Waldensian students training at the Calvinist seminaries at Geneva and Lausanne. The same meeting noted that 'upon the whole, the prospects of the Waldensians are improving. The Sardinian Government appears to be more and more favourably disposed towards them.' There were no meetings of the committee between 18 July 1833 and 14 July 1835. The annual meetings held on 14 July 1835 and 8 May 1836 were sparsely attended, with only six members, including Colonel Beckwith who was in England at the time, attending the 1835 meeting. The Bishop of Winchester chaired the 1836 meeting, but only four other members attended, including Gilly. Gilly then informed the committee about progress in founding the college at Torre Pellice. It is significant that the committee was 'informed' of this important news: it had not taken the initiative in this vital step, as Gilly was now able to operate independently of it. The five members who attended the meeting on 15 July 1837 resolved 'that the thanks of the Committee be presented to Colonel Beckwith for his long continued and benevolent exertions in furtherance of the Institutions in which the Committee takes an interest, and particularly of those connected with the public and Religious Education of the Vaudois'.

The next meeting was on 8 March 1839. This time only three members attended, including Gilly, but a printed report was circulated in which Gilly reported on his visit to the Waldensian valleys in June 1837. At this meeting Gilly recorded his apprehensions about the new code of laws introduced throughout the Sardinian states which had come into force on 1 January 1838.

Gilly's dealings with the Waldensians at this time reveal him riding his 'Waldensian hobby' for all it was worth. Both he and Beckwith appear to exhibit the arrogance of the later nineteenth-century Anglican missionary, utterly convinced that their way was the only possible way. In Gilly's case, it was exacerbated by the fact that, despite all evidence to the contrary, he held unshakeably to his belief that there had been a non-Roman, yet Catholic, church in the Piedmont valleys since Apostolic times, and that its current Calvinist nature was a temporary aberration that could easily be rectified. It is interesting to see that the Waldensians went only so far in his direction, but no further. He also reveals himself at this time as one who preferred to work on his own, using institutions such as the committee only when it suited him. Whether he would have achieved as much as he did without the Barrington-Colberg money may be questioned. In all this, both he and Beckwith were driven by two desires: first, to weaken the links with Calvinism (and, coincidentally republicanism), and second, to introduce (reintroduce, from Gilly's point of view) an episcopal model of church order.

Chapter 11

Mendicity, sanitation and culture: Durham 1840–49

Gilly was very busy in north-east England during the 1840s. As he grew older, his pace of life did not flag, and he leaves the impression that he never entertained doubt in any area of his life. During this decade he organized and conducted simultaneously two major campaigns on very different fronts. The first was to help the hinds of Northumberland, and the second to protect the Waldensians from 'extermination'. Gilly's lasting reputation as an English social reformer is due to his endeavours to improve living conditions for the agricultural labourers of Northumberland. The second campaign is covered in the next chapter (where it will be argued that Gilly was, on that occasion, more than somewhat alarmist). He also found time to preach, to carry out research in mediaeval documents, to write books, to worry about the Irish famine, and to play a prominent part in the civic affairs of the magnificent but insalubrious city of Durham.

Family affairs

Gilly was a family man, and 9 College Green and Norham vicarage must have been quite noisy places at times: between March 1816 and his death in 1855 there was always a child aged 12 or under in the household. His eldest daughter, Mary Anna, who had been born in 1816, married Lewis Morgan in 1847. Rosalie Emily, born in 1820, married the 24-year-old Rev. Cuthbert John Carr nine days after her 21st birthday on 27 July 1841.[1] She went to live at Witton Gilbert, a village near Durham City, where her new husband was the Perpetual Curate.[2] Their eldest son, Cuthbert William Carr, was born on 28 August 1844,[3] and so Gilly had a grandson. Gilly's oldest son, William Octavius Shakespear, left Harrow School in 1840, when he was 18, and became a clerk in the Admiralty in London. So by this point all Gilly's first

---

1   HN has Rosalie married to *William* Carr, citing 'Memorial in Norham Church. Also Carr family tree held by her descendants in New Zealand', but this is incorrect. The Censuses show that she married *Cuthbert John* Carr (University of Durham, BA 1841, LTh, 1842, MA 1843, deacon 1842, priest 1843 – *Crockford's*), perpetual curate of Witton Gilbert from 1850 until his death in 1888. They had five children: Rosalie Isabella (b. 1843), Cuthbert William (b. 1844), Edgar (b. 1848), Mary (b. 1849) and Emily (b. 1851). The 1851 Census shows Carr as a widower and Emily as aged 4 months, so Rosalie must have died – probably in childbirth – in 1851. He later remarried.

2   It is unclear exactly what they did between 1841 and 1850: until 1842, Carr obviously remained at the university reading theology. He must have had an assistant curacy, but his entry in *Crockford's* does not give this information.

3   HN cites 'William Carr' from the same family tree, but the 1851 Census shows him as 'Cuthbert William'. He was presumably known by his middle name to differentiate him from his father.

family had left home, and between 1840 and the end of 1843 Frederick Dawson, born on 6 February 1831, was the only child in the household.

On 26 January 1844 Jane Gilly gave birth to Alice Anne, who was baptised in Durham Cathedral two days later.[4] In November 1845 Charles Pudsey was born, and he was baptised in the Cathedral on 30 November 1845.[5] The services of the governess, Mary Shields, who lived with the family, were still to be needed. Charles Pudsey was younger than his niece, Rosalie Isabella Carr (b. 1843), and almost younger than his nephew, Cuthbert William. The family moved frequently between the prebendal house at 9 College Green in Durham and Norham vicarage, a distance of 120 km.

Some of Gilly's accounts have survived from the 1840s: those he chose to pay through the income associated with his prebendal stall. They show that he subscribed a guinea each year to the Durham Conservative Association; that he paid his window tax; drank wine; supported missions to convert both the Jews and the Catholics; opposed Puseyism; and helped the Durham Museum to purchase a lion skin.[6]

Norham and Gilly's pleas for the cottagers of the Borders

Ten years as Vicar of Norham had taught Gilly about the hard lives of the hinds, the landless farm labourers of the Borders. Between the Cheviots to the north and the Coquette to the south, agricultural practices on both sides of the Scots border were similar. Many of the hinds lived, with their families, in hovels of only one room. There was little stability in their lives, as families moved from job to job and from farm to farm, being engaged at the hiring fairs for each agricultural season. Their ancestors had lived in this way for centuries. They knew that they would be 'flitting' every a few months, and so had no incentive to improve their cottages. Most of these cottages were rural slums, lacking the most elementary decencies of life. Sanitation was almost non-existent, and it was common for whole families to live in one room, with rudimentary privacy for the parents provided by box beds. There were a few schools, but, as the families moved so often, many children received little or no education.

Yet the hinds were proud and honest people: there was almost no crime in rural Northumberland, and every family had its Bible. Many had possessions of which they were proud, including long-case clocks and ornate crockery.[7] A few of the literate hinds wrote, and spoke, about how they thought their lives could be improved. This pattern of life was peculiar to the area. The hinds' wives and grown children usually worked on the land, and it was common for a man to be employed for a fixed period

---

4   E. A. White and G. J. Armytage (eds), *The Baptismal, Marriage and Burial Registers of the Cathedral Church of Christ and Blessed Mary at Durham 1609–1896*, Harleian Society, vol. RS 23, 1897, p. 29.

5   White and Armytage, p. 30.

6   DUL, Archives and Special Collections, SRA 9/4-6; Account books of the ninth stall of Durham Cathedral, 1826–55.

7   The information about the lives of the hinds is taken from Gilly's book *The Peasantry of the Border*, discussed below.

with his wife and/or daughter as auxiliary labour. In return for the labour of himself and quite possibly his family, a man received a basic wage, some provisions and a cottage.

In 1841 Gilly joined the Highland Society.[8] This largely Scottish society was comprised principally of landowners and tenants of large farms in Scotland and the Borders. In 1841 the society held its annual General Show in Berwick-upon-Tweed, 12 km from Norham. This show was a grand affair. It was also a remarkable feat of Victorian engineering, for a huge pavilion was erected inside the Ravensdown Barracks at Berwick, with three sides of the pavilion in immediate contact with the barrack walls. Within this structure 2,000 Scottish lords, lairds and gentlemen sat down to eat and drink at 5.00 pm on Thursday 30 September 1841. His Grace the Duke of Richmond was in the chair, and the Most Noble the Marquis of Tweeddale officiated as croupier.[9] They were watched by several hundred ladies in a specially erected gallery. As the evening progressed there was much drinking, 'great the shouting and long and various the speeches'. A band was in attendance which played suitable airs, including 'See the conquering hero comes'. It was Gilly's task to propose the toast of 'The Peasantry' towards the close of the proceedings. But by then many toasts had been drunk and 'a large proportion of the company rose from their seats to leave the room, and in consequence of the noise and confusion occasioned thereby, scarcely a word which fell from the speaker was heard'. Gilly nonetheless did his best in the circumstances but his speech could hardly have been intelligible to his large but mainly inebriated audience.[10]

Gilly had prepared his speech with care, and he had a very serious message for the lords, lairds and estate owners: that the living conditions of the peasants, the hinds of Scotland and the Borders, were appalling. But if he could not get his message across verbally to a drunken audience of landlords, then he could always put pen to paper. Thus he came to publish *The Peasantry of the Border: An appeal in their behalf.*[11] This short and pungent book is the most readable of his many publications. Gilly had studied the hinds' housing, their work, their education, their finances and their outlook on life. The book contains illustrations, statistical tables and financial calculations. It was Gilly at his best, a man not afraid to speak his mind and to criticize his audience. The introductory paragraphs, which clearly show that the speech followed from the book, reads as follows:

---

8   *Prize Essays and Transactions of the Highland Society*, new series, vol. viii, Edinburgh, 1843, p. 868.

9   In this case, it means 'one who sits as assistant chairman at the lower end of the table at a public dinner', *SOED*, s.v. 'croupier', definition 3.

10   The proceedings are recorded in 'Records of the General Show of the Highland and Agricultural Society of Scotland' for 1841, held at Berwick-upon-Tweed. (Berwick-upon-Tweed, 1841). The quotations are taken from the letters. See also F. Sheldon, *History of Berwick-upon-Tweed, being a concise description of that ancient Borough, from its origin down to the Present Time*, Edinburgh, London and Berwick, 1849, pp. 327–34 for an account of the show. It attracted exhibitors from as far away as Wiltshire and Norfolk.

11   *The Peasantry of the Border: An appeal in their behalf.* Berwick-upon-Tweed, 1841; second enlarged edition with additional appendices, London 1842.

The great meeting of the Highland and Agricultural Society at Berwick affords me an opportunity of drawing attention, with more than ordinary hope of success, to the condition of
the Agricultural Labourers, and of proposing some plans for the improvement of it. Many
hundreds of landlords and tenants, eminently distinguished for their benevolence and intelligence, will shortly assemble together, from all parts of the kingdom, for the avowed purpose
of communicating and receiving information, on subjects connected with the advancement
of agriculture as a science. They will offer, severally and collectively, their contributions of
knowledge, as to the best means of improving the breed of cattle, of increasing the produc-
tiveness of the land, and of multiplying and perfecting implements of husbandry. Many of
the arts and sciences – especially chemistry, geology, and mechanics, and the experience and
observations of our ablest philosophers, theorists, and experimentalists, in the use of them
– will be brought to bear on the grand objects of the meeting. We shall hear of the beautiful
state of perfection to which horses, cattle, and sheep have been brought, by paying attention
to their nature, wants, and habits. We shall be told of the means that have been resorted to
for the purpose of improving live stock, as far as regards food, warmth, shelter, cleanliness,
and the prolongation of life. We shall hear, also, of premiums awarded, and of much that
has been done for draining and cleansing the land, for augmenting its produce, and for
making it yield things of the best quality, and in the largest quantity. In fact, everything,
'after its kind,' which belongs to the cultivation of the land, will be considered with a view
to the great command … 'Be fruitful and multiply.' That MAN, the first glorious object of
creation, may have his due place in the deliberations of such an assembly, … that the grand
implement on which all depends, *man's hand*, may not seem to be disregarded, … that the
workman, on whom the success of every improvement in agriculture depends, … that he,
the husbandman, the shepherd, or the herdsman, under whatever name or employment the
agricultural labourer be designated, … may have his interests consulted, and his condition
improved amidst the general competition in matters of agricultural reform, I venture to
submit a few statistical facts to consideration.

While some are directing attention to the flora, to the minerals, or to the romantic
localities of this fine Border District, and others to the better fabrication of various tools
and instruments, to the construction of cow-byres, pig-styes, and sheep-folds, and to the
irrational animals that are to occupy them, … I will follow the example which has been
set by benevolent members of the Society, and beg a few minutes thought, in behalf of the
cottager and the tenement which is prepared for him; and of the provision which ought to
be made for the culture of his mind, and for the advancement of his comforts, as a moral
and immortal being. Let us be doing as much for 'right minded man' (to use Sir Robert
Peel's term) in his cottage, as we have done for the ox in his crib, or for the horse in his
stable; let us take care to lodge our peasants as well as we lodge our beasts. And where shall
we find a nobler specimen of his kind than the peasant of Tweedside, and of Northumberland in general? For whether we consider the mental or physical qualities of our northern
cottagers, they equally commend themselves to our kind sympathy and most admiring
notice.

The first thing which should be improved in the condition of our northern peasantry is
their habitations.

The illustrations are not great works of art, but they are effective. They show that
many of the hinds lived in hovels which were hardly better than pigsties. There are
also illustrations showing improved cottages which had been built on some estates.

Typical and improved hinds' cottages: illustrations from Gilly's *The Peasantry of the Borders*

Gilly wrote many pamphlets in his life, and most have achieved the degree of fame common to such publications: that is, forgotten and sometimes lost. But this pamphlet gave him a modest national reputation. Throughout Britain the housing of the labouring classes was all too often appalling. There had been a cholera epidemic in 1832, and an outbreak of typhus in 1836, and these epidemics were no respecters of class. In August 1838 the House of Lords asked the Poor Law Commissioners to investigate the sanitary conditions of the labouring population of the country. Edwin Chadwick, who reported to the Poor Law Commissioners in May 1842, carried out the investigation. His report, *The Sanitary Condition of the Labouring Population of Great*

Britain, is the most important document in the social history of nineteenth-century Britain.[12] Chadwick relied upon many local correspondents for his information, and Gilly was prominent amongst these. Chadwick quoted Gilly extensively:

The *Rev. Dr Gilly*, the vicar of Norham and canon of Durham, in an appeal on behalf of the border peasantry, describes their dwellings as 'built of rubble or unhewn stone, loosely cemented; and from age, or from badness of the materials, the walls look as if they would scarcely hold together.' The chinks gape in so many places as admit blasts of wind:-
   'The chimneys have lost half their original height, and lean on the roof with fearful gravitation. The rafters are evidently rotten and displaced; and the thatch, yawning to admit the wind and wet in some parts, and in all parts utterly unfit for its original purpose of giving protection from the weather, looks more like the top of a dunghill than of a cottage.
   'Such is the exterior; and when the hind comes to take possession, he finds it no better than a shed. The wet, if it happens to rain, is making a puddle on the earth floor. (This earth floor, by the bye, is one of the causes to which Erasmus ascribed the frequent recurrence of epidemic sickness amongst the cotters of England more than 300 years ago. It is not only cold and wet, but contains the aggregate filth of years, from time of its first being used. The refuse and dropping of meals, decayed animal and vegetable matter of all kinds, which has been cast upon it from the mouth and stomach, these all mix together and exude from it.) Window-frame there is none. There is neither oven, nor copper, nor grate, nor shelf, nor fixture of any kind; all these things he has to bring with him, besides his ordinary articles of furniture. Imagine the trouble, the inconvenience, and the expense which the poor fellow and his wife have to encounter before they can put this shell of a hut into anything like a habitable form. This year I saw a family of eight … husband, wife, two sons, and four daughters …who were in utter discomfort, and in despair of putting themselves in a decent condition, three or four weeks after they had come into one of these hovels. In vain did they try to stop up the crannies, and to fill up the holes in the floor, and to arrange their furniture in tolerably decent order, and to keep out the weather. Alas! what will they not suffer in the winter! There will be no fireside enjoyment for them. They may huddle together for warmth, and heap coals on the fire; but they will have chilly beds and a damp hearth-stone; and the cold wind will sweep through the roof, and window, and crazy door-place, in spite of all their endeavours to exclude it.
   'The general character of the best of the old-fashioned hind's cottages in this neighbourhood is bad at the best. They have to bring everything with them – partitions, window-frames, fixtures of all kinds, grates, and a substitute for ceiling; for they are, as I have already called them, mere sheds. They have no byre for their cows nor sties for their pigs, no pumps or wells, nothing to promote cleanliness or comfort. The average size of these sheds is about 24 by 16. They are dark and unwholesome. The windows do not open; and many of them are not larger than 20 inches by 16; and into this place are crowded 8, 10 or even 12 persons.
   'How they lie down to rest, how they sleep, how they can preserve common decency, how unutterable horrors are avoided, is beyond all conception. The case is aggravated when there is a young woman to be lodged in this confined space who is not a member of the family, but is

---

12   *Report to Her Majesty's Principal Secretary of State for the Home Department, from the Poor Law Commissioners on an inquiry into the Sanitary Condition of the labouring population of Great Britain; with Appendices.* Presented to both Houses of Parliament, by Command of Her Majesty, July, 1842; Clowes and Sons, London; pp. 22 and 124. (Hereafter the Chadwick Report.)

hired to do the field-work, for which every hind is bound to provide a female. It shocks every feeling of propriety to think that in a room, and within such a space as I have been describing, civilized beings should be herding together without a decent separation of age and sex. So long as the agricultural system in this district requires the hind to find room for a fellow-servant of the other sex in his cabin, the least that morality and decency can demand is that he should have a second apartment where the unmarried female and those of a tender age should sleep apart from him and his wife. Last Whitsuntide, when the annual lettings were taking place, a hind, who had lived one year in the hovel he was about to quit, called to say farewell, and to thank me for some trifling kindness I had been able to show him. He was a fine tall man of about 45, a fair specimen of the frank, sensible, well-spoken, well-informed Northumbrian peasantry ... of that peasantry of which a militia regiment was composed, which so amazed the Londoners (when it was garrisoned in the capital many years ago) by the size, the noble deportment, the soldier-like bearing, and the good conduct of the men. I thought this is a good opportunity of asking some questions. Where was he going? And how would he dispose of his large family (eleven in number)? He told me they were to inhabit one of these hind's cottages, whose narrow dimensions were less than 24 feet by 15, and that the eleven would have only three beds to sleep on; that he himself, his wife, a daughter of 6, and a boy of 4 years old, would sleep in one bed; that a daughter of 18, a son of 12, a son of 10, and a daughter of 8 would have a second bed; and a third would receive his three sons of the age 20, 16, and 14. "Pray", said I, "do you not think that this is a very improper way of disposing of your family?" "Yes, certainly", was the answer; "it is very improper in a Christian point of view; but what can we do until they build us better houses?".'

The Chadwick Report made no recommendations, but left the facts to speak for themselves. Contemporary scientific knowledge knew that bad sanitation led to disease and death, and that the living conditions of the poor in both town and country areas were frequently appalling, but it did not know that bacteria caused disease.

Gilly published a second edition of his book in 1842, this time in London with an expanded appendix. This edition contained a detailed study of the hinds' living conditions and an analysis of the detailed cost of building them cottages. He concluded that a basic cottage could be built for just over £50, and an improved one for £71.10s.0d. The Durham architect Ignatius Bonomi, who was now Gilly's friend, contributed plans for a basic hind's cottage.

On 22 October 1841, a group of local gentlemen met at the White Swan Inn in Alnwick, and formed the Cottage Improvement Society for North Northumberland, with Charles Bosanquet as chairman. It was resolved unanimously 'that the thanks of the Meeting be given to the Reverend W. S. Gilly for his exertions in the cause of cottage improvement ...'.[13] In 1842 the society issued a report, which contained articles by local gentlemen and parsons. A Mr Dunn submitted a paper upon the importance of an upstairs room for the hinds' cottages as: 'it forms a sacred asylum for the females of the family to retire to'.[14]

---

13   DUL, Earl Grey pamphlets, no 727, *First Annual Report of the Cottage Improvement Society of North Northumberland*, 1842.
14   See note 13.

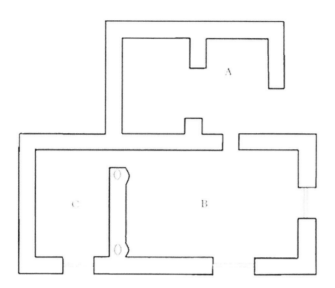

A Entrance and Pantry 10 × 6 } New.
B Day Room 14 × 12
C Bed Room 10 × 7, portion of the Old Building.

Meanwhile Gilly had started building a cottage for one of the hinds; it was finished in June 1842. The cottage was designed to accommodate a man, his wife and one child.[15] Gilly chose a piece of ground where a dry foundation could be secured, then excavated to a depth of 3 ft and filled up with stones and cinders. He ensured that the cottage had a warm aspect by facing it south. After construction, no speck of damp was found upon the walls. When completed, the cottage was 14 ft long, by 12 ft broad, and 8 ft high, with a small loft. Each of the two rooms was provided with a cast iron bedstead 6 ft long and 4 ft broad. The total cost including the bedsteads was £57.15s.7d. He also persuaded the tenant to forgo the customary box bed.[16] There were two internal fireplaces to keep the cottage warm in winter. Above is a plan of the house that Gilly built (the fireplaces are marked ()).[17]

Gilly's work for the Northumberland hinds continued for the rest of his life. His criticisms of Popery, Puseyism and pews have been largely forgotten, but he is remembered with affection as the champion of the hinds of the Borders.[18] Gilly's campaign for them was successful, and beginning in the 1840s, their living conditions began to improve. Gilly knew that the hinds were not servile. He had considerable respect for

15   We might well wonder why Gilly thought room for only one child would be adequate.
16   Although they were often seen as promoters of immorality (as in the old Welsh custom of 'bundling'), the box beds, like their ecclesiastical cousins the box pews, had the virtue of excluding draughts.
17   *Second Annual Report of the Committee of the Cottage Improvement Society for North Northumberland,* Alnwick, 1843.
18   There is a life-size effigy of Gilly preaching an indignant sermon about the hinds' living conditions in Berwick-upon-Tweed museum.

them, and pointed out that they had a 'manly independence of demeanour', and that crime was almost unknown in agricultural Northumberland, although unfortunately 'breaches of female chastity were somewhat common'.[19]

As Vicar of Norham, Gilly was widely known and respected. He deplored the divisions within the Anglican Church, and on 2 August 1845 wrote to the Rev. J. C. Crosthwaite, 'God help us all! Between the extremes of High Church and low we lie down as easily as if we had a porcupine and a hedgehog for our bedfellows.'[20] In March 1846 the Rev. James Raine, the Vicar of Meldon, County Durham, asked Gilly for a contribution for a new window for Meldon church. Apart from his parish duties, Raine had two main interests in life: writing books about the history of County Durham, and prolonged litigation about his tithes: he wrote the account of the opening of St Cuthbert's tomb in 1827, at which Gilly was present.[21] Gilly responded to Raine's appeal on 30 March 1846:

> I rejoice heartily in the prospect of your obtaining an early decision on your tithe case and devoutly hope you will succeed. Provided you will take down that caricature of the Virgin Mary, in which she is represented as a Crowned Queen, I will subscribe to a new window. But I have two reasons why I cannot be a voluntary contributor – first because the said caricature is a specimen of the trumpery which you are inclined to stick up; and secondly because my treasury is exhausted by three new schools, and a new aisle at Norham Church, erected last year: and you know who has to pay the piper, when the subscription list is closed, and bills are unsettled.[22]

It is pleasing to be able to record that after sixteen years of litigation, Mr Raine won his case about the tithes by a House of Lords decision in the same year. He also lived long enough to complete, in 1852, his *History and Antiquities of North Durham*, which he had begun in the 1820s.

Durham Cathedral

Gilly was now an experienced Canon of Durham Cathedral. Since the death of William van Mildert in 1836, the Palatine jurisdiction of the Bishop had been taken back by the Crown, so Edward Maltby was just a bishop, not a prince-bishop as his

---

19 *Second Annual Report of the Committee of the Cottage Improvement Society for North Northumberland*, 1843, p. 10.

20 Bodleian Library, Oxford, letter, Gilly to Crosthwaite. Probably John Clarke Crosthwaite, MA (Dublin), incorporated at Cambridge 1849; Rector of St Mary-at-Hill with St Andrew Hubbard (church lost in Great Fire), City of London, 1844. The patrons of this joint living were the parishioners (St Mary) and the duke of Northumberland (St Andrew) alternately.

21 See Chapter 4.

22 Raine had been Vicar of Meldon since 1822, rector of St Mary-le-Bow with St Mary-the-Less in the City of Durham since 1828, and, from 1816, librarian to the Dean and Chapter, which is how he came to know Gilly. (See further Alan Bell, 'Raine, James (1791–1858)', *ODNB*, Oxford University Press, 2004 (www.oxforddnb.com/view/article/23023, accessed 7 February 2012). Meldon lies just off the road from Durham to Norham, so Gilly quite certainly visited the church. This is an early instance of such advanced imagery being put into a parish church, and also reveals Gilly's old fashioned, anti-'Puseyite', High Churchmanship.

predecessors had been. Maltby was best known for his work on Greek prosody and metre; perhaps he was a calming influence on the more forceful members of Chapter, as, after the disputes of the late 1820s and the 1830s, dissension receded.[23] Gilly was proud of his status. He attended meetings regularly, and took his share of Chapter duties: he took his turn to preach sermons in the Cathedral; he was elected Receiver of the Cathedral in 1845, and was again Sub-Dean in 1848.[24] Towards the end of the decade he did miss several meetings, but only because he was ill.

After a very shaky start, the University of Durham was now established as an Anglican foundation,[25] under the capable leadership of the Warden, Archdeacon Charles Thorp. Gilly took little part in the governance of the expanding university, though he had endowed an annual English essay prize for students in theology in 1836. On 24 May 1845, members of the Chapter 'agreed that the consent of the Chapter be given to the conferring of the Degree of DD by Diploma upon those members of the Chapter who were founders of the University'.[26] The practice of members of august institutions awarding honours to themselves is of ancient origin, and has been followed on assorted occasions by academic institutions in many parts of the world. This did not apply to Gilly, as he was already a DD of Durham by 1842; those members of Chapter so honoured were Durrell, Ogle, Townsend and Wellesley, which reveals that not all twelve members were involved in setting up the University.[27]

Durham City: sanitation

Since his arrival in Durham in 1826, Gilly had been prominent in the affairs of this cold, wet, insanitary yet magnificent city, and he became more so in the controversies about health and sanitation in Durham City during the 1840s. He worked with his friend Ignatius Bonomi and other concerned citizens in the face of considerable opposition from the established institutions of local government. The population of Durham City was 11,163 in 1841, and 13,188 in 1851. The city was incompetently run, despite the reforms that had been attempted under the 1835 Municipal Corporations Act. In 1842 Nicholas Oliver, the medical officer of Durham, described conditions in the City:

> The city of Durham, like all ancient cities and towns, is built very irregularly, and surrounded on all sides by the river Wear, which is frequently overflown, and much wooded. These in summer and autumn, by the combined influences of heat, moisture, and decaying vegetable

---

23   Although bishops are not members of the chapters of their cathedrals.

24   Minutes of meetings of the Dean and Chapter, Durham Cathedral.

25   Whereas its contemporary, the University of London (chartered 1836) was open to all, regardless of creed (or lack of one).

26   Minutes of meetings of the Dean and Chapter, Durham Cathedral.

27   *Durham University Calendar*, 1846, p. 48, 'Degrees awarded in 1845'. Thorp was already admitted DD – probably in 1837, once the Charter was granted. A degree awarded 'by Diploma' is one in which the University concerned approaches the candidate to ask if they will accept it: if they do, the diploma is sent them. It is a full, not an 'honorary', degree.

substances, become abundant sources of malaria. The streets are very narrow, and the houses are built so much behind each other that the entrance to a great many of the dwellings is by a passage, lane, or alley, either a steep ascent or descent, where, from a proper want of receptacles and sewers, filth is allowed to accumulate, and there necessarily is a constant emanation of foetid effluvia. The majority of the houses are very old and in a dilapidated state, several not being weather proof. The great bulk of the working classes inhabit these tenements, and they seldom occupy more than two rooms, many only one, where all that is requisite in conducing to cleanliness and comfort has to be performed.

One fruitful source of generating and propagating contagious diseases is to be found in those common lodging-houses where vagrants and mendicants, or any one whatever, whether healthy or diseased, are for a trifling sum provided with lodgings. I have known 40 persons half clothed, lodged in one of those wretched dwellings, three or four lying in one bed upon straw, and only a single counterpane to cover them, which is never changed. Excrementitious matter was allowed to accumulate and be about the rooms in all directions, the stench being most revolting. In the beginning of summer fever of a typhoid type occurred in this house and affected a number of the inmates, but being in the other district, they came under the care of the other medical attendant.

The spirit of improvement, which is making such rapid strides in other parts of the country, is here quite dormant. Nothing calls louder for the attention of the constituted authorities than the improvements which might be effected in the habitations of the industrious classes, thereby increasing their health, comfort, and happiness.[28]

Sanitary conditions in Durham City improved little during the 1840s. In 1849,

---

28   Quoted in the Chadwick Report, pp. 20 and 361.

Insanitary yet magnificent: view of Durham, 1799 by Thomas Girtin

George Clark, an inspector from the General Board of Health, conducted an enquiry into conditions in the City and reported as follows:

> The civic economy of Durham is ...chiefly administered by a body of Commissioners. ...These Commissioners are about 120 in number, and include the Dean and Chapter. They are self-elected and irresponsible. Without entering into the justice of the reproaches of neglect of duty and undue attention to their individual interests, which have been cast upon them publicly by an active member of their Commission, there can be no doubt that a body so unwieldy, of which a large number of the members are placed on the roll as a mere compliment, and which is neither elected nor controlled by the rate-payers, is not likely either to expend the public money judiciously or to secure the confidence of the community.
>
> It is impossible to compliment the Commissioners upon the manner in which, during their half century of corporate existence, they have discharged their trust. The streets and drains bear no marks of the active general superintendence of a governing body.... Durham ought to be a very healthy city; it stands high, chiefly upon rock and a loamy sand, and but a small part upon clay. It is twice divided by the great valley of the Wear, and it possesses public walks, both above and below the town. Notwithstanding all these advantages, the mortality is unusually heavy. ... The extraordinary unhealthiness of Durham city is forcibly shown by contrast with other districts.[29]

At the end of the decade, on 1 May 1849, a Dr Watkin, who had great experience in the city, reported:

> In the spring of 1847 an epidemic of typhus manifested itself in the College, North and South Bailey. It thence extended to the lower part of South-street, Crossgate, Claypath, Gilesgate, and Framwellgate, and lastly appeared in the Union workhouse, lingering in that institution for eleven months, during which period (from 1st February to 31st December, 1847) there were 102 cases and 10 deaths. Owing to the number of people attacked with this fever there was a complete panic in the city, several of the leading families taking themselves out of town, the Grammar School was prematurely closed, and the boys were sent home. At the same time the University was nearly deserted, not a fourth of the students remaining to keep their term, so that those who went down lost a whole term, or one-third of the year. It is needless to remark how seriously the abrupt closing of these rising institutions militated, not only against their individual success and progress, but especially against the commercial interests of the city. I have no hesitation in saying that this epidemic was solely the result of an ill-conditioned state of the cesspools and drains, which poured forth the most noisome effluvia, vitiating the surrounding atmosphere, and infecting many who were compelled to breath it.[30]

In short, sanitary conditions in Durham were appalling throughout the 1840s. The worst conditions in the city were in the streets and alleys north of the castle. Gilly's

---

29   George Thomas Clark, *Report to the General Board of Health on a Preliminary Inquiry into the Sewerage, Drainage, and Supply of Water, and the Sanitary Condition of the Inhabitants of the Borough of Durham*, London, 1849, reprinted in 1997 by Durham County Local History Society, pp. 6, 7, 8.

30   Clark, *Report to the General Board of Health*, p. 8.

own family house was in the sedate College Green south of the cathedral, which was, and still is, an attractive and quiet part of Durham. But College Green had not escaped the typhus epidemic of 1847. Gilly must have walked many times down North Bailey to the market place, and he knew the Crossgate area well, as he had been Perpetual Curate of St Margaret's Church in that street.

On 23 November 1848, following the cholera scare of 1847, a group of concerned citizens of Durham held a town meeting, and agreed unanimously to a series of resolutions which established an interim Board of Health. This board was to be comprised of the Dean of Durham, the Warden of the university, representatives of Durham Sanitary Association (including Gilly's friend Ignatius Bonomi), the poor law guardians from the six city parishes,[31] and representatives from the Working Men's Sanitary Association. Gilly was elected chairman of this Interim Board of Health, which had no official status: it was a pressure group trying to bring about an improvement in the appalling conditions in the city. He was thus one of a small group. Meanwhile the institutions that were supposed to be administering Durham were of ancient origin, lethargic, and some influential people in the city had vested interests in their continuance. The Town Council was opposed to the introduction of the provisions of the Public Health Act in the city, on the grounds that to do so would be 'precipitate and uncalled for, and entail an unnecessary burden upon the inhabitants'.[32] The long-established Paving Commissioners met, and, after lengthy discussion, decided that the application of the Public Health Act in Durham at that time was 'premature, inexpedient and unnecessary'.[33] However, agitation by the Interim Board of Health, led by Gilly and the Durham Sanitary Association, resulted in the Government's General Board of Health instructing George Clark, a superintendent inspector, to report on public health in the City in 1849, and his observations on the disgraceful state of affairs in Durham City have been quoted above.[34]

Gilly and his fellow-campaigners for the provision of basic public health measures in Durham may have achieved little actual success in the 1840s, but, largely due to their hard work, during the next decade conditions did improve.

Durham City: mendicity

Gilly had founded the City of Durham Society for the Suppression of Mendicity in 1828. During the 1830s the society had become a prominent Durham institution, trying, in a (to us) paternalist way to relieve some of the abject misery of the poorest people in the city. As yet, no records have been located of the society's activities in the 1840s, but it presumably continued its good work based at its Vagrant Office in Claypath.

---

31 St Nicholas, St Mary-le-Bow, St Mary-the-Less, St Oswald, St Margaret Crossgate and St Giles.
32 *Durham Advertiser*, 1 December 1848, pp. 5 and 8. Quoted in Clark, *Report*, p. iv. By 'inhabitants' is meant the rate-payers – which included the Town Council, their families and their associates.
33 *Durham Advertiser*, 22 December 1848, pp. 2–5. Quoted in Clark, *Report*, p. v.
34 He took five days over his visit, 1–5 May 1849. W. Fordyce, *History and Antiquities of the County Palatine of Durham*, Newcastle[-on-Tyne], 1855, p. 210.

Durham had more than its share of the child poverty of the age. Urchins living in the city's slums had few clothes, no shoes and no schooling. They kept alive by begging, petty theft, and such relief as they could obtain from the Mendicity Office and other charities. At the end of the decade Gilly was prominent in the movement to set up a Ragged School for these children.[35] He was also involved in charities and other good works in the city: he was, for example, a trustee of the John Cock Charity, endowed in 1701, for the benefit of the poor in St Oswald's parish.[36]

Durham City: culture

Gilly was concerned that the city lacked a robust cultural life, notwithstanding that it had one of the finest cathedrals in England, and an established and expanding university. So, with a group of like-minded men, he set up the Durham Athenaeum. The inaugural meeting was held in January 1848. Gilly was, of course, the president, with J. F. W. Johnston, Professor of Chemistry at the university, and Ignatius Bonomi as members of the committee. The members were clergymen, gentlemen, prominent tradesmen and some skilled mechanics. They rented rooms above Mr Chambers' shop at the foot of Claypath, where a small reading room and library were established. They also hired halls for regular meetings, when they were addressed by visiting speakers on subjects such as literature, history, political change and the new art of photography. Ladies were not full members of the Athenaeum, but they graced the soirées.

Such a soirée was held in the public sale and exhibition room in Sadler Street in the evening of Wednesday 17 January 1849. It was a grand affair, with over 360 people attending. The hall was decorated with a profusion of evergreens, the portraits of leading Durham personalities, and 'beautiful composition figures' from the workshops of Mr Coxon, a plasterer. The Durham brass band enlivened the proceedings by playing 'a selection of choice airs' between speeches. Gilly made a lengthy speech, which was frequently interrupted by applause. He lauded the success of the Athenaeum, the virtues of the British constitution in avoiding the disturbances that had convulsed Europe in the previous year, and hoped that Britain would continue to receive divine guidance both at home and in the empire. He then introduced the other speakers, notably the Polish exile Count Valerian Krasinski, and Mr W. L. Wharton, the president of the Mechanics' Institute of Durham.[37]

Publications

Gilly wrote and published extensively during the 1840s. How he found time to do so, in view of his multifarious other activities, remains a mystery. His publications about

---

35 R. Cranfield, 'Education for the 'Dangerous Classes' in mid-nineteenth century Durham', *Durham County Local History Bulletin,* 1993, pp. 70–81.

36 F. M. Carlton, *History of the Charities in the City of Durham and its immediate vicinity,* Durham, 1872, p. 118.

37 The proceedings were reported at length in the *Durham Advertiser,* 19 January 1849. Count Valerian Krasinski was a Durham personality of the time. He was a dwarf and a Polish nationalist, who had left his native land to escape Russian repression.

the peasantry of the border have already been discussed, and those about contemporary Waldensian affairs are covered in Chapter 12. He also wrote about medieval history, Puseyism, churchyards, the Irish famine of 1840s, confirmation, and the progress of popular education.

In January 1841, the *British Magazine* published a lengthy letter from Gilly on 'The Noble Lesson and Waldensian Mss. in Cambridge University Library', which occupied twenty-two pages of the magazine. The 'Noble Lesson' (*La Nobla Leyçon*) is a medieval poem written in the Romaunt dialect of Southern France, and may or may not be an early Waldensian manuscript.[38] Academic arguments were taking place in the pages of the *British Magazine* about 'the Waldensian Question', which included accusations of 'knavery and falsification', of stealing documents from Cambridge Library, and of fraudulently antedating Waldensian tracts so as to make them appear to anticipate the Protestant Reformation. Gilly carried out extensive research in this subject, and journeyed to Dublin to examine documents in the library of Trinity College, where he was greatly helped in his researches by the Librarian, Dr J. H. Todd, and was allowed to borrow documents.[39] He concluded that the medieval Waldensian manuscripts there were genuine, and had considerable importance in the pre-Reformation history of the Waldensian Church.[40]

On 9 March 1841 Gilly wrote a second letter on the subject,[41] which was followed by a third, sent on 15 May 1841.[42] He stated that he had been toiling for years to collect authentic material about the medieval Waldensians. This material was largely written in the Pedemontano-Provençal language, which was understood on both sides of the Alps. He used this material in the academic books he published later in the decade. He believed that some seventeenth-century manuscripts by Sir Samuel Morland, author of *A History of the Evangelical churches of the valleys of Piemont* (1658), had been stolen from Cambridge University Library. However, after Gilly's death in 1855, Henry Bradshaw, a fellow of King's College, found them. They had been lost in the library, and Bradshaw took the opportunity to make pungent comments about Cambridge University librarians:

> Since the death of William Moore (in 1659), under whom every part of the library seems to have been thoroughly explored, all the librarians and their assistants have uniformly, though unaccountably, declined to make themselves in any way acquainted with the manuscripts under their charge.[43]

---

38 Audisio, *The Waldensian Dissent,* p. 153, inclines to the view that it is genuine.

39 Gilly's three long letters on this subject are printed in full in the Appendix to James Henthorn Todd, *The Books of the Vaudois: the Waldensian manuscripts preserved in the Library of Trinity College, Dublin*, London, 1865; the first is on p. 151. Todd was Senior Fellow, Professor of Hebrew, and Librarian at Trinity, and also Precentor of St Patrick's Cathedral.

40 As ever, we have to ask how far this conclusion was prompted by his 'Waldensian hobby'.

41 Todd, *The Books of the Vaudois,* p. 187.

42 Todd, *The Books of the Vaudois,* p. 197.

43 Todd, *The Books of the Vaudois,* p. 210: Henry Bradshaw, 'Discovery of the long lost Morland manuscripts' (paper originally read before the Cambridge Antiquarian Society, 10 March 1862). [I retain here HN's

So throughout the 1840s, and despite all his other activities, Gilly was carrying out academic research into medieval Waldensian documents. His subject was very obscure, and the documents difficult of access, although he was of course fluent in both Latin and French.[44] But in all his considerable academic studies, he was attempting to prove that there had been a continuous record of non-Roman, yet Catholic, Christian ministry and writings between the time of Christ and the Reformation, his 'Waldensian hobby'. Herein lay the fundamental fault evident in all Gilly's extensive research into the ancient Waldensian records: it was geared to fit the conclusions he had already reached.

In 1841 the seventh edition of the *Encyclopaedia Britannica* was published, and Gilly was asked to write the articles on the Valdenses, Valdo and Vigilantius. They duly appeared, and were also published separately as a booklet.[45] To avoid confusion, Gilly wrote that the Valdenses were otherwise known as Waldenses, Vallenses, Valdesii, Vaudes and Vaudois, but did not, oddly, include the term Waldensians, which is also widely used. He outlined their origins:

> That the Cottian Alps have been inhabited by a relatively pure association of Christians from time immemorial, who have testified for the truth, upon the same articles of faith, as the Protestant churches of modern times, is a tradition not unsupported by documentary evidence, but still open to discussion. The Valdenses of these regions maintain that they are descended from a race, who peopled the same villages, and professed the gospel, in the first centuries of the Christian era.[46]

In his article about Peter Valdo (i.e. Waldo), he described this saintly man as the founder of the fraternity of the Poor Men of Lyons in the twelfth century. These men eventually broke away from the Roman Catholic Church, were excommunicated and persecuted, and eventually reached the territory of the Waldensians in the Cottian Alps. There they found a refuge where they were able to maintain in safety opinions at variance with those of Rome. Gilly emphasized that Valdo was not the founder of the Waldensian Church, as of course he held that it was already an independent church of great antiquity. The third article was about Vigilantius, a fourth-century presbyter. Gilly was probably already writing his book about him which was published in 1843: this is discussed below.

On 2 August 1843 Gilly preached a sermon at the visitation of the Archdeacon of Lindisfarne at Berwick-upon-Tweed. It was quite an orthodox sermon:

> we may be losing time and opportunity, and putting ourselves out of the frame of mind

---

remark: 'It is understood, however, that Cambridge University librarians have improved since the 1860s: they have certainly been very helpful to the present writer.' – NWG.]

44 It is an open question to what extent he understood, or even read, the local Provençal language.

45 *Valdenses, Valdo, and Vigilantius: being the articles under these heads in the seventh edition of the Encyclopaedia Britannica*; Edinburgh, 1841.

46 *Valdenses, Valdo, and Vigilantius …*, p. 3.

necessary for a due reception of the gospel tidings, if we cumber ourselves with external things, which partake of that pride of life which is not of the Father, but of the world. ... There is nothing but the Holy Spirit which can give vitality to religion.[47]

In the same year he published *No Puseyism!*[48] This anonymous and polemical tract is eighty-four pages long. It is an attack upon the Oxford Movement, which was causing much controversy in the Church of England, as it stressed the Catholic heritage of the Church of England, which saw itself at the time as a Protestant church.[49] Edward Bouverie Pusey was a Canon of Christ Church, Oxford, and professor of Hebrew in the university, and was widely seen as a leader of the movement, although he dissoci-ated himself from some of its extremer aspects. (Nonetheless, his name was attached to it.) Many Anglicans, including 'Orthodox high-and-dry' Anglicans such as Gilly, saw the movement as embarking upon a path which would eventually lead to the triumph of Roman Catholicism in England.[50] Gilly, who was never a man to mince his words, particularly in anonymous publications, wrote as follows:

> The dormant spirit of Popery has awakened in the bosom of our church; and as the spirit ever has been carnal, and suited to the corrupt heart of man, so the sect here alluded to, and which has deeply imbibed that spirit, is likewise carnal. ... In a word, Puseyism is a religion of carnal sensations ... In a word it is High Priestcraft and low Popery ... Our national church is established on this two-fold basis, which makes Church and State to be virtually one. The Church is ... nothing more nor less than the embodied religion of the State. ... we pronounce without hesitation the adherents of Puseyism SCHISMATICS ... they can no longer maintain with honour their present anomalous position of supporting Popery without a Pope.[51]

In 1844 he published *Vigilantius and his Times.*[52] This book comprises 488 pages about Vigilantius, a presbyter of Aquitaine, who was active at the end of the fourth and beginning of the fifth centuries. He paid a visit to Saint Jerome at Bethlehem, which ended in a quarrel, and Jerome later accused him of opposing the contem-porary cults of martyrs and relics, prayers for the dead, having scant sympathy for the monastic life, and disapproving of celibacy in the clergy. Jerome attacked him in his *Contra Vigilantium* of 406; it is, as so often when Jerome was dealing with his opponents, full of invective, and Vigilantius' replies (if any) have not survived, so it

---

47   Published at Berwick-upon-Tweed.

48   *No Puseyism!* Berwick-upon-Tweed, 1843. Identified as being by Gilly by style, place of publication, and that it repeats from his 1818 book *The Spirit of the Gospel* the sentiment that Mohammed was an imposter. The BL copy bears the signature of George Townsend, Gilly's friend and fellow prebendary, and predecessor as Barrington's chaplain.

49   For further explanation of terms, see Appendix IV.

50   His opposition to the projected window at Meldon, depicting the BVM as 'a crowned queen', is noted above.

51   *No Puseyism!*, pp. 8, 9, 11, 13, 14, 82, 83.

52   *Vigilantius and his Times*, London, 1844.

is difficult to know how accurate these claims are.[53] Gilly, however, took them at face value (quite certainly because they suited his purposes), and regarded Vigilantius as an important early Christian who, long before the time of Waldo of Lyons, had carried forward the true Christian message outside the confines of the Catholic Church. Gilly wrote: 'the primitive doctrines which he was instrumental in reviving, in the vicinity of the Pyrenées and the Alps, were not lost when he perished. … these are the regions from which the so-called poison of his heresy has never been thoroughly banished'. [54] Gilly's book about Vigilantius is a formidable tome, which embodies the results of his extensive research into ancient documents. But once again, he did not write it with an open mind: it was designed to become another strand in justifying his theory of continuous apostolic succession outside the Roman Church.

In 1845 he published a sermon *On Confirmation*,[55] wherein he stressed that man was basically sinful and needed grace to improve his spiritual condition. The text is from Deuteronomy 26:17: 'Today you have obtained the Lord's agreement: to be your God; and for you to walk in his ways, to keep his statutes, his commandments, and his ordinances, and to obey him.'[56] This is standard Anglican fare: stressing grace over works, and free will over predestination.

In 1846 Gilly, the energetic Vicar of Norham, wrote about the importance of churchyards as the parish sanctuary and as a stock of local information.[57] He described his churchyard with its red sandstone memorials, and the curious spelling and antique words upon its many tombstones. He had worked hard to restore this fine churchyard as an 'agreeable resort for the public', and constructed a footpath through it to the River Tweed.[58] He had excavated in the churchyard and found Saxon remains, and studied all the documents he could find about the churchyard and Norham church. His essay remains an excellent description of this English churchyard, which has hardly changed during the past 160 years. It is fitting that Gilly and his wife should lie there in a modest grave.

In 1847 an anonymous 'Lady' wrote *Christmas 1846 and New Year 1847 in Ireland*.[59] This is a first-hand graphic description of Ireland in the grip of famine. Gilly edited it and wrote the preface, and also probably arranged for its printing in Durham. It describes men desperate to get temporary employment on the inadequate government labour schemes, and women and children starving on Christmas Day

---

53   See further, *Oxford Dictionary of the Christian Church*, s.v. Vigilantius. Jerome was not above falsely accusing his opponents of various heretical views, and wrote two further attacks on him. He nicknamed him 'Dormitianus' (the dormant) – where 'Vigilantius' means 'the watchful'.

54   *Vigilantius and his Times*, p. 481.

55   A. Watson (ed.), *Practical Sermons by Dignitaries and other Clergymen of the United Church of England and Ireland*, London, 1845, vol. II, pp. 235–49.

56   NRSV translation.

57   'On churches and churchyards', in *Proceedings of Berwickshire Naturalists Club*, vol. 2, 1846, pp. 177–90.

58   See page 126.

59   *Christmas 1846 and New Year 1847 in Ireland. Letters from a lady*, Durham, 1847. Were the letters written to Gilly? If not, how did he come by them? Or is it yet another example of Gilly writing pseudonymously?

The English churchyard: St Cuthbert's, Norham. Photo Meg Norman

1846. In his preface Gilly shows compassion for the appalling conditions in Ireland in the 1840s. He criticized the landed proprietors for their failure to help the starving peasants, but he failed to understand the basic causes of the Irish famine, which can be summarized as over-population, over-reliance on one crop (the potato), potato blight, harsh landlords and a lethargic government. The idea that the Irish famine was, at least in part, the fault of the Irish themselves runs through Gilly's introductory essay to this book. He was surely blinkered by his anti-popish beliefs, and it should be remembered that in 1824 he had claimed to be able to distinguish between Italian Protestant and Catholic peasants by the superior cleanliness of the former.[60] As we have seen, he also believed that mendicity was a matter of choice, not of necessity. In his introductory essay Gilly wrote as follows:

> I believe no better plan, and no better outlay of Capital could be adopted, than the purchase and cultivation of unclaimed land in a quiet district, on the principle of planting English or Scottish families in the proportion of one to four or five, by the side of a colony of Irish labourers, and placing all under such regulations, as new built cottages, and the providing of means for subsistence, until the land should be brought into a state of productiveness, would give the right of imposing.

In other words, Gilly's solution to the Irish famine was the further colonization of Ireland by English and Scottish immigrants.

In 1848 he published *The Romaunt Version of the Gospel According to St John*,[61] which was based on his researches in the library of Trinity College, Dublin, and also in the Royal Library in Paris: he spent October 1846 there. Part of the cost of publication was borne by the University of Cambridge. The book contains a lengthy introduction by Gilly about the history of the version of the New Testament anciently in use amongst the old Waldenses, and there are cross-references to ancient texts in Dublin, Paris, Grenoble, Zürich and Lyons. This version of the Gospel was written in the Provençal language during the Middle Ages, and Gilly wrote that 'Even in the worst periods of oppression and ignorance, vernacular translations of the Old and

---

60   See page 45.

61   *The Romaunt Version of the Gospel according to St. John, from MSS. preserved in Trinity College, Dublin, and in the Bibliothèque du Roi, Paris. With an introductory history of the version of the New Testament, anciently in use among the old Waldenses, and remarks on the texts of the Dublin, Paris, Grenoble, Zurich and Lyons MSS. of that version* London, 1848. Romaunt is an early version of the vernacular Romance languages.

New Testaments were finding their way amongst the people, in spite of the jealousy of the Romish priesthood.'[62] It is an imposing book of 182 pages, with colour facsimiles of some of the manuscripts, and shows that Gilly was quite prepared to spend a great deal of time carrying out detailed research into complex medieval documents, although again we can see that this project was at least partly inspired by a desire to have further proof of his view of the Waldensian Church.

On 1 and 2 February 1848 Gilly gave two lectures to the Mechanics' Institute of Durham on *A Comparative View of the Progress of Popular Instruction*.[63] These lectures were delivered at a time when there was increasing agitation in Durham to remedy the appalling sanitary conditions in the city. The skilled working men were becoming more organized, and Gilly complimented his listeners on spending their winter evenings listening to him after they had done a hard day's work. He stressed the importance of ballads in popular culture, and the spread of education among the labouring classes. He noted that books were becoming much cheaper, and that a fine printed Bible could be purchased in Durham for less than one shilling. He commended the virtues of education to his audience, and expressed his pleasure that many children of working-class parents were now going to primary school. Mechanics' institutes were being started throughout the country,[64] and libraries, museums and art galleries were being built. Gilly's lectures were dedicated to Professor Johnston, Lecturer in Chemistry at the university, and to Mr William Wharton, the President of the Durham Mechanics' Institute. They were timely lectures by a man who, throughout the 1840s, had worked hard to improve the lot of his fellow citizens in Durham and Northumberland.

During the 1840s Gilly was active in a number of spheres locally: improving the living conditions of the

College Green, Durham, where the Gilly family lived (No. 9, their home, has since been demolished). Photo Meg Norman.

---

62   *The Romaunt Version of the Gospel according to St. John…*, Introductory 'Advertisement', p. xv.

63   *A Comparative View of the Progress of Popular Instruction in Past and Present Times*, Durham, 1848.

64   Mechanics' institutes were educational establishments formed to provide adult education, particularly in technical subjects, to working men. They were often funded by local industrialists, as they would benefit from having better-skilled employees. A number of them still exist under other names – notably Birkbeck College, London, and the former UMIST.

hinds; improving the sanitation of Durham; presumably keeping an eye at least on the Mendicity Society, and he also found time to set up a cultural society (the Athenæum). He wrote and published extensively in support of these and other causes, and also found time to ride his 'Waldensian hobby', which caused him to travel to examine documents and resulted in yet another publication, Further activity in this field is discussed in Chapter 12. In addition he was carrying out not only the duties, of the incumbent of a large parish, but also those of a residentiary prebendary of a major cathedral. Domestically, he had a family ranging from married daughters to a son a few years old. The application of the modern term 'driven' would seem to be too weak.

Portrait of Canon Gilly by John Bannantyne, engraved by Edward Burton. Gilly is a holding a copy of *Narrative of an Excursion*, and to his left is the chalice presented to him by the Waldensians in 1844 (see p. 198).

Chapter 12

The Waldensian 'crisis' – and emancipation

Gilly made no visit to Piedmont between 1837 and 1851, but nonetheless, during these fourteen years he was much involved in the affairs of the Waldensians. They were years of hard work, tensions, arguments, polemics, patronage, praise, recriminations, setbacks, but in the end progress. The record is not complete, as most of Gilly's own papers have disappeared since his death in 1855. Yet much remains which shows that he was very busy indeed. Possibly he was too busy.

Progress in the valleys

On 16 May 1840, the London Vaudois Committee met at Winchester House in St James's Square, at which Gilly circulated a report expressing his concern at the revival of ancient repressive edicts against the Waldensian Church. He also reported that considerable progress was being made in the valleys largely through the English connections. Since 1825, two hospitals had been established; the College of the Holy Trinity had been built and opened; many books had been sent; over a hundred hamlet schools had been built or repaired; five girls' schools had been set up; and the new liturgy introduced. All this had been achieved despite the fact that:

> their national language is Italian, their vernacular tongue is a Provincial [*sc*: Provençal] dialect peculiar to that district: and the language of instruction is French, because in that only they can obtain books of devotion used by Protestants. Through a labyrinth of three tongues, therefore, the poor Waldensian has to struggle, and thread his mazy way, before he can acquire any of the elements of knowledge.[1]

Gilly took the opportunity of this meeting to again record his opposition to the traditional practice of training Waldensian pastors at the Calvinist colleges of Geneva and Lausanne in republican cantons of Switzerland:

> The education of their Clergy has hitherto been of necessity conducted in Foreign Universities, whither the youths destined for Holy Orders are compelled to go, at a great pecuniary sacrifice, and at no inconsiderable hazard to the purity of their morals and their faith.[2]

But Gilly's concerns about the threat to the students' morals applied only to Calvinist colleges on mainland Europe, for he had already embarked on his scheme

---

1   *Report of the Committee for the Relief of the Waldenses, or Vaudois, of Piedmont*, 16 May 1840 (a three-page pamphlet). The report is unsigned, but as Gilly was secretary and treasurer, it is reasonable to assume he wrote it.

2   *Report of the Committee for the Relief of the Waldenses.*

to train Waldensian students at the newly-founded, but Anglican, University of Durham.

The three Waldensian boys

The three Waldensian boys had been studying in Durham at the Grammar School since 1838. On 16 January 1840 Gilly wrote to Potts from Durham:

> Two of my protegés are distinguishing themselves by their diligence and success. One has obtained a nomination to a scholarship in Durham University and will enter next October – and the other has won a King's Scholarship in the Durham Grammar School. The third is clever and amiable and well behaved but not studious.[3]

On 17 June 1840 Gilly wrote to Pastor Vinçon reporting that the students were doing well in Durham: 'L'esprit et le caractère de Charles commencent à se developper: il montre de la diligence'.[4] On 13 August 1840 he again wrote to Pastor Vinçon protesting that three other Waldensian youths were being sent to study in Lausanne and Prussia and expressed his concern about the effect on the college:

> Je ne puis que regretter le départ des trois jeunes gens dont vous me parlez, Paradet, Janovel et Chardonnier pour le Prusse et Lausanne.
>
> Est-il dont impossible à persuader un seul jeune Vaudois de poursuiver ses études jusqu'à leur fin dans le Collège chez vous? … Depuis la reception de votre lettre, j'ai reçu une lettre d'un ami qui me dit en parlant des vallées 'J'ai visité le Collège sans avoir été très édifié de l'organization de cet Institut. – Le Governement vient d'assigner un somme considérable pour la batisse d'une Eglise Catholique à La Tour, et y fondra en autre de places de Chanoinies, dont la destination est assez évidente et [   ] pour les Vaudois et leurs enfants.'[5]

> [I can only regret the departure of the three young men of whom you spoke to me, Paradet, Janovel, and Chardonnier, for Prussia and Lausanne.
>
> Is it thus impossible to persuade a single young Waldensian to pursue his studies to their finish in the College where you are? … After receiving your letter, I received a letter from a friend who said, in talking of the valleys: I visited the College without being very well informed of the organization of this Institution – the Government has just assigned a considerable sum for the building of a Catholic Church at La Tour, and will, in addition, found Canonries there, of which the purpose is clear and [   ] enough for the Waldensians and their children.]

On 19 September 1840 he wrote to Potts: 'The boys are doing very well and have

---

3　　CUL, MS Add. 2612 letter, Gilly to Potts, 16 January 1840.

4　　ASTV, series V, vol. 38, c. 98, letter, Gilly to Vinçon, 17 June 1840. ['The spirit and the character of Charles begin to develop; he shows diligence'].

5　　ASTV, series V, vol. 38, c. 125, letter, Gilly to Vinçon, 13 August 1840 (trans. NWG. The missing word is transcribed *mendiante* in the typed version I received, which means 'mendicant'. This is clearly not what is meant, and I have not had access to the original, so I have left it blank. NWG).

lately been spending their holidays with me at Norham'.[6] On 11 December 1840 he wrote to the Moderator:

> Vous serez heureux d'apprendre que les trois jeunes gens se portent bien. Messrs les Professeurs de L'Université de Durham sont unanimes en louant la diligence de Henri Muston, qui poursuit ses études avec grand succès. Mr le Professor Johnson est très content de Charles Vinçon, qui est bien assidu, et commence à comprendre la science de la chimie. Joseph Monastier a été le premier de sa classe depuis le commencement du semestre, et sans doute il aura le prix.[7]

> [You will be happy to learn that the three young men are going on well. The professors of the University of Durham are unanimous in praising the diligence of Henri Muston, who has pursued his studies with great success. Professor Johnson is most pleased with Charles Vinçon, who is very assiduous, and is starting to understand the science of chemistry. Joseph Monastier has been first in his class since the beginning of term, and doubtless he will take the prize.]

Twenty-nine months after the arrival of the boys in England, Gilly was informing his correspondents that the scheme for educating the boys in Durham was proceeding smoothly.

Gilly continued to send reports to the Tavola about the progress of the three students. Henri Muston went home during 1841 for a vacation, and Gilly was concerned that when his studies in Durham were completed he might not return to work as a pastor in the valleys, so Henri was required to make a declaration in front of the Moderator that he would do so, before he was permitted to return to his studies in Durham. But on 8 July 1841 Gilly wrote to Potts in Cambridge:

> I regret to state that one of the three Vaudois boys does not answer my expectations and therefore I have sent him home – he was a nice lad but incorrigibly idle – His Italian blood shewed itself in the 'dolce far niente' of his countrymen, therefore he must bask in the sun in the summer and sleep away the winter as well as he can.[8]

On 26 February 1842 he again wrote to Potts about the boys: 'I have only two of the lads at present in England. One of the three returned home last summer – and I think a second will also go back this year – I do not think the transplantation of these exotics exactly answers.'[9] So quite suddenly, within two years, Gilly's plan for training the youths for the Waldensian ministry in an Anglican atmosphere at the University of Durham collapsed.

Henceforth the boys are largely lost sight of in the correspondence. Henri Muston

6   CUL, MS Add. 2612, letter, Gilly to Potts, 19 September 1840.
7   ASTV, series V, vol. 38, c. 150, letter, Gilly to moderator, 11 December 1840 (trans. NWG).
8   CUL, MS Add. 2612 letter, Gilly to Potts, 8 July 1841.
9   CUL, MS Add. 2612 letter, Gilly to Potts, 8 July 1841.

completed his education at Durham University,[10] but, despite the declaration, none of the boys returned to work as a pastor in the Waldensian valleys. Gilly's scheme for finding an Anglican alternative to the traditional Calvinist training in Switzerland had failed. Indeed, the whole project seems to have been ill thought-out from the beginning. As might have been expected, Gilly never blamed himself for this, and it was disingenuous and uncharitable of him to put the blame for the failure upon the Italian temperament. The whole experience must have been very tough upon the youths concerned, and it was foolish at best to decide that boys of that age would make suitable clerics.[11]

The Waldensian 'crisis'

On 1 January 1838 a new code of laws had come into effect in Piedmont, which Gilly considered would bear heavily on the Waldensians. He came to believe that the Catholic Church hierarchy in Piedmont was plotting against the Waldensians. In 1838 he had published anonymously a pamphlet expressing his concerns, and had also written, but probably not published, a long essay on the same lines, *The Present State of the Waldenses*.[12] But notwithstanding his concerns, the restrictions on the community did not increase during these years.

The report of the committee meeting on 16 May 1840 recorded that:

> Within the last two or three years many blows have been struck, which threaten the safety of this venerable church of the Waldenses, and which nothing but the personal feelings of kindness towards them, exercised by the King of Sardinia himself, has hitherto warded off. Among these blows may be mentioned the revival of ancient edicts of intolerance in the new Sardinian Code of 1838.

On 19 August 1840 Gilly wrote to his friend Robert Potts at Trinity College, Cambridge:

> A storm is brewing against our poor Vaudois – Bribery – threats and artifices are being employed more openly than ever to produce Apostasy – and a new establishment of a Cathedral church and four canons is to be set in place as soon as possible at La Tour. 180,000 francs are deployed by the Sardinian Government to this object. Beside this the Romanists are making purchases of land in all parts of the Valleys.[13]

The Catholics were in fact simply reacting to the construction of the new Waldensian College at the western end of Torre Pellice. They proceeded to replace the small

---

10 Henry [*sic*] Muston is listed as a Student in Arts in the 1842 *Calendar* (p 72), and that year took a second-class in the First and Second Year Examination of Students in Arts, but he is missing from the 1843 *Calendar* onwards, and does not appear in the list of graduates. The other boy does not appear at all.

11 It is perhaps interesting to see this episode in the light of what he say in *Academic Errors*, his first publication. [NG]

12 *The Present State of the Waldenses*. See Chapter 10.

13 CUL, MS Add. 2612, letter, Gilly to Potts, 19 August 1840.

Catholic chapel in the town with a large and rather ugly church, and they also built a seminary for training priests. Thus Torre Pellice acquired its present appearance, with the Catholic church and institutions at the eastern end of the small town, and the Waldensian College, and in later years the new church and other buildings, at the western end.

Little correspondence has survived for 1841. There is no record of any meeting of the London Vaudois Committee. There was a scheme that year for Waldensian emigration to Québec, where land could be acquired very cheaply. Gilly was not enthusiastic. He believed that the future of the Waldensians lay in their own valleys, from whence they would, in God's good time, act as a catalyst for the conversion of Italy to the Protestant religion. After much hesitation, the Tavola decided not to support this emigration scheme, because of the problems of sustaining the colonists during the early years whilst the land was being broken in. But in the summer of 1841 Gilly somehow became convinced that a crisis was imminent in Waldensian affairs. So he started a campaign for the redress of Waldensian 'grievances': a campaign organized and conducted without the support, or indeed the knowledge, of the Tavola.

First, in the autumn of 1841 Gilly wrote a long and impassioned pamphlet *The Crown or the Tiara? Considerations of the present conditions of the Waldenses. Addressed to the statesmen of civilised Europe.*[14] This was published anonymously in January 1842. The language is extremist, and in places reads as though the Waldensians were facing physical extermination:

> The Waldenses are on the brink of a precipice, and they will be plunged into it, unless the voice of humanity be heard against that of intolerance. … It is time that all who profess the common faith of Christendom, be they of the Reformed, the Greek, or Latin churches (the latter especially for the honour of their name), should protest against the wrongs, and plead the rights, of this helpless and unoffending branch of the Vine, against which the axe is even now raised and ready to fall. … The Crown has been friendly to them, the Tiara has doomed them to destruction. … A new code of laws received the unwilling signature of the King of Sardinia, which, unless some of its articles be repealed, must ultimately lead to the extirpation of the Protestant religion in Piedmont. … The King's signature having been once obtained to a Code reviving intolerant enactments, the enemies of the Waldenses have not been slow to take advantage of it, and children have since been taken from their parents, public worship has been interrupted, the tenure of property has been disturbed, and an interdict has been laid on the circulation of religious books, which were before permitted to be used by the Protestants in their vernacular language.[15]

---

14 *The Crown or the Tiara? Considerations of the present conditions of the Waldenses. Addressed to the statesmen of civilised Europe*, London, 1842. Gilly's authorship is certain as the copy in LPL is bound with a letter from Gilly to Howley, dated 27 January 1842, in which he acknowledges himself as author. (The 'tiara' refers to the papacy: the triple crown worn by popes (until 1979) is called the tiara.) It was reviewed, with others of Gilly's publications, in *The Quarterly Review*, vol. 73 (December 1843), pp 1–27. The alarmist sentiments expressed upset Pastor Bert, and he wrote to Moderator Bonjour (ASTV, Box 9, N7.) Bert did not know that all the publications in the review were Gilly's work.

15 *The Crown or the Tiara?* pp. 5, 8, 28, 31.

On 27 January 1842 Gilly sent a copy of this pamphlet to the Archbishop of Canterbury, when he acknowledged authorship, and pleaded for the Archbishop to urge the British government to place the Waldensians under its special protection. The Archbishop now was William Howley, who as Bishop of London had been the first chairman of the London Vaudois Committee in 1825. In his letter to Howley, Gilly wrote:

> I beg to submit a Pamphlet to Your Grace which I have lately written in behalf of the Waldenses, who are now suffering under a renewal of oppressive enactments, which must end in their destruction unless they be repealed. I have not put my name to it, for fear it should compromise these poor people, by leading to a discovery of the individuals, who have supplied me with information. ... Allow me at the same time to entreat Your Grace to receive the petition favourably, if the Waldenses should pray you to become their especial Patron, as the Primate of the Anglican Church; and if they should ask to be placed in a closer Ecclesiastical relation to our church, than they are at present. I do not know how soon a measure of this kind may be adopted: and I do not feel at liberty to do more and suggest what the ultimate results might be, if the Waldenses might hope for Your Grace's countenance and encouragement.[16]

Gilly's letter is endorsed 'Recommend prudence' in another hand – presumably that of Howley or his chaplain.

The next step was that the members of the London Vaudois Committee met on 9 April 1842, again at Winchester House, and addressed a memorial to the Earl of Aberdeen,[17] the Foreign Secretary. The Archbishop of Canterbury, the Bishop of London, the Bishop of Winchester, Sir Robert Inglis MP,[18] Gilly and four other members of the Committee signed this memorial.[19] It was another alarmist document:

> We, the undersigned, Members of the London Committee, instituted in 1825 for the relief of the Vaudois of Piedmont, earnestly request your Lordship to submit to Her Majesty the Queen, our humble entreaty that Her Majesty will be graciously pleased to intercede in behalf of that ancient community with their Sovereign the King of Sardinia. ... Among other grievances, it has been represented to us, that the Vaudois have now to complain, that children are taken away from their parents by the Priests and Local Authorities, when one of the parents is said to be a Roman Catholic, under the pretence of their being illegitimate; that their Religious Services are interrupted; that their intercourse and traffic with their fellow-countrymen, beyond certain limits, are placed under grievous restrictions; that some of them are deprived of the means of subsistence, being forbidden to purchase, to farm or to cultivate lands, except within boundaries too narrow for their population; and

---

16 The letter is bound into the copy of *The Crown or the Tiara?* in Lambeth Palace Library.

17 George Hamilton-Gordon, 4th earl; Foreign Secretary 1841–46; Prime Minster 1852–55.

18 Sir Robert Harry Inglis, Bart (1786–1855); Conservative MP for Dundalk 1824–26, for Ripon 1828–29, and then for Oxford University until 1854. He was a prominent parliamentarian, known especially for his interest in the Established Church, the slave trade, and the Factory Acts. In 1845 he was the leading MP in opposition to the proposed Maynooth Grant.

19 George H. Rose, W. R. Hamilton, William Cotton and Sir Thomas Dyke Acland (either the 10th or 11th baronet) were the other signatories.

that others, to their great disadvantage and detriment, have been ordered to sell property, which they have legally acquired beyond the territories to which they are confined. ... We are the more anxious to bring this subject before your Lordship, from our conviction that the present vexations of this people are not afflicted upon them with the entire consent of their Sovereign, for it is but justice to say, that ever since this Committee have taken an active interest in their behalf, we have repeated proofs of the favourable disposition of His Sardinian Majesty towards them.[20]

Gilly again sought to absolve King Carlos Alberto from personal responsibility for the persecution of the Waldensians. All these perturbations were of course based upon the presumption that the Waldensians really were being persecuted by the Sardinian authorities: the august signatories of the memorial to the Earl of Aberdeen certainly believed this to be the case. But there is absolutely no evidence of such a persecution in the archives of the Waldensian Church. The Waldensians continued to operate their new college with the support of funds regularly remitted from England. Admittedly, the Roman Catholics were building their large new church and seminary at the eastern end of Torre Pellice in reaction to the building of a Waldensian College at the western end of the town, but that could hardly be classed as persecution. Otherwise, the traditional restrictions remained in force: the Catholics could proselytize, the Waldensians were forbidden to do so; the Waldensians were forbidden to purchase land outside their traditional limits, as had been the case for hundreds of years, while the Catholics could purchase land in the valleys; the Catholics were forbidden to enrol in Waldensian schools; and there were, as there always had been, allegations of children being removed from their parents by zealous priests and nuns.

Lord Aberdeen took action on the memorial he had received from the London Vaudois Committee and passed the concerns on to the Sardinian government, but no reply was received. On 7 December 1842 Lord Canning, the Under-Secretary of State for Foreign Affairs, informed the committee of the situation.[21] Meanwhile, Colonel Beckwith had, on 28 September 1842, written a letter to Gilly which was laid before members of the committee:

An Evening prayer and Sunday School in the Grammar School (at La Tour) has been stopped. A severe, false, and ungentlemanlike letter from the Prefect (of Pignerol [Pinerolo]) based upon Edicts has been addressed to the Pastors, imputing to them many things that they have not done, such as mixed marriages, baptising illegitimate children, endeavouring to make proselytes, – permitting Romanist children to frequent Protestant schools, – and allowing Romanists to go into Protestant Churches; and all this by undue influence and underhand means.[22]

The next meeting of the committee was held on 13 December 1842, when it was

---

20   Contained in *Report of the Committee for the Relief of the Waldenses*, 9 April and 13 December 1842. It will be noted that the whole of what it has to say is based on hearsay.
21   LVC Minutes, 13 December 1842.
22   Quoted in LVC Minutes, 13 December 1842.

resolved 'That the Bishop of London and Sir Robert H. Inglis be requested to take an early opportunity of bringing the subject of the Vaudois again under the notice of the Secretary of State for Foreign Affairs.' Archbishop Howley wrote to Gilly on 21 December 1842, commending the action of the Committee:

> I have received the resolution of the Vaudois Committee and am persuaded that the course they have taken in deputing the Bishop of London and Sir Robert Inglis to converse with Lord Aberdeen on the claims of this oppressed and injured little community is the most likely to secure the object which they have in mind.[23]

The Bishop of London[24] and Sir Robert Inglis met Lord Aberdeen in early 1843, when

> His Lordship expressed himself in such a manner as to assure them, that he took a deep interest in the present condition of the Vaudois, and would lose no opportunity of pressing their care on the attention of the Sardinian Government, as far as might be thought to be beneficial to the Vaudois themselves, and consistent with the Treaties.[25]

Sir Robert reported to the meeting of the London Vaudois Committee on 1 June 1843, when the Committee resolved:

> That Sir Robert Inglis be requested to have another interview with the Earl of Aberdeen on the subject of the present Grievances of the Vaudois, and that, after such interview, the Lord Bishop of London, and Sir Robert Inglis be further requested to exercise their judgement as to the expediency of moving in Parliament for the production of the memorial, addressed to his Grace the Archbishop of Canterbury, and other members of the Committee to Lord Aberdeen, on 9 April 1842.

All of this is a highly diplomatic method of appearing to act while in fact doing nothing at all, which might lead us to think that the politicians had the measure of Gilly. Possibly he realized this, or maybe things were not moving as quickly as he would have liked, since as early in 1843 he wrote another polemical pamphlet, *Statement of the Grievances of the Waldenses*.[26] This was a forty-page pamphlet expressing the same concerns as set out in *The Crown or the Tiara* of the previous year, but with appendices which include copies of edicts against the Waldenses between 1476 and 1842, and a copy of the memorial addressed to Lord Aberdeen by the London Vaudois Committee on 19 April 1842. The publication also contained an eight-page postscript containing *An analysis of Ancient Edicts and Intolerant Regulations issued by the Dukes of Savoy and Kings of Sardinia, against the Waldenses, and revived and put into force by the decrees of 21 May, 1814, and 1 January, 1838, and by orders of a more recent date, up to the present*

23   Manuscript letter pasted into the LVC Minute book.
24   Charles James Blomfield, Bishop 1828–56.
25   LVC Minutes, 1 June 1843.
26   *Statement of the Grievances of the Waldenses*, Durham, 1843.

year, 1843. Again, the pamphlet was issued anonymously. Three copies of the publication are known to exist, each of which is endorsed in Gilly's hand: 'For Private use only. Not published, W. S. G.' Despite this statement it was extensively and sympathetically reviewed in the December 1843 edition of *Quarterly Review*.[27] So at least one copy of this supposedly unpublished pamphlet became public. Was it 'leaked' by its author – or was a copy sent to the *Quarterly* by some other interested party?

Gilly had now published three alarmist statements about the current condition of the Waldensians, in 1837, 1842, and 1843. But his information did not come from the Waldensian authorities. Indeed, during 1843 he was complaining that they were neglecting him. On 31 July 1843, he wrote an unhappy and personal letter to Pastor Amedée Bert in Turin. Gilly had met Pastor Bert's father (Pastor Pierre Bert) in 1824. There was, of course, no Waldensian church building in Turin, but the Protestant services held in the Prussian embassy chapel were attended by the staff of the Protestant embassies and conducted by Pastor Bert.

Gilly's letters to Bert are more personal than those to the Moderator. He began by informing the pastor that a portrait of himself had been finished and dispatched to Count Waldburg Truchsess, the Prussian ambassador in Turin, who would doubtless forward it to the Waldensian authorities so that it could be placed in the library of the college.[28] He continued:

> Of late years I have had reason to complain that the intercourse between the Vaudois authorities and myself has not been as intimate, and unreserved as it used to be – Something seems to have been raised as a partition wall between me and my friends in the Valleys. My name is never mentioned either in the publications, or in their communications with other churches – and in the letter addressed to the Church of Scotland, although allusion was made to those who have contributed to the promotion of Education in the Valleys, an entire silence was preserved in regard to myself. It no longer appears in the face of any document put forth by the Vaudois that I am in their confidence, or that their devoted friend exists, and still continues to devise plans for their benefit – to plead for them – to keep their wants and condition before the people of England as far as he can – I am not indulging in *amour propre* when I thus confide my complaints to you, but I am frank and candid in my observations, because if I am no longer mentioned as the accredited agent and instrument of the Vaudois, I lose the means of promoting their cause, and am supposed to know little about their true position, and therefore my appeals in their behalf lose their force.[29]

On the same day he wrote to the Moderator and Tavola:

---

27 *Quarterly Review*, vol. 73 (December 1843), pp. 1–27. See also p. 89, note 14. The copies are in the British Library; Cambridge University Library (bound with other works); and the Library of the Waldensian Cultural Centre, Torre Pellice.

28 This is the portrait by Richard Evans which now hangs in the Red Room of the Vaudois Church in Torre Pellice. A version of the same portrait hangs in the Great Hall of Durham Castle, and is reproduced on the cover of this book. It was lithographed by Edward Morton. Copies of the engraving are displayed in the Vaudois museum in Torre Pellice and in other museums in the valleys.

29 Letter, Gilly to Bert, 31 July 1843. ASTV, series V, vol. 39, c. 377. This and the following extract reveal a good deal about Gilly's character, and how he saw himself.

Pardonnez-moi si je remarque que j'ai lu la lettre addressée a L'Eglise d' Ecosse par la Table, dans laquelle les noms et les services d'autres amis de Vaudois sont mentionnés, mais le mien n'y paroit pas. Dans les efforts que je fais pour l'amélioration des Vaudois mes mains sont affaiblis par le non-apparence de mon nom dans de tels documens publics qui proviennent de la Table.[30]

[Pardon me if I remark that I have read the letter addressed to the Church of Scotland by the Tavola, in which the names and services of other friends of the Waldensians are mentioned, yet mine does not appear there. In the efforts which I have make for the amelioration of the Waldensians, my hands are weakened by the non-appearance of my name in such public documents which originate from the Tavola.]

News of the alarmist publications in England reached the Moderator and Tavola late in 1843, following the publication of a twenty-seven-page article about the Waldensians in the December 1843 edition of the *Quarterly Review*. This article reviewed Gilly's anonymous publications of 1842 (*The Crown or the Tiara?*) and 1843 (*Statement of the Grievances*), the 1842 report of the London Vaudois Committee, and an extract from Gilly's 1831 book *Waldensian Researches*. The author of the *Quarterly Review* article is not known, but he appeared to have a good knowledge of Waldensian affairs, and endorsed Gilly's alarmist conclusions that the Waldensians were suffering severe persecution. It was probably not Gilly himself, as it criticizes him for having 'coloured his landscape too highly'.

This time there was a Waldensian reaction, for a copy of the *Quarterly Review* reached Pastor Bert in Turin and he was very concerned indeed. He wrote to Moderator Bonjour in Torre Pellice on 9 January 1844:

Il a paru dans le dernier No du quarterly [*sic*] Review en Angleterre un article assez long sur les Vaudois. On y raconte au long nos affaires de Ventes forceés, la Réponse que le Roi t'a fait ce printemps, etc, etc, et l'on y dit que l'on a recourir directement au Gouvernement Anglais pour qu'il intervienne activement en notre faveur. Les ministres de Prusse et d'Angleterre craignent beaucoup qu'un tel article ne compromette le Modr, la Vaudois et le Cl Beckw[ith] – J'ai assuré que nous etions innocente de cela – Que le Cl peut certainement aussi, car il est loin de nous exciter à faire des démarches semblables, bien au contraire, et que si les expressions même du Roi sont référées, tu n'en peux rien. Car tu peux avoir rapporté ton entretien avec S[a] M[ajesté] a des amis – et naturellement tu as dit faire – mais si ceux ci ont ensuite fait des démarches quelconques pour nous, en sommes-nous réspons-ables en aucune manière?[31]

[There appeared in the last number of the *Quarterly Review* in England a fairly long article

30   ASTV, series V, vol. 39, c. 377, letter, Gilly to Vinçon, 31 July 1843 (trans. NG). For the Church of Scotland, see 'the Scottish mission' below.
31   Bert to Bonjour, 9 January 1844 [trans NWG]. This forms a hasty (judging by the handwriting and the sketchy puncuation) postscript to Bert's letter to Bonjour about the three chalices that were to be sent to Gilly, Beckwith and Truchsess (see p. 197). HN's photocopy, from which I have worked, notes that the letter is in ASTV, but does not give its reference. [NWG]

on the Waldensians. In it are recounted at length our affairs of forced sales,[32] the reply which the King made to you this spring, etc, etc, and it also says that recourse has been made directly to the English Government so that they may intervene actively in our favour. The ministers of Prussia and of England believe strongly that such an article will not compromise the Moderator, the Waldensians, nor Colonel Beckwith — I have made sure that we are innocent of that — the Colonel is also certain, for he is a long way from urging us to make such approaches, very much to the contrary, and that if these expressions are referred even to the King, you can do nothing about it. For you can report your interview with His Majesty to friends — and naturally you have done so — but if the latter then make any approaches on our behalf, are we responsible for them in any way?]

The Waldensian leaders thus became concerned about the situation. But their worries were not that they were facing persecution: rather, it was a concern that extremist articles were being published in London about their society which could well upset the Sardinian authorities, King Carlos Alberto, and ultimately of course, affect the welfare of the Waldensians themselves.

Presumably matters were sorted out, and the 'crisis' averted; Gilly was to receive official recognition from the church for his services in 1844. It is doubtful if a crisis ever really existed (though it could have been all too real, thanks to Gilly's meddling), for the Waldensians themselves did not appear to know about it, but it had enhanced Gilly's reputation as the English spokesman of the Waldensians, and again brought him into contact with leaders of the national church and state. Throughout his life Gilly cultivated relations with important people, yet this facet of his character should not detract from his record of untiring work for the Waldensians for more than thirty years. But there was another 'crisis' looming, one which equally seems to have come to nothing.

The Scottish mission

Several references have already been made to this. In 1842 the Scots had reached the Waldensian valleys. The Reverend Robert Walter Stewart made a tour of the valleys that year, and established contacts with the Moderator and Tavola. Three years later he published an account of this visit. He noted that 'their discipline is now Presbyterian, very much resembling that of the Church of Scotland'. His visit came in the years after Beckwith had tried to persuade the Waldensians to appoint a Moderator for life. Stewart recorded that:

During my visit to the valleys in 1842, I learned that an attempt was being made in certain influential quarters to alter their present form of church of government for a modified form of episcopacy by introducing a bishop under the title of Perpetual Moderator. ... Formerly the Vaudois students were ordained at Geneva, or where they had completed their studies,

---

32   This must refer to the practice whereby any Waldensians who had bought land outside the valleys were forced by a decree cancelling the contracts of sale to re-sell the land to Roman Catholics by a specified date. See further *Quarterly Review*, Dec. 1843, p 22. [NWG]

but now on the wise suggestion of Dr Gilly this system has been discontinued. The Vaudois church has resumed the ordination of its own ministers, and none can now hold office who have been ordained elsewhere.[33]

Stewart's essay gives a good account of contemporary Waldensian society. Theologically, the Calvinist Scots had much more in common with the Waldensians than did Beckwith and Gilly, who were both High Church Anglicans.[34] Stewart was, however, distressed to see that the Waldensians enjoyed themselves on Sundays, and wrote:

> The desecration of the Sabbath is certainly the foulest blot in their character ... After the services of the morning, the Sabbath is converted into a day of amusement ... they may be seen congregating in groups, singing, dancing, and pursuing their other favourite pastimes, as though the day were their own.[35]

When Stewart returned home the Church of Scotland was in a state of excitement. A bitter dispute about the right of the presentation of ministers to parishes had been rumbling for years. On 18 May 1843, 474 ministers, out of a total of 1,203, seceded from the state church and founded the Free Church of Scotland. Thus occurred the Disruption, the most dramatic event in the ecclesiastical history of nineteenth-century Scotland. Scottish society was split for the next eighty-three years. The new body, the Free Church of Scotland, rapidly gathered strength, and within a few years had become one of the world's great missionary churches. Stewart was one of the seceding ministers, and he spent the rest of his life working for the Italian Protestant churches; his portrait now hangs in the Red Room, the inner sanctum of the Waldensian Church in Torre Pellice, beside those of Gilly and Beckwith.

So by the end of 1843, the Tavola was in touch with the Free Church of Scotland. As revealed in his letter to the Tavola of 31 July 1843, quoted above, Gilly was very upset when he found out. On 12 March 1844 he wrote to the Moderator:

> Jai l'honneur de vous avertir que le portrait, que quelques uns de mes amis Vaudois ont temoigné le désir de posséder pour le Bibliothèque du College, est confié aux soins de Mr Amadée Bert à Turin, qui le mettra a votre disposition. Je vous prie de l'accepter comme un temoinage de mon affection, et de mon respect. ...
>
> Une lettre addressée a Mr Stewart, daté 4 Oct 1843, et signée par Monsieur le Modera-teur, et trois officiers de la Table Vaudois a été circulée (en Anglais) partout dans les journaux publics, et elle a causé une vive sensation tant en Ecosse qu'en Angleterre parmi ceux qui se sont toujours montrés les vrais amis des Vaudois, et qui ont soutenu[36] leur cause en toute

---

33   R. R. Stewart, 'On the present condition and future prospects of the Waldensian Church', in *Lectures on Foreign Churches delivered in Edinburgh and Glasgow, in Connection with the Objects of the Committee of the Free Church of Scotland on the State of Christian Churches on the Continent and in the East*, Edinburgh, 1845, p. 217.

34   See Appendix IV.

35   Stewart, 'On the present condition and future prospects of the Waldensian Church', p. 250. In this, of course, he agreed with Gilly.

36   This word was transcribed 'santenic' in HN's original typed draft, and I have not had access to the original

occasion. Nos mains sont affaiblés par les resultes de la publication de cette lettre, puisque vous êtes chargé de vous être melés sans aucun necessité dans les controvers étrangeoirs, et de vous être identifiés avec une faction de separatistes.

Je vous supplie d'avoir la bonté de m'envoyer immediatement une copie litterale de la lettre au fin que je puisse vous justifier des animadversions auxquelles vous êtes [...??][37] et vous rétablir dans les affections que vous avez risqués par l'apparence de vous être unis avec les ennemis declarés de toute établissement Ecclesiastique, soit Presbyterian, soit Episcopale. [38]

[I have the honour of informing you that the portrait, which several of my Waldensian friends have expressed a desire for the Library of the College to possess, is consigned to the care of M. Amadée Bert at Turin, who will put it at your disposition. I beg you to accept it as an expression of my affection, and of my respect ...

A letter addressed to Mr Stewart, dated 4 October 1843, and signed by Monsieur the Moderator, and three officers of the Vaudois Tavola, has been circulated (in English) everywhere in the public papers, and it has caused a lively sensation, as much in Scotland as in England, amongst those who have always shown themselves to be the true friends of the Vaudois, and who have supported their cause on every occasion. Our hands are weakened by the results of the publication of this letter, seeing that you are charged with being involved, without the least necessity, in foreign controversies, and of identifying yourselves with a separatist faction.[39]

I ask you to have the goodness to send me immediately an exact copy of the letter, so that I may justify you against the animadversions with which you are [?charged?], and to re-establish you in the affections which you have risked by the appearance of having united yourselves with the declared enemies of all ecclesiastical establishment, be it Presbyterian or Episcopal.]

It is unlikely that the Tavola realized that they had become involved in a bitter Scottish dispute, and it may not be too fanciful to see Gilly yet again fomenting discord where there was none. Certainly the Waldensians must have found the Disruption a strange piece of British ecclesiastical politics: as puzzling to them as their involvement in the Oxford Movement dispute which had occurred a few years previously. But Gilly's last sentence is telling: the emphasis is on Establishment.

Twenty years on ...

January 1844 saw the completion of twenty years since Gilly had begun his work for the Waldensians. The Tavola decided to honour the three foreigners who had worked so hard for their church, Count Waldburg de Truchsess (the Prussian ambassador), Beckwith and Gilly. So each of them was presented with a silver chalice bearing the Waldensian emblem (a candle and seven stars) and motto (*Lux lucet in tenebris*) and an inscription. Gilly's reads:

---

     text. 'Soutenu' seems to be a reasonable guess. [NWG]
37   This word was left blank in the draft: I suggest in my translation it should be something like 'charged'.
38   ASTV, series V, vol. 40, c. 43, letter, Gilly to Vinçon, 12 March 1844 (trans. NWG).
39   *I.e.* the Free Church of Scotland.

Two views of the chalice presented to Dr Gilly

Lux Lucet in Tenebris
au très RD.
Docr. W. S. Gilly
Chanoine de la
Cathédrale
de Durham
Les Vaudois du Piemont
Reconnaissants 1844.[40]

Gilly was very touched. On 15 April 1844 he wrote to the Moderator:

Vous m'avez honoré du témoignage d'affection le plus précieux, et le plus touchant qu'il m'eut été possible de concevoir, et je suis vraiment accablé au les sentimens profonds qu'il a produit. ... Comment vous exprimer les sentimens d'affection pour vous, et pour vos compatriotes, qui dominent mon coeur?[41]

---

40   'The light shines in the darkness. To the very Reverend Doctor W. S. Gilly, Canon of the Cathedral of Durham: the Vaudois of Piedmont with grateful thanks, 1844'.

41   ASTV, series V, vol. 40, c. 152, letter, Gilly to Moderator, 15 April 1844. This is just a month after he had written in strong terms about the Scottish Disruption.

[You have honoured me with the most precious and touching expression of affection which it is possible for me to conceive, and I am truly overwhelmed by the profound sentiments which it has produced …. How to express the sentiments of affection for you, and for your compatriots, which dominate my heart?]

Several years later John Ballantyne, a notable Scottish artist, painted a portrait of Gilly with the chalice and holding a copy of *Waldensian Researches,* his first book about the Waldensians (see page 184). After Gilly's death in 1855 the chalice disappeared from sight, but in 1999 it was discovered to be in Wellington Cathedral, New Zealand. This somewhat unlikely resting place for it is explained by the fact that Cuthbert, the son of Gilly's daughter Rosalie Emily and her husband Cuthbert Carr, emigrated to New Zealand in the 1880s. The family kept it until 1958, when it was presented to Wellington Cathedral, as a memorial to family members killed in battle.[42] Ballantyne's portrait has disappeared,[43] as has Beckwith's chalice.[44]

The later 1840s and Waldensian emancipation

The London Vaudois Committee next met on 22 March 1844 and decided that henceforth they would meet annually on the second Thursday of June. It was a short meeting, chaired by the Bishop of London, with only four members present: the Bishop, Sir Robert Inglis, Mr W. R. Hamilton and Gilly. It was resolved to appoint Gilly's son, W. O. S. Gilly, as assistant secretary. Otherwise little business was done, except to arrange for the transfer of the regular sums to Piedmont.

The next meeting was thus on 12 June 1845, again at Winchester House, chaired by the Bishop. Eight other members attended, including the Bishop of London (Blomfield), Sir Robert Inglis and the Gillys, father and son. The Committee approved a thirty-seven-page report prepared by Gilly. This document is replete with factual information about the work of the committee and the current state of Waldensian society. The payments of the Royal Bounty of £277.1s.6d. had been remitted regularly; about fifteen pastors were working in the valleys with the support of the Committee; and over 4,000 Waldensian children were receiving some education. Also, five girls' schools were operating; the college had been established; three new churches were being built (with some help from the Free Church of Scotland); the king had relaxed his measures against the Waldensians; and a Protestant asylum had

---

42 The extra inscription reads: 'Presented to Wellington Cathedral by the CARR family in 1958 in Commemoration of Cuthbert Owen Carr, 1916, Charles Emil Carr, 1917, Raymond Batley, 1942. Killed in action.' H. Norwood, 'The Vaudois chalice in Wellington Cathedral', *History Now*, vol. 8, no. 1, February 2002, pp 14–17. It is interesting that Carr had the chalice, for, as will be seen in the next chapter, by Gilly's will, his widow had had a life interest in the plate and the family pictures, which were to be divided among his three sons after her death, which occurred in 1899. As none of the three sons became clergymen, it was presumably felt fitting that the chalice should go to the son-in-law who was.

43 It was engraved by Edward Burton, and prints made. A copy of it exists at Norham Church, and also in DUL, Prints and Drawings Collection, no. 570.

44 We have to wonder exactly what use Beckwith might have had for a liturgical vessel! (NWG)

been established in Turin. In short, the London Vaudois Committee report for 1845 showed a much more rosy position than that portrayed in Gilly's publications of the late 1830s and early 1840s, when he was worrying about the 'Waldensian crisis'.

Gilly was always a prolific correspondent. He wrote frequently to the Moderator and Tavola encouraging, and on occasion lecturing, the church authorities. On 3 December 1844 he wrote:

> Si les Vaudois seront fidèles a eux-mêmes, et a la Sainte Religion qu'ils professent, tous les pouvoirs de la terre et de l'enfer ne previendront point contre eux.[45]

> [If the Waldensians will remain faithful to themselves, and to the Holy Religion which they profess, all the powers of the earth and of hell with not prevail against them.]

On 12 December 1845:

> Au milieu des agitations et les divisions, qui déchirent presque toutes les Églises contemporaines, la paix, et l'unité, et la pure doctrine regnent dans celle des Vallées.[46]

> [In the middle of the agitations and divisions, which rend almost all the contemporary churches, peace, and unity, and pure doctrine reign in that of the Vallées.]

The committee next met on 21 May 1846. Gilly reported that sixty-five students had passed through the College of the Holy Trinity since its foundation in 1837; that the schools were thriving; the church in Torre Pellice was dilapidated and needed rebuilding; that the disturbed state of Switzerland, which was engaged in the Sonderbund, a civil war between Catholic and Protestant cantons, was likely to result in the withdrawal of students from Lausanne because of 'the Democratic influences pervading there'; and that 'no complaints are now made' about the attitude of the Piedmontese authorities towards the Waldensians.

The committee met again the following month, on 23 June 1846, when a pamphlet marked 'Private' was issued. This included a paragraph:

> For many years the young Waldenses intended for the ministry have been compelled to complete their education in foreign universities, chiefly at Lausanne, in Switzerland. The great expenses and other inconveniences of such an expatriation have always been regretted, and repeated attempts have been made in England to provide a remedy for this evil.

An appeal was also made for more funds to complete the building of the college in Torre Pellice:

> Their most pressing want, however, is the completion of the College of the Holy Trinity; for this they require forthwith more professors, and an enlarged building sufficient to

---

45   ASTV, series V, vol. 40, c. 266, letter, Gilly to Vinçon, 3 December 1844 (trans. NWG).
46   ASTV, series V, vol. 40, c. 505, letter, Gilly to Vinçon, 12 December 1845 (trans. NWG).

afford apartments for their accommodation, as well as a library for the use of professors and students. Should there be any surplus, after placing the College in a condition to ensure its efficiency, it will be applied towards rebuilding the church and pastors' house at La Tour and placing them, if permitted, on a site more convenient for the population, and nearer to the College so as to complete a group of buildings, which will have the desired effect of rendering the Waldensian institutions conspicuous and acceptable in the principal Waldensian village – on a plan recommended by one of the well-known friends of the Waldenses, who has spent much of his time and money in erecting schools, and super-intending proceedings beneficial to the cause of religion and education in the Protestant valleys of Piedmont.[47]

The well-known friend was, of course, Colonel Beckwith.

The next meeting of the committee, held on 31 June 1847, was attended by only three people, of whom two were the Bishop of Winchester and Gilly's son. Gilly himself was ill.

On 20 February 1848 there occurred the most important event in nineteenth-century Waldensian history: emancipation. Most of the restrictions, which had been an integral part of the lives of Waldensians for hundreds of years, were lifted. They were now free to live outside their traditional valleys, and could build churches throughout the king of Sardinia's domains of Piedmont, Genoa and Sardinia. The men of the valleys celebrated by lighting bonfires on the peaks of the Cottian Alps, and 800 Protestant peasants marched through the streets of Turin to demonstrate their loyalty to the King: the people of Turin shouted, 'Evviva i Valdesi' along the route. 1848 was a time of great excitement for liberals throughout Europe. Gilly hoped that the time would be opportune for Waldensian advancement from the Valleys to Turin, and on 30 August 1848 he wrote from Durham to Pastor Bert in Turin, giving sensible advice:

> ... the political fermentation must subside before the religious feeling can become active and efficacious, but you had better be preparing the way for a successful appeal to the Protes-tant Church of Europe in behalf of your project by making a beginning among yourselves. Here in England when the wants of a locality are to be brought before the public, a stir is first made on the spot, neighbours are solicited, a subscription list is opened, and when the utmost has been done on the spot, then the co-operation of distant friends is asked. You must do the same. Plead your cause with the people of Turin and the Valleys, and then obtain a Representation from the Table setting forth the necessity of the case, the amount of contributions raised in Piedmont, and the sum total required to complete the design.[48]

The committee met again on 23 March 1848 at Winchester House. William Howley, whom Gilly had known since 1819, first as Bishop of London then as Archbishop of Canterbury since 1828, had just died at the age of 80. He had been a stalwart

---

47   *The Waldenses*; four-page pamphlet, London, 1846. Signed by the Bishop of Winchester as chairman, and Gilly as secretary.
48   ASTV, series V, vol. 42, c. 137, letter, Gilly to Bert, 30 August 1848 (trans. NWG).

supporter of the committee since its inception, and had presided over its first meeting on 26 May 1825. Gilly prepared a report on the state of the schools, hospital and the College:

> The emancipation of the Waldenses was completed by a Royal Edict last month, (February) which placed them on the same foot as the other subjects of His Majesty, King Charles Albert; and as soon as the Protestant population heard of it, they repaired to their churches to offer up public thanks to Almighty God. ... On the day of the proclamation of the new Constitution and at Turin, (Feb. 27) the people, who defiled before the King, in organised bodies, gave, by acclamation, the first place to 800 Waldenses, as a public expression of their approbation of the event which restored to them their civil rights, and rendered them eligible to offices of every description; and shouts of *Evviva i Valdes,* were heard throughout the whole line of march. ... the summits of the Alps, which overhang the three valleys, were also blazing at night with bonfires, and proclaimed the welcome intelligence, in the face of the plains of Piedmont. ... It may be, that there will be soon be a completely new page in the History of the Waldensian Church, and the Committee may have to consider, whether the time be at hand for the termination of their duties; but for the present it seem to be advisable for them to retain their management of the Waldensian Front.[49]

However, only four days after this meeting of the Committee, there were further alarms about the restrictions placed on the Waldensians. The new Archbishop of Canterbury,[50] the Bishop of Winchester,[51] Lord Ashley, Sir Robert Inglis, Mr T. D. Acland and Gilly wrote to Lord Palmerston, the Foreign Secretary, asking for his intervention 'at the present crisis'. The crisis was the king's decision to sign a new law which removed most of the civil disabilities of the Waldensians but restricted the activities of the Waldensian College, and gave Catholic priests the power of proselytizing children over 10 years old. Lord Palmerston replied on 6 April 1848 informing the Archbishop, 'I have the honour to inform Your Grace that I have instructed Her Majesty's Minister at Turin to endeavour to persuade the Sardinian government to remove those remaining grievances.' The committee was concerned because they had received letters from Piedmont, probably from Beckwith, which included the following:

> The atmosphere darkens on all sides. Neither forethought nor experience can tell what will happen next, it is impossible to count on men or things. Tremendous effects will probably arise at all that is going on. But what will be their effect on existing churches none can conjecture. We scarcely know how to shape our conduct towards any given end. But we must do all we can to make the Vaudois Church manifest to the world. God has protected it hitherto and as we have given it succour, we must continue to do so. Our political horizon is again clouded.[52]

---

49 *Report of the Committee for the Relief of the Waldenses, or Vaudois, of Piedmont,* London, 1848.

50 John Bird Sumner, Bishop of Chester 1828–48; also a Prebendary of Durham 1820–48, and thus known to Gilly.

51 Charles Richard Sumner, Bishop of Llandaff May 1826–November 1827; Winchester 1827–69. Younger brother of John Bird Sumner.

52 LVC records.

Gilly was again feeling aggrieved that the Waldensians were not keeping him fully informed about the uses to which cash sent from England was being spent. On 23 February 1848, he had written to the moderator asking for more details of the ways in which the money being sent from England was being spent.

On 21 December 1848 Gilly wrote to the Moderator setting out in detail the uses to which the various monies raised for the Waldensians since 1825 had been put:

> J'ai le plaisir de vous authoriser à tirer sur moi, comme le Trésorier du Comité Vaudois, chez Messieurs [..] quet,[53] Banquiers, Londres, pour les deux sommes de £138 10s 9d (étant le second semestre de 1848 du subside Royale) et de £111 sterl[ing], pour l'hôpital, les écoles de filles, etc.
>
> J'ai avèrté Messieurs ?Nigre? à Turin de payer à l'ordre de Mr le Moderateur, la somme de £81 5s 0d pour le Collège, etc – et à l'ordre de Mr Lantaret [...] sterl[ing] pour Oscar Concourde.[54]
>
> Je vous prie de m'envoyer chaque semestre une quittance sous-signée par les Professeurs du Collège, et par les autres récipients pour la somme de £81 5s 0d de la même manière que vous m'envoyez des reçus pour les subsides que je vous remet de la part du Comité Vaudois. J'ai déjà démandé une pareille quittance mais je ne l'ai reçu qu'une seule fois. Ce fut avant la formation de la nouvelle Table, et probablement les officiers actuels n'en savent rien.
>
> Je prends cette occasion de communiquer aux Membres de la nouvelle Table les détails suivants de nos relations financiales avec vous.
>
> Depuis mes premières relations avec les Vaudois pres de £19000 [footnote Underlined three times in Gilly's MS.] sterl[ing] ont été appliquées par le Comité de Londres, dont je suis le Trésorier et Secrétaire, au profit des Vaudois, c['est] à d[ire]:
>   £7200 placées aux fonds publics;
>   £3996 l'intérêt de £7200 remis aux Vallées;
>   £6095 le montant du subside Royale depuis 1827;
>   £382   remises pour divers objects d'instruction, ou de charité;
>   £1300 en Exchequer Bills, collecte faite pour le Collège
>   £18,973 sterling.
>
> Outre la susdite somme j'ai moi-même dépensé en faveur de l'Eglise Vaudoise la somme de £12,261 (sterling) dont la plupart m'a été confiée par des amis person[nnels], c['est] à d[ire]:
>   £5125 placées aux fonds publics pour le Collège;
>   £3401 l'intérêt remis pour le Collège, etc;
>   £1074 dépensées pour l'entretien, l'education, etc, des trois Etudiants: Muston, Vinçon, et Monastier;
>   £1361 remises, pour des objets d'instruction ou des benefactions aux Vallées;
>   £1300 en Exchequer Bills, déstinées pour le nouveau Presbytère, et pour l'Eglise nouvelle _____ à La Tour
>   £12261 sterling.

---

53   Unfortunately the supplied photocopy has a piece of paper overlaying the left-hand half-inch of the text, and the start of the bankers' name is obscured.

54   As with note 53, the sum is obscured by the overlay. It is not clear who Oscar Concourde was.

	£18973
	£12261
En total	£31234 sterl[ing], ou 780,850 Francs.[55]

[I have the pleasure of authorizing you to draw on me, as Treasurer of the [London] Vaudois Committee, on Messrs ...., bankers, London, for the two sums of £138 10s 9d, being the second half-year for 1848 of the Royal Subsidy) and for £111 sterling, for the hospital, the girls' schools, etc.

I have alerted Messrs ?Nigre in Turin to pay to the order of M. le Moderateur the sum of £81 5s 0d for the College, etc – and to the order of M. Lantaret £xxx sterling for Oscar Concourde.

I ask you to send me each half-year a receipt signed by the Professors of the College, and by the other recipients for the sum of £81 5s 0d in the same way that you send me receipts for the subsidies which I send you on behalf of the Committee. I have already asked for a similar receipt, but I have not received it even once. This was before the formation of the new Table, and probably the officers themselves know nothing of it.

I take this opportunity to communicate to the members of the new Table the following details of our financial relations with you.

Since my first relations with the Waldensians nearly £19,000 have been applied by the London Committee, of which I am the Treasurer and Secretary, for the profit of the Waldensians, that is to say,

£7200 placed in public funds;

£3996 the interest of the l £7200 sent to the Valleys;

£6095 the total amount of the Royal subsidy since 1827;

£ 382 sent for various objects of instruction or charity

£1300 in Exchequer Bills, collection for the College

£18,973 sterling.

Beyond the above-mentioned sum, I myself have spent in favour of the Waldensian Church the sum of £12,261, of which the greater part has been imparted by personal friends; that is to say:

£5125 placed in public funds for the College;

£3401 the interest remitted for the College etc;

£1074 spent on the maintenaince, education etc, of the three students: Muston, Vinçon, and Monastier;

£1361 remitted for the objects of instruction or benefactions in the Valleys;

£1300 in Exchequer Bills, set aside for the new presbytery, and the new church, at La Torre.

£12261 sterling.

	£18973
	£12261
Grand total	£31234 sterl[ing], or 780,850 Francs]

The sums seem impressive, but most of the capital sums remained in England, and

---

55   ASTV, series V, vol. 42, c. 210, letter, Gilly to Rollier, 21 December 1848. (trans. NWG).

had never been transmitted to the Waldensians. Money sitting in a British bank account was of no serious value to the Waldensian Church. We might also suspect that the £12,261 Gilly had spent on his own, contributed by 'personal friends', was the money of Anne Colberg.

Despite the various setbacks, educational and health services were being improved in the valleys. In 1848 there were still only thirteen young men studying at the college at La Tour, but in the valleys there were fifteen parochial schools, 129 hamlet schools (open only during the winter), six girls' schools and two infant schools. Out of a total population of 20,650 living in the valleys, 4,517 (or about 22 per cent of the total population) were receiving some form of education. These statistics are impressive for the 1840s, for they show that almost all Waldensian children were able to read and write. It is doubtful whether any other European country could, at that time, show such a record.

In June 1849 Gilly was upset to hear of the death of Pastor Bert's wife in Turin. He had known Pastor and Mme Bert since 1823. On 23 June 1849 he wrote to the Moderator:

La nouvelle de la mort de ma chère et excellente amie Madame Bert m'afflige vivement ....
M. et Madame Bert furent mes premiers amis Vaudois.[56]

[The news of the death of my dear and excellent friend Madame Bert affects me greatly ....
M. and Mme Bert were my first Waldensian friends.]

In the same letter he expressed the hope that one of the young men educated in the Waldensian College would become an evangelist for the Protestant religion, 'Un missionnaire Italien et Protestant!!! Quelle vocation glorieuse!'

Following emancipation in 1848, the Waldensians were able to live outside their three small valleys. Naturally their first thought was for the great city of Turin, which was only 50 kilometres away, and there had been an informal Waldensian community in that city for many years. A proposal was formulated for the construction of a Waldensian church there, and Gilly was approached about helping. His initial response was one of caution: on 22 October 1849 he wrote to the Moderator pointing out that much remained to be done in the valleys. The College in Torre Pellice needed improving and there was a need for a presbytery and houses for the professors.

And so the decade of hopes, fears, and considerable achievement ended. Gilly still had five years to live. He was to achieve much more in these years.

---

56   ASTV, series V, vol. 40, c. 308, letter, Gilly to Rollier, 23 June 1849, trans. NWG.

Chapter 13

'The place of usefulness he occupied': the final years and after

The last five years of Gilly's life saw him as active as ever.[1] He lectured locally, made three further trips to Piedmont, and was involved in activities in England concerned with the Waldensians. However, his health deteriorated during this period, which curtailed his participation in some events. He died, after a sudden illness, in 1855.

Events in England

In January 1850 Gilly gave a lecture to the Mechanics' Institute at Gateshead on 'Cottage life', which was later repeated at Morpeth, and then published.[2] This was linked with his desire for permanent and effective improvements to the housing of the working classes, already adumbrated in his concern for the hinds of the borders. In the same year, he contributed a twenty-six page preface to his son's book on naval shipwrecks.[3] It contains a few pieces of autobiographical information,[4] largely as justification for writing the preface; otherwise there is a good deal of highly partial discussion of the relative merits of the French and British navies, and some reflections of the proper duties of naval chaplains. Although the book was revised and expanded twice (1851 and 1864), the preface remained unaltered.

In 1850 also, Gilly participated in the foundation of a female penitentiary in Durham, which was eventually opened in April 1852. 'Penitentiaries', sometimes called Houses of Mercy, were establishments to which unmarried women, usually of the poorer classes, who had fallen pregnant could go if they were turned out by their families. The name expresses the contemporary view: that it was the woman's fault, and that extra-marital pregnancy brought shame on her father's household.

Gilly resigned two presidencies in this period. The first, in September 1851, was the presidency of the Berwickshire Naturalists' Club, to which he had been elected only the previous year: he had been a member for a long time. This decision was apparently motivated by the fact that his own researches had not brought any new information to light on the topics usually discussed.[5] He had also, as noted in

---

1   I am indebted for the core matter of this chapter, for which Hugh Norwood did not write a draft, to an outline list of events provided by Dr Viviana Genre (NWG).

2   *A Lecture on Cottage Life*, Durham, 1850.

3   W. O. S. Gilly, *Narratives of Shipwrecks of the Royal Navy: Between 1793 and 1849. Compiled Principally from Official Documents in the Admiralty*, London 1850.

4   See Chapter 2.

5   'Address to members of the Berwickshire Naturalists' Club', in *Proceedings of the Berwickshire Naturalists' Club*, vol. III, 1851.

Chapter 9, been president of the Durham Athenæum since its inception in 1848, with J. F. W. Johnston, Professor of Chemistry at the university, and his architect friend Ignatius Bonomi as members of the committee, but in 1854 he resigned in favour of Johnston. Possibly this was to do with his failing health, but there seem to have been tensions within the society, and evidently Johnson wanted the presidency.

It is worth noting that the vast majority, if not all, of Gilly's travelling, both in England and on the continent, was by horse and carriage. The railway, a branch-line of the North Eastern Railway, was authorized in 1845, but did not arrive at Berwick until 1847, and at Norham until 1849. The line is that still taken by the East Coast Main Line, but there was a branch line running from Berwick to Alnmouth via Norham and Coldstream. To go to Durham, Gilly could travel via either Berwick or Coldstream, although there is no evidence that he ever used the railway.

Waldensian matters

Gilly undertook his fourth trip to the Waldensian valleys in May 1851, accompanied by his wife, and was present at the opening of the Synod of the Church. He wrote about this visit in a pamphlet, *The Protestant Church in Turin*, in which he also appealed for funds to build a Waldensian church in Turin (members of the church who lived there had to worship in Protestant embassy chapels).[6] A further attempt to clarify, and perhaps to give currency to, his idea of the origins of the Waldensian Church took the form of a long letter to the editor of *La Buona Novella*, which published it in two parts, on 23 and 30 July 1852.[7]

The Turin church building seems to have suffered from a problem familiar today: a shifting completion date. The consecration ceremony was set for 29 September 1853,[8] but work had not finished, so it was postponed to 20 October.[9] Even that was not time enough, so it was put back again, to 15 December.[10] Although Gilly had been informed of this further change of date,[11] he still went ahead with his fifth visit in October, assuming he would assist at the consecration: he was of course disappointed.[12]

---

6   *The Protestant Church in Turin*, four-page pamphlet, Glasgow, 1851. This visit had hitherto not been known about. It was discovered by Dr Viviana Genre during the course of her research into Charles Vinçon, one of the Waldensian boys sent by Gilly to study at Durham. ASSV, carte J. Vinçon, letter to Charles, 6 June 1851.

7   'Lettera dall'Inghilterra alla Buona Novella intorno l'origine della Chiesa Valdese': *La Buona Novella*, no. 36, 23 July 1852, and no. 37, 30 July 1852. *La Buona Novella* was an Italian-language newspaper published by the Waldensians; it was launched in October 1851, replacing the French-language *L'Echo des Vallées Vaudoises*, established 1848.

8   ASTV, series V, vol. 44, c. 364, letter, Burgess to Revel 27 June 1853; ASTV, series V, vol. 44, c. 422, letter, Gilly to Revel, 20 September 1853. A letter from Gilly to the *Christian Times*, 26 August 1853, ascribes the postponement to the accidental incineration of the principal contractor's daughter.

9   ASTV, series V, vol. 44, c. 398, letter, Beckwith to Revel, 15 August 1853; ASTV, series V, vol. 44, c. 398 bis, letter, Revel to Beckwith, 5 September 1853.

10 ASTV, series V, vol. 44, c. 427, letter, Beckwith to Revel, 27 September 1853.

11 Ibid.

12 ASTV, series V, vol. 44, c. 486, letter, Gilly to Revel, 30 November 1853; ASTV, series V, vol. 44, c. 487, pastors' newsletter, 1 December 1853.

Interior of the Waldensian church in Turin. Photo by David Peyrot (1856–1915) (via Wikimedia Commons).

He had written to Revel that 'neither distance, nor winter, nor the Alps, nor should have prevented my being at Turin on the day of consecration', but that:

> the fatigue of the long journey last month, disappointment, and the continued anxiety which I have felt on this subject, added to the cold caught between Turin and Chamberai, have prostrated me, and my recovery will be slow. [13]

Nonetheless his health did not prevent him producing another book: this fifth expedition was described in *Piedmont and the Waldenses*, although for some reason he chose to print it for private circulation only.[14]

A British Waldensian venture independent of Gilly, the British Ladies' Association for Establishing an Orphan Asylum and Industrial School in the Valleys of the Waldensians, Piedmont, was founded in Clifton by a group of English travellers who had visited the valleys and discovered the needs of the orphans. Both Gilly and his wife were members, and as might be expected, Gilly became involved in the running of it, and Jane Gilly was a patron. The orphans were taught 'useful industries, such as straw-hat plaiting, lace, and needle-work. Articles thus made are disposed of for the benefit of the institution, which provides a home for sixty children.'[15]

---

13   ASTV, series V, vol. 44, c. 486, letter, Gilly to Revel, 30 November 1853.
14   *Piedmont and the Waldenses*, London, 1854.
15   J. N. Worsfold, *The Vaudois of Piedmont*, London, 1873, p. 55. He stated that the work was to be a pocket volume to supplement 'the large and learned works of Muston, Monastier, Gilly, and others'.

A sixth visit was considered in 1854, but was postponed for two reasons. First, there was a likelihood of war; and second, the Synod was to discuss important topics at which the presence of foreigners would have been awkward. The Crimean War indeed came to pass, and that made travel impossible. Even had this not been so, Gilly had further health problems, and wrote to the Tavola later that year that 'Grace à la bonté de Dieu ma Santé est à peu près retablie, après une attaque violente d'une maladie très pénible'.[16] It is not clear what the illness was, but it seems to have been a recurrence of it that killed him the following year. His sixth (and in the event, final) trip to Piedmont happened in June 1855. An initial desire to participate in the Synod in May that year was again scotched by the nature of the business: this time, changes to the church's constitution of which he did not approve.[17]

The end

What was to be Gilly's final public appearance took place on 26 August 1855, when he preached to an enormous crowd at the reopening of Berwick-upon-Tweed parish church.[18] Shortly afterwards he fell seriously ill, and after a week's sickness he died at Norham on 10 September 1855. Jane Gilly wrote to the Tavola:

> Mon bien aimé tomba malade si soudainement après son retour chez-nous qu'il n'a pas eu le temps d'arranger quoique ce soit; pas même de tout déballer, car il trouva une telle accumulation d'affaires suivie à son absence, que c'était presque trop, d'abord, même our son industrieuse habitude de travailler.[19]

> [My well-beloved fell ill so suddenly after his return that he did not have the time to put things in order; not even to unpack everything, for he found such an accumulation of things to do following from his absence, that it was almost too much, indeed, even for his industrious method of working. (trans. NWG)]

He is buried at Norham, in a grave alongside the path from the Vicarage to the church, where he was joined many years later (in 1899) by Jane. There is a memorial inside the church, by the sculptor Lough, which takes the form of a recumbent effigy of Gilly vested in surplice, scarf, bands and presumably hood, holding a prayer book. He lies on a late medieval-style chest tomb, and the whole is enclosed by a Norman-style arch. The inscription reads:

TO THE MEMORY OF
THE REV'D WILLIAM STEPHEN GILLY
VICAR OF NORHAM AND CANON OF DURHAM

---

16   ASTV, series V, vol. 45, c. 203, letter, Gilly to the Tavola, 29 June 1854. ('Thanks to the goodness of God my health is almost re-established, after a violent attack of a most painful illness' – trans. NWG.)

17   ASTV, series V, vol. 46, c. 92, letter, Gilly to Revel, 30 March 1855; ASTV, series V, vol. 44, c. 128, letter, Gilly to the Synod, 7 May 1855.

18   This work included the building of a chancel onto the 1650 building, as well as general restoration.

19   Quoted from ASTV, series V, vol. 46, c. 294, the Tavola's newsletter to the parishes about Gilly's death.

Gilly's memorial in Norham Church

AND FRIEND OF THE VAUDOIS
WHOEVER SHALL LOOK UPON THIS MONUMENT
LET HIM REMEMBER
THAT BY WORKS OF FAITH AND LABOURS OF LOVE
A NAME MAY BE MADE IMPERISHABLE

Further memorials are to be found in the form of a stained glass window in the quire of Norham church; the rose window over the chancel arch in Berwick-upon-Tweed church; and a bust at the entrance to the Dean and Chapter Library at Durham. In the Waldensian valleys, the Synod of 1856 decided to erect a monument to commemorate Gilly and his work for the Waldensians. A stone was placed in the hallway on the first floor of the College of the Holy Trinity, which reads

À LA MÉMOIRE
DU REV^D DOCTEUR W^M ST^N GILLY
FONDATEUR DU COLLÈGE
HISTORIEN BIENFAITEUR

The bust of Gilly at the entrance to the Dean and Chapter Library, Durham

ET AMI DES VAUDOIS
LES VALLÉES RECONNAISSANTES
ANNÉE 1858
NÉ À HAWKEDON LE 28 JANVIER 1789
MORT À NORHAM LE 10 7ᴮᴿᴱ 1855[20]

A final memorial to Gilly is the clergy house at Torre, built in 1863, and dedicated to his memory. This was his last, but unrealized, Waldensian project, and so the London Vaudois Committee decided to complete it in his memory. Again there is an inscription:

---

20 'To the memory of the Reverend Doctor William Stephen Gilly, founder of the college; historian, bene-factor, and friend of the Vaudois: the valleys are grateful. Born at Hawkedon 29 January 1798; died at Norham, 10 September 1855' (trans. NWG).

AEDES HASCE PASTORALES
IN MEMORIAM SIMUL AC HONOREM
GUGLIELMI GILLY S.T.P.
ECCLESIAE DUNELMENSIS OLIM CANONICI
RERUM VALDENSIUM SI QUIS ALIUS APPRIME STUDIOSI
COLLATIS ULTRO PECUNIIS
EXTRUI CURAVERUNT
AMICI VALDENSIUM ANGLICANI
MDXXXLXIII[21]

Many of Gilly's responsibilities to the Waldensians passed to his son, William Octavius Shakespear, and in 1856 he was nominated secretary and treasurer of the London Vaudois Committee – a post he vacated after three years, owing to health problems.[22]

Gilly's will – and its codicil

Gilly's will, witnessed on 5 November 1852 by Bolton Simpson, a Minor Canon of Durham, and Charles Reynolds, Gilly's butler, is relatively straightforward. He left to Jane the sum of £500 outright, and such items of household furniture, books, linen and wines as she might choose. She also had a life interest in the plate and the family pictures. After her death, these were to be divided among his three sons. To each of his children he left £100 outright. The residue of the estate was to form a trust, with Jane, his sons and his brother-in-law Rowland Colberg as trustees. The proceeds were for Jane's use; there is an involved series of instructions on how it was to be administered after her death.

However, there is also a codicil. Executed on 6 November 1854, and witnessed by Mary Shields, the governess, and W. Willoby, solicitor of Berwick-upon-Tweed, it revokes all provision made in the will for Frederick Dawson. It does not say why, but it is quite certain that Frederick had made a marriage his father disapproved of, since on 3 November 1854, three days before the codicil was executed, Frederick had married Emma Latter at St Michael, Chester Square. In 1851 he had rooms with his brother William Octavius at 84 Mount Street; he was a clerk in the Home Office, and William a clerk in the Admiralty,[23] but at the time of the marriage the residence of both him and Emma was 10 Chester Terrace.[24] Emma's father, Richard Henry Latter, is described as 'Captain in the Indian Navy'.[25] It is not known exactly what triggered Gilly's vicious response: was it the fact they had been living together? If so,

---

21   'In memory and honour of William Gilly, DD, sometime canon of the Church of Durham, scholar of the Waldensians superior to everybody. He having spontaneously gathered the money, the Anglican friends of the Waldensians built this parsonage, 1863' (trans. NWG).

22   ASTV, series V, vol. 47, c. 90, letter, W. O. S. Gilly to Revel, 28 April 1856.

23   1851 England Census.

24   Marriage certificate for Frederick Dawson Gilly and Emma Latter. The witnesses appear to have been local people, possibly impressed for the occasion.

25   He was deceased, although this is (unusually) not noted on the certificate. Emma was two years older than Frederick.

surely the marriage regularized the situation. More likely, as the codicil followed hard on the marriage, he objected to Emma herself, though it is not clear why. Possibly it was class-motivated, and Gilly was certainly acutely aware of his exact social standing. Whatever the case, it is highly significant that Frederick was willing to stand up to what were presumably his father's non-negotiable demands on the matter, even to the extent of being disinherited.[26]

Gilly in retrospect

It is hard to make an exact judgment of Gilly. Even allowing for differences in perceptions over 150 years, there can be no doubt that he was a social climber: he enjoyed, and indeed cultivated, the society of those of higher social standing than himself. His first cure, North Fambridge, served solely to give him the desired status of a beneficed incumbent of the established church; he never went near the place, and was indeed reprimanded by his bishop for this.[27] It was given him through an exercise of patronage at the highest levels, something which was to be severely curtailed in the near future. He attempted to use his connections to gain a living at one of the new London churches, though this failed, at least initially. He utilized an invitation to call on Shute Barrington to its utmost, and his second wife was the niece of a member of Barrington's household – a very wealthy woman. An appointment to a Durham canonry followed from this connexion, with the large income attached to it.

He was a pluralist. He held North Fambridge with his appointment to St Mary, Somers Town, relinquishing both on his appointment to Durham, but then taking in succession two Chapter livings – St Margaret Crossgate and then Norham. In this, he was merely following accepted custom, and as noted already, he was by no means the worst offender in this context. Most of his fellow prebendaries held other appointments – three as diocesan bishops.

He was not, as it would now be expressed, 'a team player': he effectively ran the London Vaudois Committee by himself, and indeed seems to have regarded the Waldensians as his special preserve, becoming quite annoyed if others presumed to write or speak about them. He could act in an alarmist manner: see the 'Irish papers episode' (Chapter 2) and the 'Waldensian crisis' (Chapter 12), neither of which came to anything. And there remains the oddity of the codicil disinheriting Frederick. In other spheres he invariably figures as chairman or president: the Durham Athenæum, the Mendicity Society. It is telling, therefore, that van Mildert and Thorp managed to keep him at arm's length over the founding of the University of Durham, despite the funds he had available via Anne Colberg.

On the other hand, he does show a more acceptable side. His work for the Waldensians stands pre-eminent here, of course, and he seems to have been an effective and well-liked parish priest – at least at St Margaret Crossgate and at Norham. He busied

---

26   Of a significant sum, too: his brother Charles Pudsey left £10,000 – approximately £800,000 in 2011.
27   He is omitted from the list of rectors – see Chapter 2, note 37.

himself in good works, and these included such apparently non-ecclesiastical things[28] as sanitation in Durham and reform of the housing and employment of the border peasantry; the Mendicity Society; and the Penitentiary. His first book had been a cry against the corrupt and corrupting public schools of the day; his second book was written with an view to getting his name in the public eye; but his later works (the Waldensian books excepted) are, to an extent, no more than one would expect of any residentiary canon in a small cathedral city. On the other hand, he had taken the living of Norham and fulfilled its duties alongside those of his canonry, when many might have been tempted to live comfortably on just the canonry, with its comparatively light duties.

Further information on this side of Gilly can be gleaned from his obituary, allowing for the usual conventions of obituary writing.[29] It was published in the *Berwick-upon-Tweed Advertiser*.[30] He was a magistrate, though he rarely acted as such, preferring 'to win people from their vices by encouraging the virtuous than by punishing the evil-doer'.[31] He 'extended the means of religious worship' in Norham: he built daughter churches at Duddo and at Shoreswood Moor, and employed several curates, and his own parochial visiting was 'incessant': he was known on occasion to make over fifty visits in one day.[32] A further appreciation of Gilly has already been quoted in Chapter 6.

As a churchman, he was among the last generation of the 'old-fashioned orthodox': the original High Churchmen, before the rising Ritualist movement of the 1860s and 1870s took that title to itself and redefined it. As such, he was equally opposed to Rome and to Dissent: while accepting that the Church of England was part of the Church Catholic (in the sense of universal), he was unshaken in his view that it was also a Protestant church. This stance caused him to see the contemporary social order as ordained by God: to alter it in any way was to rebel against divine ordinances.[33] It also explains why he could not countenance the idea that the Waldensians had Reformed theology and influences, though they might be Protestants. On the other hand, he disapproved of the Tractarian party, and its offshoot the Ritualists, both of which attempted to emphasize the Catholic heritage of the Church of England at the expense of its Protestantism. It was as much a political stance as a theological one, and High Churchmen were usually Tories and supporters of the Hanoverian dynasty. However, Gilly changed political horses: having realized that 'his party was opposed to men of eminent talent, of conscious rectitude, and aptitude for business – while

---

28   Except that, at this time, the Church of England was also the effective purveyor of social services.

29   '... the possibility of a successor to Dr Gilly ever filling the place of usefulness he occupied seems to be considered altogether hopeless'.

30   *Berwick-upon-Tweed Advertiser*, 15 September 1855. Hereafter 'Obituary'.

31   Obituary.

32   Obituary.

33   His concern for the peasantry was a pastoral one, to improve their living standards; it did not encompass bringing them out of 'the state of life, unto which it shall please God to call [them]' (BCP Catechism). Indeed, the Catechism instructs them to 'order [themselves] lowly and reverently to all [their] betters'.

to these qualities was only opposed a puny imbecility'[34] he became as ardent a Liberal has he had been a Tory: 'like a man of good sense he turned his advocacy to the party where the greatest qualifications for office existed'.[35]

He certainly appears to have been able to carry out a number of responsibilities simultaneously, any one of which could have been made to occupy a full-time appointment.[36] It is not desirable to sum up characters in a single sentence, but we are left in the case of Gilly with the impression of a very busy, possibly hyperactive, man; one who, in his own view, knew best; one who was adept at climbing the social tree and at making his name known; but also one who, within the constraints of his day, exhibited a good deal of social concern.

---

34 Obituary.
35 Obituary.
36 And indeed, in the case of the parish appointments, probably ought to have. He was among the last representatives of the 'old way' of doing things: the changes in attitude to ministry brought about by the second-generation Tractarians were not to take place until some years after his death.

Appendix I: List of published works by Gilly

This list is based on an annotated bibliography produced by Hugh Norwood and Viviana Genre in 2004. It is arranged chronologically. Items not bearing Gilly's name as author, but identifiable either internally or externally as his work (e.g. pamphlets) are marked *. Letters to newspapers and other very minor pieces are omitted, as are the various annual reports of the Committee for the Relief of the Vaudois.

1. *Academic Errors; Or, recollections of youth.* A. J. Valpy, London, 1817.
2. *The Spirit of the Gospel; Or, the four Evangelists elucidated by explanatory observations, historical references, and miscellaneous illustrations.* London: A. J. Valpy, 1818.
3. *Narrative of an Excursion to the Mountains of Piemont and Researches Among the Vaudois, or Waldenses, Protestant inhabitants of the Cottian Alps.* London: C. & J. Rivington, 1824.
4. *Narrative of an Excursion to the Mountains of Piemont in the year MDCCXXIII and Researches among the Vaudois, or Waldenses, Protestant inhabitants of the Cottian Alps.* London: C. & J. Rivington, 1825. Second edition of three. Third edition, 1826; fourth edition 1827.
5. *The Vaudois, or Waldenses, Protestant subjects of the King of Sardinia, and Inhabitants of that Part of the Alps, Which Lies Between Mount Viso and Fenestrelle.* Pamphlet, 3 pp. Undated, but internal reference dates it at 1824.
6. **Subscription for the Vaudois.* Pamphlet, 3 pp., 1825.
7. **Subscriptions for the Relief of the Waldenses, or Vaudois of the Vallies of Piemont, Protestant Subjects of His Majesty the King of Sardinia; More especially for the purpose of endowing an hospital, in aid of which they have received permission from their Sovereign to solicit Foreign Contributions.* Pamphlet, 4 pp., 1826.
8. *Subscriptions for the Relief of the Waldenses, or Vaudois of the Valleys of Piemont.* Pamphlet, 4 pp., 1825. Slightly altered version of no. 6.
9. *The Waldenses, or Vaudois, Protestants of Piemont.* Pamphlet, 4 pp.
10. *Copy of a letter to Lord Liverpool.* Pamphlet, 3 pp., 1826.
11. *Sermon Preached Before the Royal Humane Society in the Church of St Martin in the Fields on the Fifty-Third Anniversary.* London: Royal Humane Society, 1827.
12. *Horæ Catecheticæ; or, an Exposition of the duty and advantages of Public Catechising in Church. In a letter to the Lord Bishop of London.* London: C. & J. Rivington, 1828. Republished by W. Marshall, Philadelphia, USA, with introduction by G. W. Doane, 1836.
13. *Waldensian Researches During a Second Visit to the Vaudois of Piemont.* London: C. J. G. & F. Rivington, 1831.
14. *Extracts from Waldensian Researches.* London: Gilbert & Rivington. Pamphlet, 32 pp., extracts from no. 13, 1831.

15. *'Education among the Waldenses', *Quarterly Journal of Education*, November 1831, pp. 201–15.

16. *A Memoir of Felix Neff, Pastor of the High Alps; And of his labours among the French Protestants of Dauphine, a remnant of the primitive Christians of Gaul.* London: J. G. & F. Rivington, 1832; Boston, Mass.: W. Hyde & Co., 1832. Second and third editions (abridged), 1833; fourth edition 1835, with *Appendix to the fourth edition of the Rev. Dr Gilly's Memoir of Felix Neff*, fifth edition 1840; sixth edition, 1855; all Rivington.

17. 'The power of prayer', pp. 1–18 in *Sermons Contributed by Clergymen of the Church of England*, vol. II. London: L. Seeley, 1834.

18. 'The enduring obligation of the Sabbath', pp. 375–89 in *Original Family Sermons*, vol. III. London: J. W. Parker, 1834.

19. *Report of Sixth Annual Meeting of the City of Durham Society for the Suppression of Mendicity*, single-page flyer. 1834.

20. *Our Protestant Forefathers.* Pamphlet, 35 pp.London: Rivington, 1835. Republished twice in 1835. Reissued in 1836 as vol. IV of *Religious Tracts Circulated by the Society for Promoting Christian Knowledge*.

21. *'God is with Us': A sermon preached before the Society of the Sons of the Clergy of Northumberland, north of the Coquet, at Almwick.* Berwick-upon-Tweed: Thomas Ramsey, 1836.

22. *The Church of England: Her strong and weak points.* Berwick-upon-Tweed: Thomas Ramsey, 1836. (Sermon preached at Berwick at the Bishop's Visitation.)

23. **Who is the Arian? – In reply to 'An Epistle to the Priesthood, etc.'.* Pamphlet, 27 pp. Berwick-upon-Tweed: Thomas Ramsey, 1838.

24. **Present State of the Waldenses.* Sole proof copy (103 pp.) in CUL, bound up with other documents by Gilly, the property of Mary Shields, governess to the family. No title page; no date, but internal referencing suggests 1838.

25. *The Cause of Missions, the Cause of God.* New York: Swords, Stanford & Co., 1839. Sermon preached at St Margaret Crossgate in aid of funds for the SPG.

26. *Valdenses, Valdo, and Vigilantius: Being the articles under these heads in the seventh edition of the Encylopædia Britannica.* Pamphlet, 41 pp. Edinburgh: A. & C. Black, 1841.

27. Speech at the Grand Banquet of the General Show of the Highland and Agricultural Society of Scotland for 1841, in *Records of the General Show of the Highland and Agricultural Society of Scotland for 1841.* Berwick-upon-Tweed: Warder Office, 1841.

28. *The Peasantry of the Border: An Appeal in their Behalf.* Pamphlet, 54 pp. Berwick-upon-Tweed: Warder Office, 1841. Second, enlarged, edition, London: John Murray, 1842. First edition republished Edinburgh: Bratton Publishing, 1973, and Aylesbury: Square Edge Books, 2001.

29. **The Crown or the Tiara? Considerations on the present condition of the Waldenses.*

Addressed to the Statesmen of Civilised Europe. Pamphlet, 38 pp. London: John Murray, 1842.

30. 'Letter to the Secretary of the Society for the Improvement of Cottages, etc., in Northumberland' in *Second Report of the Committee of the Cottage Improvement Society for North Northumberland,* Alnwick, 1843, pp. 3–12.

31. **Statement of the Grievances of the Waldenses.* Pamphlet, 40 pp. Durham: W. Humble & Son, 1843.

32. **No Puseyism.* Pamphlet, 84 pp., Berwick-upon-Tweed: Warder Office, 1843.

33. *A Sermon Preached at the Visitation of the Archdeacon of Lindisfarne at Berwick on 2 August.* Pamphlet, 16 pp. Berwick-upon-Tweed: Warder Office, 1843.

34. *A Sermon Preached before the Rose and Thistle Lodge of Odd Fellows, Manchester Unity, at Berwick, on Monday, 4 September.* Pamphlet, 15 pp. Berwick-upon-Tweed: James Jaffrey, 1843.

35. *Vigilantius and His Times.* London: Seeley, Burnside & Seeley, 1844.

36. 'On confirmation', pp. 235–49 in A Watson (ed.), *Practical Sermons by Dignitaries and other Clergymen of the United Church of England and Ireland,* vol. II. London: John Parker, 1845.

37. 'National Treaties in favour of the Vaudois'. Appendix to *Lectures on Foreign Churches. Delivered in Glasgow, May 1845, in connection with the objects of the Committee of the Free Church of Scotland on the State of Christian Churches on the Continent and in the East.* Edinburgh: W. P. Kennedy, 1845. This is an extract from his letter to Lord Aberdeen of 1829, printed in full in no. 14. Pages 2 and 3 are transposed.

38. *The Waldenses.* Pamphlet, 4 pp., appeal circulated by LVC, 1846.

39. 'Our churches and churchyards' pp. 177–90 in *Proceedings of the Berwickshire Naturalists' Club,* vol. II, 1846.

40. Preface to *Christmas 1846 and the New Year 1847 in Ireland. Letters from a Lady.* Pamphlet, 5 pp. Durham: G. Andrews, 1847.

41. *The Romaunt Version of the Gospel according to St John, from MSS preserved in Trinity College, Dublin, and in the Bibliothèque du Roi, Paris.* London: J. Murray, 1848.

42. *A Comparative View of the Progress of Popular Instruction in Past and Present Times. Two lectures given to the Mechanics' Institute of Durham.* Pamphlet, 36 pp. Durham: G. Andrews, 1848.

43. Speech as president of the Durham Athenæum, *Durham Advertiser,* 19 January 1849.

44. *A Lecture on Cottage Life.* Lecture given to the Mechanics' Institute of Gateshead and repeated at Morpeth. Pamphlet, 20 pp. Durham: Ann Humble, 1850.

45. Preface to W. O. S. Gilly, *Narratives of Shipwrecks of the Royal Navy between 1793 and 1849.* London: J. W. Parker, 1850.

46. 'Address to members of the Berwickshire Naturalists' Club delivered at the

Anniversary Meeting held at Grant's House, 3 September 1851', pp. 51–62 in *Proceedings of the Berwickshire Naturalists' Club*, vol. III, 1851. London: Taylor & Francis.

47. *The Waldenses in Italy.* Pamphlet, 4 pp. Appeal for funds for a church in Turin. Undated, but internal evidence suggests 1851.
48. *The Protestant Church in Turin.* Pamphlet, 4 pp. Norham, 1851.
49. 'Lettera dall'Inghilterra alla Buona Novella intorno l'origine della Chiesa Valdese' in *La Buona Novella,* nos 36, 23 July (pp. 549–54) and 37, 30 July (pp. 656–68), 1852.
50. *Piedmont and the Waldenses.* Pamphlet, 16 pp. London: W. Clowes & Sons, 1854.
51. *The Waldensian Church in Genoa.* Pamphlet, 4 pp. Durham: Advertiser Office, 1854.
52. Copy of a letter addressed to the Rt Hon Sir George H Rose, GCH: in *Explanation of the late Proceedings of the Vaudois Table.* Pamphlet, 3 pp. Durham, 1854.
53. Preface to J. L. Willyams, *A Short History of the Waldensian Church in the Valleys of Piedmont from the Earliest Period to the Present Time.* London: J. Nisbet, 1855.

The following items cannot be dated:

An appeal in behalf of the Vaudois or Waldenses, Protestant subjects of the King of Sardinia, and natives of the Alps. Pamphlet, 3 pp. Unsigned, but identified as being by Gilly by style and reference to Apostolic Succession.

An appeal in behalf of the Vaudois, or Waldenses, Protestant subjects of the King of Sardinia, and natives of that region of the Cottian Alps, which is situated on the eastern side of Mount Viso and Fenestrelle. Unsigned, but identified as being by Gilly as it is a mixture of three different appeals, two of which were by Gilly (and see no. 5).

Catalogues of ancient Waldensian MSS. Pamphlet, 16 pp, bound with 'Note to Perrin's account of Waldensian MSS' and eight pages of parallel Biblical texts in French and Provençal. No publisher or date; two copies in CUL are bound up with other documents by Gilly, the property of Mary Shields, governess to the family – see no. 24.

La Nobla Leyçon. Pamphlet, 2 pp. Parallel texts in French and Provençal. No publisher or date; two copies in CUL are bound up with other documents by Gilly, the property of Mary Shields, governess to the family – see no. 24.

Appendix II

The immediate family after Gilly's death

Gilly's widow, his second wife Jane, went to live in Northgate, Bury St Edmunds, where she sent Charles Pudsey to school.[1] They then moved to 15 Trumpington Road, Cambridge, and Charles entered St Catherine's College in 1864; he did not take a degree.[2] After W. O. S. Gilly resigned from the London committee, Jane took charge of sending money to the Waldensians herself until 1896, when she entrusted the task to the committee. She paid a visit herself to the valleys in 1869, accompanied by her daughter Alice Anne, and stayed with Mrs Beckwith. She died at Layer Breton, Essex, on 12 February 1899, and was buried, as noted above, at Norham, in her husband's grave.

In 1861 the disinherited Frederick was living at York Cottage, North End Road, Fulham, with his wife Emma and her 16-year-old sister Augusta, and was still a clerk in the Home Office. No children are listed in the 1861 Census entry, so presumably Frederick had not made Emma pregnant before the marriage (which could have been a possible cause of the disinheritance) – or if he had, then the child had either miscarried or died in infancy. Some kind of reconciliation took place, as in 1871 he and Emma[3] were living with Jane Gilly at Cambridge, together with his sister Alice Anne, and Mary Shields (described in the Census entry as 'resident friend').[4] Frederick was by then a 'retired clerk in the Home Office' – aged 40. Shortly after this they emigrated to Canada,[5] where Frederick died in 1880. In the 1891 Canadian Census, Emma was living with her sister Augusta and brother-in-law, Charles Arkoll Boulton, a lumberman, whom Augusta married there in 1874.[6]

---

1   He attended the King Edward VI Free Grammar School there from 1855 to 1863 (S. H. A. Hervey (comp.), *A Biographical List of Boys Educated at the King Edward VI Free Grammar School, Bury St Edmunds, from 1550–1900*, Bury St Edmunds, 1908). It is at present unclear why this choice was made: Gilly's Suffolk heritage may have been a factor. The *Edinburgh Academy Register* says he was at that school from 1857 to 1864 (T. Henderson and P. J. Hamilton-Grierson (eds), *The Edinburgh Academy Register*, Edinburgh, 1914, p. 226). It is hard to see how to reconcile these dates. However, as it gives his father as 'Archdeacon Gilly', and under W. O. S.'s entry (p. 70) says he was the son of 'William Gilly, India', it would appear that the *EAR* is less than accurate. It also states that W. O. S. was there from 1832 to 1839, and this would be feasible if the family was living at Norham, though the *Harrow School Register 1801–93* has him as entering there in September 1835 (p. 109).

2   Venn, *Alumni Cantabrigienses*. This may have been dictated by lack of money as much as inability to reach the required standard.

3   The 1871 Census entry has her as 'Ellen', but this must be an error on the part of the enumerator. She is clearly listed as Emma in 1861, and also on the marriage certificate.

4   As she had witnessed the codicil, this may have been an awkward relationship, unless she was coerced into doing so by Gilly.

5   Probably October 1871: the passenger list for the SS *Sarmatian* contains a Mr and Mrs Gilly (no initials are given) travelling from Liverpool to Québec. Under 'Rank or profession' they are listed as 'Gent' and 'Lady' respectively.

6   Schedule of Marriages, Simcoe County, Orellia Village, 007997, 4 February 1874.

Of the children of his 'first family', Mary Anna had married Lewis Morgan, and she died in 1888; they had no children. Rosalie Emily, married to Cuthbert John Carr, had already died in 1851. They had four children of whom one, Cuthbert William, emigrated to New Zealand, which explains the presence of Gilly's Vaudois chalice there. His brother Edgar became a clergyman, married, and had four children. After Rosalie's death Carr married her cousin Frances Mansel, the daughter of Gilly's sister Harriet: they had four more children.

William Octavius Shakespear died unmarried in 1860. Of the rest of the 'second family', Alice Anne married George Holmes Blakesley, a barrister, in 1878, and died, aged 90, in 1934; they had no children. Charles Pudsey appears to have been in New Zealand between about 1871 and 1891.[7] The 1901 England Census lists him as married, but his wife was away from home on Census night, so she is not listed at their house; probably they had married in New Zealand. He died in 1904 at Layer Breton; probate was granted to his sister Alice Blakesley, which may suggest that his wife had predeceased him.[8] It is not clear whether they produced any children.

---

7   I am grateful to Eileen Tristram for this information. He appears in the Electoral Roll for 1880 for Oamaru, Otago, where he is listed as 'settler'. He is not there in 1881, but of course may have moved elsewhere. The *Edinburgh Academy Register* says he went to the Argentine, but the *Bury School Register* gives Australia. As noted above, the *EAR* must be suspect in its accuracy.

8   He left just over £10,000.

Table A2.1 Tree to show Gilly's marriages and descendants

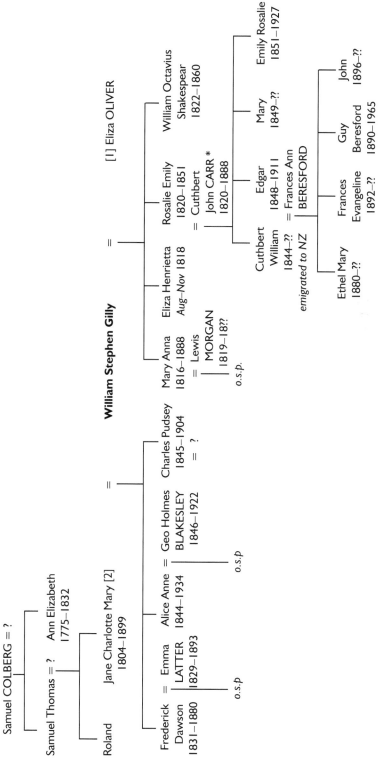

*After Rosalie's death, C. J. Carr married her cousin, Frances MANSEL: see Table 1.1.

Appendix III

The Waldensians and the Apostolic Succession

A great deal of Gilly's interest in the Waldensians was rooted in his belief that they preserved unbroken the Apostolic Succession parallel to that preserved in the Church of Rome and, so far as he was concerned, in the Church of England.[1] The doctrine of apostolic succession holds that the Apostles ordained their successors, who in turn ordained theirs, and so on down the ages:[2] it is possible, in theory, for any clergyman to trace his 'ancestry' back through the bishop who ordained him, and then through the bishops who consecrated him, all the way to the Apostles. Thus Gilly could work back both through Richard Beadon, Bishop of Bath and Wells, who ordained him deacon, and also through William Howley, Bishop of London, who ordained him priest.

For High Churchmen such as Gilly, this was very important, as they held that anyone who was ordained outside the succession was invalidly ordained: this included all dissenting ministers, such as Baptists, Congregationalists and Presbyterians, as well as those of the various Lutheran and Calvinist churches. An invalid ordination meant that any sacraments administered by such a person were also invalid, as he was no more than a layman. Of course the members of the dissenting churches see things otherwise, and see no need for a 'valid' succession: 'validity' of Orders for them is conferred, not automatically by a bishop because he himself is validly ordained, but by agreement of the present-day church that this is a proper person to be ordained; it is the gathered church that confers the Order. The point at stake here was that the Church of Rome held that the Church of England's succession had been invalid since 1550,[3] and Gilly was attempting to find a valid, non-Roman, succession which Rome would have to acknowledge.

As we have seen, Gilly thought that the origins of the Waldensians lay far back in the past – as far as 820, although there is no evidence of the existence of the Waldensian Church before about 1200. However, it has now been questioned whether the body Gilly knew is in fact the same as the one that separated from Rome around 1200. The basis of this argument, put forward by Audisio,[4] is that, by adopting Reformation principles, the whole basis of Waldensian theology changed, and along with it their concept of ministry, and thus, as explained above, the succession was no longer of import to them, if it ever had been.

---

1   The Church of England still technically holds the doctrine, though more so in its 'higher' reaches than in the 'lower'.
2   A good deal depends on exactly how the Apostles and their successors are perceived: they were certainly not operating as 'bishops' as that term was later understood.
3   The date of the first English Ordinal. Rome held (and still holds) that it was invalid in intent.
4   G. Audisio (trans. C. Davison), *The Waldensian Dissent: Persecution and survival, c1170–c1570*, Cambridge, 1999.

When the news of the Reformation reached the Waldensian valleys, a Synod held 1526 in Laus, a town in the Chisone valley, decided to send envoys to examine the new movement, with the result that the Tavola Valdese decided to seek fellowship with the nascent movement. In 1532 they met with German and Swiss Protestants, and adapted their beliefs to those of the Reformed Church. A Confession of Faith, based on Reformed doctrines, was formulated, and the Waldensians decided to worship openly in French. The French Bible was translated by Pierre Robert Olivétan with the help of Calvin, and published at Neuchâtel in 1535. It was based in part on the Romaunt New Testament.

So the Waldensian adoption of the Reformers' principles led to their transformation from a group on the edge of Catholicism, which shared many Catholic beliefs, into a Reformed church adhering to the theology of John Calvin, which differed greatly from the beliefs of Peter Waldo. The Waldensian Church had thus become the Italian branch of the Reformed Church. So even if it had preserved a 'valid' succession throughout the Middle Ages, it had been broken in the sixteenth century. This inconvenient fact was ignored by Gilly, although he must have known about the theological shift in the sixteenth century, and of course this is the reason he wanted the Waldensians to stop sending their ordinands for training and ordination to Calvinist seminaries in Switzerland. The present-day Waldensian Church does not claim to be a 'pipeline' for the Apostolic Succession.

Appendix IV

Church party terminology

The terms 'High Church' and 'Low Church', together with 'Protestant' and 'Evangelical', have been used a good deal in this work, as have to a lesser extent 'Tractarian', 'Ritualist' and 'Anglo-Catholic'. It is necessary to define these terms, as they all underwent major semantic changes during Gilly's life, and what they meant in 1820 was not what they meant in 1860, and they mean different things again today. The exact usage of the terms has been well discussed by Peter Nockles,[1] and what follows is to a large extent based on his work. In order to make matters totally clear, the discussion here goes beyond Gilly's death in 1855, noting how the second generation of the Oxford Movement, the Ritualists, deliberately changed the meanings, and also notes what the terms mean now. Gilly, an orthodox High Churchman of the 1820s, would probably be seen as Low Church today.

A great deal of the problem is rooted in both in the later redefinition of party terms by the Tractarians and their successors,[2] and the degree of imprecision with which these terms were used in earlier years: 'The Tractarians altered the nomenclature of Anglican church parties, as a result of their distortion of the pre-existing theological spectrum.'[3] There is also the question of shifting perceptions: what was regarded as extreme Ritualism in 1850 had become mainstream practice by 1880. I shall examine the terms High Church, Tractarian, Ritualist and Anglo-Catholic, and then the terms Protestant, Evangelical and Low Church. As with the various 'High Church' labels, popular usage caused a blurring of edges between the various 'Low Church' terms too; perhaps more understandably, as, while it would be easy to pick out the difference between a Ritualist and a High Churchman on the externals of worship alone, it was almost impossible to do so between the various degrees of 'Low' Churchmanship.

High Church

This is perhaps the term that is surrounded with the greatest amount of imprecision. Starting life in the 1650s, by the 1700s it had become a derogatory label, and remained so, especially when used by Whigs; those to whom the label was applied, such as Gilly, preferred to call themselves 'Orthodox'.[4] Between about 1715 and 1830, it was, as

---

1 P. B. Nockles, *The Oxford Movement in Context*, (Cambridge 1994), ch. 1, especially pp. 25–43.

2 It should also be noted that until well into the twentieth century, Anglican church history was written almost exclusively from an Anglo-Catholic point of view (albeit of varying degrees), and has thus come to be the accepted version. A particular thread of this historiography is the denigration of the eighteenth and early nineteenth centuries – something that is much overdone.

3 Nockles, *Oxford Movement*, p. 33.

4 Nockles, *Oxford Movement*, pp. 27–8.

J. D. Walsh says, 'a Protean label, with variations doctrinal, ecclesiastical and political'.[5] Nockles' definition of the pre-Tractarian High Churchman is a useful starting point, and it certainly fits Gilly:

> [He] tended to uphold in some form the doctrine of apostolical succession as a manifes-tation of ... the Church's catholicity and apostolicity as a branch of the universal church catholic, within which he did not include those reformed bodies which had abandoned episcopacy .... He believed in the supremacy of Holy Scripture, and set varying degrees of value on the testimony of authorised standards such as Creeds, the Prayer Book and the Catechism ... valued the writings of the early Fathers ... upheld in a qualified way the primacy of dogma ... laid emphasis on the doctrine of sacramental grace. ... He tended to cultivate a practical spirituality based on good works ... rather than on any subjective conversion experience ... stressed the divine rather than the popular basis of political alle-giance and obligation. ... upheld the importance of a religious establishment but insisted on the duty of the state as a divinely-ordained rather than merely secular entity, to protect and promote the interests of the church.[6]

Thus it can be seen why Gilly was prepared, indeed anxious, to work with the Walden-sians: his unshakeable belief that they effectively had the apostolic succession made them an ideal subject for cooperation.

Much of this was to be found in the thinking of the Tractarians and the Ritual-ists, although they and their successors developed and added to the basis. Those who continued in 'the old way' were dubbed 'High and Dry'; they continued well into the early twentieth century, and often came to be seen by their more 'advanced' brethren, as a result of their refusal to adopt any but the mildest ceremonial innovations, as 'Low Church', which they quite certainly were not. The term 'High Church' also came to be applied in a derogatory manner by extreme Anglo-Catholics to clergy who had a taste for modified but dignified ritual, and were happy to have lighted candles and wear vestments, but who did not promote the more decidedly 'catholic' teachings which were supposed to go with it – auricular confession, transubstantiation, and later the cult of the Virgin and so on. 'He's not a proper Catholic, he's just High Church' was a phrase frequently heard.

Tractarian

The word derives from the series of pamphlets produced under the generic title *Tracts for the Times* (1833 *et seq.*). Its initial application was narrow: those who had written, edited or approved of these Tracts. But as the Tracts held a wide variety of doctrinal content, it is impossible to set down a standard to which they all adhere, and thus inappropriate in many ways to use the term 'Tractarian' to define a particular party line. Some of the earlier authors distanced themselves from the later direction

---

5   J. D. Walsh, 'The origins of the Evangelical revival', in G. V. Bennett and J. D. Walsh, *Essays in Modern English Church History* (London, 1966), p. 138.

6   Nockles, *Oxford Movement*, pp. 25–6.

the movement took. There were others, too, who were enthusiastic followers of the movement, but who had neither written, nor even in many cases read, the Tracts. And to cloud the issue further, there were many who inhabited the debatable land between the old High Church (being more advanced) and full-blown Tractarianism (being not so far advanced): this was especially the case in the 1840s and 1850s. Tractarianism itself came to comprehend a wide variety of opinion, from those who merged imperceptibly with the more advanced end of the High Church, to the Romanizing party. Another term that came to be almost synonymous with Tractarian was the opprobrious 'Puseyism', much used by the more militant detractors, especially about the more Romanist end of the spectrum.[7]

Ritualist

Ritualism was partly a product of second-generation Tractarianism, but also (and possibly more so) a product of nineteenth-century interest in things medieval and Gothic. This was given force by the Cambridge Camden Society (later the Ecclesiological Society), which promoted the revival of the 'true' Gothic church (whether built anew or a restored medieval original), as opposed to the Gothick churches which were being built from about 1750, which were simply Wren-style auditory churches in Gothic dress.[8] Arguably this was *ceremonialism* – a revival of perceived pre-Reformation ways of conducting services – as opposed to *Ritualism* (which is, strictly, concerned with the order of service, rather than its mechanics), but the term was in contemporary use and therefore I use it in the sense in which it was understood.

The Ritualists represent, then, the more extreme end of the spectrum of the terms under consideration here, and although as a phenomenon they did not really get under way until after Gilly's death, we should be aware of them as they are the people who appropriate the term 'Anglo-Catholic' to themselves, and make it susceptible of a very narrow definition only.[9] They are disowned by the old High Church or Orthodox as 'un-Anglican'. But the term must be constantly redefined, or at least be capable of a shifting definition, as what is initially seen as extreme Ritualism (for instance, wearing a surplice in the pulpit) later becomes the accepted norm, and those who hold to the previous norm are seen as Low Church, even though in many cases they are merely conservative. That they were making inroads early on is seen in Gilly's refusal to subscribe to Raine's window, and also his book *No Puseyism!*

Anglo-Catholic

This is another term that has undergone a variety of meanings since it first saw the light of day somewhere in the seventeenth century. It was original ly interchange-

---

7   Name for Edward Bouverie Pusey (1800–1882), Regius Professor of Hebrew at Oxford. While he subscribed to many 'advanced' theological views, he did not approve of advanced ritual.
8   Such as St Mary Somers Town.
9   Exactly how far 'Ritualist' and 'Anglo-Catholic' are coterminous is a moot point.

able with Anglican;[10] it meant simply 'the branch of the Catholic (that is, universal) Church that is in England', and it retained this meaning well into the nineteenth century, being used in this sense by Newman in his *Lectures on the Prophetical Office of the Church* (1837), and by the editors of the series *Library of Anglo-Catholic Theology* (1841 et seq.). Likewise, William Palmer[11] used the word to mean the 'orthodox Church of England position' in his *Treatise on the Church of Christ* of 1838, and more importantly it was used in this sense in William Gresley's *Anglo-Catholicism* of 1844. The latter, which seems to be the first time that the suffix *-ism* was added, allowed a more precise interpretation of the term. Gresley intended it to mean 'a reinvigorated version of traditional High Churchmanship',[12] but it was gradually appropriated by the Tractarian (and later the ritualist) party – who saw themselves increasingly as the 'true' catholic church – and the hitherto neutral term became a party label. The hijacking of the term did not go unchallenged, especially by the old High Church school, who indeed accused the Tractarians of ceasing to be real Anglo-Catholics.[13] Nonetheless, the term did become associated with the Ritualist school (and especially its more extreme adherents), and certainly by the end of the century (if not earlier) could be used to refer only to those churches with fully developed ritual and teaching, and to their clergy and laity, as it still is today.

Protestant

Initially a term which goes back further than any of those so far discussed, it originally meant those who protested at the Diet of Speyer (1529) against the Catholic powers who wished to halt the reforming movement.[14] By the seventeenth century, in an Anglican context it had come to mean those opposed equally to Roman Catholicism and to Puritanism, and at the start of the nineteenth century it still held this meaning. Thus Gilly could be both a High Churchman and a Protestant, something which was to be an oxymoron by about 1870. Although it is not used in any of the official formularies of the Church of England, most, if not all, of her members would have regarded themselves as protestant – but also as catholic, though with a small 'p' or 'c' in each case.[15] During the latter part of the century the term tended to take on a rather militant tone; the party that eventually appropriated the name seemed to define itself almost entirely by what it disapproved of. We can think here of Kensit's Protestant Truth Society of 1890, which organized resistance to Ritualism, and published propaganda to support this aim.

---

10 Nockles, *Oxford Movement*, p. 41.
11 William Palmer of Worcester, not William Palmer of Magdalen, who visited the Waldensian valleys – see Chapter 10.
12 Nockles, *Oxford Movement*, p. 42.
13 Gresley quotes Charles Wordsworth, who in his *Annals* of 1891 lamented that the Movement ceased so soon to be ' "bona fides" Anglo-Catholic'.
14 It is often confined to the followers of Luther; those of Zwingli and Calvin are termed 'Reformed'.
15 Although in the literature of the period, capitals were used, simply because they were used more freely in any case.

Evangelical

In Britain, the Evangelicals as a group go back to about 1730.[16] As with many of the other terms under consideration, exactly what constitutes 'an Evangelical' changed over time, but David Bebbington suggests that four 'qualities', which remain constant, may be used as yardsticks. These are 'conversionism' – the idea that lives need to be, and are, changed by Christ; 'activism' – the expression of the gospel in works; 'biblicism' – a special regard for the Bible; and 'crucicentrism' – a particular stress on the Atonement through Christ's sacrifice on the cross.[17] What changes over the years is the relative weight put upon them. In the early days of the movement the stress was on the first and last of them, while later generations stressed the supremacy of scripture, probably as a result of the increased importance given by other schools of thought to the Church or to Reason.[18] While all Evangelicals believed in the divine inspiration of Scripture, it was the precise interpretation of this doctrine that led to a split. Originally they were concerned to spread the devotional use of the Bible, and the message it contains, but from about 1820, there appears the idea of plenary verbal inspiration, and after 1918 the party split into liberal and conservative wings over this point. The older, liberal, view was that Scripture was inspired in its matter, but not the actual words in which that matter was expressed; the new concept of plenary verbal inspiration, originating with Robert Haldane, a Scottish Evangelical, was that the actual words themselves were inspired, and that anything that appeared incomprehensible should nonetheless be received with 'adoring faith and love'.[19]

After about 1830, the Evangelical movement changed its direction, largely because of the rise of a new generation with fresh attitudes. This has been interpreted in various ways, but the (to an extent) most popularly held view is that it was a reaction to the Oxford Movement, although as Bebbington points out, it was in force long before the Movement's genesis.[20] The principal features of this change of direction were a revival of Calvinism, which by 1820 was the vogue at Oxford, centring round Henry Bulteel, the curate of St Ebbe's; and a rise in the doctrine of pre-millenarianism (the idea that Christ's second advent would inaugurate, rather than conclude, the Millennium, his thousand-year rule on earth).

A major difference was their attitude towards dissent. The Anglican Evangelicals were very willing to cooperate with non-Anglican English and Welsh Protestants; the 'old-fashioned orthodox' and the High Churchmen, while willing in some cases to collaborate with foreign Protestants such as the Waldensians (as being the equivalent of *Ecclesia Anglicana*), would not do so with domestic dissent, as they regarded it as

---

16   I ignore the growing use of 'evangelical' by Tudor historians to describe 'the religious reformism which developed in England during the 1520s and 1530s': D. MacCulloch, *Thomas Cranmer: A life* (New Haven and London, 1996), p. 2.

17   D. W. Bebbington, *Evangelicalism in Modern Britain*, London, 1989, p. 3.

18   Bebbington, p. 3.

19   Many high churchmen also subscribed to the doctrine of scriptural (but not necessarily verbal) inspiration.

20   See Bebbington, *Evangelicalism*, p. 75.

schismatic. The Ritualists would have no dealings with any form of Protestantism, preferring to look towards Rome.

There are several bonds between the two movements, of whom the best known is Newman, who moved from Evangelicalism in the 1820s to Tractarianism, a move in which he was followed by the sons of William Wilberforce, and also Henry Manning (who, together with Robert and Henry Wilberforce, followed him in the further step to Rome). In 1833, Newman was able to publish letters in *The Record*, asking for the support of Evangelicals for the Oxford Movement, but the affinity was dissolved, and indeed forgotten, once suspicion of the Tractarians had been aroused among the Evangelicals – especially after 1838, with the publication of Froude's *Remains*. But the true foe of Evangelicals and Anglo-Catholics was not each other, but the Broad Church movement.[21]

Low Church

Again, loose popular usage has tended to confuse this term with the other two. But before 1833, an Evangelical could not be a Low Churchman: the term was confined to the Latitudinarian school, in that it was used to refer to values that provided much latitude in matters of discipline and faith, and the term was used in contradistinction to the term 'High Church', which applied to those who valued the exclusive authority of the Established Church, the episcopacy and the sacramental system. The Low Church position was criticized as severely by the Evangelicals as it was by the old High Church.[22] Again, it would seem to be the Tractarians who are responsible for the shift in definition: by the end of the 1840s, their polemicists were describing the Evangelicals as 'Low Church', although as Nockles points out,[23] by then the Evangelicals did not object to the label.

Current usage

Nowadays, in popular usage, and to an extent within the Church of England, these terms usually fall into two groups: High Church/Anglo-Catholic and Low Church/Protestant/Evangelical, and refer solely to the theological beliefs and forms of worship of specific people or congregations, whereas around 1800 each of them had very specific meanings, and referred as much to politics as to theology.

---

21   The Broad Church started as a liberal movement, which questioned the historicity of the Bible. The term eventually came to mean 'middle-stump' Anglicanism: neither markedly high nor low. It was never an organized party in the way that the other two were.

22   Indeed, a visiting American High Churchman described the Evangelical Bishop Ryder as a High Churchman (Nockles, *Oxford Movement*, p. 32, n. 133).

23   Nockles, *Oxford Movement*, p. 32.

Appendix V

Composition of the Durham Chapter

This appendix contains various details about the Chapter. Tables A5.1 and A5.2 show what other preferments the prebendaries held in addition in 1826, the year Gilly joined it, and in 1831, the year he became Vicar of Norham. This is listed in stall order, as some prebendaries moved between stalls. Table A5.3 gives the income for each stall in 1841, and Table A5.4 the composition of the Chapter in 1853, two years before Gilly's death, again with other preferments held in plurality. Table A5.5 shows how many diocesan bishops held pluralities in 1841: Durham was unusual, though not unique, in having two diocesan bishops on its chapter (in 1831 it had had four, of which one was the Dean).

Table A5.1 Other preferments held by members of the Durham Chapter in 1826, listed in stall order

Person	Stall	Date	Other posts held at the same time
Thomas Gisborne, MA (Cantab)	1st	1826–46	V of Croxall, Derbs, 1838–46
John Banks Jenkinson, MA, DD (Oxon)	2nd	1825–27	Bishop of St Davids, 1825–40
	Dean	1827–40	*Cousin of Lord Liverpool, PM*
John Bird Sumner, MA, DD (Cantab)	2nd	1827–48	V of Mapledurham, Oxon, 1818–28
(Sumner demonstrates a common procedure: that of proceeding from a prebend with a small income to another with a larger one.)	5th	1826–27	Bishop of Chester, 1828–48
	9th	1820–26	(Archbishop of Canterbury, 1848–62)
Richard Prosser, MA, DD(Oxon)	3rd	1804–39	R of Gateshead, 1796–39
			Archdeacon of Durham, 1808–31
			R of Easington, 1808–39
Charles Thorp, MA, DD(Oxon), FRS	4th	1829–62	R of Ryton, 1807–62
			Archdeacon of Durham, 1831–62
			First Warden of Durham University, 1833–62

Gerald Valerian Wellesley, MA (Cantab) DD (Lambeth)	5th	1827–48	R of St Luke with Holy Trinity, Chelsea, 1805–32 Preb and Canon of St Paul's, 1809–48 R of Therfield, Herts., 1822–32 R of Bishop Wearmouth, Co. Durham
William Nicholas Darnell, MA, BD (Oxon)	6th	1820–31	V of St Mary-le-Bow, Durham, 1809–15
	9th	1816–20	PC St Margaret Crossgate, 1820–27 V of Norham, 1827–31 V of Lastingham, 1821–28 R of Stanhope, Co Durham, 1831–65
Robert Gray, MA, DD (Oxon),	7th	1804–34	R of Bishop Wearmouth, 1805–27 Bishop of Bristol, 1827–34
David Durell, MA (Oxon)	8th	1809–52	R of Mongewell, Oxon, 1791–1852 *(Bishop Shute Barrington's estate)* R of Twining, Glos, 1791–1802 R of Crowmarsh, Oxon, 1793–1843
William Stephen Gilly, MA, DD (Cantab)	9th	1826–55	PC St Mary Somers Town, 1826–2; Domestic chaplain to Bishop of Durham, 1825 PC St Margaret Crossgate, 1827–31 V of Norham, 1831–55
George Townsend, MA (Cantab) DD(Dunelm)	10th	1825–57	Domestic chaplain to Bishop of Durham, 1822–25 V of Northallerton, Yorks, 1826–39 PC of St Margaret Crossgate, 1839–42
George Barrington, MA (Oxon)	11th	1801–29	R of Sedgefield *5th Viscount Barrington, 1814–29* *(nephew of Bishop Shute Barrington)*
John Savile Ogle, MA (Oxon)	12th	1820–53	Preb of Salisbury, 1794–1838

R = Rector; V = Vicar; PC = Perpetual Curate, Preb = Prebendary

Table A5.2 Composition of the Chapter in 1831, when Gilly became Vicar of Norham

Stall	Name	Date of installation	Other preferments
Dean	John Banks Jenkinson MA, DD (Oxon)	1827	Bishop of St David's
1	Thomas Gisborne MA (Cantab)	1826	V of Croxall, Derbs, 1838–46
2	John Bird Sumner MA, DD (Cantab)	1827	V of Mapledurham, Oxon, 1818–28 Bishop of Chester, 1828–48 (Archbishop of Canterbury, 1848–62)
3	Richard Prosser MA, DD (Oxon)	1804	R of Gateshead, 1796–39 Archdeacon of Durham, 1808–31 R of Easington, 1808–39
4	Charles Thorp MA, DD (Oxon), DD (Dunelm), FRS	1829	R of Ryton, 1807–62 Archdeacon of Durham, 1831–62 First Warden of Durham University, 1833–62
5	Gerald Valerian Wellesley MA (Cantab) DD (Lambeth)	1827	R of St Luke with Holy Trinity, Chelsea, 1805–32 Preb and Canon of St Paul's, 1809–48 R of Therfield, Herts, 1822–32 R of Bishop Wearmouth, Co. Durham
6	William Nicholas Darnell MA, BD (Oxon)	1820–31	PC St Margaret Crossgate, 1820–27 V of Norham, 1827–31 R Stanhope, Co. Durham, 1831–65
	Henry Phillpotts, MA, DD (Oxon)	1831	Bishop of Exeter, 1831 PC St Margaret Crossgate, 1810–27
7	Robert Gray MA, DD (Oxon),	1804	R of Bp Wearmouth, 1805–27 Bishop of Bristol, 1827–34
8	David Durell MA (Oxon)	1809	R of Mongewell, Oxon, 1791–1852 R of Twining, Glos, 1791–1802 R of Crowmarsh, Oxon, 1793–1843
9	William Stephen Gilly MA, DD (Cantab)	1826	PC St Mary Somers Town, 1826–28 Domestic chaplain to Bishop of Durham, 1857– PC St Margaret Crossgate, 1827–31 V of Norham, 1831–55
10	George Townsend MA (Cantab) DD (Dunelm)	1825	Domestic chaplain to Bishop of Durham, 1822–57 V of Northallerton, Yorks, 1826–39 PC St Margaret Crossgate, 1839–42

11	Thomas Gaisford MA, DD (Oxon) *exchanged Durham stall with Smith for Deanery of Christ Church*	1829–31	Preb St Paul's, 1823–55 Preb Llandaff, 1823–55 Preb Worcester, 1825–29 R Westwell, Oxon, 1815–47 Dean Christ Church, 1831–55
	Samuel Smith, MA, DD (Oxon)	1831	Canon Christ Church, 1807–24 Dean Christ Church, 1824–31 Preb Southwell, 1800 Preb York, 1801–41 Chaplain House Commons, 1802 R Dry Drayton, Cambs, 1808–41
12	John Savile Ogle MA (Oxon)	1820	Preb Salisbury, 1794–1838

Table A5.3 Incomes of the Chapter in 1841 (in pounds sterling), listed in stall order

Person	Prebend	Date	Annual income	Notes
George Waddington	Deanery	1840	3,000	
Thomas Gisborne	1st	1823	706	
John Bird Sumner	2nd	1820	813	also Bishop of Chester (1828), £3,250
Henry Jenkyns	3rd	1839	486	
Charles Thorp	4th	1829	402	also Archdeacon of Durham (1831), £17
Gerald Valerian Wellesley	5th	1827	391	
Henry Phillpotts	6th	1831	565	also Bishop of Exeter (1831), £2,700
Henry Douglas	7th	1834	687	
David Durell	8th	1801	576	
William Stephen Gilly	9th	1826	312	
George Townsend	10th	1825	1,043	
Samuel Smith	11th	1831	1,400	(the so-called 'golden stall')
John Savile Ogle	12th	1820	872	

In addition, there were eight minor canons with stipends varying between £148 and £174, and the other archdeacon, Thomas Singleton of Northumberland, with a stipend of £213.

In 1841, £100 was worth about £7,000 in 2011, using the Retail Price Index <www.measuringworth.com/ppowerus>.

Table A5.4 Durham Chapter in 1853; listed in order of appointment to Chapter

Person	Prebend	Date	Annual income	Notes
George Waddington	Deanery	1840	3,000	Dean
George Townsend	10th	1825	1,043	
William Stephen Gilly	9th	1826	312	
Charles Thorp	4th	1829	402	also Archdeacon of Durham (1831) £17
Henry Phillpotts	6th	1831	565	also Bishop of Exeter (1831) £2,700
Samuel Smith	11th	1831	1,400	
Henry Douglas	7th	1834	687	
Henry Jenkyns	3rd	1839	486	
John Edwards	11th	1841	——	
William Forbes Raymond	1st	1846	——	also Archdeacon of Northumberland (1842) £213
H. J. Maltby	8th	1852	——	

In accordance with the 1841 Act (Stat. 3 & 4 Vic, chapter 113, section 8),[1] six canonries were to be suspended as follows: the first and second canonries to become vacant were to be suspended, the third to be filled; the fourth and fifth to be suspended, the sixth to be filled; and the seventh and eighth to be suspended. These turned out to be the second (Sumner), fifth (Wellesley), seventh (Douglas), eighth (Maltby) ninth (Gilly), and twelfth (Ogle) prebends; thus Gilly was the last holder of the ninth stall. This process took from 1848 (Sumner) to 1863 (Maltby).

In addition, the first and fourth were annexed to archdeaconries as above; and the eleventh annexed to the chair of Greek at the university. There were now three archdeacons, the junior, George Bland of Lindisfarne, not being on the Chapter. There were also seventeen honorary canons and six minor canons, none of whom had any income from the Chapter. It will be noted that the incomes of the various prebends remained stationary from 1841.

---

1   This Act affected all collegiate bodies, and reduced the prebends at all places to six; at the same time, the new concept of 'honorary canons' was introduced.

Table A5.5 Episcopal pluralities, 1841 (not counting sinecure posts such as Provincial Dean, Clerk of the Closet, all of which still exist)

See	Bishop	Posts in plurality
Carlisle	Hugh Percy (1827–56)	Prebendary of Finsbury in St Paul's (1816–56) Chancellor of Salisbury (1811–56)
Chester	John Bird Sumner (1828–48)	Prebendary of Durham (1827–48)
Exeter	Henry Philpotts (1830–69)	Prebendary of Durham (1831–69)
Gloucester and Bristol[2]	John Henry Monk (1830–56)	Canon of Westminster (1830–56)
Llandaff	Edward Copleston (1828–49)	Dean of St Paul's (1827–49)
Oxford	Richard Bagot (1829–45)	Dean of Canterbury (1827–45)
Rochester	George Murray (1827–60)	Dean of Worcester (1828–45) Rector of Bishopsbourne

Sources: 'Canons of Durham'; *Fasti Ecclesiae Anglicanae 1541–1857*: vol. 11: Carlisle, Chester, Durham, Manchester, Ripon, and Sodor and Man dioceses (2004), pp. 86–113 (www.british–history.ac.uk/report.aspx?compid=35857). Some dates are at variance with those given in Forster, *Alumni Oxoniensis.*

---

2   This was arguably a plurality in itself. The diocese of Bristol was united to that of Gloucester in 1836; they were again divided in 1897. Monk was Bishop of Gloucester from 1830, adding Bristol in 1836. The total of pluralist bishops in 1841 was seven out of twenty-eight – the four Welsh dioceses were part of the Province of Canterbury until 1920 – and they were not necessarily holders of the poorer sees.

Appendix VI

Holders of nationally important posts

For the sake of convenience, this appendix lists the holders of various important posts during Gilly's adult lifetime (from 1812, the year he graduated BA, to 1855, when he died).

North Fambridge and Wanstead were in the London diocese, and Hawkedon in Norwich, for the whole of Gilly's life. The episcopal careers of the various bishops are noted, as are episcopal pluralities of the deans of Durham.

Monarchs

1760–1820 – George III (Regency from 1811)
1820–30 – George IV
1830–37 – William IV
1837–1901 – Victoria

Prime Ministers

1812 – Earl of Liverpool [T]
1820 – Earl of Liverpool [T]
1827 – George Canning (Apr–Aug) [T]
1827 – Viscount Goderich (from Aug) [T]
1828 – Duke of Wellington [T]
1830 – Duke of Wellington [T]
1830 – Earl Grey [W]
1834 – Viscount Melbourne (July–Nov) [W]
1834 – Duke of Wellington (from Nov) [T]
1834 – Robert Peel [C]
1835 – Viscount Melbourne [W]
1837 – Viscount Melbourne [W]
1841 – Robert Peel [C]
1846 – Lord John Russell [W]
1852 – Earl of Derby (Feb–Dec) [C]
1852 – Earl of Aberdeen (Dec) [Peelite]
1855 – Viscount Palmerston (to 1858) [W]

[T] = Tory; [W] = Whig; [C] = Conservative.

Archbishops of Canterbury

1805–28 – Charles Manners Sutton; Bishop of Norwich 1792–1805
1828–48 – William Howley; Bishop of London 1813–28
1848–62 – John Bird Sumner; Bishop of Chester 1828–48

Bishops of Durham

1791–1826 – Shute Barrington; Bishop of Llandaff 1769–82; Bishop of Salisbury
1782–91
1826–36 – William van Mildert; Bishop of Llandaff 1819–26
1836–56 – Edward Maltby; Bishop of Chichester 1831–36

Bishops of London

1813–28 – William Howley; Archbishop of Canterbury 1828–48
1828–56 – Charles James Blomfield; Bishop of Chester 1824–28

Bishops of Norwich

1792–1805 – Charles Manners Sutton; Archbishop of Canterbury 1805
1805–37 – Henry Bathurst (died in office)
1837–49 – Edward Stanley (died in office)
1849–57 – Samuel Hinds (resigned 1857)

Deans of Durham

1794–1824 – James Cornwallis; also Bishop of Lichfield 1781–1824
1824–27 – Charles Henry Hall
1827–40 – John Banks Jenkinson; also Bishop of St Davids 1825–40
1840–69 – George Waddington

Bibliography

This lists the sources consulted by HN and NWG. The primary sources consulted by HN alone are marked *. For works by Gilly, see Appendix I; the vast majority of these are to be taken as having been consulted.

Primary sources (MS)

Archivio Centro Cuturale Valdense, Torre Pellice (ACCV)
*Beckwith Papers.

Archivio Storico S...... Valdense (ASSV)
*Carte Beckwith, fasicole 1, 2, 12.

Archivio Storico Tavola Valdense, Torre Pellice (ASTV)
*Series V, vols 33–46.
*Registre, 76–93.

Archivio di Stato di Torino
*File *Eretico e protestante: Carta toptgrafica del capolvogo del Pomaretto e suoi controni.*

Balliol College, Oxford
*Jenkyns Papers.

British Library (BL)
Beach, ES: *Notes on the Parish of North Fambridge*; typescript, 1948.
Peel Papers, vol. CLXXX.

Cambridge University Library (CUL)
Minutes of the London Vaudois Committee. (LVC)
MS Add. 2612: Correspondence relating to the Library at La Tour, 1838–1855.

Camden Borough Local Studies and Archives Centre
*P/PN1//M/1/ and M/2/: Minutes of St Pancras Select Vestry.

Centre for Buckinghamshire Studies, Aylesbury (CBS)
PR 27/1/10: Brill Parish Registers, Marriages, 1813–37.

Durham Cathedral Chapter Library
*Chapter Minutes …

Durham University Library - Archives and Special Collections (DUL)
*SRA/9/4-6: Account Books of the Ninth Stall.
*Probate Records, Will of William Stephen Gilly, 5 November 1852.
*Thorp Correspondence.

Essex Record Office, Chelmsford (ERO)
D/P 206/1/6: North Fambridge Parish Registers, Baptisms, 1813–1981.
D/P 206/1/7: North Fambridge Parish Registers, Burials, 1813–1982.
D/P 206/1/8: North Fambridge Parish Registers, Marriages, 1831–38.
D/P 206/1/9: North Fambridge Parish Registers, Marriages, 1838–1925.
D/P 292/1/5: Wanstead Parish Registers, Baptisms, 1813–37.

D/P 292/1/6: Wanstead Parish Registers, Burials, 1813–37.
D/P 292/1/7: Wanstead Parish Registers, Marriages, 1813–37.

Guildhall Library, London
Ms 12818, vol. 13: Christ's Hospital Admission Register.

Lambeth Palace Library (LPL)
Fulham Papers, Howley, vol. 17.
Palmer Papers: no. 2816, Journal of William Palmer.

Suffolk Record Office, Bury St Edmunds (SRO)
ACC 2220/4: Inventory of Goods and Chattels of William Gilly, late of Bury St Edmunds, 1716.
FL 579/4/2: Hawkedon Parish Register, 1786–1812.
FL 579/4/3: Hawkedon Parish Registers, Baptisms, 1813–97.
FL 579/4/7: Hawkedon Parish Registers, Burials, 1813–1997.
FL 579/4/8: Hawkedon Parish Registers, Marriages, 1838–1996.
HA 535/4/7: Indenture of Sale of Perpetual Right of Presentation to Hawkedon Rectory, 1796; 'Next Presentation to the valuable Rectory of Hawkedon', 1833.
HA 535/4/21: Pedigree of William Stephen Gilly … 1810.
HA 535/5/351: Drawing of Hawkedon Parsonage.

University College, London (UCL)
*Brougham Papers.
*Archives of the Society for the Diffusion of Useful Knowledge.

Newspapers and periodicals

(Various dates consulted except where specific dates are noted)
Berwick-upon-Tweed Advertiser.
British Critic, Quarterly Theological Review and Ecclesiastical Record, vol. 3, 1826; vol. 13, 1833.
Bury & Norwich Post.
The Christian Remembrancer, vol. 6, 1824.
Crockford's Clerical Directory, London.
Dublin Review, vol. 3, 1837.
Durham Advertiser.
Durham Chronicle.
Durham University Calendar.
The Gentleman's Magazine, vol. 88, April 1818.
The Literary Gazette and Journal of Belles Lettres, Arts, Sciences, etc., no. 400, 18 September 1824.
London Gazette.
Parson & White's Directory, Norhamshire, Newcastle, 1828.
Prize Essays and Transactions of the Highland Society, new series, vol viii, Edinburgh, 1843.
The Times.
Whellan's Directory, Norhamshire, London and Manchester, 1855.

Other primary sources (printed)

Records of the General Show of the Highland and Agricultural Society of Scotland for 1841. Berwick-upon-Tweed, 1841.

Report to Her Majesty's Principal Secretary of State for the Home Department, from the Poor Law Commissioners on an Inquiry into the Sanitary Condition of the Labouring Population of Great Britain; with Appendices. Presented to both Houses of Parliament, by Command of Her Majesty, July 1842.

Report of the Commissioners appointed by his Majesty to Inquire into Ecclesiastical Revenues of England and Wales, 1835.

First Annual Report of the Cottage Improvement Society of North Northumberland, 1842.

Second Annual Report of the Committee of the Cottage Improvement Society of North Northumberland, Alnwick, 1843.

Cane, C. *Brief Notes on North Fambridge.* Privately printed, 1909.

Clark, G. T. *Report to the General Board of Health on a Preliminary Inquiry into the Sewerage, Drainage and Supply of Water, and the Sanitary Conditions of the Inhabitants of Durham,* London, Stationery Office,1849. Repr. as D. J. Butler (ed. and intro.), *Public Health Act, Report to the General Board of Health on Durham.* Durham County Local History Society, 1997.

Foster, J. *Alumni Oxonienses, 1715–1886* (4 vols). Oxford, 1887.

Holdstock, J. *A Reply to a letter addressed to Mt HH Breen by Mr Roberts, upon his relapsing into the errors of the Church of Rome;* London, 1828.

Lockhart, A. W. (ed.) *Christ's Hospital, List of University Exhibitions 1566–1885,* London, 1876.

Powell, W. R. (ed.) *Victoria County History: A History of the County of Essex,* vol. 6. 1973.

Romilly, J. *Graduati Cantabrigienses.* Cambridge, 1856.

Venn, J. and J. A. *Alumni Cantabrigienses, A Biographical List of All Known Students, Graduates and Holders of Office at the University of Cambridge, from the Earliest Times to 1900,* 10 vols. Cambridge, 1922–1953.

Welch, R. G. (ed.) *The Harrow School Register, 1801–1835.* London, 1834.

White, E. A. and Armytage, G. J. (eds) *The Baptismal, Marriage, and Burial Registers of the Cathedral Church of Christ and the Blessed Virgin Mary at Durham, 1609–1896.* Harleian Society, vol. RS 23, 1897.

Secondary sources

a. Books

Armytage, W. H. G. *Civic Universities: Some aspects of a British tradition.* London, 1955.

Audisio, G. *The Waldensian Dissent: Persecution and survival c1170–c1570.* Cambridge, 1999.

Barrington, S. *Vigilance: A counterblast to past concessions and preventive of future prodigality. Recommended in two charges and a letter to the clergy of the diocese of Durham.* London, 1806.

Baveystock, J. A. *The Centenary Book.* London, 1926.

Bowden, E. (ed.) *The Correspondence of Robert Southey with Caroline Bowles,* Dublin ,1881.

Bracebridge, C. H. *Authentic Details of the Valdenses, in Piemont and Other Countries; With abridged translations of 'L'Histoire des Vaudois' par Bresse, and La Rentrée glorieuse, d'Henri Arnaud, etc.* London, 1827.

Brickstock, R. *Durham Castle, Fortress, Palace, College:* Durham, 2007.

Cameron, E. *The Reformation of the Heretics, the Waldenses of the Alps 1480–1580*. Oxford, 1984.

Carlton, C. M. *Monumental Inscriptions of the Cathedral, Parish Churches, and Cemeteries of the City of Durham,* vol. 1. Durham, 1880.

Carlton, F. M. *History of the Charities in the City of Durham and its Immediate Vicinity.* Durham, 1872

Crosby, J. *Igatius Bonomi of Durham*. Durham, 1987.

Dewey, C. *The Passing of Barchester*. London, 1991.

Ellerby, T. S. *Memorials of Felix Neff, the Alpine Pastor*. London, Manchester and Liverpool, 1833.

Emerson, R. W. *English Traits*, XIII. London, 1856.

Fordyce, W., *History and Antiquities of the County Palatine of Durham,* Newcastle-on-Tyne, 1855.

Fowler, J. T. *Rites of Durham.,* vol. 197. Surtees Society, 1903.

Gibson, W. *A Social History of the Domestic Chaplain, 1530–1840*. Leicester, 1997.

Gilly, W. O. S. *Shipwrecks of the Royal Navy between 1793 and 1849*. London, 1850.

Harte, N. *The History of the University of London, 1836–1989: An illustrated history*. London, 1986.

Henderson, E. *The Vaudois: Comprising observations made during a tour to the Valleys of Piedmont, in the summer of 1814: together with remarks, introductory and interspersed, respecting the origin, history, and present condition of that people*. London, 1845.

Hunt, L. *The Autobiography of Leigh Hunt, with reminiscences of friends and contemporaries*. 3 vols. London, 1850; rev. edn by R. Ingpen, 1903.

Meile, J. P. (trans. W. Arnot). *General Beckwith: His life and labours among the Waldenses of Piedmont*. London, 1873.

Miller, F. *St Pancras Past and Present*. London, 1874.

Morland, S. *History of the Evangelical Chuches of the Valleys of Piemont*. London, 1658 (repub. 1985).

Nichols, J. *Illustrations of the Literary History of the Eighteenth Century*, 6 vols. London, 1817–31.

'Parish Priest, A'. *The State of the Curates of the Church of England – A letter addressed to the Archbishop of Canterbury*. London, 1828.

Park, T. *St Bees College: Pioneering higher education in 19th century Cumbria*. St Bees, 2008.

Pevsner, N. *The Buildings of England: Northumberland*. Harmondsworth, 1957.

Pevsner, N. *The Buildings of England: Suffolk*. Harmondsworth, 1961.

Pevsner, N. *The Buildings of England: Cheshire*. Harmondsworth, 1971.

Port, M. H. *Six Hundred New Churches : A Study of the Church Building Commission 1818–1856 and its Church Building Activities*. Spire, 2006.

Price, D. T. W. *A History of St David's University College, Lampeter*. Cardiff, vol. 1 (to 1898), 1977; vol. 2 (1898–1971), 1990.

Raine, J. *Saint Cuthbert: With an account of the state in which his remains were found upon the opening of his tomb in Durham cathedral, in the year MDCCCXXVII*. Durham, 1828.

Raine, J. *The History and Antquities of North Durham as sub-divided into the Shires of Norham, Island, and Bedlington*. London, 1852.

Sheldon, F. *History of Berwick-upon-Tweed, being a concise description of that ancient Borough, from its origin down to the Present Time*. Edinburgh, London and Berwick, 1849.

Sims, T. *An Apology for the Waldensians …* London, 1827.

Sims, T. *Visits to the Valleys of Piedmont*. London, 1864.

Stephens, P. *The Waldensian Story: A study in faith, intolerance, and survival*. Lewes, 1998.

Stranks, C. J. *The Sumptuous Church: The story of Durham Cathedral*. London, 1973.

Teignmouth, Lord *Memoir of the Life and Correspondence of John, Lord Teignmouth*. London, 1843.

Todd, J. H. *The Books of the Vaudois: The Waldensian manuscripts preserved in the Library of Trinity College, Dublin*. London, 1865.

Tweedy, J M. *Popish Elvet*. Durham, 1981.

Varley, E. A. *The Last of the Prince-Bishops*. Cambridge, 1992.

Watson, A. (ed.) *Practical Sermons by Dignitaries and other Clergymen of the United Church of England and Ireland*, 2 vols. London, 1845.

Wheeler, J. *A Brief Reply to Dr Gilly's Tract*. Durham, 1836.

White, W. *Northumberland Border*. London, 1859.

Wilson, J. *The History of Christ's Hospital*. London, 1821.

Worsfold, J. N. *The Vaudois of Piedmont*. London, 1873.

Yates, N. *Liturgical Space: Christian worship and Church buildings in western Europe, 1500–2000*. Ashgate, 2008.

b. Articles

Anon. 'Memoir of the Rev. Henry Martin, BD, late fellow of St John's College, Cambridge, and chaplain to the Honourable East India Company'. *Quarterly Review*, vol. 25, no. 50, pp. 437–54.

Anon. 'Memoir of the Hon and Rt Rev. Shute Barrington'. *Imperial Magazine*, June 1826, p. 617.

Anon. 'On churches and churchyards'. *Proceedings of the Berwickshire Naturalists Club*, vol. 2, 1846, pp. 177–90.

Barrington, J. S. 'A brief memoir of Shute Barrington, the late bishop of Durham'. *The Theological Works of the First Viscount Barrington*, vol. 1. London, 1828, p. li.

Cranfield, R. 'Education for the "Dangerous Classes" in mid-nineteenth century Durham'. *Durham County Local History Bulletin*, 1993, pp. 70–81.

Lamb, C. 'Christ's Hospital five-and-thirty years ago'. *Essays of Elia*, London.

Pakenham, C. *General John Charles Beckwith: The Man behind the Myth*. lecture to Waldensian 'away-day'. 1998.

Pinnington, J. 'The Waldenses as the Evangelical pipeline'. *Australian and New Zealand Theological Review,*, vol. 3, 1969, pp. 229–37.

Stewart, R. W. 'On the present condition and future prospects of the Waldensian Church'. *Lectures on Foreign Churches delivered in May 1845 in connection with the objects of the Committee of the Free Church of Scotland on the state of Christian Churches on the Continent and in the East*. Edinburgh, 1845, pp. 205–68.

Williams, R. 'Cambridge English and beyond'. *London Review of Books*, vol. 5, no. 12, July 1983.

Index

Also published by the Lasse Press

King Herod. The census that brought Joseph and Mary to Bethlehem. The guiding star. The building of the temple at Jerusalem. The crucifixion. These are among the events that we know of from the Bible that might be used to set the life of Jesus in the historical record. But generations of researchers have found that it is far from easy to reconcile the different accounts of Jesus's life given in the four Gospels, and to tie them to independently verifiable historical dates. In contrast to his massive significance in the centuries since his life, Jesus of Nazareth was known by only a few during his lifetime, and left little mark on the historical records of his time. As a result there is still much debate about the exact dates of his life. When was he born? When did his ministry begin, and when did he die?

Stephen J. Dudley takes a mathematician's approach to the issue. He looks not only at the events in the Gospels that might be linked to independent histories, but also at the difficulties of dating each one. Using a careful process of logical analysis, *The Road to Golgotha* tries to identify both the evidence and the pitfalls in interpreting it. Its conclusions are arguably the most accurate yet obtained about what we can and cannot know of the chronology of Jesus's life.

For details of all our titles visit

www.lassepress.com

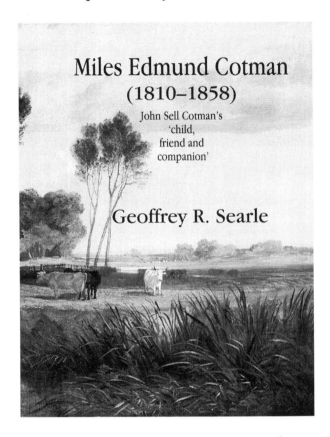

Miles Edmund Cotman (known to his contemporaries as Edmund) was given the role of sheet anchor to a family of outstanding artists, little as it may have suited his personality. Much of his output was determined by the needs of his family, not least his father, the brilliant Norwich School painter John Sell Cotman. It is perhaps unfair that as a result, he has sometimes been dismissed as an inferior hack artist. While he did not show the genius of his father, he did in fact produce a variety of interesting and well-executed work. Geoffrey Searle looks at Edmund Cotman's background, the circumstances of his work, and the work itself that survives for us today. Illustrated with a representative sample of Cotman's works (including oils, watercolours and etchings), this is an important addition to the literature about the Norwich School.

Geoffrey R. Searle is an emeritus professor of British history at the University of East Anglia and a fellow of the British Academy. He is the author of eight books on political history. This is his first foray into the history of art.

For details of all our titles visit

www.lassepress.com